HANDBOOK OF
FEDERAL ACCOUNTING
PRACTICES

HANDBOOK
OF
FEDERAL

ADDISON-WESLEY PUBLISHING COMPANY

CORNELIUS E. TIERNEY

Partner,
Arthur Young & Company

Visiting Professor
School of Business Administration
Georgetown University
Washington, D.C.

ACCOUNTING PRACTICES

Reading, Massachusetts • Menlo Park, California • London •
Amsterdam • Don Mills, Ontario • Sydney

Production Editor: William J. Yskamp
Designer: Margaret Ong Tsao
Illustrator: Robert Trevor
Cover Design: Richard Hannus

Library of Congress Cataloging in Publication Data

Tierney, Cornelius E
    Handbook of Federal accounting practices.

    Includes index.
    1. Finance, Public — United States — Accounting.
I. Title.
HJ9801.T54   657′.835′0973   80-27965
ISBN 0-201-07713-2

ISBN 0-201-07713-2
ABCDEFGHIJ-AL-8987654321

Preface

The objective of this book is to provide an introduction to federal accounting and reporting for governmental managers—particularly attorneys, program managers and analysts, accountants, budget officers, auditors, and planners. Similar professional personnel serving at state and local governmental levels will also find the book to be a ready reference work concerning the basis for requirements that have been imposed by federal agencies upon their governmental programs.

This book provides sufficient explanations, definitions, and illustrations to permit it to be used by those colleges desiring to supply accounting majors and graduate students with an insight into financial management within the federal government. Heretofore such knowledge could be acquired in only two ways: (1) by serving in federal budgeting, accounting, auditing, and planning positions with a variety of federal agencies and (2) by being sufficiently interested in the process to review the numerous documents relating to various aspects of the subject (such as public laws, General Accounting Office decisions and publications, Office of Management and Budget and Treasury circulars, and other agency directives, regulations, and procedures).

Discussions with college professors and federal personnel involved with the training of financial managers disclosed the fact that the literature had a conspicuous void with respect to the federal accounting practices. To everyone's knowledge, no other book is devoted exclusively to this subject. No college provides a course in federal accounting. If the subject is covered at all, it is as a small part of the broader subject of fund accounting, which is generally viewed as the accounting procedures and practices of municipal and local governmental units.

Special acknowledgment must be given to Andrew J. Kapfer, Director of Accounting Systems and Procedures for the Federal Department of Health and Human services, and to Ronald J. Points, Associate Director of the Accounting and Financial Group of the United States General Office, both of whom are lifelong professionals in the practice of governmental accounting in the federal sector. Their contributions, assistance, and advice were invaluable in the final structuring of this publication.

I, however, have the responsibility for the contents of this book. The blame for any errors, omissions, or interpretations rests solely with me. The views, opinions, or positions are mine and they do not necessarily reflect the thoughts of others, the firm of Arthur Young & Company, or Georgetown University.

Washington, D.C.   C. E. T.
December 1981

Contents

CONTENTS

CONTENTS

PART IV **ACCOUNTING FOR FEDERAL EXPENDITURES   221
AND RECEIPTS**

PART V   ACCOUNTING FOR ASSETS, LIABILITIES, AND INVESTMENT OF THE GOVERNMENT   327

CONTENTS

The Nature of Federal Accounting

chapter 1

INTRODUCTION

Tens of thousands of persons are involved daily with planning, budgeting, accounting, processing, or reporting on the financial activities of the federal government. Little, though, has been published on this important segment of governmental finance. Even less is taught about federal accounting in universities, colleges, and business schools. Many more individuals are indirectly affected by federal financial management because their responsibilities include accounting for federal funds received by 50 states, 80,000 local governmental units, and several thousand firms, institutions, and individuals. Further, the accepted and practiced federal accounting principles and procedures are neither the generally accepted accounting principles of the private sector nor of the other levels of government.

THE SIGNIFICANCE OF FEDERAL ACCOUNTING

Each President talks about the minimal requirements in his budget, the austerity of his budget requests, and promises to hold down federal spending levels of prior years. He also outlines reasons why the federal budget cannot help but be larger than in prior years. Regardless of, or in spite of explanations and good intentions, the federal government's budget for the fiscal year ending September 30, 1982, will approach $700 billion. This amount, approaching three quarters of a trillion dollars, will exceed 20 percent of the estimated Gross National Product (GNP) of the United States for that same period. Yet this budget does not consider many other fiscal activities or assistance provided by or guaranteed by the federal government. For example, the "off-budget" direct loans and guaranteed and insured loans for the fiscal year 1980 are estimated to be another $390 billion.

This is the universe of accounting in the federal sector. The procedures and practices will differ from the accounting applied to the finances of state, local, and municipal governments. The variances from generally accepted corporate accounting are even greater. For some reason though, if federal accounting is mentioned at all in college courses, the coverage is brief at best. Text and reference books on governmental accounting generally delegate only a chapter or two to this sphere of finance. No reference work exists that is devoted exclusively to the budgeting, accounting, and reporting of federal financial matters.

GENERALLY ACCEPTED ACCOUNTING PROCEDURES There is no single publication in which one will find the body of concepts or theory comprising generally accepted accounting procedures. "Generally accepted" is a relative term that must be applied with care to specific circumstances. For example, the accepted accounting procedures for corporate reporting are not viewed as totally relevant to the accounting for public sector activities and funds.

Private Sector Accounting

For decades, the generally accepted accounting procedures were espoused and monitored by the American Institute of Certified Public Accountants (AICPA). Initially, these acceptable procedures and practices were made known by the Institute through its several Accounting Research Bulletins (51 in all). Later, the Institute's Accounting Principles Board issued another 31 opinions on several accounting issues. More recently, the Financial Accounting Standards Board, established in 1972, has assumed the leading role in researching, developing, and issuing standards for accounting in the private sector. Of course, the Securities and Exchange Commission provides considerable guidance and direction to accountants and enterprises with published securities.

While judgment must always be applied to the specific event, the burden is on the practitioner to justify material departures from these several bodies of technical accounting guidance for corporate organizations.

Public Sector Accounting

Public sector accounting has been informally segregated into two groups: (1) that which is required for state and local governmental units, and (2) that which is required for federal agencies and departments. The accounting at all levels of government is closely related to the budget process, which in turn is founded in law or legislation, but differences among levels of government do exist.

State and Local Government

There are some 80,000 state and local governmental units. Within the local governmental units groupings are counties, cities, townships, municipalities, school districts, and special districts. The special districts are numerous and diverse, including such entities as airports, roads and bridges, authorities, hospitals, housing developments, and parks and recreation facilities. The accounting practices and procedures for these governmental units have been published by the National Committee on Governmental Accounting (now the National Council on Governmental Accounting (NCGA)) that was affiliated with the Municipal Finance Officers Association. That publication is known as *Governmental Accounting, Auditing, and Financial Reporting* (reissued in 1980, often referred to as the "bluebook") and describes the generally accepted accounting principles for these governmental units.

The *GAAFR* sets forth several generally accepted principles and practices or requirements to be followed by the states and thousands of local governmental units. No single unified set of accounts or a system of accounting is prescribed. Rather, the accounting for these governmental units is accomplished through a series of funds or groups of accounts. The funds and groups of accounts are segregated in the records as separate accounting entities, each of which has its own set of financial statements. Exhibit 1.1 lists and provides a summary definition of each of these prescribed funds and account groupings.

The *GAAFR* views governmental accounting as an integral but separate branch of accounting, sharing many concepts, procedures, and practices applicable to the private sector. The *GAAFR* recognizes that

Exhibit 1.1 **FUNDS AND ACCOUNT GROUPINGS PRESCRIBED BY** *GAAFR* *

FUND TITLE	FUND DESCRIPTION
	Governmental Funds
General fund	To account for all externally, unrestricted resources not accounted for in another fund
Special revenue fund	To account for proceeds of specific revenue sources restricted by law or administrative action to specified expenditures
Capital projects fund	To account for financial resources segregated for acquisition of major capital facilities (other than those financed by special assessment and enterprise funds)
Debt service funds	To account for the accumulation of resources for, and payment of, interest and principal on general obligation long-term debt (other than special assessment and enterprise debt)
Special assessment funds	To account for financing of public improvements or services benefiting properties against which special assessments are levied
	Proprietary Funds
Enterprise funds	To account for provision of goods and services to the public on a continuing basis when costs are financed by user charges or when the periodic determination of revenues earned, expenses incurred, and net income or loss is appropriate
Internal service fund	To account for financing of goods or services provided by one department to other departments of the governmental unit on a reimbursable basis
	Fiduciary Funds
Trust and agency funds	To account for assets held by a governmental unit as trustee or agent for individuals, private organizations, or other governmental units (governmental trust funds are expendable trust funds, pension trust funds, and agency funds: proprietary trust funds include nonexpendable trust funds)
	Account Groups
General fixed assets account group	To account for fixed assets of governmental unit, except for fixed assets accounted for in proprietary funds
General long term debt account group	To account for long-term, unmatured general obligation liabilities of the governmental unit

*Governmental Accounting, Auditing, and Financial Reporting, 1979, National Council on Governmental Accounting.

certain private sector principles of accounting and reporting as also being the generally accepted accounting principles for governmental units. The *GAAFR Restatement* of 1979 by the NCGA stated that the principal sources of authoritative guidance with respect to generally accepted accounting principles applicable to states and local governments are the NCGA and, more recently, the AICPA.

Federal Government Accounting

At the federal level, the responsibilities for accounting are split between the United States General Accounting Office (GAO), which is a legislative agency, and the Office of Management and Budget (OMB), the Treasury, and the individual departments and agencies of the executive branch. By several laws, the GAO is required to prescribe the forms, systems, procedures, and the principles and standards of accounting to be observed by federal agencies. Also by law, the head of each department or agency is required to develop and maintain a system of accounts in accordance with the GAO-prescribed principles and standards. While fund accounting is the practiced form of accounting, the procedures, terms, and practices vary considerably from those in use by state and local governmental units.

Much of the accounting guidance provided by the GAO to government agencies parallels conventions of the private and state and local governmental levels. But no reference is made in the GAO principles and

Exhibit 1.2 *GAO MANUAL* **FOR GUIDANCE OF FEDERAL AGENCIES**

STATED PURPOSE AND SCOPE:

The manual is the official medium through which the Comptroller General of the United States promulgates (1) accounting principles, standards, and related requirements and material for the guidance of federal agencies in the development of their accounting and internal auditing systems; (2) uniform procedures for use by federal agencies; and (3) regulations governing the relationships of the GAO with other federal agencies, individuals, and private concerns doing business with the federal government.

Titles of Manual	Summary of Content
Title 1—*The United States General Accounting Office*	Historical material relating to GAO and general information on its basic mission and objectives
Title 2—*Accounting*	Accounting principles and standards of GAO and instruction relating to GAO review and approval of agency accounting systems
Title 3—*Audit*	Reference material, regulations, requirements for auditing in the federal government, including guidelines and principles for agency internal auditing programs
Title 4—*Claims, General*	Regulatory material relating to claims by and against the government and procedures for collecting, waiving, or settling such claims
Title 5—*Transportation*	Regulatory material and information for procurement, billing, and payment of freight and transportation services furnished to the government
Title 6—*Pay, Leave, and Allowances*	Principles, standards, and requirements applicable to federal departments and agencies for development, installation, and operation of systems for pay, leave, and allowances of personnel
Title 7—*Fiscal Procedures*	Principles, standards, and requirements relating to the fiscal transactions of an agency's financial management system
Title 8—*Records and Management*	Responsibilities of GAO for preservation and disposal of fiscal and accounting records of the government and certain procedural instructions to federal departments and agencies relating to accounting and fiscal records

General Accounting Office Policy and Procedures Manual for Guidance of Federal Agencies, 1957, GAO, Washington, D.C.

standards to adherence to "generally accepted accounting principles." The applicable principles, standards, and related accounting requirements for federal accounting are those prescribed by the Comptroller General (the head of the GAO) after consultation with the Secretary of the Treasury and the Director of the Office of Management and Budget.

The official medium for promulgating accounting principles, standards, and related requirements is the *GAO Manual for Guidance of Federal Agencies*. Published initially in 1957, the manual comprises several titles. (These are listed and briefly described in Exhibit 1.2.) This manual, along with numerous issuances of the GAO over the years, the requirements of the Treasury and OMB, as well as specific restrictions, limitations, and other guidance set forth in various congressional enactments form the generally accepted accounting principles, procedures, and practices of the federal sector. It is this body of knowledge that this book addresses.

FACTORS INFLUENCING FEDERAL ACCOUNTING

Over the years several factors have influenced federal accountants and have resulted in the emergence of practices that are not consistent with generally accepted accounting principles as known in the private sector. There are instances in which the governmental practices are more appropriate and necessary to account for the financial management of the government. On the other hand, certain commercial accounting applications would have relevancy and could improve the controls of federal managers.

It is not the purpose of this book to try to resolve or postulate the ideal procedures but rather to identify the procedures and practices in use by federal financial managers. Changes are being examined, but change will come slow. Several basic considerations are being examined by the GAO and others interested in improving and enhancing the accounting of government. However, without a modification of the conditions to which systems must respond, government accountants and managers find themselves in a position of accounting for conditions set forth in law and externally mandated reporting requirements and, only secondarily, addressing the financial information that might be required to monitor the activities and operations of government programs.

Terminology

Federal accounting, like other disciplines, has generated phrases, terms, and words having specialized meaning and import within the government. These descriptives are often associated with or related to actions or events of specific organizations as the President, Congress, GAO, OMB,

Treasury, and the several individual executive departments and agencies. The terms permeating the budget, accounting, and reporting process are defined and illustrated in several sections of this book. Most specialized are the terms relating to the monitoring and accounting for the fund balance comprising the investment of the government in the programs of each agency. Additionally, the requirements of concurrently performing budgetary and proprietary accounting have resulted in the emergence of accounting procedures and processes applicable only to the accounting performed in the federal sector.

APPROPRIATIONS AS THE ACCOUNTING ENTITY

The appropriation of funds or the approval of budgetary authority by Congress provides the basis for departments and agencies of the federal government to collect taxes and other revenues from the public and incur obligations and make expenditures from the federal treasury.

The appropriation by Congress becomes the accounting entity, not, as is sometimes believed, the agency. There are complicating circumstances, e.g., when an agency receives many appropriations whose resources must be merged to support the operations or programs desired by Congress. Alternatively, an agency might be required to operate programs without having received a direct appropriation, but rather is provided funding through an allocation from another agency's appropriation. The ideal condition, of course, would exist for those agencies whose total program is supported by a single Congressional appropriation, a condition that considerably simplifies the accounting and reporting complexity.

Because the appropriation is the accounting entity, the recipient agency must record assets, liabilities, and the government's investment by the individual appropriation. Stated in another manner, while an integrated set of accounting records is required to account fully for the entire agency, the details with respect to each appropriation for which an agency is responsible must be separable in the records of the agency.

Governmental Financial Statements

It is important to understand the purpose of federal financial statements and the entity being reported on. While a consolidated financial statement might be prepared in a manner approximating a corporate statement, these values would be of minimal concern or interest to Congress, the OMB, the Treasury, or the GAO. The agency's accounting must provide a stewardship and reporting on an appropriation-by-appropriation basis.

Further, one should be aware that, with few exceptions, none of the agency financial statements are independently audited for the purpose of expressing an opinion on the reasonableness of the information reflected in the statements or whether there was compliance either with generally accepted accounting principles or the GAO standards and principles.

Relevance of Financial Statements

As mentioned, unless financial statements are prepared for individual appropriations and funds, agency reporting will be of limited value in assessing performance of agency managers. The consolidation or combination of appropriation and fund balances will permit a determination of the total resources under the control of a single agency, but such aggregations of data will answer few of the questions most often asked of financial managers.

GAO has grouped the required agency reports into two categories

▲ External reports required by control agencies (Treasury, OMB, and GAO) and others

▲ Internal reports useful to agency management

In its principles, GAO has defined the basic internal reports as including (1) statements of assets and liabilities, and (2) statements of operations of an agency's programs and activities.

Within an agency few but accountants will have an interest or concern in the preparation or analysis of data reflected on an agencywide statement of assets and liabilities. To comply with laws and manage funds in the manner outlined by the Congressional appropriations, it is necessary to consider the appropriation as the accounting entity in contrast to the agency. Unless information is provided about the currency and status of the individual appropriation and the amount of carry-over obligations that will fund future operations, for example, an agencywide balance sheet or statement of assets and liabilities has limited value.

Statements of operations have more value but, again, only if the information is provided on an appropriation-by-appropriation basis. Consolidated reporting of operations on an agencywide basis may have some general public utility, but will be of limited value to agency managers and executives in the Treasury or the OMB.

Responsibility for Financial Statements

The head of each federal agency is required to prepare financial statements reflecting the financial position, results of operations, and the status of individual appropriations. GAO, in its *Accounting Principles and Standards* for the guidance of federal agencies, has interpreted this reporting requirement to include the following statements.

▲ *Statement of Assets and Liabilities*—similar in content to a corporate balance sheet, showing assets, liabilities, and appropriation equity.

▲ *Statement of Changes in Investment*—reporting on the fund balance of an appropriation

▲ *Statement of Operations*—disclosing revenues and expenses of agency activities

▲ *Sources and Applications of Funds*—reporting the appropriation and other related sources of funding

The arrangement of accounts in financial statements for commercial organizations typically reflect the liquidity or convertibility of the assets and liabilities. Statements for regulated industries, having a different objective, are often prepared giving prominence to capital assets, long-term debt, and earned surplus. In federal accounting no such segregation is mandated. The following chapters discuss many of the accounts used by agencies financed by Congressional appropriations. There is no absolute limit on the number of accounts that might be used by an agency nor does a standard governmentwide uniform chart of accounts exist at the federal level. Additionally, the nature of the operations will dictate the type of reporting to be made. For example, working capital and revolving funds will generally require financial reporting, paralleling the corporate sector because such disclosure provides the most meaningful information to those fund managers. Other reporting will be dictated by legislation and other compliance criteria imposed on the agency. Further, statements unique to the agency must often be designed to provide data on performance indicators and operations.

The earlier placement of chapters on expenditures and collections was prompted by the nature and emphasis given to aspects of federal accounting that differ from those that exist in the private sector. The accounting for assets is almost secondary within the federal government. This is not to say that assets and the accounts normally comprising the more commonly known balance sheet are less important or should not be emphasized, but it is merely a statement of fact.

FEDERAL FINANCIAL MANAGEMENT POLICY AND PROCEDURES

The responsibility for setting financial management policy and mandating procedures is fragmented among several agencies and between the legislative and executive branches of government. The Congress and, by law, the General Accounting Office have prescribed the accounting requirements for the executive branch only. The OMB, the Treasury, the

President by executive order, and the numerous department and agencies of the executive branch have all contributed to the development of policy and procedures of federal accounting as well.

There is a system, although considerable research is necessary for one to grasp the purposes and process for federal accounting. The budget process, from its preparation through execution, is probably the single continuum on which federal accounting rests. It is money or revenue and expenditure authority given by Congress that forms the accounting entity to be planned, budgeted, controlled, managed, and reported by departments and agencies. Over the years, various concepts have been attempted to provide more precision in estimating the budget, in monitoring expenditures, and in accumulating the costs of government programs. These concepts, such as zero-based budgeting (ZBB), planning, programming, and budgeting systems (PPBS), and, to a lesser degree, management by objectives (MBO), have been required by various Presidents, although not always with the full agreement or concurrence of Congress.

Another factor that contributes to the development of federal accounting has been the Treasury and its need for specific information to maintain and operate the central accounting and financial reporting system of the federal government. As the "keeper of the government's purse," the Treasury must, pursuant to the Constitution and other laws, render regular statements of receipts and expenditures of the government.

These processes, policies, and procedures are described in several chapters.

▲ Chapter 2, Federal Financial Management Policy, identifies several laws governing fiscal and financial policies of federal departments and agencies and those organizations and agencies responsible for setting government-wide financial policy.

▲ Chapter 3, Federal Budget Process, Controls, and Monitoring: (I), outlines the phases of the federal budget cycle, the changes resulting from the passage of the Congressional Budget and Impoundment Act and some of the planning and budgeting concepts applied to federal financial management over the years.

▲ Chapter 4, Federal Budget Process, Controls, and Monitoring: (II), discusses the budget preparation process and outlines several events that occur during the execution of the budget by departments and agencies.

ACCOUNTING STANDARDS, PRINCIPLES, PROCESSES, AND CONCEPTS

For decades, accounting standards, principles, and reporting requirements have existed in the federal government. To ensure compliance with these criteria, GAO has exercised a process for reviewing and approving government financial systems. Systems achieving the GAO approval are a source of pride to agency financial managers. Because of these standards and principles, and the unique requirements imposed by Congress, the Treasury, and the OMB, certain accounting concepts have evolved, and the several agencies rather consistently adhere to them. These concepts, in turn, have generally evolved into an accounting process that rather effectively integrates the budgetary requirements of a governmental entity with the type of proprietary information also considered by corporate organizations as necessary to monitor operations.

An overview of the standards and principles and the nature in which these guidelines have been incorporated into agency accounting systems is set forth in four chapters.

▲ Chapter 5, Central Accounting and Financial Reporting, identifies the legal basis for federal accounting and the reporting required by the Treasury for the central fiscal accounts of the government, which differs from the accounting practices of individual agencies.

▲ Chapter 6, Government Accounting Standards and Principles, describes the accounting standards, principles, and reporting requirements published by the GAO and outlines the GAO system's review and approval procedures.

▲ Chapter 7, Accounting Concepts in the Federal Government, summarizes several concepts involved with federal sector accounting, such as fund, budgetary, accrual, cost, and cash basis accounting.

▲ Chapter 8, The Accounting Process, describes the fiscal nature of agency systems, requirements that must be included in the accounting process, and the elements comprising the more recent automated integrated financial systems.

BUDGETARY ACCOUNTING PROCESSES AND PRACTICES The budgetary accounting of the federal government has given rise to a body of terminology descriptive both of events in the fiscal process of government and of actions required of certain organizations. Some examples follow.

▲ Congress must *authorize* and *appropriate* funds or budget authority to permit the collection of revenues or expenditure of federal money.

▲ Permission to *allocate* a portion of an appropriation between agencies is a prerogative of Congress, as well.

▲ OMB has the responsibility to *apportion* the various funds appropriated or allocated by the Congress to regulate the rate of fund use by agencies.

▲ The individual agencies are responsible for *allotting, obligating, expending, disbursing,* and *costing* the funds of the appropriation or other budgetary authority.

Procedures are required by law to ensure that there is compliance with governmentwide criteria and that the necessary controls exist within an agency to properly manage the funds and assets required for operations. Failure to adhere to required controls could result in actions being taken against responsible officials, involving financial penalties or imprisonment, or both.

An understanding of the budgetary accounting process is a prerequisite to understanding federal accounting. The many aspects of this form of accounting are highlighted in the following chapters.

▲ Chapter 9, Appropriations, Allocations, and Apportionments, defines these important fiscal events, describes the process for controlling federal monies external to a federal agency, and illustrates the nature of the accounting that would be required to reflect the actions of agency management in committing appropriated funds.

▲ Chapter 10, Allotments and Obligations, defines these events, sets forth specific legal criteria applicable to agency obligations, identifies the standard object classifications, and describes the accounting required to properly reflect such activities in the agency records.

▲ Chapter 11, Expenditures and Applied Costs, defines these terms and describes accrual accounting as it is applied to governmental accounting. Methods used to determine accruals and applied costs are summarized along with certain control procedures and accounting practices.

▲ Chapter 12, Disbursements, describes a system of accountable officers existing in the federal service and the responsibilities and liabilities attached to such positions. The disbursement process is identified, selected controls are summarized, and the desired accounting for disbursements is highlighted.

It is in accounting for the events above that federal accounting differs from other applications of accounting.

ACCOUNTING FOR FEDERAL EXPENDITURES AND RECEIPTS

The preponderance of federal accounting, in practice, revolves around the recording, accumulating, monitoring, and reporting of expenditures and receipts. For each of the categories, definitions have been provided, the applicable process has been illustrated, the important events requiring accounting recognition have been demonstrated, and reporting has been described. The following major expenditures and classes of receipts have been described in this manner.

▲ Chapter 13, Pay, Leave, and Allowances
▲ Chapter 14, Travel and Transportation
▲ Chapter 15, Contracts
▲ Chapter 16, Grants

▲ Chapter 17, Selected Interagency Transactions and Other Expenditures

▲ Chapter 18, Receipts, Transfers, Reimbursements, and Refunds

An understanding of these transactions requires knowledge of the requirements of several organizations such as GAO, OMB, and the Treasury. Additionally, Congress has provided much guidance and imposed specific compliance criteria with respect to certain of these transactions that must be considered in the accounting and reporting process as well.

ACCOUNTING FOR ASSETS, LIABILITIES, AND INVESTMENTS OF GOVERNMENT

Accounting for the assets, liabilities, and investments of the government in an agency's operations is similar to the process used in the private sector. Congress and GAO require that systems of accounting and internal controls exist to acquire, safeguard, account, report, and dispose of these properties and settle debts of the government. Illustrations have been provided of the several types of reporting existing within a federal agency to ensure proper accountability. Each of these types of transactions has been treated in separate chapters.

▲ Chapter 19, Current Assets

▲ Chapter 20, Fixed Assets and Other Assets

▲ Chapter 21, Liabilities

▲ Chapter 22, Investments of the Government

▲ Chapter 23, Financial Reports and Statements

The definitions that appear in these chapters are similar to those used in the private sector. Specific accounting treatments, however, are illustrated, which are generally followed to comply with the requirements of GAO or other central agency directions.

ACCOUNTING FOR REVOLVING FUNDS

Within the federal government, numerous funds have been established by Congressional action to support the conduct of certain business operations. Generally, these operations are conducted pursuant to the requirements of working capital and revolving funds. Under these structures, agencies operate supply and industrial funds, performing services ranging from wholesaling to manufacturing. Charges for these services are "billed" to the appropriations of user organizations.

Business or private sector accounting is generally applied to these activities. Often cost accounting is an integral aspect of the financial management of such entities. It is necessary to monitor cost closely to ensure that the "selling prices" of such funds are adequate to replenish or reimburse the fund for the costs incurred in providing goods or services for other organizations. This funding mechanism is described in two chapters.

▲   Chapter 24, Revolving Funds
▲   Chapter 25, Industrial Funds

The requirements for such funds are described and the accounting process used by agencies has been illustrated to provide an insight into how the budgetary accounting process is capable of being integrated by organizations utilizing, essentially, generally accepted accounting principles of the corporate world.

FEDERAL FINANCIAL MANAGEMENT POLICY AND

PART I **PROCEDURES**

Federal Financial chapter 2 Management Policy

INTRODUCTION The overall responsibility for prescribing policy relating to federal financial management rests with the Congress of the United States. By various laws, Congress has directed that certain central agencies establish standards, principles, and set administrative guides for other departments and agencies of the government. The central agencies group comprises the General Accounting Office, the Office of Management and Budget, Treasury Department, and the General Services Administration. The individual departments and agencies themselves have considerable discretion for determining the specific procedures and practices for the programs and activities within their statutory control.

Historically, Congress has provided the general requirements for fiscal, accounting, reporting, financial management, and auditing. Much information implementing these general requirements has also been published by the central agencies. These implementing guidelines have taken various forms. Some of the more common forms are described in this chapter.

SELECTED LEGISLATION GOVERNING ACCOUNTING

Several laws are directed toward the manner in which government agencies receive, account, spend, and report on the status of federal appropriations. In addition to laws primarily addressed to accounting and financial management matters, oftentimes the authorizing or appropriating legislation related to the programs of a specific agency will contain requirements on the management of appropriated funds. In this section, selected provisions of laws having a general impact on fiscal and financial management are highlighted.

Constitutional Authority for Appropriations

The initial legislation making reference to revenues and expenditures of the federal government is the Constitution. Portions of Article 1, Sections 8 and 9 outline the financial responsibility vested in the Congress:

▲ *Section 8, clause 1,* The Congress shall have power to lay and collect taxes, duties, imposts and excises, to pay the debts and provide for the common defense and general welfare of the United States . . . .

▲ *Section 8, clause 2,* To borrow money on the credit of the United States . . . .

▲ *Section 9, clause 7,* No money shall be drawn from the Treasury, but in consequence of appropriations made by law; and a regular statement and account of receipts and expenditures of all public money shall be published from time to time.

To date, this forms the underlying authority by which the Congress provides for federal revenues and authorizes the expenditure of public funds.

Establishment of GAO and Bureau of the Budget

Broad changes were made in federal financial management with the passage of the Budget and Accounting Act of 1921. The more significant provisions of that law included

▲ Title II of the Act that established a national budget system requiring the President to formally transmit the national budget to the Congress at the beginning of each session. Additionally, the Bureau of the Budget was created in the Department of the Treasury.

▲ Title III of the Act that established the General Accounting Office, headed by a Comptroller General of the United States. The GAO was independent of the executive branch, responsible only to the Congress.

A later amendment gave GAO the responsibility for settling and adjusting all claims and demands by or against the government.

The act gave the Comptroller General the power to prescribe the forms, systems, and procedures for the administrative controls and accounting for the funds appropriated to the various government departments and agencies. GAO was also given the responsibility to make administrative examinations of fiscal officer's accounts and claims against the government.

The same Title of the Act of 1921 required that the Comptroller General investigate ". . . at the seat of government or elsewhere, all matters relating to the receipt, disbursement, and application of public funds . . . ."

Government Corporation Control Act

For some years, there had been growing concern by the public and Congress over the number of government corporations and the need for closer scrutiny and independent audit.

Since 1927, pursuant to a Supreme Court decision, it was believed that government corporations, in certain respects, were free from accountability to the Treasury and from the audit jurisdiction of the GAO. Further, the Supreme Court held that the corporations generally were free of Congressional control over the corporation's expenditures for administration and operations. As a consequence, most government corporations did not submit their records for review by the GAO.

Following an investigation by Congress in the 1940s, legislation was passed to provide for closer Congressional scrutiny of the many government corporations and required that these organizations undergo independent audits. The resulting legislation was referred to as the Government Corporation Control Act of 1945. The significant provisions, from a financial management view, were that this law

▲ Specified that wholly owned government corporations were required to submit budgets of a business type annually to the Congress, and

▲ Required the Comptroller General to audit the financial transactions of the wholly owned government corporations.

These audits were to be made in accordance with the procedures applicable to commercial corporate audits and under any regulations that may be prescribed by the Comptroller General.

The Act of 1945, as amended, provided for reviews of two types of government corporations: wholly owned corporations and mixed-ownership corporations.

The mixed-ownership government corporations were defined by the Act of 1945, as amended, to mean organizations such as the Central Bank for Cooperatives, Federal Land Banks, Federal Intermediate Credit Banks, Federal Home Loan Banks and the Federal Deposit Insurance Corporation. Wholly owned government corporations were defined by the act to include such entities as the Commodity Credit Corporation, the Government National Mortgage Association, the Inland Waterways Corporation, the Federal Prison Industries, the Federal Savings and Loan Corporation, the Tennessee Valley Authority, and the Pension Benefit Guaranty Corporation. The financial transactions of mixed-ownership corporations for any period during which federal government capital has been invested were required to be audited by the GAO in accordance with the principles and procedures applicable to commercial corporate transactions and under such rules and regulations as may be prescribed by the Comptroller General of the United States. GAO was to conduct an annual audit and make a report to Congress describing the scope of the audit and including a statement of assets and liabilities, capital and surplus or deficit, an analysis of surplus or deficit, a statement of income and expenses, a statement of sources and application of funds and other comments necessary to keep Congress informed of the operations and financial conditions of the corporations.

Antideficiency Legislation

Probably the most quoted, and most closely monitored, of all financial legislation are the provisions of the Antideficiency Act, more commonly cited by governmental financial managers as the "Section 3679" (of the Revised Statutes) provisions. The purpose of this legislation, dating back to 1870, was to prevent agencies from having expenditures in excess of amounts appropriated by the Congress. By later amendments, the fiscal restrictions of the statutes were made increasingly stringent, requiring the apportionment of appropriations by the Bureau of the Budget, placing limitations on both expenditures and obligations in excess of appropriated funds, and establishing specific prohibitions relating to officers and employees of the government.

The salient provisions of Section 3679 of the Revised Statute related to the apportionments, administrative controls, and the prohibitions of federal funds follow.

▲ The Director of the Bureau of the Budget (now the Office of Mangement and Budget) was required to apportion or reapportion in writing appropriated funds, by months, calendar quarters, operating seasons, other time periods, or by activities, functions, projects or objects, or by a combination thereof.

▲ No apportionment is permitted that would indicate a necessity for a deficiency or supplemental estimate unless such an action is required because of

Laws enacted after the transmission of the estimates for an appropriation to the congress that require expenditure beyond administrative control, or

Emergencies involving safety of human life, protection of property, or the immediate welfare of individuals in cases in which an appropriation has been made requiring sums to be paid to such individuals.

▲ Any officer of the government having administrative control of an appropriation is required to prescribe, by regulation, a system of administrative control that is designed to

Restrict obligations or expenditures against each appropriation to the amount of apportionments, and

Enable such officer or agency head to fix responsibility for the creation of any obligation or the making of an expenditure in excess of an apportionment or reapportionment.

Each agency was directed to have a simplified system of subdividing appropriations among operating units, with the objective of maintaining control at the highest practical level within the agency. The implementation of this act has generally resulted in the design of a detailed system of signatory authorization and approval by appropriate agency officials as well as in the adherence to detailed fiscal review and fund certification procedures.

Budget and Accounting Procedures Act of 1950

The Budget and Accounting Procedures Act of 1950 established additional improvement in areas of budgeting, accounting, and auditing in the federal government. This act was really three acts: Title I dealt with budgeting and accounting; Title II addressed appropriations; and Title III contained repeals or deletions of prior legislation that was no longer applicable. Parts of the Act of 1950 amended the Budget and Accounting Act of 1921. The more significant provisions of the Act of 1950 related to the preparation of budgets and the accounting for and reporting on budget execution.

Budget Regulation

The preparation of performance-based budgets was authorized by the Act of 1950 requiring agency financial information to be displayed in terms of functions and activities of the government. Each agency head was directed to take the necessary action, in consultation with the Bureau of the Budget, to achieve

▲ Consistency in accounting and budget classifications;

▲ Synchronization between accounting and budget classifications and organizational structures; and

▲ Support of the budget justifications by information on performance and program costs by organizational units.

Accounting Legislation

Part 2 of Title I was actually an "act within an act," and is cited as the Accounting and Auditing Act of 1950. There are several pertinent provisions that have become the underlying legal base for much of the accounting that now exists in the federal government.

By the Act of 1950, the maintenance of accounting systems and production of financial reports on operations of executive agencies are the responsibility of the executive branch. The auditing for the government, conducted by the Comptroller General, was to be directed at

▲ Determining the extent to which accounting and related financial reporting fulfill the purposes specified;

▲ Determining that financial transactions have been consummated in accordance with laws, regulations, or other legal requirements, and

▲ Determining that adequate internal financial control over operations is exercised, and that the controls afford an effective basis for the settlement of accounts of accountable officers.

Additionally, the Comptroller General, after consultation with the Secretary of Treasury and the Director of the Bureau of the Budget, was required to prescribe the principles, standards, and related requirements for the accounting to be observed by each executive agency. However, it was the head of each executive agency who was responsible for establishing and maintaining systems of accounting and internal controls. These systems and controls were to be designed to accomplish

▲ Full disclosure of the financial results of the agency's activities;

▲ Adequate financial information needed for the agency's management purposes;

▲ Effective control over and accountability for all funds, property, and other assets for which the agency is responsible, including appropriate internal audit;

▲ Reliable accounting results to serve as a basis for preparation and support of the agency's budget request, for controlling the execution of its budget, and providing financial information required by the Bureau of the Budget; and

▲ Suitable integration of the accounting of the agency with the Treasury Department in connection with its central accounting and reporting responsibilities.

The established accounting systems of executive agencies were required to conform to the principles, standards, and related requirements prescribed by the Comptroller General.

The Act of 1950 was later amended by 84 PL 863 and each executive agency was required to maintain the accounts of the agency on an accrual basis to show the resources, liabilities, and costs of operations of the agency with a view to facilitating the preparation of cost-based budgets. The accounting principles and standards for the accrual accounting were to be prescribed by the Comptroller General. The accounting system was also required to include adequate monetary property records as an integral part of the system.

Performance Budgeting

Title III of the 1950 act provided that the budget was to be presented on a performance basis, with emphasis on functions, activities, and justified on the basis of possible work load and unit-cost data. The President was given authority to determine the form and detail of the budget, but Congress, by the act, required that certain specific information be included, such as

▲ Functions and activities of government and other desirable classification data

▲ Reconciliation of expenditures with appropriations

▲ Estimated expenditures and proposed appropriations for the ensuing year

▲ Estimated receipts of the government during the ensuing fiscal year

▲ Actual and estimated appropriations, expenditures, and receipts during the last completed fiscal year and fiscal year in progress, respectively

▲ Balanced statements of conditions of the Treasury at the end of the last complete year, estimates for the end of the year in progress, and the estimated condition of the ensuing fiscal year if the financial proposals contained in the budget are adopted

▲ All essential facts regarding the bonded and other indebtedness of the government

▲ Such other financial statements and data as the President deems necessary or desirable to make known the financial condition of the government

By the act, Congress required that accounting objectives of the government provide for full disclosure of results of financial operations, adequate financial information for operating and budgetary purposes and effective control over receipts, expenditures, funds, property, and other assets. Congress also mandated that the needs and responsibilities of both the executive and legislative branches be fully considered in establishing accounting and reporting systems and requirements.

Cost-based Budgets and Accrual Accounting

Public Law 84-863 amended the Budget and Accounting Act of 1921 and the Budgeting and Accounting Procedures Act of 1950 to permit the President to include annual budget information on program costs and accomplishments. Additionally, this law directed agency heads to take the necessary action to achieve

▲ Consistency in accounting and budget classifications,

▲ Synchronization between these classifications and organizational structure, and

▲ Support of budget justifications by information on performance and program costs.

The stated objective for cost-based budgets was that both management and Congress would be able to review the total resources on hand, on order, and being procured, rather than limiting the budget review only to money sought from Congress in the form of new obligational authority. A *cost-based budget* was defined as one identifying the cost of the program in terms of goods and services consumed. The budget discloses the balances of the goods and services on hand, obtained through the use of prior appropriations, and the extent that any unconsumed services and goods would be available to support current or future years' budget programs. A cost-based budget would show the obligational authority necessary to support the current year activities. Such a budget is particularly revealing in identifying carry-overs of available resources from one year to another.

The heads of agencies were also directed to maintain accounts on an accrual basis to show the resources, liabilities, and costs of operations of such agency in a manner that facilitated the preparation of cost-based budgets and to include adequate monetary property accounting records as an integral part of the accounting system. Under this legislation *accrued expenditures* were defined as charges incurred for goods and services received and other assets acquired, whether or not payment has been made and whether or not invoices have been received.

This same act also amended the Antideficiency Act, cited above, to achieve simplified controls over the subdivision of appropriations and funds. Each agency was directed to work towards the objective of financing its operating units through a minimum of administrative subdivisions of the appropriations, consistent with the requirements of the applicable funding legislation.

Supplemental Appropriation
Act of 1955

Section 1311 of the Supplemental Appropriation Act of 1955 resulted from the Congressional difficulties in obtaining accurate data on obligations from executive agencies. This act established statutory criteria to define valid obligations. According to Section 1311 (a) of the act, no amount shall be recorded as an obligation of the government unless it is supported by one of the eight forms of documentary evidence set forth in this act.

Congress intended these eight forms of documentary evidence (defined in Chapter 7, Accounting Concepts in the Federal Government) to encompass all types of obligations incurred in the course of governmental activities.

Section 1311 required that each report of year-end unliquidated obligations and unobligated appropriation balance be certified by officials designated by the agency head having overall responsibility for recording obligations.

Congressional Budget and Impoundment
Control Act of 1974

More recently, important legislation affecting governmental finances was enacted. The Congressional Budget and Impoundment Act of 1974 made considerable changes in the federal financial process and provided for

▲ A new Congressional budget process

▲ Committees on the Budget in each House of Congress

▲ A Congressional Budget Office

▲ Procedures providing Congressional control over the impoundment of funds by the executive branch

▲ A new fiscal year of the government, changing from July 1 to June 30 of each year to October 1 to September 30 of each year

The revised timetable, with respect to the Congressional Budget process for any fiscal year, was also set forth in this act. (See Chapter 3.)

RESPONSIBILITY FOR ACCOUNTING IN THE FEDERAL GOVERNMENT

The responsibility for accounting is dispersed among several agencies. Each is required by some legislation or other directive to perform certain functions to ensure or promote sounder accounting practices in government. The principal organizations include the General Accounting Office, the Office of Management and Budget, and the Treasury. Departments and agencies themselves are responsible for designing, implementing, and maintaining their own systems of accounting.

These and other responsibilities have been highlighted by the Joint Financial Management Improvement Program (in its publication *Financial Management Functions in the Federal Government*, September 1974).

The General Accounting Office

The General Accounting Office is an independent agency in the legislative branch, headed by the Comptroller General of the United States. As mentioned earlier, the agency was created by the Budget and Accounting Act of 1921 and is responsible to the Congress of the United States. By various laws, the GAO has been charged with several responsibilities with respect to accounting in the government. For example, GAO

▲ Prescribes principles, standards, and related requirements for accounting;

▲ Cooperates in the development and improvement of agency accounting and financial management systems;

▲ Reviews and approves agency accounting systems;

▲ Examines and reports on accounting systems periodically;

▲ Renders decisions to departments and agencies relating to questions concerning the legality of government expenditures;

▲ Settles or final audits the accounts of the government's accountable officers; and

▲ Prescribes the guidance relating to the retention and preservation of records, books of accounts, and documents.

Along with the OMB and the Treasury, the GAO also shares responsibility for developing and maintaining standardized data processing and information systems and develops and publishes standard terminology, definitions, classifications and codes for federal fiscal, budgetary, and program-related data and information.

Over the years, the General Accounting Office has published considerable information concerning the criteria to be used by federal agencies in accounting for appropriated monies. The GAO standards and principles are discussed in several chapters of this book. As noted in Chapter 1, the principal body of knowledge related to governmental financial management exists in an eight-volume manual entitled *Policy and Procedures GAO Manual for Guidance of Federal Agencies*, which covers several fiscal and financial subjects in considerable detail.

▲ Title 1—*The United States General Accounting Office*

▲ Title 2—*Accounting Principles and Standards and Internal Auditing Guidelines*

▲ Title 3—*Audit*

▲ Title 4—*Claims-General*

▲ Title 5—*Transportation*

▲ Title 6—*Pay, Leave, and Allowances*

▲ Title 7—*Standardized Fiscal Procedures*

▲ Title 8—*Records' Management and Services*

The listing above is not an exhaustive outline of the guidelines issued by the GAO. From an auditing viewpoint, the GAO has published *Standards for Audit* of governmental organizations, programs, activities and functions, along with several audit guidelines to assist in the implementation of these standards. Considerable information has also been published relating to the design and approval of governmental accounting systems.

Further, the GAO regularly issues the Comptroller General's decisions on a variety of subjects relating to the expenditure of government monies. These administrative decisions have the full effect of law upon the various government agencies. Additionally, under other legal mandates, the GAO issues hundreds of audit and evaluative reports to the Congress giving GAO's observations and recommendations concerning the application of federal monies by departments and agencies.

The Office of Management and Budget

The Office of Management and Budget was established by the Reorganization Plan No. 2 of 1970, effective July 1, 1970. All functions of the predecessor agency, the Bureau of the Budget, were transferred to the Director of the OMB. The Bureau of the Budget itself was established, along with GAO, by the Budget and Accounting Act of 1921. In 1939, the bureau was made a part of the executive office of the President.

The OMB has accounting-related responsibilities that have been established by several laws. A partial listing of significant responsibilities follows.

▲ Developing and improving the government's system of budget control and review,

▲ Developing governmentwide information systems policy and fiscal and policy overseeing of automatic data processing in the executive branch,

▲ Planning and promoting a continuous program for improving accounting and financial reporting in the government,

▲ Making improvements in governmental budgeting and accounting methods and procedures, and

▲ Establishing a system of apportionments of appropriations to monitor expenditures of federal monies.

Along with the GAO and the Treasury, the OMB shares the responsibility for developing and maintaining standardized data processing and information systems for fiscal, budgetary, and program-related data and information and, additionally, to develop and publish standard terminology, definitions, classifications, and codes for federal fiscal, budgetary and program-related data and information.

A principal medium through which the OMB publishes financial management policy to the federal government is a system of circulars and bulletins. As outlined in OMB Circular A-1, the subject matter of these documents applies to all departments and establishments, which include any executive department, independent commission, board, bureau, office, agency, government-owned or government-controlled corporation, or other establishment of the government, including regulatory commissions or boards. OMB circulars are issued when the nature of the subject is of a continuing effect. The circulars are identified by the letter "A" and a number (e.g., OMB Circular A-11). Excluded are the legislative and judicial branches of the government.

Bulletins, on the other hand, are used when the nature of the subject requires a single or ad hoc action by departments and establishments or is of a transitory nature. Bulletins are issued in an annual series, numbered in chronological order. The last two numerals of the fiscal year of issuance are used to indicate the annual series (e.g., 80-3).

Exhibit 2.1 identifies the principal OMB Circulars dealing with or impacting upon the accounting practices of the federal government.

The Treasury

The Treasury, headed by the Secretary of the Treasury, is the official fiscal agency of the federal government. The department was created in 1789. Some of its fiscal and accounting responsibilities follow.

▲ Maintaining the central accounts of the government to provide the consolidated position of the government's financial transactions

▲ Collecting and recording receipts of the government from taxes, duties, fees, and other sources

▲ Making disbursements at the direction of properly supported requests from other agencies of the government

▲ Prescribing reporting requirements for receipts and disbursement and appropriations balances

▲ Providing operating instructions to agencies for central accounting and reporting and other fiscal matters

Exhibit 2.1 **OFFICE OF MANAGEMENT AND BUDGET CIRCULARS THAT IMPACT UPON ACCOUNTING FEDERAL FUNDS**

OMB CIRCULAR NUMBER	SUBJECT OF OMB CIRCULAR
A-1	Bureau of the Budget's systems of circulars and bulletins to executive departments and establishments
A-10	Responsibilities for disclosure with respect to the budget
A-11	Preparation and submission of budget estimates
A-12	Object classification
A-25	User charges
A-31	Distribution of appropriations and other budget authority made to the President
A-34	Instruction for budget execution
A-40	Clearance of public reporting and record-keeping requirements under the Federal Reporting Act
A-44	Management review and improvement program
A-115	Zero-based budgeting

From time to time, the Treasury has issued Joint Regulations with the General Accounting Office on fiscal and accounting-related matters having governmentwide significance. Additionally, the Treasury maintains a series of notices and circulars that are used to issue guidance to departments and agencies on specific subjects. The more permanent or continuing guidance is set forth in the Treasury's *Fiscal Requirements Manual for the Guidance of Departments and Agencies*.

The General Service Administration

The General Services Administration (GSA) is an executive branch agency, established in 1949 by the Federal Property and Administrative Services Act, to perform a variety of property management and other services. Among its responsibilities are those related to automated data processing and telecommunications. GSA personnel must provide for the

▲ Management, operation, and utilization of federal data processing centers and communication facilities to provide services to GSA and other agencies of the government;

▲ Promotion and coordination of purchase, lease, maintenance, operation, and utilization of automated data processing equipment by federal agencies; and

▲ Guidance, assistance, and coordination to agencies in procurement and utilization of automated data processing and communication services.

Federal Budget Process, chapter 3 Controls, and Monitoring: (I)

INTRODUCTION The budget process, from preparation through execution, is an integral part of federal financing. It is the money appropriated or the budget authority given by Congress that forms the accounting entity that must be controlled, managed, and reported by the agencies and departments of the federal government. An individual agency could be responsible for one or several appropriations, each of which could require special expenditure and reporting conditions. Additionally, the activities of several agencies might be financed by the appropriation of another agency responsible to the Congress for compliance with the appropriation law. For these reasons, an understanding of the federal budget process is important to the study of federal government accounting.

This chapter describes the phases of the budget cycle, the requirements of the Congressional Budget and Impoundment Control Act of 1974, and selected budgeting concepts. Chapter 4 provides details concerning the preparation and the execution of an agency budget.

IMPORTANCE OF THE FEDERAL BUDGET CYCLE

Within the federal government, the budget is viewed as considerably more than a guide for planned expenditures. The budget is a legal mandate of Congress to collect, obligate, and expend federal money in a prescribed manner and for specified purposes. Often, a time limitation is placed on the period during which the funds may be used. As will be seen in this and other chapters, the federal budget is at one and the same time

▲ A listing of the priorities of the federal government as determined by the President and the Congress of the United States;

▲ The operating criteria for agencies to commence, continue, or cease specific government programs and activities;

▲ The legal authority to collect revenues and incur obligations and expenditures that must be paid;

▲ An operating plan for managing the government during the fiscal year; and

▲ The financial authority dictating the acceptable accounting and reporting procedures and practices.

Governmental accounting is fund accounting. Fund accounting or appropriation accounting of governmental organizations is directly responsive to the legal mandates, limitations, and specific fiscal requirements of the budgets passed by Congress. It is the budget, with its legal basis, that is also responsible for the development of auditing concepts unique to governmental entities. The execution of the federal budget, which is dispersed among many appropriations to many agencies, must be continually reviewed during the execution period to ensure its compliance with Congressional intent. Deviations from budget could constitute statutory violations for which there often must be a reporting to both the President and Congress.

Budget activity in the federal government continues throughout the year. Traditionally, though, the budget cycle can be viewed in several phases. In practice, seldom is a department clearly addressing a single phase: the current year's budget must be monitored and accounted for; next year's budget is being defended before the Congressional committees; the department's budget for two years hence is being discussed with the analysts of the Office of the Management and Budget.

Budget Preparation Phase

This phase begins some 15 to 18 months before the start of the fiscal year. It is a period of continuous exchange of information and decision making for the President, assisted by the OMB and agencies and advisors. The preparation phase proceeds from the evaluation, issue-identification period during the spring of the year to the general budget and more final fiscal policy decisions of fall and early winter.

During this phase, there is considerable discussion among the President, Congress, agencies, and outside experts. In addition to being the financial plan of the government, the budget is, as importantly, the culmination of the political process and thoughts. As this phase nears conclusion, the executive branch prepares to make its oral and written submission to the Congress and to the general public.

Historically, this phase concludes with the President making his State of the Union message and formally transmitting his budget to the Congress shortly after it convenes in January preceding the start of the fiscal year concerned.

Congressional Action Phase

It is up to Congress to approve, change, or disapprove the President's budget. The Congressional phase is marked by two sets of hearings (1) for authorization of the program and (2) for the funding or approval of an appropriation for the program.

This phase often comprises several types of activities involving many interested parties.

▲ The President, OMB, and the heads and key officials of the executive branch agencies appear before committees of Congress to defend, explain, and justify the need for the requested programs and the programmed level of dollars.

▲ Congress holds hearings that are also attended by citizens, occasionally by representatives of foreign governments, and by organizations as well as by the general public, supporting particular programs and proposed initiatives.

▲ Special reviews and studies are made and submitted to Congress; Congress, itself, will authorize independent reviews to provide data valuable in reaching a conclusion on the various budget requests.

▲ Executive sessions or private meetings are held among members and committees of Congress and persons or organizations involved or interested in particular programs.

▲ Continual releases are made to the public media relating to suggested alternatives, programs, possible tax consequences, and projected debt ceilings of various budgets for the purpose of generating interest and support for particular positions.

▲ Ultimately, Congress, through its committees, must develop a summary legislative package resulting from the many authorization and appropriation bills proposed during the session.

▲ Once a Congressional consensus is reached, the various appropriations are submitted to the President for his review and approval or veto.

The Congressional approval for a program, with the permission to obligate and expend funds, is referred to as an *appropriation*. An appropriation is the legal or budget authority that makes funds available to the department or agency. This authority can last for a year, or several years. In some cases, the authority can be permanent. In the last instance, funds become available annually without further Congressional action.

On occasion, Congress will not complete action on all budget requests before the beginning of a fiscal year. In such circumstances, Congress may enact a *continuing resolution*, providing funding authority for the agency to continue operations usually, but not always, until an appropriation is approved. In unusual circumstances, when an appropriation is never passed for a fiscal year, the continuing resolution is the basis for agency financing for the entire year. Under a continuing resolution, the agency may generally not undertake any new initiatives and must maintain its rate of expenditure at the same level of the preceding program year. If one House of the Congress has acted, the agency may not exceed the rate of expenditure of that action or the expenditure rate of the last year's appropriation, whichever is less.

Execution Phase

Once passed by the Congress and approved by the President, the budget forms the operating plan for the government over the next fiscal year. At the federal level several activities will occur, although not all will be performed by a single agency.

▲ Taxes must be levied, duties are imposed, fees are charged, and all must be collected to provide the funds necessary to support the expenditure budgets approved.

▲ Obligations will be made, expenditures will be accrued, and liabilities of the government must be paid.

▲ Both receipts and expenditures will be closely monitored by the responsible agencies to ensure compliance with the budget legislation; periodic reports will have to be made to the President, Congress, and to the public on the status of compliance with the budget.

▲ Within the individual agencies there must exist a system for allocating the appropriated funds throughout the year to ensure that a deficiency does not result and to achieve the legislated goals and objectives.

After approval, or appropriation, by Congress, the budget becomes the financial plan for operating the agency. The activities of the plan must be controlled and costed to ensure full compliance with the intent of Congress.

Once funds are appropriated, the OMB by law must apportion the appropriation to the individual agencies. The *apportionment* is a division of the appropriation by time (often quarterly), activity, or purpose. Should additional funds be required during the fiscal year, supplemental requests for appropriations must be made to the Congress. As described in later chapters, the apportioned funds are then allocated by the agency head to various activities and programs; transfers of funds to other agencies may be required to meet Congressional or Presidential directives.

Review and Audit

Departments and agencies, by law, are required to establish systems of controls and accounting to ensure that obligations and outlays are consistent with the authorizing and appropriations of Congress. These organizations must also establish their own programs for reviews, evaluations, and audits. Additionally, the General Accounting Office and the Office of Management and Budget will regularly make reviews and evaluations of the manner in which the executive agencies and other organizations are complying with the intent of Congress.

CONGRESSIONAL BUDGET AND IMPOUNDMENT CONTROL ACT OF 1974

The Congressional Budget and Impoundment Control Act of 1974 significantly altered certain aspects of financial management in the federal government, including the budget cycle. In summary, the act provided for

▲ A new Congressional budget process;
▲ Committees on the Budget of each House;
▲ A Congressional Budget Office;
▲ Procedures for providing Congressional control over the impoundment of funds by the executive branch;
▲ A revised fiscal year to start on October 1 and end on September 30 of each year.
▲ A revised timetable for submission of the budget to the Congress.

Under the act "impoundment" refers to the process by which the President reduces the amount provided by Congress for programs by failing to spend at the level authorized by Congress.

Revised Budget Process Timetable

The following constitutes the revised Congressional budget process, as defined by the Act of 1974.

On or before	Action to be completed
November 10	President submits *current services budget*.
Fifteen days after Congress meets	President submits his budget.
March 15	Committees and joint committees submit reports to the *Committees on the Budget*.
April 1	*Congressional Budget Office* submits report to Budget Committees.
April 15	Budget committees report *first concurrent resolution* on the budget to their Houses.
May 15	Committees report bills and resolutions authorizing new budget authority.
May 15	Congress completes action on first concurrent resolution of the budget.
Seventh day after Labor Day	Congress completes action on bills and resolutions providing new budget authority and new spending authority.
September 15	Congress completes action on second required concurrent resolution on the budget.
September 25	Congress completes action on reconciliation bill or resolution, or both; implementing the *second required concurrent resolution*.
October 1	Fiscal year begins.

New Budget Terminology

The Act of 1974 introduced and defined several new terms that have subsequently become part of the governmental budget process terminology.

Current Services Budget

The *current services budget*, to be submitted by the President on or before November 10, is a summary of the estimated outlays and proposed budget authority that would be included in the budget to be submitted for the ensuing fiscal year if all programs and activities were carried on during such ensuing year at the same level as the fiscal year in progress and without policy changes in such programs and activities.

The estimated outlays and proposed budget authority submitted pursuant to the act shall be shown by function and subfunctions. Accompanying these estimates shall be economic and programmatic assumptions underlying the estimated outlays and proposed budget authority, such as the rate of inflation, the rate of real economic growth, the unemployment rate, program case loads, and pay increases.

Concurrent Resolution

The *concurrent resolution* of Congress on the budget, according to the act, means

▲ A concurrent resolution setting forth the Congressional budget for the government for a fiscal year,

▲ A concurrent resolution reaffirming or revising the Congressional budget for the government for a fiscal year, and

▲ Any other concurrent resolution revising the Congressional budget for the government for a fiscal year.

Committees on the Budget

The *Committee on the Budget* of each of the Houses has been defined as a committee that shall have the duty

▲ To report the matters required to be reported under the Congressional Budget Act;

▲ To make continuing studies of the effect on budget outlays of relevant existing and proposed legislation and to report the results of such studies to the House or Senate, as appropriate;

▲ To request and evaluate continuing studies of tax expenditures, to devise methods of coordinating tax expenditures, policies, and programs with direct budget outlays, and to report the results of such studies to the House or Senate, as appropriate;

▲ To review, on a continuing basis, the conduct by the Congressional Budget Office of its functions and duties.

Congressional Budget Office

By the act, a *Congressional Budget Office* was established to assist the Committees on the Budget of both Houses in discharging matters within their jurisdiction, including the development of

▲ Information with respect to the budget, appropriation bills, and other bills authorizing or providing budget authority or tax expenditures;

▲ Information with respect to revenues, receipts, estimated future revenues and receipts, and changing revenue conditions; and

▲ Such related information as these and other committees may request.

First Concurrent Resolution

The *first concurrent resolution,* to be completed by May 15 of each year for the fiscal year beginning on October 1 of the year, shall include

▲ The appropriate level of total budget outlays and total new budget authority;

▲ An estimate of budget outlays and an appropriate level of new budget authority for each major functional category, for contingencies, and for un-distributed intragovernmental transactions, based on allocation of the appropriate level of total budget outlays and of total new budget authority;

▲ The amount, if any, of the surplus or the deficit in the budget that is appropriate in light of economic conditions and all other relevant factors;

▲ The recommended level of federal revenues and the amount, if any, by which the aggregate level of federal revenues should be increased or decreased by bills and resolutions to be reported by the committees;

▲ The appropriate level of the public debt, and the amount, if any, by which the statutory limit on the public debt should be increased or decreased by bills and resolutions to be reported by the appropriate committees; and

▲ Such other matters relating to the budget as may be appropriate to carry out the purposes of the Act of 1974.

Second Concurrent Resolution

The Act of 1974 provides for a *second required concurrent resolution* to be completed by the Congress on or before September 15 that shall, to the extent necessary,

▲ Specify the total amount by which the new budget authority for the fiscal year, the budget authority provided for prior fiscal years, and new spending authority contained in bills and other resolutions within the jurisdiction of the committee is to be changed and to direct that committee to determine and recommend changes to accomplish a change in the total amount;

▲ Specify the total amount by which revenues are to be changed and direct that the committees having jurisdiction to determine and recommend changes in the revenues laws, bills, and resolutions to accomplish a change of the total amount;

▲ Specify the amount by which the statutory limit on the public debt is to be changed and direct the committees having jurisdiction to recommend such change.

BUDGETING CONCEPTS OF THE FEDERAL GOVERNMENT Over the years the federal government has utilized various concepts in attempts to achieve more precision in estimating required resources, in monitoring the expenditure rate of budgeted funds, and in determining the cumulative cost of agency programs. These efforts were dictated, in part, by concerns over the efficiency and effectiveness with which budgeted funds were being utilized. Probably as important, though, is the fact that the budget is also a statutory directive, violations of which must be reported to the President and Congress, as mentioned earlier.

To varying degrees, government agencies are applying at least three budgeting or planning concepts to the management of appropriated funds. The most recent is zero-based budgeting. Currently in use by many agencies, but more popular during the 1960s, is PPBS (i.e., planning, programming, and budgeting systems). Other agencies have found some merit in attempting to apply MBO, Management By Objectivies, to the activities of federal personnel.

Zero-based Budgeting

By Presidential directive, agencies were instructed to use zero-based budgeting (ZBB) as the sole basis for the preparation of the budget requests for fiscal year 1980. Thus the President was eliminating the traditional process used by agencies to justify budgets.

Defined

Zero-based budgeting is defined as a systematic process by which management undertakes the careful examination of the basis for allocating resources in conjunction with the formulation of budget requests and program planning.

The policies and procedures relating to this concept have been published by the Office of Management and Budget in its Circular, A-115, *Zero-Base Budgeting*.

The concept implies that ideally all planning and budgeting decisions are examined in total and that resource requests must be justified by the agencies in their entirety, i.e., a zero-based budget. In the federal sector this concept has been considerably modified by OMB.

Goals of ZBB

The goals of zero-based budgeting as applied to federal finances were summarized by OMB as being to

39

▲ Examine the need for and accomplishments and effectiveness of existing government programs as if they were being proposed for the first time;

▲ Allow proposed new programs to compete for resources on a more equal footing with existing programs;

▲ Focus budget justifications on the evaluation of discrete elements, and programs or activities of each decision unit; and

▲ Secure extensive managerial involvement at all levels in the budget process.

While success is claimed, governmental programs are probably not the fairest test of this concept. Agencies, with few exceptions, do not have the sole discretion to transfer funds between appropriations to the more effective programs, as determined by an executive branch zero-based budget analysis. Significant program changes, dissolutions, or expansions must be approved by the Congress in the same manner as it makes its other decisions. There is some discretionary power provided to the President by the Congress; however, even here significant program changes are not made without informing Congress.

ZBB Process

Exhibit 3.1 provides an overview of the process for developing a zero-based budget. The process consists of four general steps: (1) identify decision units, (2) develop decision packages, (3) rank programs or activities by priority and (4) consolidate or summarize budget justification.

Identify Decision Units. The *decision unit* is the basic program or organizational entity for which budget requests are prepared and that require significant decisions on the amount of spending and scope or quality of work to be performed. It is the definition of decision units that lay the foundation for zero-based budgeting. If the decision unit is defined too broadly, no meaningful analysis can result; if too detailed, the process will be immersed in minutia and again no meaningful conclusions will be reached.

Develop Decision Packages. Decision packages are the lowest practical level of accountability or responsibility under the ZBB approach. A package will be prepared for each unit and will consist of a brief jurisdiction document including information to permit judgments on program or activity levels and resource requirements.

In practice, series of decision packages are prepared that attempt to summarize a series of alternative scenarios. For fiscal year 1980, agencies were directed to prepare the packages at various levels.

Exhibit 3.1   **HIERARCHICAL PROCESS FOR DEVELOPMENT OF A ZERO-BASED BUDGET**

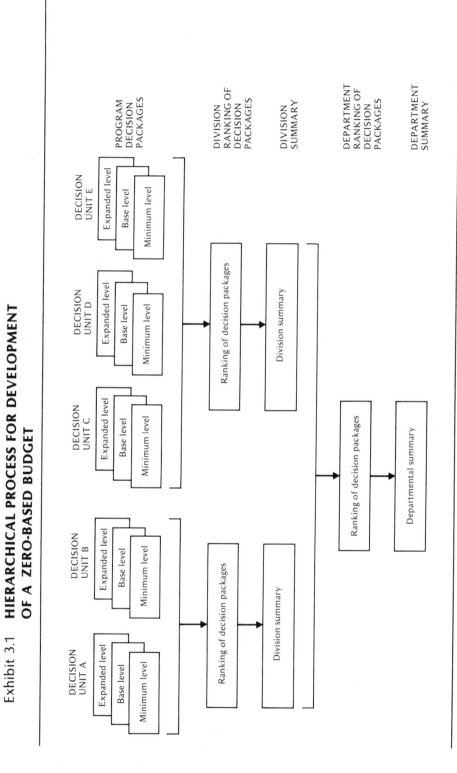

Source: Cornelius E. Tierney, *Governmental Auditing*, Chicago: Commerce Clearing House, p. 26.

▲ *Minimum Level*—level of performance below which it is not feasible for the decision unit to continue because no constructive contribution can be made toward fulfilling stated objectives.

▲ *Base or Current Level*—level of performance that would be reflected if activities for the budget year were carried on at the current year service or output levels. There could be some internal program realignments.

▲ *Expanded or Enhancement Level*—level above current level requiring increased output or services that are expected to require review by higher management.

Exhibit 3.2, from OMB Circular A-115, is an example of a current level decision package.

Rank Programs or Units. Agency management must participate in a prioritizing of units, activities, and programs. Consideration must be given to the various funding levels as well as to administration objectives. It is during this process that evaluating and arraying takes place. Each decision package must be placed in a relative order of priority.

Consolidate or Summarize Budget Justification. The consolidated or summarized priorities form the basis for the detailed budget justification of the agency. Priorities, while important, must be tempered with anticipated resources that could be obtained by the agency. To minimize paperwork, agencies are permitted to consolidate the units by program units.

At the conclusion of the process above, the agency ZBB justification will consist of numerous decision units packages, ranking sheets displaying the relative priority of the many decision units, and an overview of the decision units. For the fiscal year 1980, each decision package was required to present the effect of the budget year request for the budget year, plus the next four years.

Unlike PPBS, discussed in the next section, zero-based budgeting is viewed as a resource allocation tool. The structuring and later prioritizing of units at various levels of resource availability make it difficult to provide a financial tracking during the execution years. Further, there may be little relation between the requested unit funding levels and those passed by the Congress. These conditions do not permit the incorporation of the concept in the agency's costing system. Cost of programs and activities may be recorded and reported, but cost, by decision units, will seldom be distinguishable in the accounting records of the agency.

Exhibit 3.2 **CURRENT LEVEL DECISION PACKAGE**

(Department of Water Quality, Water Enforcement Water Resources Control:
09-2650-0-1-301 Water Enforcement Unit-1452)

ACTIVITY

In addition to the activities contemplated in packages 1* and 2†, the unit will conduct the following activities.

1. Conduct preenforcement evaluations on self-monitoring reports for half of the nonfederally funded municipal permittees.
2. Conduct technical enforcement evaluations on 6% of the self-monitoring reports for half of the nonfederally funded municipal permittees.
3. Conduct compliance sampling and evaluation inspections on 15% of the major nonfederally funded municipal permittees (344) and 5% of the major industrial permittees (203).
4. Conduct follow-up in 250 administrative enforcement actions.

RESOURCE REQUIREMENTS:

			19BY			PLANNING ESTIMATES		
	19PY	19CY	This package	Cumulative total	19BY + 1	19BY + 2	19BY + 3	19BY + 4
Budget authority ($000)								
In-house	13,412	13,546	976	12,012				
Contracts	963	814	1,663	2,398				
Total budget authority	14,375	14,360	2,639	14,410	14,925	15,470	16,020	16,600
(Headquarters)	(3,266)	(2,725)	(1,710)	(4,303)				
(Laboratories)	(11,109)	(11,635)	(929)	(10,107)				
Outlays ($000)	14,362	14,351	2,638	14,395	14,910	15,455	16,005	16,580
Positions								
Full-time/permanent	542	546	39	471				
Other	47	47	0	47				

SHORT-TERM OBJECTIVE

Concentrate on settlement of adjudicatory hearings to a level that permits 86% of all major sources to be placed on compliance schedules.

OUTPUT/WORK LOAD MEASURES:

			19BY	
	19PY	19CY	This package	Cumulative total
1. Conduct preenforcement evaluation of self-monitoring reports.	100,000	100,000	8,700	92,000
2. Conduct technical enforcement evaluations of self-monitoring reports.	6,000	6,000	500	5,500
3. Conduct compliance inspections.	1,450	1,470	547	1,501
4. Issue follow-up administrative orders and notices of violations.	1,014	1,758	250	1,500

IMPACT ON MAJOR OBJECTIVES:

1. All major permit holders will be inspected every six years (17% annually).
2. Ninety-two percent of the self-monitoring reports will be evaluated annually.
3. Twenty-five percent of new requests from polluters for adjudicatory hearings will be settled each year.

* Minimum-level decision package
† Intermediate-level decision package

Source: Office of Management and Budget Circular A-115, Zero-Base Budgeting, Washington, D.C.

Planning, Programming, Budgeting System

Implemented governmentwide by Presidential directive, PPBS was intended to be the integrated process by which agency heads made decisions concerning types, nature, and funding of agency programs and supporting activities. Where PPBS was successfully integrated into the decision-making process of an agency, the concept provided a sound basis for determining, monitoring, and accounting for programs and activities. Properly implemented, information systems were developed that provided a uniform structure between the programming, planning, budgeting, and accounting.

Defined

Planning, programming, budgeting was an effort by the executive branch (beginning with the Department of Defense in 1961 and later mandated by the President on all agencies for years after August 1965) to prepare budgets in a systematic way to improve the usefulness of the documents in establishing priorities and to measure costs against meaningful performance criteria.

Objectives of PPBS

In summary, there were several goals attributed to the adoption of PPBS. PPBS, as envisioned by executive branch officials, was to result in

▲ The design of an output-oriented program structure under which data on each agency's operations and activities could be presented in categories reflecting the agency's purposes or objectives;

▲ Analyses in terms of costs and benefits of possible alternative objectives for an agency and possible alternative programs for meeting the objectives;

▲ Translation of program decisions to be carried out into financial budgets for consideration and action by the President and Congress; and

▲ Development of agency operating budgets and accounting systems to permit management to monitor the progress of programs and activities.

The several phases of PPBS include

▲ *Planning*—Studying of agency objectives, constructing alternative approaches to achieve objectives, identifying and assessing contingencies;

▲ *Programming*—The structure of activities consistent with the agency's objectives and expected outputs in relation to the cost of resources needed to attain the programmed objectives and outputs; and

▲ *Budgeting*—Requesting funds of the President and Congress in support of the programmed activities; once approved, the budget became the operating plan for the agency.

PPBS Process

The PPBS was designed to include several processes or stages. Financial managers are involved in different phases for different fiscal years. For example, at the same period, an agency might be involved with planning agency objectives for a period three years into the future; programming activities would be underway for the budget fiscal year; the operating plan was being executed in the current fiscal year. For any one fiscal year, though, a series of sequential processes was completed. These processes have been summarized in Exhibit 3.3.

Exhibit 3.3 **PROCESSES OF PLANNING, PROGRAMMING, AND BUDGETING SYSTEMS**

PROCESS	ACTIVITY
Planning	Established agency program objectives and broad requirements to achieve objectives within specified time period
Programming	Established programs consisting of time-phased action schedules and estimated funding and staff resources to achieve objectives
Budgeting	Established detailed projections of funds for programs, obtains and allocates funds, balances priorities among competing resources
Program Operating	System by which authorized funds and resources were spent to achieve program objectives
Progress Reporting	Financial and nonfinancial information on status and results of program operations transmitted to appropriate levels of agency management
Program Change	System and procedures by which changes were introduced to multiyear programs, financial plans, and operating plans
Evaluation	Systematic reviews and examinations of accomplishments by program operations

Source: *Planning, Programming, Budgeting System* (PPBS), Office of Economic Opportunity, 1968.

The PPBS, in addition to consisting of the several processes, required the participation and active involvement of several federal agencies. At differing times in the cycle, the President, the Office of Management and Budget, Congress, and heads of agencies, and agency program officials provided information, made reviews, or gave approvals to the system. Exhibit 3.4 highlights the responsibilities of these organizations. To monitor compliance with the operating plans, agencies were required to structure their charts of accounts to provide expenditure and cost information in relation to programs and program elements, as well as other activities, functions, and object classes of expenses.

Management By Objectives

Defined

Management By Objectives is a method of planning and monitoring performance (of an organization, work group, or an individual) in relation to predetermined objectives. Generally, objectives have been established to be attained within a specified time period.

MBO was more popular in the federal government during the early 1970s. At that time the Office of Management and Budget emphasized the development and utilization of MBO. Agencies were to describe goals and objectives in installing systems to permit monitoring of achievement. Like zero-based budgeting, and unlike PPBS, MBO reporting systems were not developed nor was there a detailed accounting of initial or revised objectives.

MBO Process

MBO can be viewed as a series of negotiated goals and objectives planned to be accomplished with specified resources within a predetermined time period. Typically, the media was a series of conferences between superiors and subordinate organizations and individuals—between individuals and their bosses, and between program managers and the head of the agency. Once the objectives were established, responsibility for performance was determined, resources assigned to accomplish the objective, and a form of information reporting or feedback established to monitor achievement or lack thereof. To be effective the objectives of an MBO program had to be

▲   *Specific*, providing clear statements of work or activity to be accomplished, within a negotiated time period, and by designated persons or organizations;

▲   *Measurable*, permitting an evaluation of achievement on a predetermined, quantitative basis; and

▲   *Attainable*, allowing the realization of success by establishing reasonable standards of performance.

Exhibit 3.4 **RESPONSIBILITIES FOR PLANNING, PROGRAMMING, AND BUDGETING IN FEDERAL GOVERNMENT**

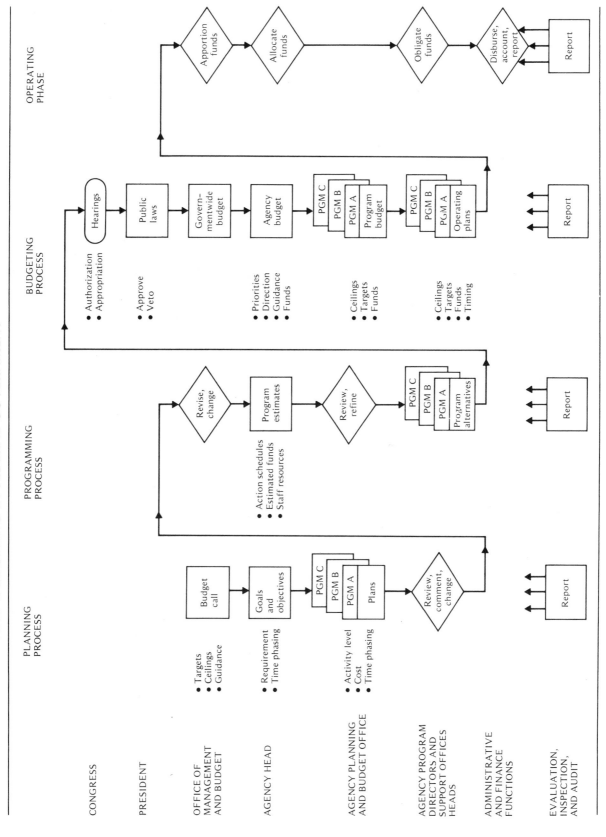

Exhibit 3.5 outlines the MBO process. As may be evident, MBO is most effective when applied to exceptions, i.e., individuals or organizations not performing to expectations. The goals and objectives must be specific to solve the problems or provide the incentive to alter or improve performance. It is not feasible to view MBO as being applicable to an entire agency.

Exhibit 3.5 **MANAGEMENT BY OBJECTIVES PROCESS**

PROCESS	CONSIDERATIONS
Define organization goals and performance measures	Generally set forth in policy statements.
Objective-setting meetings	Between organizations, supervisors and employees to ensure mutual agreement on objectives, performance measures, period for achievement.
Feedback on performance against established milestones	Based upon acceptable management information system; not directed toward punitive aspects; permits corrective actions and reaction to variances on current basis.
Revision of objectives	Permits the achievement of alternatives; flexibility to take corrective actions; modification of activities to be measured.
Periodic reviews of results against targeted objectives	Typically done quarterly or more frequently, supervisors must meet with employees; permits adjustments in objectives and resource allocations to optimize performance of individual and organization within the specified time period.
Overall review of organizational performance and related to initial step in process for next planning period	Usually done annually to evaluate completed year and provide inputs for development of appropriate goals and objectives for next year. Review concentrates on the achievement of overall organization.

Source: Cornelius E. Tierney, *Governmental Auditing*, Chicago: Commerce Clearing House, p. 23.

Federal
Budget Process,
Controls, and
chapter 4 # Monitoring: (II)

INTRODUCTION   Chapter 3 described the phases of the federal budget cycle, the requirements of the Congressional Budget and Impoundment Control Act of 1974, and selected budgeting concepts. This chapter is concerned with the details prescribed by the Office of Management and Budget for preparing and executing a federal agency budget.

   The procedures and practices relating to accounting, controlling, and reporting on the status of federal appropriations and funds are described in greater detail in several succeeding chapters.

DISCLOSURE   Information relating to the preparation of a federal
OF BUDGET   budget has been historically viewed as privileged infor-
INFORMATION   mation of the executive branch of the government. A specific OMB Circular, A-10, established the policy with respect to the responsibilities for disclosing budget data. By law, the President is required to transmit an annual budget to the Congress; the same law, the Budget and Accounting Act of 1921, prohibits an agency submission in any other manner unless at the formal request of either House of Congress.

Circular A-10 emphasizes that the executive branch communications that led to the preparation of the budget are not to be disclosed by agencies or by those who have prepared the budget. Maintaining the confidential nature of agency submission, requests, recommendations, supporting materials and similar communications is important because these documents are an integral part of the decision-making process by which the President resolves budget issues and develops recommendations to the Congress. Budget decisions are not final until the President transmits the budget to Congress.

PREPARATION AND SUBMISSION OF BUDGET ESTIMATES

Under Reorganization Plan No. 2 of 1970, the Bureau of the Budget was designated as the Office of Management and Budget. It is the OMB that is responsible for providing budget guidance to all federal agencies, compiling the agency budget information, and assisting the President with presentation and defense of the budget before Congress.

Budget Guidance

OMB annually issues guidance relating to the preparation and submission of budget estimates in its Circular A-11. In fiscal year 1980, for example, a multiyear budget planning system was established in that Circular A-11, expanding the planning to include two years beyond the budget year.

Overall ceilings are initially provided by OMB to all agencies on an individual basis. Circular A-11 outlines detailed governmentwide guidance concerning the formats, table and schedule content, definitions, and codes to be used in submitting the final budget estimates to the President.

Bases for Estimates

The financial estimates submitted to OMB by the agencies are prepared on several bases: costs, budget authority, outlays, transfer of funds, obligated balances, unexpended balances, and refunds, and collections to cite several. Circular A-11 defines these terms as follows.

Costs. Costs represents the value of resources consumed or used. For procurement and manufacturing programs, costs represents the value of material received or produced. For capital investment programs, costs for public works will cover the value of work put in place. Costs for loan activities will represent assets required.

Budget Authority. The budget authority provided by law to an agency to enter into obligations that will result in immediate or future outlays of government funds. Most authority is in the form of appropriations; other types may include contract authority or authority to borrow.

Outlays. Outlays are payments of obligations incurred that are reported and estimated on a "checks-issued, net" basis. These are interpreted as being gross payments or obligations (cash payments or issuance of checks) less reimbursements received and credited to the appropriation or fund account.

Transfer of Funds. Transfers are the legal authorization to move all or part of a fund balance to another account. Such transfers may be between agencies, different types of funds, and appropriations. In any event, a transfer must be formally authorized by OMB and, in some instances, the Congress.

Obligated Balances. Obligated balances are the unpaid obligations incurred for which disbursements have not been made.

Unexpended Balances. Unexpended balances are obligation balances plus the unobligated balances of an appropriations or funds (including investments in United States securities).

Unobligated Balances. The unobligated balance is merely the total of the unexpended appropriation or fund balance less the obligated balance.

Collections. Collections would be any money received by a government agency.

These bases would apply to the budget estimate prepared by all agencies. With variations (identified in later chapters), these definitions are also applicable to agency accounting and reporting.

Fiscal Years of the Budget Cycle

The Congressional Budget Act of 1974 established new budget procedures for the federal government and changed the fiscal year. Subsequent to the act, the government moved to a fiscal year of October 1 to September 30. The compilation of the budget requires that several fiscal years be considered.

Past year—the fiscal year immediately preceding the current year; the last completed fiscal year.

Current year—the fiscal year immediately preceding the budget year.

Budget year—the next fiscal year for which estimates are to be submitted.

Budget year + 1 (and BY + 2, BY + 3)—the first (or later) fiscal year(s) following the budget year.

The definitions above, set forth in Circular A-11, apply to the budget estimates of all agencies. The fiscal year is identified by the calendar year in which it ends. For example, fiscal year "1980" refers to the twelve months ending on September 30, 1980. The word "agency" is described by OMB as including departments and establishments; "bureau" designates principal subordinate organizational units.

SUBMISSION OF BUDGET ESTIMATES FOR APPROPRIATIONS OR FUNDS

Materials Required

As mentioned above, the OMB annually issues a revised Circular A-11 to provide guidance on a governmentwide basis to executive departments and establishments on the manner in which to prepare and submit budget estimates to OMB. Exhibit 4.1 lists the data required from department and establishment for each appropriation or fund or group of accounts constituting a unit pursuant to the above OMB definition. Exhibit 4.2, also from Circular A-11, is typical of the listing statements and other material required by OMB to support agency requests for new appropriation and budgetary authority. This information relates to the federal budget for the fiscal year 1980. The submission requirements will vary from year to year.

In both Exhibits 4.1 and 4.2, the notations to section numbers refer to sections and paragraphs of Circular A-11, that provide specific and detailed guidance to nature, content, format, and other requirements to ensure uniform submissions by all agencies.

Arrangement of Data

Agency submissions are assembled by bureaus or other subordinate organizations if such organizations are responsible for separate appropriations or funds. Otherwise, the data are accumulated agencywide by appropriation or fund or group of accounts, pursuant to OMB criteria. The budget materials must be arranged in the following fund order:

▲ General fund and special funds by
   Accounts for which appropriations are requested for the budget year
   Accounts for which current appropriations were received in the current year

Exhibit 4.1 CMB REQUIREMENTS FOR DATA-SUPPORTING BUDGET ESTIMATES

DETAILED MATERIAL FOR APPROPRIATIONS AND FUNDS
(See section 21.3 for sequence of accounts)

Type of material	General and special fund accounts	Revolving funds (including trust revolving funds)	Management funds	Trust funds (excluding trust revolving funds)
Appropriation language sheet (sections 31.1–31.5).	Required (if there is language for the current year or budget year).	Required (if there is language for the current year or budget year).	Required (if there is language for the current year or budget year).	Required (if there is language for the current year or budget year).
Schedule of amounts available for appropriation (section 38.2).	Required only for the few special funds where applicable.	Not required.	Not required.	Required only for the few funds where applicable.
Program and financing schedule (sections 32.1–32.8).	Required.	Required for funds and for annual limitations.	Required.	Required for funds and for annual limitations.
Schedule on status of unfunded contract authority (section 38.1).	Required only in the few cases where applicable.	Not generally applicable.	Not generally required.	Required only in the few cases where applicable.
Schedule on status of loan guarantees (section 38.4).	Required for accounts with loan guarantee activities.	Required for funds with loan guarantee activities.	Not generally required.	Not generally required.
Narrative statement on program and performance (sections 36.1–36.4).	Required, except where there is no activity after the past year. For permanent appropriations, see special instructions in section 36.4.	Required (special instructions in section 36.3).	Required.	Required (special instructions in section 36.4).
Statement of revenue and expense; statement of financial condition; and supplementary schedules (sections 37.1–37.5).	Not required.	Required for each fund.	Not generally required.	Not required.
Schedule of object classification and personnel summary (sections 34.1–34.6).	Required.	Required for funds and for annual limitations.	Required.	Required for funds and for annual limitations.
Supplementary source document (sections 33.1–33.5).	Required.	Required.	Required.	Required.

NOTE.—1. In the case of trust or revolving funds that have annual limitations, the material pertaining to limitations will appear following the other material on the fund.

2. For informational foreign currency accounts, material will be similar to requirements for corresponding types of dollar accounts (general fund, trust fund, etc.) with slight modifications (section 38.3).

3. For proposed supplementals, only the program and financing schedule and a narrative statement on program and performance are required in the initial submission. OMB representatives will inform agencies of any additional material needed for the supplementals to be transmitted with the budget.

Source: Circular A-11, *Preparation and Submission of Budget Estimates*, May 1978, Washington, D.C.: Office of Management and Budget.

Exhibit 4.2 OMB BUDGET ESTIMATE SUBMISSION REQUIREMENTS

Sequence of material	Section number	Minimum requirement: 3 basic copies plus additional copies (number of copies)
SUMMARY STATEMENTS		
Summary and highlight memorandum	22.1	-------------
Relationship of decision units to account structure	22.2	1
Statement of receipts	22.3	1
Statement of numbers of personnel	22.4	-------------
Grade reduction targets	22.5	1
Multi-year planning estimates and long-range projections	23.1–23.3	1
DETAILED MATERIAL FOR APPROPRIATIONS AND FUNDS		
Appropriation language sheet	31.1–31.5	1
Schedule of amounts available for appropriation	38.2	1
Program and financing schedule	32.1–32.8	1
Schedule on status of loan guarantees	38.4	1
Schedule on status of unfunded contract authority	38.1	1
Narrative statement on program and performance	36.1–36.4	1
Statement of revenue and expense	37.2	1
Statement of financial condition	37.3	1
Schedules of selected supporting data for business-type budgets	37.4	1
Schedule of object classification	34.1–34.3	1
Personnel summary	34.4–34.6	1
Supporting schedules of object classification and personnel summary for allocations	34.3–34.4	1
JUSTIFICATIONS AND EXPLANATIONS		
Zero-base budget justifications (decision unit overviews, decision packages, and ranking sheets)	24.1	-------------
Information on rental payments to GSA	24.5	-------------
OTHER MATERIAL FOR ANALYSIS		
Detail of permanent positions schedule	35.1–35.3	1
Data on acquisition, operation, or use of ADP and telecommunications systems	43.1–43.3	2
Data on research and development	44.1–44.4	-------------
Data on Federal income security programs	49-1.49.6	-------------
Data on employment and training programs	50.1–50.4	-------------
Data on environmental programs	52.1–52.4	-------------
Data on Federal statistical programs	54.1–54.5	-------------
Data on research and development by agency missions	55.1–55.3	1

(b) The following material is required as specified or at a later date, usually when agencies are advised of budget determinations:

	Section number
COMPUTER MATERIALS AND OTHER MATERIALS FOR SPECIAL ANALYSES	
Data on deposit funds	32.7(n)
Supplementary source document	33.1–33.5
Current services estimates	40.1–40.3
Data on Federal credit programs	42.1–42.8
Data on health programs (October 16)	45.1–45.9
Data on education and related programs	46.1–46.6
Data on agency borrowing and investment	47.1–47.2
Data on Federal civil rights activities (November 27)	53.1–53.4

Source: Circular A-11, *Preparation and Submission of Budget Estimates*, May 1978, Washington, D.C.: Office of Management and Budget.

Other unexpired accounts

Expired accounts

Headings and notes of allocations from other agency appropriations

Special fund budget data will be submitted following the general fund presentation and be in the same order.

▲ Permanent general and special fund appropriations

▲ Public enterprise funds

▲ Intragovernmental revolving funds and management funds

▲ Trust funds

▲ Trust revolving funds

It should be recognized that not all agencies are responsible for all of the funds listed above. However, many agencies must provide budget estimates and data for multiple appropriations and funds.

Funds Defined

According to OMB, as mentioned above, federal *funds* are the accounting units established for segregating revenues and assets in accordance with law. The segregation is required to assure that revenues and assets are applied only to financial transactions for which they were appropriated or authorized by Congress. There are several types of federal funds.

▲ *General* funds are credited with all receipts not earmarked by law and charged with payments out of appropriations and out of general borrowings.

▲ *Special* funds are credited with receipts earmarked for specific purposes. Generally an operation of a business type will be classified as a public enterprise fund, however.

▲ *Public enterprise* funds are revolving funds, credited with collections, primarily from outside government, earmarked to finance a continuing cycle of operations of a business type.

▲ *Intragovernmental* funds facilitate financing of transactions within and between agencies. There are two types of intragovernmental funds: (1) Intragovernmental revolving funds whose collections from other agencies and accounts are earmarked to carry out a continuing cycle of operations and (2) management funds whose corpus is merged with monies from two or more accounts to carry out a purpose or project, but not involving a cycle of operations.

▲ *Trust* and *deposit* funds are funds credited with collections used for specific purposes and programs according to trust agreement or statute.

Exhibit 4.3 illustrates these funds in relation to unrestricted (funds arising from general taxing powers or business operations) and restricted (trust and deposit) funds.

EXECUTION OF FEDERAL AGENCY BUDGET

In addition to the preparation of the budget, OMB is also responsible for budget execution, including financial planning, apportioning of funds, approving systems for administrative controls, and monitoring compliance by government agency with various laws. The governmentwide guidance relating to the budget execution is set forth in OMB's Circular A-34 entitled *Instructions on Budget Execution.*

The control over budget resources provided by Congress is monitored by OMB through its apportionment process. The required reporting on budget execution required by OMB, is an integral requirement of agency accounting systems.

Requirement for Systems of Administrative Controls

Section 3679 of the Revised Statutes requires the head of each agency, subject to approval by the OMB, to prescribe a system of administrative control of funds. The system of control can not be inconsistent with any accounting procedures prescribed by law and must be designed to

▲   Restrict obligations and expenditures against each appropriation or fund to the amount of apportionments or reapportionments, and

▲   Enable the agency head to fix responsibility for the obligation or expenditure in excess of an apportionment or reapportionment.

A system would be found deficient by the General Accounting Office if it merely performed these accounting functions because compliance with OMB requirements is but one of many external fiscal and financial criteria agency systems must achieve. Additional principles and standards of agency systems are discussed in later chapters.

Apportionment Process

As defined by OMB, in Circular A-34, the apportionment process is intended to

Exhibit 4.3 **FUND STRUCTURE OF THE FEDERAL GOVERNMENT**

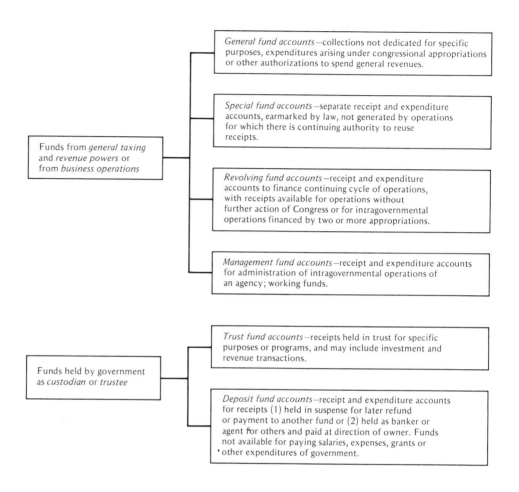

General fund accounts —collections not dedicated for specific purposes, expenditures arising under congressional appropriations or other authorizations to spend general revenues.

Special fund accounts —separate receipt and expenditure accounts, earmarked by law, not generated by operations for which there is continuing authority to reuse receipts.

Revolving fund accounts —receipt and expenditure accounts to finance continuing cycle of operations, with receipts available for operations without further action of Congress or for intragovernmental operations financed by two or more appropriations.

Management fund accounts —receipt and expenditure accounts for administration of intragovernmental operations of an agency; working funds.

Funds from *general taxing* and *revenue powers* or from *business operations*

Trust fund accounts —receipts held in trust for specific purposes or programs, and may include investment and revenue transactions.

Deposit fund accounts —receipt and expenditure accounts for receipts (1) held in suspense for later refund or payment to another fund or (2) held as banker or agent for others and paid at direction of owner. Funds not available for paying salaries, expenses, grants or other expenditures of government.

Funds held by government as *custodian* or *trustee*

Source: *Accounting Principles and Standards for Federal Agencies,* Comptroller General of the United States, Revised 1972.

▲ Prevent obligation of an account in a manner that would require deficiency or supplemental appropriations and

▲ Achieve the most effective and economical use of amounts made available.

Apportionment actions by OMB divide amounts available for obligation by (1) specific time periods (generally quarterly) or (2) activities, projects, objects, or a combination thereof. Reapportionments are made when the earlier apportionments are no longer appropriate or because of a change in amounts available for obligation or the occurrence of unforeseen events. Amounts, although appropriated by Congress, may be deferred through the apportionment process. These funds are temporarily not available to the agency for obligation until released by OMB.

Circular A-11 defines an *apportionment* as a distribution by OMB of amounts available in an appropriation or fund account into amounts available to agencies for obligation in specified time periods, or for activities, projects, objects, or a combination thereof.

Appropriations

An *appropriation* is a *fund account* in Treasury to record amounts available for obligation and outlay, including not only money directly appropriated by Congress but also revenues available for use without current Congressional appropriation action. The latter would include revolving funds and trust funds. Appropriations may be available for obligation and expenditure by an agency for varying periods of time. For example, each of the following appropriations would expire at a different time.

▲ *One-year account*—available for obligation only during a specified fiscal year.

▲ *Multiple-year account*—available for obligation for a definite period in excess of one fiscal year.

▲ *No year account*—available for obligation for an indefinite period, usually until the objective has been accomplished.

▲ *Unexpired account*—an account in which the authority to obligate has not ceased to be available.

▲ *Expired account*—an account in which the authority to obligate has ceased, but from which outlays can be made to pay for obligations previously incurred and adjustments can be made.

Types of Budget Authority

It is the available budget authority that OMB regulates through the apportionment process. In any year, the budget authority becomes the dollar ceiling provided by law for obligation and expenditure. The several basic forms of budget authority provided by the Congress include

▲ *Appropriation*—The most common form of budget authority that allows agencies to incur obligations and make payments out of the Treasury for specified purposes.

▲ *Authority to spend debt receipts*—Permits an agency to incur obligations and make payments for specified purposes out of borrowed money.

▲ *Public debt authority*—Derived from the sale of public debt securities of the federal government.

▲ *Agency debt authority*—Derived from sale of agency debt securities (bonds, assumption of mortgages, participation certificates in pools of loans).

▲ *Contract authority*—Statutory authority under which contracts or other obligations may be entered into prior to an appropriation for the payment of such obligations.

▲ *Reappropriation*—Authority to obligate and make payment amounting to all or part of the unobligated balance of an otherwise expired one-year or multiple-year appropriation, whether for the same or different purpose.

In federal financial management, other terms may be used to describe the nature of budget authority available to agencies. These other terms, definite or indefinite and permanent or current, are not mutually exclusive.

▲ *Definite authority*—A specific sum at the time budget authority is granted by Congress, including authority stated as "not to exceed" a specific dollar amount.

▲ *Indefinite authority*—Not stated as a specific sum when the authority is granted by Congress, but is determinable only at some future date, such as an appropriation of all or part of a receipt from a certain source.

▲ *Current authority*—New budget authority enacted by Congress in or immediately preceding the fiscal year involved.

▲ *Permanent authority*—New budget authority available each year by virtue of one-time or standing legislation, not requiring further action by Congress. Such authority is considered "current" in the first year and "permanent" in succeeding years.

Estimates of Budgeting Authority

OMB Circular A-34 contains the prohibition that inclusion of estimates in determining the amounts available for apportionment in no way authorizes any agency to obligate or make expenditures in excess of the budgetary authority available for obligation from such source at the time the obligation or expenditure is made. The amount apportioned of any appropriation that includes unrealized reimbursements or other anticipated receipts will not be alloted unless there is reasonable assurance that such collections will be made and deposited to the credit of the appropriation involved. Circular A-34 states that in the case of reimbursable work, budgetary resources available to an agency for obligation and expenditure would include

▲ Entitlement to reimbursement based on goods and services furnished, and as authorized by law;

▲ Amount of orders received from within the government that represent valid obligations of the ordering account to the extent that the reimbursements will be placed in the current account when collected; and

▲ Amount of unfilled customers' orders from the public for which advance payment has been made.

The administrative system of the agency must be designed to keep obligations and expenditures (1) from exceeding apportionments and allotments, or (2) from exceeding budgetary resources available for obligation, whichever is smaller. These controls must be an integral part of the accounting system.

Agency Allocation, Allotment, and Obligation

As mentioned, Congress appropriates monies; OMB apportions appropriations; the individual agencies allot and obligate funds. These terms frequent the accounts, transactions, and reports of government agencies. In Circular A-34, OMB defines these terms to include the following actions.

▲ *Allocation*—The transfer of obligational authority from one agency to a "transfer appropriation account" established by another agency to carry out the purposes of the parent appropriation.

▲ *Transfer appropriation account*—A separate account established to receive (and later obligate and expend) allocations from an appropriation of another agency; these accounts carry symbols identified with the original appropriation and later transactions are usually reported with the transactions of the parent account.

▲ *Allotment*—Authority delegated by the head or other authorized employees of an agency to other employees to incur obligations within a specified amount, pursuant to OMB apportionment or other statutory authority making funds available for obligation.

▲ *Obligations incurred*—Amounts of orders placed, contracts awarded, services received, and similar transactions that will require payment in the same or a future fiscal period.

▲ *Obligated balance*—Unpaid obligations applicable to an account less the amount collectible as repayments to the appropriation.

▲ *Unobligated balance*—The amount remaining after deducting the cumulative obligations from the amount available for obligation.

As described more fully in later chapters, the term "obligations" has a precise legal connotation as well as detailed accounting implications within a federal agency.

Accruing, Disbursing, and Costing Funds

In federal budgeting and accounting, accruing and disbursing funds and costing of activities and operations have meanings slightly different from similar terms in corporate accounting. For example, accrual in the private sector refers to the appropriate matching of costs to revenues, often the terms "accrual" and "cost" are synonymous. OMB Circular A-34 defines the terms in the following manner, which is the generally accepted usage today in governmental financial management.

- ▲ *Accrued expenditures*—Charges to an account in a given period that reflect liabilities incurred and the need to pay for services performed, goods and other property received, and amounts becoming owed under programs for which no current service or performance is required (annuities, insurance claims, etc.).
- ▲ *Disbursement, or outlays*—Amount of checks issued, interest accrued on public debt, other payments made (including advances to others), net of refunds and reimbursements.
- ▲ *Costs applied*—The value (purchase price) of goods and services used, consumed, given away, or lost (or destroyed), regardless of when ordered, received, or paid for. Applied costs become the financial measure of resources consumed or applied in accomplishing a specific purpose, performing a service, carrying out an activity, or completing a unit of work or specific project.

The accrued expenditures that are unpaid are shown as liabilities. Payments made for which expenditures have not accrued (as advances, prepayments, etc.) are assets (generally receivables) until the expenditure accrues. Loan transactions are accounted for on a cash basis; an accrued expenditure occurs when cash payment is made.

With few exceptions, federal agencies do not disburse cash or issue checks. This function is generally performed by the Treasury for the government as a whole. The individual agencies make a formal, written request to the Treasury for checks to be issued to identified payees. Upon issuance, the disbursement is recorded on the central accounts in the Treasury and as well as on the agency's accounts.

The accounting procedures and practices for each of the above transactions are described more fully in later chapters.

REPORTING ON BUDGET EXECUTION OMB monitors agency performance and budget execution of the several agencies and departments by requiring adherence to an apportionment process prior to the time an agency may incur obligations or make expenditures. Additionally, OMB has prescribed governmentwide reporting on budget execution.

Each agency or department must complete and submit an apportionment and reapportionment schedule, to the OMB in advance of incurring obligations from an appropriation or fund. This form is required to obtain OMB authority permitting the agency to obligate existing funds. This request for apportionment is generally supported by a proposed obligation plan by time period or project or activity. A report on budget execution must also be submitted monthly by agencies to report the actual status of appropriations and funds.

BUSINESS TYPES OF BUDGET STATEMENTS

Financial Statements

OMB requires that business types of budget statements be submitted to it for (1) all enterprises pursuant to the provisions of the Government Corporation Control Act, and similar legislation, and (2) all other revolving and (3) trust revolving funds.

These business types of statements are required in addition to the program and financing schedules cited in an earlier section.

▲   A condensed statement of revenues and expenses

▲   A condensed statement of financial condition, with an appended analysis of changes in government equity

▲   A schedule of selected supporting data

▲   When applicable, a schedule showing the position of the fund with respect to lending, guarantee, or insurance authority

▲   Other schedules to assist OMB in the analysis of program

OMB, in Circular A-11, requires that data on these statements be in agreement with receipt and disbursement data reported on the agency's statement of financial condition or statement of income and retained earnings that are submitted to the Treasury.

Statement of Revenue and Expense

When the enterprise is engaged in two or more major programs, this statement of revenue and expense should reflect separately the revenue, expense, and net operating income or loss for each program and the net operating income or loss for all programs. This statement closely parallels a corporate profit-and-loss statement in both content and format.

Statement of Financial Condition

The condensed statement of financial condition contains three principal sections, required by Circular A-11.

ASSETS

Fund balance with the Treasury

United States Securities (at par)

  Public debt securities

  Agency securities

Accounts receivable

Advances made

Loans receivable

Inventories

Real property and equipment

Other assets

  Total assets

LIABILITIES

Accounts payable including funded accrual

Advances received

Unfunded liabilities

Debt issued under borrowing authority

  Borrowing from the Treasury

  Borrowing from federal financing bank

  Agency securities issued

Other liabilities

  Total liabilities

GOVERNMENT EQUITY

Unexpended balances

  Unobligated balance

  Undelivered orders

Unfinanced budget authority

  Unfilled customer orders

  Contract authority

  Borrowing authority

Invested capital

  Total government equity

This statement resembles the corporate balance sheet and is used by agencies in a similar manner to disclose the financial conditions of the enterprise or revolving or trust fund as of a specific date.

Changes in Government Equity

As mentioned earlier, the statements must also include an analysis of changes in government equity, setting forth paid-in capital and retained income, as appropriate, the beginning balance, transactions or changes during the year, and the ending balance. These tabulations when required, must conform to the following format.

PAID-IN CAPITAL:
  Opening balance
  Transactions
    Appropriation
    Appropriation transfers
    Other transactions
  Closing balance

RETAINED INCOME OR DEFICIT
  Opening balance
  Transactions
    Net operating income or loss
    Net nonoperating income or loss
    Dividend payments
    Capital transfers
    Other transactions
  Closing balance

TOTAL GOVERNMENT EQUITY

In both content and purpose, this statement parallels the statement of changes in net worth, published by corporate organizations.

chapter 5

Central Accounting and Financial Reporting

INTRODUCTION The Treasury is the "keeper of the government's purse." Congress, by the Constitution, is responsible for authorizing expenditures and prescribing the sources from which revenues will be raised to meet the expenditures. The Treasury's role is to ensure that the desired cash flow is monitored and maintained.

The Treasury is among the oldest agencies in government, founded in 1789, as the principal fiscal agent of government. As the fiscal agent, the Treasury maintains the central accounts of government; controls the collection, accounting, and makes disbursement of cash; and prescribes a uniform system of fiscal reporting for government agencies. However, there are numerous other functions of the Treasury. A few examples include the managing of the public debt, serving as the government's banker for a system of commercial depositaries and the Federal Reserve banks and Federal Deposit Insurance Corporation; printing or minting money, to mention a few.

LEGAL BASIS FOR CENTRAL ACCOUNTING Initially, the statutory basis for the government's central accounting system was the Act of 1789, establishing the Treasury, and the later Dockery Act of 1894 that reorganized the Treasury's accounting function.

The requirement for making an accounting of receipts and expenditures originates with Article I, Section 9, of the Constitution, which states in part, that

> . . . a regular statement and account of all public money shall be published from time to time.

Later, by the Act of 1894, the reporting requirement was superseded and it now became the duty of

> . . . the Secretary of Treasury annually to lay before Congress, on the first day of the regular session thereof, an accurate combined statement of the receipts and expenditures during the last preceding fiscal year of all public moneys. . . .

The Act of September 12, 1950, further provided that

> . . . the Secretary of the Treasury shall prepare such reports for the information of the President, the Congress, and the public as will present the results of the financial operations of the Government. . . .

Central Accounting System

The central accounting system maintained by the Treasury must be consistent with the overall principles, standards, and related requirements for accounting prescribed by the Comptroller General. With the exception of the financial transactions handled directly by the Treasury, all accounts are maintained on the basis of the financial information reported by other federal agencies. Within the central accounts of Treasury, receipt and outlay accounts have been classified according to (1) budget accounts and (2) other accounts.

Budget Accounts

The budget accounts are numerous in number and include, in summary, the following accounts.

General Fund Receipt Accounts. These accounts are credited with all receipts which are not earmarked by law for a specific purpose. The general fund receipts primarily include internal revenue collections (income taxes, excise taxes, estate, gift, and employment taxes). Also included are custom duties and variety of other receipts.

Special Fund Receipts Accounts. These accounts are credited with receipts from specific sources earmarked by law for specific purposes, but which are not generated from a cycle of operations. Congress may appropriate these receipts on an annual basis for indefinite periods of time. (Examples would include rents and royalties under the Mineral Leasing Act, revenues from visitors to Yellowstone National Park, proceeds from the sale of certain timber.)

General Fund Expenditure Accounts. These accounts are maintained to record amounts appropriated by Congress to be expended for the general support of the government. These general expenditure accounts are classified according to (1) limitations established by Congress as to the period of availability for obligation (one-year, multiple-year, no-year) and (2) with respect to the agency authorized to enter into obligations and approve outlays.

Special Fund Expenditure Accounts. These accounts are established to record appropriated amounts of special fund receipts to be expended for special programs in accordance with specific provisions of law.

Revolving Fund Accounts. These funds are authorized by law to finance a continuing cycle of operations in which outlays generate receipts that are available for outlay generally with no further action of Congress. Such funds may be classified as public enterprise funds (receipts coming from outside the government); and intragovernmental funds (receipts coming from other appropriations or funds within the federal government). These are usually no-year type funds and may be expended without limitation as to period of availability for outlay.

The Tennessee Valley Authority and the Commodity Credit Corporation are examples of public enterprise revolving funds. The General Supply Fund of the General Services Administration and the Government Printing Office Revolving Fund are examples of intragovernmental revolving funds.

Consolidated Working Fund Accounts. These accounts are established to receive and disburse advance payments from agencies pursuant to Section 601 of the Economy Act or other laws. Consolidated working funds may be credited with advances from more than one appropriation for procurement of goods or services to be furnished by the performing agency with the use of its own facilities within the same fiscal year.

The monies in these accounts are subject to the same fiscal year limitations of the appropriation or funds from which advanced; that is, one-year monies advanced by an agency to a consolidated working fund must be obligated within the fiscal year of availability. Limitations applied to appropriations do not change by the mere transfer of agency funds to a consolidated working capital fund.

Management Fund Accounts. These accounts are authorized by law to facilitate accounting for and administration of intragovernmental activities (other than a continuing cycle of operations) that are financed by two or more appropriations. This classification also applies to the consolidated working fund defined earlier.

Trust Fund Accounts. These accounts are maintained to record receipts and outlays of money held in trust by the government for specific purposes or programs in accordance with terms of a trust agreement or statute. Receipts of many trust funds not needed for current payments are invested in public debt and government agency securities. Generally, separate receipt and outlay accounts are established. However, when the trust corpus is established to perform a business kind of operation, the fund entity is called a "trust revolving fund," and combined receipt and outlay accounts are used. (Major trust fund accounts are Federal Old Age and Survivors Insurance trust fund, Unemployment trust fund, Civil Service Retirement trust fund, Highway trust fund.)

Transfer Appropriation Accounts. Transfer appropriation accounts are established to receive and disburse allocations that are nonexpediture transactions of the government at the time the allocation is made. That is, at the time of transfer from one agency to another no disbursement has been made outside of the government. These would also include certain transfers made pursuant to Section 601 of the Economy Act and other laws.

Other Accounts. The Treasury also maintains other accounts. These are *deposit fund accounts* combining receipts and outlay accounts established to account for money received that is held by the government (1) in suspense and later refunded or paid into some other fund upon the legal determination of the proper disposition or (2) as banker or agency for others and paying the funds at the direction of the depositor. Typically, these deposit funds are not available for paying salaries, expenses, grants or other outlays of the government.

The central system of the Treasury provides a consolidated record of the governmentwide financial transactions and permits reporting on the fiscal state of the government to the Congress and the public. Note that central accounts are *not* the government's overall general ledger for all assets and liabilities. The central accounts reflect only the assets and liabilities of the United States to which receipts and expenditures and the Treasury's cash activities can be related monthly and annually. The central system reports expenditures and appropriation balances on a cash or "checks-issued" basis. This information is obtained from the monthly statements received from the various departments and agencies. Receipts are entered by Treasury into the central accounts on the basis of collections or deposits reported in statements submitted by disbursing and collecting officers.

Sources of Receipts

The cash receipts of the government as shown in the central accounts arise from several sources. Statements are rendered monthly to the Treasury by the many disbursing officers and collection officers showing funds collected and deposited. When classed as to *nature* of the receipts, the following titles would generally apply.

▲　*Governmental receipts*—resulting from the sovereign rights to levy and collect taxes (e.g., income taxes, duties)

▲　*Proprietary receipts*—resulting from business types of operations of various agencies (e.g., sales of publication, licenses, fees)

▲　*Intrabudgetary receipts*—resulting from activities between various federal accounts that are not a net increase of the funds of the government

Other classifications are used to identify receipts by the *type of fund*. This classification would define receipts in the following manner.

▲　*General fund receipts*—include all receipts not earmarked by law for specific purposes (e.g., internal revenue taxes, custom duties, and several types of miscellaneous receipts)

▲　*Special fund receipts*—include receipts from specific sources that are earmarked by law to finance specific programs of government

It is the general fund receipts that are used by executive agencies to finance the discretionary programs of government set forth in the President's budget. It is the President's budget that is approved by Congress in the form of appropriations.

Receipts might also be referred to by the *source* of the receipts. In this instance, internal revenue receipts, alcohol and tobacco taxes, and custom receipts, for example, would be collected by agencies within the Treasury. The terms above are not mutually exclusive and, in practice, some confusion exists.

Basis for Expenditures

As a result of the budget process, outlined in earlier chapters, agencies are recipients of expenditure appropriations that provide the authority for incurring obligation and making expenditures on behalf of the government. Periodically, often monthly, quarterly, and at year end, the expenditure accounts of the several individual agencies must be reconciled to the receipt and disbursement transactions reflected on the records of the Treasury. The assets, liabilities, government investment, and details of receipts and expenditures are maintained in the accounts of the separate agencies.

In its role as fiscal agent, the Treasury monitors the rate of expenditures, debt ceiling, and other fiscal and monetary indicators. When necessary, the Treasury will issue guidance to govern the rate at which agencies may expend and disburse money.

ACCOUNTING FOR RECEIPTS AND EXPENDITURES

Supporting the system of central accounts is a receipts and expenditure fund coding structure. The Treasury annually publishes certain governmentwide fund symbols that must be used in reporting to OMB, GAO, Congress, and the Treasury. There is no restriction on an agency with respect to the degree of detailed coding deemed to best meet the needs of the individual agency.

Appropriation Symbols

While the term appropriation is most often used in reference to obligational and expenditure authority, the term applies equally to receipts as well as expenditures.

The symbols assigned by the Treasury must be used by all agencies for central reporting on appropriations for which they have responsibility. These symbols identify the department or agency, the fiscal year or years of availability, and the appropriation number. The account symbol structure is similar for both receipts and expenditure appropriations.

Exhibit 5.1 **ACCOUNT SYMBOLS AND TITLES FOR MAJOR CLASSES OF RECEIPTS BY FUND**

TYPE OF FUND	ACCOUNT SYMBOL
General Fund	
Governmental Receipts	
Taxes	0100
Custom duties	0300
Receipts from monetary power	0600
Fees for regulatory and judicial services	0800
Fines, penalties, and forfeitures	1000
War reparations and recoveries under military occupations	1100
Gift and contributions	1200
Clearing accounts	3800
Proprietary Receipts	
Interest	1400
Dividends and other earnings	1600
Rent	1800
Royalties	2000
Sale of products	2200
Fees and other charges for services and special benefits	2400
Sale of government property	2600
Realization upon loans and investments	2800-2900
Recoveries and refunds	3000
Special Fund	5000
Trust Fund	
Department and agencies	7000-8999
District of Columbia	9000-9999

Source: *Treasury Fiscal Requirements Manual,* Treasury Department, Washington, D.C., June 1980.

Receipt Appropriation Symbols

The vast majority of the receipts of the federal government are recorded in two general fund accounts: 0100—Taxes; and 0300—Customs Duties. Exhibit 5.1 lists the principal receipt appropriation fund symbols. The symbol used by a collection agency consists of a six-digit code: the first two digits identify the department or agency; the next four digits identify the fund or type of receipt. (See Exhibit 5.2 for an illustration.)

At present, the Treasury has identified over 1000 separate appropriation receipt accounts; however, only a few are applicable to most departments and agencies.

Expenditure Appropriation Symbols

A Congressional appropriation is required to provide an agency with the authority to obligate and expend funds. These appropriations could be related to general, special, or trust fund appropriations and other authority that may be conferred by the Congress. Once appropriated, the Treasury must inform the responsible agency of the amount available for obligation and expenditure. This is done by a formal document referred to as an appropriation or Treasury *warrant*.

The Treasury account symbols for expenditure appropriations may contain varying numbers of digits, possibly up to ten. As with the receipt appropriations, there is an agency identifier—the same code as used for receipts. Account symbols, four digits, have also been assigned to designate the type of fund from which the expenditure is to be made. Additionally, though, the expenditure symbol describes the duration for which obligational authority exists, by identifying the date the authority expires, for example:

▲   A *one-year appropriation* is available for obligation for a period of one fiscal year and is designated by the last digit in the fiscal year. Years 1980 and 1981 would be shown as a "0" and a "1," respectively.

▲   A *multiple-year appropriation* is available for obligation for more than one fiscal year and is designated by showing the first and last years for which obligational authority exists. A three-year appropriation beginning in fiscal year 1980 and expiring in 1982 would be shown as 0/2.

▲   A *no-year appropriation* is generally available for the accomplishment of a specific purpose or is available for obligation until exhausted and is designated by the letter "X" in lieu of the fiscal year digit.

▲   An *expired appropriation* is no longer available for obligation, the authority to obligate having expired at least two fiscal years earlier and the unliquidated obligated balances have been transferred to and merged with the Treasury's central accounts. These accounts are designated by the letter "M" in lieu of a fiscal year digit to signify "merged" accounts.

Exhibit 5.2 illustrates the coding that might be used for a multiple-year expenditure appropriation. Exhibit 5.3 lists the major expenditure fund appropriation account symbols of the federal government.

CENTRAL REPORTING   The central reporting system of the Treasury includes four general areas of fiscal activity.

▲   All receipts and expenditures of the federal government must be reported to a single source, the Treasury;

▲   Receipts and expenditures of foreign currency acquired without payment of dollars are monitored by the Treasury;

Exhibit 5.2 **ILLUSTRATION OF TREASURY RECEIPT AND EXPENDITURE APPROPRIATION ACCOUNT SYMBOLS**

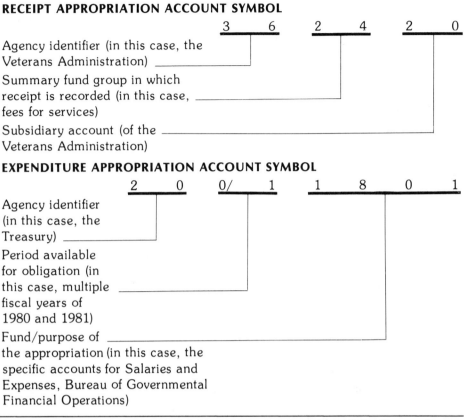

RECEIPT APPROPRIATION ACCOUNT SYMBOL

Agency identifier (in this case, the Veterans Administration) _____

Summary fund group in which receipt is recorded (in this case, fees for services) _____

Subsidiary account (of the Veterans Administration) _____

EXPENDITURE APPROPRIATION ACCOUNT SYMBOL

Agency identifier (in this case, the Treasury) _____

Period available for obligation (in this case, multiple fiscal years of 1980 and 1981) _____

Fund/purpose of the appropriation (in this case, the specific accounts for Salaries and Expenses, Bureau of Governmental Financial Operations) _____

Source: *Receipts, Appropriations, and Other Fund Account Symbols and Titles,* Treasury Department, 1980.

Exhibit 5.3 **APPROPRIATION AND OTHER EXPENDITURE ACCOUNT SYMBOLS BY FUND**

TYPE OF FUND	ACCOUNT SYMBOL
General Fund	0000-3899
Management, including consolidated working fund	3900-3999
Revolving fund	
Public enterprises	4000-4499
Intragovernmental	4500-4999
Special fund	5000-5999
Deposit fund	6000-6999
Trust fund	
Departments and agencies (exclusive of the District of Columbia)	7000-8999
District of Columbia	9000-9999

Source: *Treasury Fiscal Requirements Manual,* Treasury Department, Washington, D.C., June 1980.

▲ A reporting is required for the proprietary accounts of the government as shown by the combined statements of financial condition and income and expense submitted by individual agencies to the Treasury; and

▲ Activities of major trust funds and statistical data in relation to fiscal operations for certain governmental programs must be made known to the Treasury.

For the typical government agency, the reporting to the Treasury has been routinized and consists of a few principal reports, although special data or other reporting may be requested by Treasury from time to time.

Reporting to the Treasury by Agencies

General Nature of Reporting

The receipts and expenditures and the related budget surplus of deficits are published monthly by the Treasury based on the information contained in the accounts submitted by disbursing and collecting officers of the government, as reflected in the central accounts of the Treasury. The monthly Treasury statement reconciles the central accounts and the accounts of the various agencies. The classifications of the information is comparable to other Treasury reports and budget estimates.

Expenditures are shown, exclusively, on the "checks-issued" basis. This would include both cash payments and withdrawals under letters of credit. Receipts are shown on the basis of collections reported in the accounts of disbursing and collecting officers.

The central reporting is streamlined, involving minimal forms. The reporting varies, depending on whether the transactions are handled directly by the Treasury or by an exempted department. Agencies, such as the Department of Defense, other offices, and certain government corporations, disburse their own funds and do not report by the standard statement of transactions form to the Treasury. In the exempted agencies, the reporting of collections and disbursements is through the disbursing officer without separate reporting by the Agency.

Examples of Reports to the Treasury

Exhibit 5.4 illustrates the several types of reporting required by the Treasury from federal agencies for payments. The nature of the reporting formats vary, depending on whether the Treasury makes the disbursement or the agency does its own disbursing.

Exhibit 5.4 **REPORTS SUBMITTED BY FEDERAL AGENCIES TO TREASURY DEPARTMENT FOR PAYMENTS MADE**

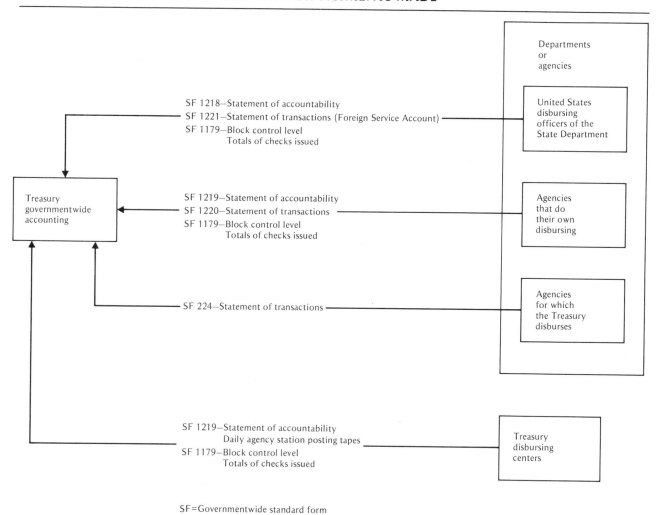

SF = Governmentwide standard form

Source: *Federal Financial Transactions*, Treasury Department, Washington, D.C., June 1980, p. 78.

Exhibit 5.5 illustrates several reports required from federal agencies for collections made on behalf of the government.

Financial Condition and Income and Retained Earnings Reporting

The statements of financial condition and a related statement of income and retained earnings must be submitted quarterly, semiannually, and annually to the Treasury. These reports are required from each revolving fund and business types of general and special funds.

Exhibit 5.5 **REPORTS SUBMITTED BY FEDERAL AGENCIES TO THE TREASURY FOR COLLECTIONS MADE**

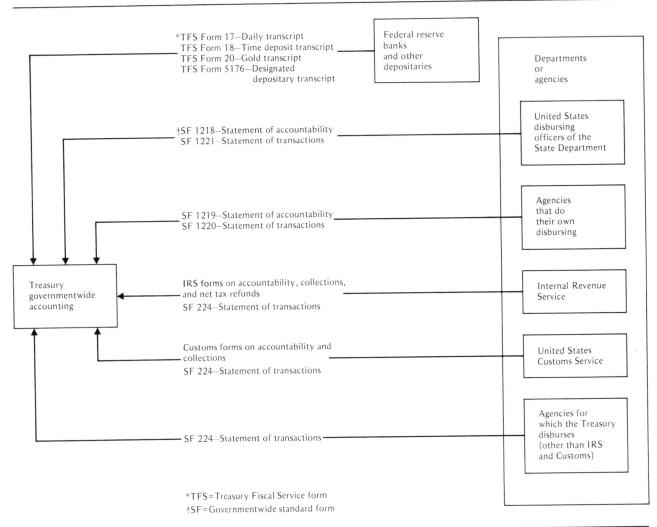

Source: *Federal Financial Transactions*, Department of Treasury, Washington, D.C., June 1980, p. 79.

Statement of Transactions

The reporting of most agencies includes the monthly completion and submission of (SF) 224, Statement of Transactions. This form is the official agency report to the Treasury showing total agency receipts and disbursements for the month. The report is submitted together with a list of confirmed deposits and debit vouchers within three working days of the end of the month.

The Statement of Transactions along with another report submitted monthly by disbursing officers (called their Statement of Accountability) must be in balance. Receipts and disbursements must be reported showing the related appropriation, fund, or receipt symbol.

As mentioned above, certain agencies are exempted. Depending on the agency, two types of statements of accountability would also be submitted by the disbursing officers to the Treasury: the standard form 1218 for foreign service accounts, or SF 1219 for United States disbursing officers.

Two types of statements of transactions are submitted by the disbursing officers to the Treasury: SF 1221 for foreign service accounts, or SF 1220 for United States disbursing officers accounts.

Statement of Obligations

The Report on Obligations (SF 225) is submitted by agencies to the Treasury no later than 20 calendar days after the close of the month. This reporting is made for each general fund, management fund, (as well as consolidated working funds), revolving fund, special fund, and trust fund when it is anticipated that the reportable amounts of the fund will exceed $1 million in a fiscal year.

Amounts on the Report of Obligations must be in agreement with related data submitted to the Office of Management and Budget on SF 133, Report on Budget Execution, required by the OMB Circular A-34.

Statement of Unexpended Balances of Appropriations (or Year-end Closing Statement)

This statement, TF 2108, is used by agencies to make an annual report on the unexpended balances of appropriations as reflected on the agencies records and to reconcile the reported balances with the amounts shown on the central accounts maintained by the Treasury. The statement displays a comparison and analysis of the Treasury's unexpended appropriation balance and the agency's after giving consideration to reconciling item such as transfers to "M" accounts (the "merged" or expired appropriation accounts maintained by the Treasury), withdrawn or restored balances to "M" accounts, reimbursements and receivables, undelivered orders and contracts, and accounts payable and other liabilities.

It is this report that is used to monitor compliance with the provisions of Section 1311 of the Supplemental Appropriation Act relating to the validity of reported obligations and the need for supplemental appropriations.

Accrual Reporting

For several years, two statements were required by the Treasury that reflect the agencies accounts on an accrual basis. The genesis of this reporting is a position taken by the President's Commission on Budget Concepts that concluded, in the 1960s, that expenditures reported on an accrual basis probably represented the best measure of the economic impact of the federal budget. The commission's conclusion, in essence, was that expenditures should be reflected in the budget and federal financial reporting at the time the liability is incurred or on the accrual basis, rather than on the cash basis. Treasury reporting has historically been done, and to this day, is still done primarily on a "checks-issued" or cash basis accounting.

Statement of Appropriation Account

The Statement of Appropriation Account (TF 6727) is required quarterly, although within the agency the information is available on a monthly basis. The primary purpose of the statement is to reconcile accrued expenditures to the net cash disbursements for each appropriation for which the agency is responsible. A separate statement must be submitted for each appropriation.

In the case of disbursements versus accrued expenditures, TF 6727 provides the following formula to reconcile the two concepts.

Net disbursements (appropriation and fund accounts)
+   Balance of applicable liability accounts, end of period
−   Balance of applicable liability accounts, beginning of period
−   Balance of applicable asset accounts, end of period
+   Balance of applicable asset accounts, beginning of period
=   **Net accrued expenditures (appropriation and fund accounts)**

Statement of Receipt Account

The Statement of Receipt Account, TF 6728 must be submitted quarterly by agencies to the Treasury. The primary purpose of the statement is to reconcile accrued revenues for the period to net cash receipts for each appropriation under the agency's control. A separate statement must be submitted for each appropriation. The statement, TF 6728, provides the following formula to reconcile the two concepts.

Net cash receipts (receipts accounts)
+   Balance of applicable asset accounts, end of period

  −   Balance of applicable asset accounts, beginning of period
  −   Balance of applicable liability accounts, end of period
  +   Balance of applicable liability accounts, beginning of period
  =   **Net accrued revenues (receipt accounts)**

Reporting by the Treasury

The principal financial reports prepared by the Treasury on the operations of the government as a whole include

▲   The Daily Statement of the United States Treasury
▲   The Monthly Statement of Receipts and Outlays of the United States Government
▲   Combined Statement of Receipts, Expenditures and Balances of the United States Government

For a few years, the Treasury also experimented with the preparation of consolidated financial statements for the entire federal government.

Daily Statement

The Treasurer of the United States, each day, publishes a report of transactions affecting the central accounts of the Treasury. At month-end, this report (The Daily Statement of the United States Treasury) is supplemented by additional information. These statements include the following information concerning the fiscal position of the government.

▲   Statement of assets and liabilities comprising only the central accounts
▲   Summary of changes in the balance of the central accounts, for the month, year to date, and the corresponding periods of the prior year
▲   Summary of cash deposits and withdrawals for the month, year to date, and the corresponding periods for the prior year
▲   Summary of certain transactions reflecting increased value of outstanding public debt securities sold at a discount during the periods

At month end, certain additional information is published to supplement the Daily Statement. The additional contents issued on the last day of each month relates to

▲   A detailed statement of public debt receipts and expenditures for the month, year to date, by major debt categories;
▲   A summary of public debt and guaranteed debt outstanding for the current date and corresponding date for the prior year;

▲ A detailed statement of outstanding public debt, showing the amount of each obligation issued, retired, and outstanding;

▲ A statement of the guaranteed debt of the government, at the end of the month;

▲ A summary of direct and guaranteed debt outstanding at certain dates;

▲ A summary of the amount of savings bond issued and retired for the month, year to date compared with the corresponding periods for the prior year; and

▲ A statement of securities of government corporations and other agencies held by the Treasury at month end.

Monthly Statement of Receipts and Outlays

The Monthly Statement of Receipts and Outlays reflects the budget surplus or deficit. Receipts are reported as collected; outlays are reported on the basis of "checks issued" and cash payments made. The exception is public debt interest that is reported on the accrual basis. This monthly statement comprises several tables containing the following information.

▲ Budget receipts, outlays and related surplus or deficit for the prior year, current year to date, and estimates for the full current year as well as the means of financing the budget (Table I)

▲ Budget receipts for the current year to date, classified by major sources and budget outlays classified by departments, agencies, and other organizations and compared to budget estimates for the year (Table II)

▲ Budget receipts and outlays for the current month, year to date, and the corresponding period for the prior year by divisions in the budget document to permit comparison to budget estimates (Table III)

▲ Means of financing the budget classified by assets and liabilities directly related to the budget showing net transactions for the month and current and prior fiscal years to date and account balances at the beginning of the current year and month and the balances at the close of the month (Table IV)

▲ Budget receipts and outlays for each month of the current year, cumulative totals year to date, and a comparison to the prior year to date (Table V)

▲ Summary of trust fund receipts and outlays for the current month, year to date, and securities held as investments at the beginning of the current year and month and at the end of the month (Table VI)

▲ Summary of net receipts by source and outlays by function for the month, current year to date and the corresponding period of the prior year

This monthly report is published on a preliminary basis shortly after the close of the fiscal year; not all receipts and disbursements have been included in the accounts. It is the balance of this preliminary statement that is used to announce the budget surplus or deficit for the year. The final statement, issued some four months later, will contain the official positions for the fiscal year and may vary slightly from the earlier preliminary statement.

Combined Statement of
Receipts, Expenditures,
and Balances

Annually, the Treasury issues the *Combined Statement of Receipts, Expenditures and Balances* of the United States Government. The statement is in book form containing tabulations of financial data, segregated into several parts.

Part I. Part I comprises three statements: the federal government's balance sheet, statement of receipts and outlays, and a financing statement showing when financing was provided and applied. Supporting schedules provide details on the International Monetary Fund, public debt, agency securities issued, federal securities held as investments of the government, cash and other assets held outside the Treasury by disbursing, collecting and other fiscal officers.

Part II. Part II of the Combined Statement provides details concerning internal revenues, customs, and miscellaneous receipts for the fiscal year. This information is shown by source, categories and organizational unit. Data are also provided on individual income and FICA taxes, capital transfers, customs collections by district and ports, and internal revenue receipts by states and districts.

Part III. Part III consists of detailed statements of appropriations, outlays, and balances for the fiscal year by (1) budget expenditure accounts, (2) deposit fund accounts, and (3) summary of budget authority, appropriations, outlays, and balances.

Part IV. Part IV contains informational tables on appropriations and authorizations, public debt, and status of special and trust fund receipts.

Part V. Part V contains information relating to each foreign currency account for currencies acquired by the government without payment of dollars or other means.

The tables of Parts I, II, and III are compiled from the central accounts of the government maintained by the Treasury and other information reported to the Treasury by agencies. The information for Parts IV and V is obtained from various organizations both inside and outside of the Treasury.

Consolidated Financial Statements

For fiscal years 1975, 1976, and 1977, the Treasury issued prototype consolidated financial statements for the federal government in an attempt to provide a comprehensive financial reporting on the full range of federal government activities structured in a manner similar to a commercial or corporate financial statement. While an attempt was made, it was not possible to reflect the government's financial status on the basis of generally accepted accounting principles. Several problems and issues were identified, such as valuing assets, recording unfunded pension and other government benefits, selecting equitable depreciation methods, determining a uniform method of fixed asset accounting, establishing methods for accruing costs and revenues, to mention a few.

FISCAL POLICIES AND PROCEDURES The preceding reporting requirements are set forth along with related policies and procedures in the *Treasury Fiscal Requirements Manual* (TFRM). The manual is a codification of instructions to federal agencies concerning the fiscal responsibilities of the Treasury and reporting and accounting requirements imposed by the Treasury on other agencies of the government. In its publication, *Federal Financial Transactions*, the Treasury states that the manual comprises three volumes: Volume 1 provides instructions for the guidance of departments and agencies; Volume II provides instructions for the guidance of Federal Reserve Banks and general depositaries; Volume III provides procedures for Federal Reserve Banks for canceling, verifying, destroying, and accounting for Federal Reserve notes unfit for circulation. Volume I of the *TFRM* is of particular relevance to government agencies and their accounting considerations. This volume contains guidance on the following matters.

▲ The form, content, and reporting frequencies for submitting the financial data needed by the Treasury to fulfill the central accounting and reporting responsibilities

▲ The procedures and standard forms relating to payrolls, including the various types of deductions, and for other matters related to federal agency pay systems

▲ The disbursing procedures of the government, particularly those related to vouchering of payments by cash, checks, letters of credit, and other systems. Additionally, the TFRM contains guidance for the designated depositaries of government.

▲ The process, requirements, and standard forms for recording and accounting for the deposit of public money through the depositary system of the government.

As mentioned earlier, agencies by law are required to incorporate the requirements of the Treasury into the appropriation accounting systems, recognizing that the requirements of the TFRM are but a portion of the financial data needed to manage a federal program.

PART II

ACCOUNTING STANDARDS, PRINCIPLES, PROCESSES, AND CONCEPTS

Government Accounting Standards and Principles

chapter 6

Although the General Accounting Office is an agency in the legislative branch of government, many laws have given this organization, headed by the Comptroller General of the United States, the authority and responsibility for prescribing the accounting standards and principles of governmental accounting for each executive agency. In contrast, the reporting requirements, while influenced by GAO, have been imposed upon government agencies principally by the Treasury and the Office of Management and Budget, generally to ensure compliance with one or more laws.

In addition to prescribing the desired accounting and monitoring the reporting, the GAO is also responsible for examining the "application" of federal money by the executive branch. This latter responsibility is discharged by conducting numerous audits of agencies' systems. This chapter highlights the broad guidelines, published by GAO, that should form the structural base upon which federal accounting systems are designed and operate.

LEGAL BASIS OF STANDARDS AND PRINCIPLES

The Budget and Accounting Procedures Act of 1950 directed the Comptroller General of the United States to prescribe accounting standards for executive federal agencies and departments. These standards have been published in Title 2 (revised 1978) of the General Accounting Office's *Policy and Procedures Manual for Guidance of Federal Agencies.* While acknowledging that no single set of standards can be devised to fit the diversity of governmental operations, GAO established several standards as guidance to agencies and departments. These standards are the requirements against which agency systems are reviewed, evaluated, and approved.

ACCOUNTING STANDARDS

The several standards for federal accounting systems that have been established include

- ▲ Usefulness of financial data
- ▲ Accounting for responsibilities
- ▲ Consistency of accounting and other classifications
- ▲ Technical requirements
- ▲ Qualified personnel
- ▲ Truthfulness and honesty
- ▲ Simplicity
- ▲ Reliability and materiality
- ▲ Necessity for updating accounting systems

Each of the standards is summarized in the following paragraphs.

Usefulness of Financial Data

The financial data produced by the agency system must be useful to the governmental officials. The data must be of benefit in the planning, controlling, managing, and reporting of agency performance. Needs external to the agency must also be met, including those of the President, Congress, other agencies, and the public.

In recent years, many agencies have been upgrading their accounting and management systems. Critical evaluations of the historical systems often disclose that considerable attention was given to fiscal activity and externally imposed reporting requirements. The information needs of agency management were often not considered in the original systems.

Accounting for Responsibilities

The accounting system provides a method of reporting as one basis for evaluating performance. The accounting should be structured to permit reporting by areas of responsibility and activity.

A system designed to account by responsibilities and activities provides the vital information on the budget and monitoring functions. Such an accounting permits the identification of individuals and organizations to whom resources have been allotted and a basis for assessing performance. This standard has not been fully implemented across agencies at this time although, as agencies modernize systems, this feature is one of the more important objectives sought.

Consistency of Accounting and Other Classifications

To be of maximum use to management as well as serving external needs, the agency's accounting must be consistent with its other financial activities. Programming, planning, budgeting, accounting, and reporting classifications should be consistent.

When the accounting and reporting structure of the resource allocation systems and the accounting systems are not consistent, minimal management can be exercised over the expenditure of agency resources. Planning, budgeting, and accounting systems should be designed in a similar manner, permitting the aggregation of actual resources consumed in a manner that will permit a comparison with anticipated resource requirements.

Technical Requirements

An agency's accounting system comprises the formal books and accounts, supporting records, documents, papers, reports, and related procedures used to account for resources and operations.

Financial transactions must be adequately supported with pertinent documents readily available for audit. Interagency and interfund transactions shall be separately identified. Accounts should be sufficiently detailed to meet all management needs as well as external requirements.

This standard is much easier to verbalize than to implement. Students of system design will testify to the challenge of a transaction and account coding structure that will meet all of the multidimensional accounting and reporting needs of federal agency management. (Examples of these requirements are discussed later in the chapter.)

Qualified Personnel

Technical competence is important to the continual improvement of accounting. The design, implementation, and maintenance of satisfactory accounting systems require competent leadership and capable staff.

While this standard might appear obvious, it was not until the late 1950s and early 1960s that one began to notice a preponderance of personnel having accounting and financial education and experience holding governmental accounting and financial management executive positions. The GAO itself was staffed principally with investigators rather than with professional accountants and auditors until the 1950s.

Truthfulness and Honesty

The highest standard of truthfulness and honesty must be applied in accounting for the receipt, disbursement, and application of public funds; transactions should not be recorded in agency accounts in a manner that will produce materially inaccurate or false or misleading information.

The Treasury, the OMB, Congress and all recipients of federal reports have a right to presume that published information is (1) accurate and (2) supported by the agency's accounting system. While estimations (e.g., determination of end-of-period accruals) are permissible, the criteria of reasonableness and materiality should be applied to all reported data.

Simplicity

Accounting procedures shall be as simple and readily understandable as practicable; excessive details and unnecessary refinements shall be avoided. Undue precision is often neither necessary nor desirable to the achievement of accurate and reasonable reporting of an agency.

The continuing emphasis placed on agencies has been for orderly improvements resulting in simplified and more effective accounting and the elimination of requirements and procedures that involve duplication or that do not serve a purpose commensurate with the costs involved.

Reliability and Materiality

Accounting processes require estimates and judgments. In determining the degree of precision to be employed in allocating costs and income and computations in which estimates must be employed, due consideration should be given to the materiality and relative significance of the items involved.

To a degree, this standard is related to the simplicity and understandability of the the system, mentioned above. The cost and relative benefits must always be considered when refining the account and transaction structure of an agency's system.

Necessity for Updating Accounting Systems

Organizational arrangements, shifting emphasis on program activities, revised legislation, and technological changes require updating the accounting systems to maintain the currency and continued usefulness of the systems.

This is particularly true with the changes that have occurred in the technology for processing data. Many agencies installed automated data processing techniques during the 1950s and early 1960s. Then, the principal improvement seemed to be the ability to process data faster. Manual systems were speeded up essentially by computer applications. In the late 1970s and at present, agencies are again upgrading systems. This generation of changes, though, is directed toward improving the quality and timeliness of information and appears to be taking advantage of the latest methodology to design new and improved systems.

GOVERNMENTAL ACCOUNTING PRINCIPLES The Budget and Accounting Procedures Act of 1950 also directed the Comptroller General of the United States to prescribe accounting principles, and other requirements to be observed by federal agencies and departments. These principles have been published in Title 2 of the General Accounting Office's Policy and Procedures Manual for Guidance of Federal Agencies.

Several accounting principles have been established by GAO relating to several subject areas such as

▲ Accrual accounting
▲ Fund control

▲ Account structure

▲ Asset control

▲ Accounting for liabilities

▲ Accounting for the federal investment

▲ Cost information

▲ Financial reporting, and

▲ Central accounting and reporting

A summary of each of these standards is provided in the following paragraphs.

Accrual Accounting

The maintenance of accounts on the accrual basis is a basic requirement for federal agencies. The accrual basis of accounting consists of recognizing in the books and records the significant and accountable aspects of financial transactions or events as they occur.

Expenditures accrue as goods and property are received, services performed, and when amounts become owed under programs for which no performance or current services are required. Expenditures accrue regardless of when cash payments are made, invoices received or, in some cases, property is physically received. Revenue transactions are to be recorded in the accounts when earned or accrued to provide an official record of amounts to be collected and the revenue-producing operations of the agency.

Fund Control

Federal agency accounting must reflect the need to comply with laws, including those prohibiting incurring obligations and expenditures in excess of appropriations (the Antideficiency Act), restraining or otherwise impounding appropriated funds (the Impoundment Control Act of 1974), and other legislation relating to fiscal or financial matters. Agency accounting systems must incorporate appropriate techniques to assist in achieving fund control.

Account Structure

The account structure is the system of general ledger and subsidiary accounts to be established and maintained. The design, establishment, and maintenance of accounts must be defined in light of an agency's legal authorities, assigned responsibilities, and reporting requirements. The accounting entity, for which separate groups of accounts must be established, may be an entire agency, a subdivision thereof, or one or more legally established funds.

Asset Control

Effective procedures must be devised to provide assurance that assets are used properly and only for authorized purposes, and that assets do not leave the possession of the government unless authorized. No assets are written off, written down, or disposed of without proper authorization.

Accounting for Liabilities

Specific principles must be observed with respect to liabilities.

▲ All liabilities shall be measured and recorded in the agency accounts in the period incurred and removed from the accounts in the period liquidated.

▲ Liabilities recorded shall represent amounts owed.

▲ Incurred liabilities shall be accounted for and reported irrespective of whether funds are available or authorized for their payment.

▲ Separate accounts shall be maintained for major categories of liabilities to facilitate clear and full disclosure.

▲ All transactions related to liabilities must be included as of the end of the accounting period.

Accounting for Federal Investment

The major elements of the federal investment shall be separately accounted for and disclosed in the financial reports. With respect to individual agencies, these elements include

▲ *Additions* to the federal investment such as
+ Congressional appropriations
+ Property and services obtained from other federal agencies without reimbursement
+ Donations received
+ Accumulated net income from operations

▲ *Deductions* from the federal investment such as
− Funds returned to the Treasury
− Property transferred to other federal agencies without reimbursement
− Accumulated net loss from operations

Until October 1978, borrowings from the Treasury were included as an addition to the federal investment of an agency. However, after that date the General Accounting Office required that borrowings be accounted for as liabilities of agencies rather than as part of the investment of the government.

Cost Information

The production and reporting of significant cost information are essential ingredients of effective financial management. Information must be available to agency management, Treasury, Office of Management and Budget, and Congress for devising and approving realistic financial plans, making reasonable comparisons, and controlling costs with limits established by law or adminstratively.

Financial Reporting

Financial reports should be prepared to clearly disclose significant financial facts about agency operations and activities. The reports should be prepared and issued as often as necessary to be of maximum use to management and meet prescribed external requirements.

Central Accounting and Reporting

The system of central accounts is maintained by the Treasury to comply with statutory requirements for central accounting and the production of overall financial reports for the federal government. These accounts and reports shall be consistent with the overall principles, standards, and related requirements for accounting prescribed by the Comptroller General.

PRESCRIBED REPORTING STANDARDS Full disclosure of agency operations was required by the Budget and Accounting Procedures Act of 1950. To achieve full disclosure and comply with other sections of the same act, the Comptroller General prescribed reporting standards. These standards are published in Title 2 of the General Accounting Office's Policy and Procedures Manual for Guidance of Federal Agencies.

As detailed in 2-GAO-17, the achievement of full disclosure in financial reporting requires observance with several GAO reporting criteria.

▲ Fairness of presentation
▲ Compliance with prescribed requirements
▲ Timeliness
▲ Usefulness

These reporting standards have been defined by the GAO in the following manner.

Fairness of Presentation

Fairness of presentation of financial reports refers to the overall propriety in disclosing financial information. Fair presentation through full disclosure in reporting requires observance with the following GAO requirements.

▲ *Completeness and clarity* of all essential facts related to scope, purpose, and period of time of each report must be included and clearly displayed.
▲ *Accuracy, reliability, and truthfulness* are required of all financial data; appropriate steps should be taken to avoid bias, obscurement of significant facts, and presenting misleading information.
▲ *Accounting support* shall be the basis of all financial reports; bases or sources other than the accounting system should be clearly explained.
▲ *Excluded costs* shall be clearly explained in accompanying notes along with estimates of the amounts excluded.
▲ *Form, content, and arrangement* shall be simple and designed to communicate significant information clearly to users of the reports.
▲ *Extent of detail* shall be sufficient to provide a clear and complete report; unnecessary detail shall be avoided, particularly when inclusion would obscure significant information.
▲ *Performance under limitations* prescribed by higher authority shall be specifically reported.
▲ *Consistency* of accounting shall be the basis of reported financial data; material accounting changes or methods and the effect must be clearly explained.
▲ *Terminology* consistent and not technical shall be used in financial reports to promote clarity and usefulness.

Compliance with Prescribed Requirements

Financial reports of federal agencies must comply with

▲ Requirements of applicable laws and regulations relating to nature, accounting basis, content, frequency, and distribution; and

▲ Restrictions concerning classified information.

The reports must be based on the agency's official accounting system and maintained in accordance with the requirements of the GAO.

Timeliness

To be of maximum usefulness, reports must be timely. The publication should not be delayed to produce relatively minor refinements of data.

As mentioned in an earlier chapter, the reporting requirements of the Treasury are stringent, in some instances requiring agencies with multi-billion dollar budgets to submit financial status information within a few days of month end. To meet such mandates, systems must be automated and structured to record and aggregate financial transaction in a manner that is readily conducive to preparation of reports. It is hoped such reports will be generated in an accurate and timely fashion with minimal analytic effort or attempts to make minor refinements to data.

Usefulness

Financial reports should be designed to present needed information useful to report recipients. Unnecessary or excessively detailed reports should be avoided.

Historically, the emphasis on agency reporting was directed toward fiscal accountability. All agencies gave a priority to providing the reports required by the Treasury, OMB, and Congress as well as other external users. These types of reports, however, were typically of minimal value to agency managers responsible for allocating and managing activities within finite resources. Until recently, few agency systems provided for the generation of information on not only an obligation and disbursement basis but also on a cost base. Similarly, information aggregated by activity, organization, cost, or performance centers was also sparse.

GAO REVIEW AND APPROVAL OF AGENCY ACCOUNTING SYSTEMS The head of each executive department and agency is responsible, under Section 113 of the Budget and Accounting Procedures Act of 1950, for establishing and maintaining systems of accounting that conform to the principles, standards, and other requirements prescribed by the Comptroller General.

Section 112 of the same act requires that the executive department and agency accounting systems and the central accounting system of the Treasury be approved by the Comptroller General.

Phases of Accounting System Approval Process

Over the years, the approval process adopted by the Comptroller General has been refined and consists of two phases or stages: (1) the department or agency submission of its accounting principles and standards established to govern agency accounting systems and (2) the design of the accounting systems.

In practice, the agency's request for approval of its systems takes the following form.

▲   The development of an overall plan for the financial management of the agency, including a thorough study of the total financial management needs

▲   The application of the GAO principles and standards to the specific operational and management features of the agency

▲   The design of an accounting system concept to integrate the details of the plan and the requirements of the specific principles and standards into an approvable system.

Statements of Principles and Standards

The statement of accounting principles and standards may be submitted by an agency to the General Accounting Office for the entire department or agency, for individual systems within the entity, or for appropriate groupings of individual systems.

The submission of principles and standards may be in the form of statements of complete principles and standards or amendments to previously approved principles and standards. These principles and standards will, typically, discuss or describe

▲   Variations in substantive accounting matters (such as depreciation, annual leave, unfunded costs, handling and storage costs, etc.) must be identified and discussed.

▲   Techniques (such as cost-finding techniques, estimating techniques, analyses and periodic summations of documentary data) may be utilized in lieu of formally recording in the accounting system every significant or accountable aspect of transactions.

▲   The significant aspects of transactions (such as recording revenues, receipts, obligations, accrued expenditures including asset acquisitions, disbursements, and applied costs).

General System Design

An agency's system design presented to the Comptroller General for approval must be comprehensive, containing where appropriate narrative descriptions, charts, and diagrams. The general system design documentation would not include procedures and instructions necessary to operate the system. However, according to Title 2 of the GAO Manual, the documentation must include or address the following subjects.

A General System Description

The system description must include the overall design concept; the relationship of the accounting system to the agency's budget and program structure, mission, functions and management information system; a summary coding classification; interfacing relationships with other accounting systems.

Financial Reports to be Produced

The reports section must include an overview of the recurrent reporting plan to satisfy both internal and external requirements; a listing by title and form number of all recurring internal and external reports (including details as frequency, period covered, recipients, sample formats).

The Accounting Records to be Maintained

The accounting records include general ledger accounts title, number, definition, content of account, control functions in respect to subsidiary ledgers; subsidiary ledger accounts; description of books of original entry or transactions files (in case of computers) locations and organizational levels maintaining accounts and documents.

Major Accounting Processes

The accounting processes must be documented by flowcharts of data describing actions relating accounting objectives, records, internal control, financial reporting requirements, methods for determining and recording and accounting for accrued expenditures, revenues, and costs.

Accounting for Costs

The role of cost accounting must be defined as well as the refinement for operational classification for costing purposes, rationale and criteria for accruing expenditures; role of cost centers and other accounts for allocating, charging, and accumulating costs; explanation of coding structure for distributing and summarizing costs by activity; relationship of cost accounts to cost-based budgeting; areas where cost-finding techniques will be used in lieu of cost accounts.

Extent and Nature of Automation

The documentation must include a statement of objectives, descriptions and flowcharts of information flow in the system; description of equipment configuration and capabilities and computer languages to be utilized in programming the processing operations; design specifications describing the logic of the computer system (sequence of operations performed, each proposed computer program, physical characteristics of data elements contained in transactions files, controls, and audit trails).

Internal Controls Maintained

Descriptions of controls for safeguarding personnel and property resources; controls over quantity, timeliness, reliability and accuracy of inputs, processing and outputs; basis for auditability of system should be included in the submitted documentation.

Plans for Implementing
the System

The proposed conversion process and methods for testing logic and reliability of the accounting system must be described.

In connection with an automated system, the General Accounting Office does not require computer programmer and operator's instructions to be submitted for its review.

GAO System Review Guides

The General Accounting Office has issued several guides to assist departments and agencies in determining whether their accounting principles and standards and general system design meet the system's approval criteria of GAO. A partial listing of these include

▲ *Review Guide for Federal Agency Accounting Systems: Accounting*
▲ *Review Guide for Federal Agency Accounting Systems Designs: ADP Application*, September 1974, and
▲ *Review Guide for Federal Agency Payroll System Designs*, January 1976.

These guides are generally consulted prior to submitting formal requests for GAO approvals. It should be noted that it is the policy of the GAO to approve the accounting system design without waiting for implementation or operation of the system. Significant deviations or changes from the approved principles, standards, or system design will require the agency to obtain GAO's approval to maintain the approved status of the system.

Additionally, the Joint Financial Management Improvement Program issued, in February 1979, a checklist designed to provide assistance to new or reorganized departments and agencies in developing basic financial management systems. This checklist summarizes the requirements of financial management systems by addressing four principal processes.

▲ Planning, organizing, and staffing financial activities
▲ Budget system design, implementation, and operation
▲ Accounting system design, implementation, and operation
▲ Program control, feedback, and evaluation.

Accounting Concepts in the Federal Government

chapter 7

INTRODUCTION

Federal accounting, like other disciplines, requires the use of phrases, terms, words, and concepts that have specialized meaning and import to practitioners within the federal government community. These descriptors are often associated with or related to actions of specific parties or organizations as the President, Congress, Office of Management, Treasury, or the individual agencies.

In addition to the application of phrases with specific implications in the federal financial community, the accounting concepts or applications are further complicated by the legal requirements that a single system must provide for the total accounting of an agency's resources. The system of an agency must be sufficiently integrated to provide complete disclosure for each appropriation or fund for which the agency is responsible as well as the total of all such resources received from Congress. The same system must be capable of providing data on several accounting bases: fund, budgetary, accrual, cost, and cash disbursement. Additionally, the system must provide financial information by the agency's programs, activities, functions, organizations, and cost or responsibility centers. These bases are discussed in greater detail in later chapters.

Unfortunately, practitioners do not use these terms and concepts as if they were mutually exclusive. At times, too, formal discussions and publications may improperly treat these methods or concepts of agency accounting as if they were separable processes.

Chapters 3 and 4 contain definitions of appropriations, apportionments, allotments, obligations, and other terms used throughout this and later chapters.

FUND ACCOUNTING

Requirements for Fund Accounting

The Congressional concern with appropriation of funds to pay debts and provide for the common defense and general welfare has its roots in the Constitution of the United States. Congress, properly so, jealously guards the Constitutional mandate that "no money shall be drawn from the Treasury, but in Consequence of Appropriations made by Law." Similarly, the same article continues with a system of reporting that has remained intact to the present day. For example, the Constitution requires that ". . . a regular Statement and Account of Receipts and Expenditures of all public Money shall be published from time to time."

Abuses and liberties taken by executive agencies over the years have led Congress to reinforce its controls over the appropriation and expenditure of federal monies. Today, several laws exist that provide for and impose civil and criminal sanctions on any person violating limitations, ceilings, or restrictions on an appropriation of Congress, either through applying funds for unauthorized purposes or for committing or expending sums beyond the amounts appropriated or approved by Congress.

Related to the Congressional prerogatives is the fact that most appropriations are for a one-year period. This is not to say that Congress has not appropriated money to complete a project spanning more than one fiscal year or provided that the appropriation would remain available, possibly for several years, until expended for the purpose enacted. Generally, though, the overwhelming proportion of appropriations are one-year funds.

Funds Defined

In federal accounting, the term *fund* is viewed as being synonymous with a Congressional appropriation of money or legal budget authority to incur obligations and expenditures and make disbursements on behalf of the federal government.

Fund accounting or, more accurately, *appropriation accounting* is the principal basis of accounting in the federal government. Agencies must maintain an integrated system of accounts and control to provide for a complete reporting of their stewardship of all funds or appropriations, individually and in total, for which they have responsibility. The more common and continuing interests of Congress, the Treasury, and the Office of Management and Budget are with the status of each appropriation or budget authority as a separate accounting entity.

Objectives of Appropriation Accounting

The overall objectives of fund or appropriation accounting are directed toward fiscal accountability and compliance with the express or imposed intent of Congress. These would include

▲ Ensuring that the federal monies are spent for the purposes and within the time periods desired by Congress;

▲ Preventing obligations, expenditures, or disbursements in excess of the appropriations or budget authority approved by Congress;

▲ Fixing personal responsibility with designated federal executives for any violations or noncompliance with Congressional limitations; and

▲ Assisting in the increased effectiveness and economy in the application and rate of expending federal money.

Implicit in an agency's systems of controls and accounting are the checks and balances to ensure that the several criteria of a federal appropriation are considered by federal executives prior to the obligation or expenditure of funds. All appropriations and budget authority have three specific compliance considerations, relating to timing, purpose, and amounts.

▲ *Timing*—The commitment and, on occasion, the expenditure of appropriated funds must be made during the time period permitted by the Congress in the legislation.

▲ *Purpose*—Appropriated funds may be obligated and expended only for those purposes intended or expressed in an agency's authorization or appropriation legislation.

▲ *Amount*—The total amount of obligations and expenditures may not exceed the appropriation or budgetary authority provided by the Congress.

As explained in Chapter 12, certifying and disbursing officers are personally liable for obligations or expenditures in excess of appropriated amounts.

Distinctions in Fund Accounting

Other chapters have defined and illustrated several aspects of the types of funds existing in the federal government. While the term "fund accounting" is applied to both federal financial management and to state and local accounting, the concept has been implemented in a different way at the federal level. The general fund of the federal government is all-encompassing and of minimal concern except to those interested in only the greatest of governmental financial matters.

To the individual financial manager, "fund accounting" is almost immediately equated to "appropriation accounting." It is the integrity of the appropriation that must be controlled, monitored, and reported upon. Agency program managers, while not adverse to receiving information on the accrual basis of accounting, have difficulty using such information to resolve questions concerned with obligations and expenditures, items of prime significance to the Congress, OMB, and the Treasury. Also, the initial indication of any program progress will be revealed through the rate and trends of obligations and expenditures.

The basic premise of government accounting is that if obligations are controlled in relation to ceilings or other limitations, it is unlikely (although not impossible) to overexpend or overdisburse an appropriation or budget authority.

The Process

Recording the Appropriation

While an agency must develop and maintain a system to account for the total resources for which it is responsible, the accounting controls and procedures are directed toward monitoring and reporting on the status of the individual appropriations and the required administrative subdivision of each funding authority. The agency must account for the execution of its approved budget authority. This will include several steps.

The appropriation must be made available to the agency by the Treasury. This process is formalized by the issuance of a Treasury *warrant* notifying the agency of the available Congressional appropriation. This notification is recognized by a journal entry in the agency's accounts, establishing a "cash balance" with the Treasury against which the agency will request that disbursements be made.

Recording the Apportionment

Apportionments by the Office of Management and Budget divide the appropriated amounts. An apportionment will restrict the amounts that may be obligated or expended by an agency through limiting fund amounts by time period, activity, project, objects, or some other criteria. As explained in Chapters 3 and 4, the apportionment is supported by a formal written notice subdividing the appropriated amounts into category "A" or "B" apportionments. The apportionment actions are recognized by an agency through entries in its accounting records.

Recording Allotments

Once the agency head has received the apportioned amounts, a formal delegation will often be made giving obligational and expenditure authority to subordinate agency program heads and heads of offices. This transfer of obligational and expenditure authority is done by the issuance of a document referred to as an *advice of allotment*. The advice is formal notification to other agency executives or allottees of their responsibility for funds allotted to them within the amounts apportioned to the agency. Accounting entries are made to reflect this delegation of authority to different allottees.

Allowances

In some agencies, funds are further subdivided through the issuances of allowances to other agency personnel. While this subdivision is formally documented by the issuance of *advices of allowances*, generally no formal accounting entry is made to record the event.

The detailed accounting and fund tracking occurs at the program or allottee level although there may be instances in which certain funds are recorded and accounted for above the allottee level. The balances of allotments, which constitute the unobligated apportionments, are the remaining obligational authority of the program official or allottee for which he or she is personally responsible. Allotment balances are closely monitored by the maintenance of manual or computerized allotment (or, if used, allowance) registers.

Following chapters provide more detail concerning specific accounting procedures and practices relating to the events above.

BUDGETARY ACCOUNTING The term "budgetary accounting" is used in the federal government to describe a detailed accounting process instituted to account fiscally and continually for the obligation of funds in relation to expenditures, obligations, allotments, apportionments, and ultimately the appropriations for which the agency is responsible. While the budgetary accounting might be construed to be a separate accounting requirement, this process is actually more in the nature of a bookkeeping refinement of the overall fund accounting of an agency.

Budgetary Accounts

In practice, concurrent accounting entries are made to a set of balancing budgetary accounts and to proprietary accounts in order to provide financial information of value to those concerned with monitoring the appropriations as well as to managers concerned with the cost of resources required to support a government program.

The following listing of accounts is illustrative of the accounts concurrently affected.

BUDGETARY ACCOUNTS	PROPRIETARY ACCOUNTS
Unapportioned appropriations	Assets
Unallotted apportionments	Liabilities
Unobligated allotments	Invested capital
Unliquidated obligations	Revenues
Accrued expenditures—capital	Cost and expenses
Accrued expenditures—operating	

Legal and Accounting Views of Obligations

The term *obligation* has both an accounting and legal connotation. From an accounting view, the incurrence of an obligation represents an accounting event that must be entered in the official records of an agency. From a legal view, an obligation must take a precise form to be recognized as a commitment of government funds and a possible liability that the government may ultimately pay.

With respect to the legal aspect, the Supplemental Appropriation Act of 1955 (Section 1311 of the Revised Statutes) requires that an obligation of the government be supported by specific documentary evidence. The eight forms of obligations include

▲ A *binding agreement* in writing between the parties in a manner and form and for a purpose authorized by law, executed before the expiration of the period of availability for obligation of the appropriation or fund for specific goods to be delivered, real property to be purchased or leased, or work or services to be performed

▲ A *valid loan agreement*, showing the amount of the loan to be made and the terms of repayment

▲ An *order required by law* to be placed with a government agency

▲ An *order* issued pursuant to a law authorizing purchases without advertising when necessitated by public exigency or for perishable subsistence supplies or within specific monetary limitation

▲ A *grant or subsidy payable* from appropriations made for payment of, or contributions toward, sums required to be paid in specific amounts fixed by law or in accord with formulas prescribed by law; or payable pursuant to agreement authorized by, or plans approved in accord with an authorized law

▲ A *liability* that may result from *pending litigation* brought under authority of law

▲ *Employment or services* or persons or expenses of travel *in accord with law,* and services performed by *public utilities*

▲ Any other *legal liability* of the government against an appropriation or funds legally available.

Availability for Obligation

In addition to meeting these formal requirements, an obligation may be legally incurred only if there is a current or unexpired appropriation in existence for the period during which the obligation is incurred. Certain general rules, by the GAO, govern conditions under which obligations may be incurred.

▲ The general rule regarding obligation of a fiscal year appropriation for payments to be made in a succeeding year is that the contract or other instrument imposing the obligation must be made within the fiscal year sought to be charged and the contract must be to meet a bona fide need of that fiscal year. (33 Com. Gen. 57,61)

▲ The bona fide need of the service of a particular year depends upon the facts and circumstances of the specific case; no general rule for application to all situations exist. (73 Com. Gen. 155,159)

▲ The obligated balance of an appropriation available for a definite time period must be transferred at the end of the second full fiscal year following the close of the period of availability of the appropriation. (The transfer will be to the successor or "M" or merged accounts of the Treasury, Chapter 5). (7 GAO 19.6, 31 U.S.C. 701-708)

▲ Working capital or revolving type funds cannot operate to divest appropriate funds of their identity or change the requirement that they must be expended solely for the purpose for which the appropriation was made available. (26 Com. Gen. 545, 548)

▲ The use of a specific appropriation to pay obligations under another appropriation, *even during a temporary exhaustion of funds is in contravention* of 31 U.S.C. 628, even though the repayment is contemplated after a supplemental appropriation might be made. (36 Com. Gen. 368)

The GAO decisions above are important to federal accounting and compliance with each is a requisite for properly controlling and complying with appropriation requirements. In practice, some confusion and discussion arise over whether appropriated funds may be obligated in one fiscal year and liquidated in a succeeding fiscal year. As indicated, unless set forth in an appropriation or otherwise precluded, it is *not* necessary for the obligation and its liquidation to occur in the same fiscal year. Even obligated balances transferred to the "M" accounts, remain available to meet expenditures until exhausted or until the expiration of a time period that might be specified by Congress.

It is also important to note that another appropriation or working capital or revolving fund cannot be used to incur obligations or make expenditures for a "customer" appropriation that are prohibited by the conditions of that appropriation. In other words, other appropriations or funds may not be used to "change the color" (i.e., terms, conditions, limits, prohibitions, etc.) of another appropriation.

The Process

Accounting for the Budget

As explained in Chapters 3 and 4, the appropriation, once approved by the President and apportioned by OMB, becomes the operating plan or program budget of agency officials. The actions of agency executives, accounting controls, and procedures are directed to monitoring compliance in accordance with the program budget. The initial reservation, in most agencies, of budget funds occurs when the program official executes one of the eight obligation forms above.

Recording the Obligation

As mentioned, allottees are the authorized officials permitted to incur obligations on behalf of the government. Prior to the execution of a formal obligating document, allottees or their delegates must certify to the availability of funds to meet the intended obligations. By this certification, the agency official is acknowledging that there is sufficient money remaining unobligated from an unexpired appropriation to meet the amount of the obligation being considered.

In some agencies, the period of time between the issuance of a committing document (such as a procurement request or a travel order) is prolonged. In these cases, the commitment may be recorded in the accounting records in advance of the formal recordation of the intended obligation. As a general practice, though, only the later obligation is recorded.

In many instances, amounts originally obligated must be later adjusted up or down to reflect changes in the potential liability of the government. Should a downward adjustment be made to recorded obligations prior to the expiration of the appropriation or obligational authority, the released obligational authority could be used for other authorized expenditures. However, once the appropriation has expired, the obligated funds generally remain available only to meet the liability for which it was initially obligated. A new obligation may not be incurred.

Liquidating the Obligation

Established obligations must be reduced or "liquidated" upon the receipt of goods or services or performance, depending on the purpose of the original obligation. The liquidation of the obligation is also referred to as the accruing of the expenditure. Of course, an obligation could be liquidated by the cancellation of the obligation. The liquidation of the expenditure obligation requires that accounting entries be made to the budgetary accounts.

▲ Unliquidated obligations

▲ Expended appropriation—capital

   or

▲ Expended appropriation—operating

A concurrent or parallel entry must be made to the proprietary accounts to record the asset acquired or expense incurred. The offset for these accounts would be a cash disbursement or incurrence of an accounts payable.

The objective of the concurrent entries or budgetary accounting is to provide a formal, continuous accounting reconciliation between the funds appropriated and apportioned and the rate, level, or purpose of funds being expended. The budgetary accounts of an agency provide a current record of the status of the program budget or financial plan and the manner in which it is being executed. However, as indicated in succeeding paragraphs, the financial management cycle is not complete with the liquidation of the obligation.

ACCRUAL ACCOUNTING One aspect of accrual accounting of an agency relates to the accounting for revenues and expenditures in the appropriate accounting period and *not* to the matching of revenues and expenses. There will often be no relationship of receipts to expenditures at the agency level. The law governing the receipts may be totally different from the legal requirements for expenditures. Further the actual cash receipt or outlay may have taken place in an earlier period (in, possibly, the form of an advance) or later period.

Accrued Revenues and Expenditures Defined

The *accrued revenues* of an agency consist of amounts earned, but neither received nor past due. The accrued amounts may be billed or unbilled at the reporting date, in which case the appropriate distinction should be made.

Accrued expenditures consist of liabilities incurred for goods and services received, other assets acquired, performance accepted, and other goods or services consumed. Accrued expenditures occur even though invoices may or may not have been received and payment may or may not have been made.

Benefits of Accrual Accounting

Accrual accounting provides several benefits to an agency in its ability to conduct meaningful analyses of its status of revenues, expenditures, and fund balances. For example,

▲ Information is provided to permit the development of cost-based budgets.

▲ More accurate information is provided to permit program management and relating costs to work performance.

▲ Increased precision of historical data exists to later assign actual costs to appropriate accounting periods.

▲ A full and more representative disclosure of financial results is presented to more accurately assess the status of any projected overruns or underruns.

▲ A sounder basis exists for controlling and allocating available dollars to competing programs, activities, and functions.

Acceptance of Accrual Accounting

Accrual accounting is a much discussed and debated subject among federal accountants, budget officials, managers, and even Congress. Despite numerous statements by Presidents, pronouncements by the General Accounting Office, the Office of Management and Budget, and the Treasury, not all agencies have accounting systems that provide for accrual kind of information. Additionally, alternative methods might be used to arrive at accrual reports and financial statements, although the accounts are maintained on a cash basis. Often, too, the distinction is not maintained between accrued expenditures and accrued expenses or costs. *Accrued expenditures* relate to services received or performance accepted whereas *accrued expenses or costs* are defined as the consumption or use of goods or services. A more appropriate term for accrued costs, used by financial managers in recent years, is applied expenses or costs.

The accounting for a fixed asset might best illustrate the distinctions above. Assume that an asset is acquired for an amount of $10,000, estimated to have a service life of ten years, with no salvage or residual value at the end of that period. The specific entries and distinction between accrued expenditures and accrued expenses or cost would be

Accrued Expenditure at the Time
of Receipt of Fixed Asset

BUDGETARY ENTRY:

DEBIT: Unliquidated obligation $10,000
     CREDIT: Expended appropriation—capital
                                                         $10,000

PROPRIETARY ENTRY:

DEBIT: Fixed asset $10,000
     CREDIT: Accounts payable $10,000

The entries above reflect the accruing of an expenditure. Again, a billing may or may not have been received from the vendor from whom the asset was acquired. Further, payment for the asset is not relevant. The budgetary entry provides for an adjustment to the program budget or financial plan amounts. The proprietary entry records the asset acquired and the liability of the agency.

Accrued Expenses or Cost

Later, possibly the end of a fiscal period, the expense or cost applied or consumed by the agency would be recorded in the following manner.

BUDGETARY ENTRY:

—None—

PROPRIETARY ENTRY:

DEBIT: Depreciation on fixed assets $1,000
     CREDIT: Accumulated depreciation $1,000

111

This entry reflects that portion of the asset consumed by program operations during the fiscal period. Thus, from a cost standpoint, a program could consume and be charged for costs during a period different from the one in which the accrued expenditure occurred.

GAO Definition of Accrued Expenditures

Accrued expenditures, as defined by GAO in its *Accounting Principles and Standards,* are charges incurred during a given period that require the provision of funds. An expenditure would accrue or mature, by this definition, when

▲   Goods and other tangible property are received, or

▲   Services are performed by employees, contractors, grantees, lessors, and other payees, or

▲   Amounts become owed by the government under programs for which no performance or current services are required.

Examples of the latter would be amounts due for annuities, insurance claims, benefit payments, and certain cash grants. As noted earlier, expenditures accrue whether or not cash payment is made and, in some instances, whether or not goods or tangible property have been physically received. An unpaid expenditure is reflected in the accounts as a liablity.

Note, though, it is possible that a payment could be made although no expenditure has been accrued. Such a condition exists when an agency made a cash advance, at which time an asset (accounts receivable due) is established but no services have been received or accrued. This is common for federal grant programs in which the government's policy is to permit the recipient to operate with federal capital rather than its own.

Liquidating Obligations

The accruing of expenditures, as illustrated earlier, is one method of "liquidating" or reducing a previously established obligation. There are three events that result in the liquidation or reduction of an earlier obligated amount.

▲   The complete or partial cancellation of the obligation,

▲   The receipt of services or materials in full satisfaction of the amount previously obligated, or

▲ The accrual of expenditures for which a prior obligation had not been established (e.g., in the case of salaries) where, for pratical purposes, the obligation and accrued expenditure occurs almost simultaneously.

An "unliquidated" obligation is merely an outstanding obligation against which no expenditures have accrued and which has not been cancelled.

ACCOUNTING FOR COST

Cost Defined

In its Title 2, *Accounting,* the GAO states that every expenditure in its primary form should be conceived as a cost of some essential, planned activity. Costs furnish important measures of performance. GAO has defined *costs* as

> . . . the financial measure of resources consumed in accomplishing a specified purpose such as performing a service, carrying out an activity, or completing a unit of work or a specific project.

GAO requires that agency accounting systems classify costs according to acquisition of assets and current expenses. Additionally, the systems should provide for classification of the kinds of costs as between labor, material, or contractor services.

Other terms as "costs applied (to program activity)" or "cost consumed" or "accrued costs" or "accrued expenses" are synonymous to "cost," as defined above. The objective is to provide for an accounting of the resources required or consumed in a fiscal period to support the services or activities performed during that period.

Some comments, though, concerning the limitations or usefulness of cost data to program managers are discussed in the next section.

Utility of Cost to Federal Managers

The General Accounting Office, and federal accountants, in general, support the premise that cost-based information is essential to the conduct of economical and efficient operations. Public law 84-863, which amended the Budget and Accounting Act of 1921 and the Budgeting and Accounting Procedures Act of 1950, directed heads of agencies to, among other things, support budget justifications by information on performance and program costs.

However, the utility of cost-based information may be limited in government operations due to various circumstances. Given the one-year life of most operating appropriations, it may be difficult to obtain cost-based reporting prior to the expiration of the appropriation. Additionally, the long-term nature of other programs could require significant capital investment, covering several years, before operations commence and cost is known before the appropriation expires. Further, the timing difference for consummating various transactions compounds the reporting problems and usefulness of cost as a valuable statistic to program managers.

Exhibit 7.1 illustrates what is probably a typical life cycle of a government program. Note that it is not possible to report cost in the first or second year of program, as illustrated. It may not be until the third year that cost becomes available to be used by program managers. Presumably after that time the program activity has entered a leveling-off or period of stability. Although this cost information is useful, the top managers of an agency must be concerned with the funds being considered by the Congress for the next fiscal year. Typically, little interest will be shown in the cost being reported for a program that was initiated some three years earlier.

Even when the life cycle of a transaction does not cover several years, as it did in the example given, cost-based budgets are not generally

Exhibit 7.1 **TIMING OF THE RECORDING OF PURCHASE OF MATERIALS UNDER THE ACCRUAL METHOD OF ACCOUNTING**

NATURE OF TRANSACTION	RECORDED IN PERIOD IN WHICH			
	Order is placed	Materials are delivered	Materials are used	Bill is paid
Placing an order for materials	As an obligation			
Materials delivered		As an accrued expenditure		
Materials used or consumed			As an applied cost or expense	
Payment made for materials				As a disbursement of cash
Program period	1	2	3	4

Source: Adapted from *Frequently Asked Questions about Accrual Accounting in the Federal Government,* United States General Accounting Office, Washington, D.C., 1970.

available for presentation to Congressional committees and others concerned with planning or programming agency funds. For example, an agency typically prepares its budget for a fiscal year some 15 months in advance of the start of a fiscal year. Congressional hearings and the appropriation process may be completed several months before the fiscal year closes. Cost-based information does not exist within this time frame. Often, final cost data are not known until 90 to 120 days following the close of a fiscal year.

Few take issue with the premise that cost-based information provides the most appropriate data upon which to base decisions or manage programs. However, the timeliness of such data probably results in such information being of more utility for after-the-fact assessments of program economy and efficiency than for day-to-day management decisions.

OMB Definition of Costs

The accounting and reporting procedures at the federal level are not necessarily consistent. GAO has generally required the definition above with respect to the accounting for costs or applied costs. However, OMB by its Circular A-34 has prescribed a method of reporting that is not totally consistent among the different types of resources consumed or applied by an agency. For example, Circular A-34, relating to the reporting required for budget execution by an agency, cites the following permissible variations in determining applied costs of different resources.

▲ For operating programs, applied costs will represent the value of resources consumed or used (which is consistent with the GAO definition).

▲ For procurement and manufacturing programs, applied costs will represent the value of material received or produced.

▲ For capital outlay programs, applied costs for public works will equal the value of work put in place.

▲ For loan activities, applied costs will represent assets acquired, even though no resource has been consumed.

▲ For operating programs, funded by appropriations, equipment will be included in costs when it is placed in use.

▲ For all programs, when the data are provided in the accounting system, accrued annual leave will be included in costs when earned, rather than when taken. This is true even though the leave may be unfunded at the time. Depreciation costs and other unfunded costs will be included where appropriate as well.

Circular A-34 views applied costs as associated with program outputs so that such costs are financial measures or resources consumed or applied in accomplishing a specific purpose, performance of a service, carrying out an activity, or completing a unit of work.

CASH BASIS ACCOUNTING

Cash Defined

Probably due to the immediacy with which the Treasury requires the reporting of cash disbursements, many agencies, to this day, essentially operate on a cash basis.

References are made to "cash expenditures," "checks issued," "cash disbursements," and "cash." These terms are synonymous and refer to the simultaneous accounting recognition of a liquidated obligation, accrued expenditure, and cash disbursement. An agency on this basis of accounting recognizes these accounting events at the time it forwards a schedule and voucher of payments to the Treasury for the issuance of checks to the listed payees.

Limitations of Cash Accounting

A system designed for cash basis accounting does not provide for the recognition of legitimate timing differences actually occurring between the accruing of an expenditure, the costing of an event or consuming resources, and the disbursing of cash. Financial statements published on such a basis will typically understate the liabilities of an agency and never reflect the actual cost of program activity.

Alternatively, an agency may have a system designed for accrual accounting, but fiscal practices could result in the accounting being performed essentially on a cash or checks-issued basis. For example, an agency may not adhere to a system procedure of recording a contractor's invoice when it is received or the receipt of an asset when that event occurs. That is, the accrued expenditure and the obligation are not recorded in a manner consistent with the facts. Agency personnel might delay processing the invoice or posting the asset until the point at which the actual amount due is determined. Generally, the accounting is performed when the documents are compiled for transfer to the Treasury for disbursement purposes. Such practices subvert the intent of the accounting system and result in the accounts being maintained on a cash basis.

Hybrid Accrual Accounting

To comply with OMB, GAO and Treasury requirements for accrual type of information, agencies may resort to a hybrid method of accounting that permits accrual reporting. The accounts of the agency still remain on a cash or checks-issued basis. The accrual reporting is accomplished by inventorying the receivables, payables, and accruals at the end of the period. No amounts are reflected in the formal accounting records.

Another alternative, is to inventory the receivables, payables, and accruals and to post an adjusting entry to the accounts at the end of the fiscal period. A reversing entry is made for the accruals at the beginning of the next fiscal period thereby returning the accounts to the cash basis.

While reasonable data may result for accrual reporting purposes, such accounting information, which could be of value to agency managers, is not available for their review between reporting periods. A cursory study of the events and timing of transactions outlined in Exhibit 7.1 illustrates the limitations of a cash-basis system. Little or no information is available to agency executives for monitoring programs and activities.

chapter 8 The Accounting Process

INTRODUCTION
The fundamental objective of accounting in the federal government is to provide a reporting on the receipts and expenditures and the economy, efficiency, and effectiveness with which management applied these funds to agency operations. Historically, the accounting objectives, in practice, were limited to the fiscal stewardship reporting of receipts, obligations, and disbursements. Today such a limited accounting is not permitted. Agencies are required to have multidimensional systems, integrating the controlled-oriented aspects with the capabilities to provide cost, segregate operating from investment items, permit the operation of working capital and management funds, and provide information for both budget preparation as well as budget execution.

FISCAL ACCOUNTING
Numerous laws notwithstanding, not all agencies have accounting systems capable of achieving the broader, integrated reporting desired by the General Accounting Office and Office of Management and Budget. In these instances, emphasis continues to be given to the fiscal

accounting and control criteria, in some cases to the exclusion of any consideration of accrual accounting, cost accounting, or management's operating needs.

Input Systems

The prescription of many required standard fiscal forms and fiscal-type requirements to support transactions of a government agency is necessary for governmentwide uniformity and certain cost efficiencies. In the design of systems, some organizations have given primary consideration to the types of expenditures. Generally, such systems are referred to as "input-oriented" systems: the account structure accumulates fiscal information by the type of document or "inputs" supporting fiscal transactions (e.g., personnel salaries and benefits, travel, contracts, grants, utilities). In these instances one of the primary concerns is not support of management, but meeting reporting requirements that are imposed externally (e.g., by the Treasury, the OMB).

The consequences are predictable. With such account structures, the support of a multiple-purpose accounting system is not possible; aggregations or summarizations of data are restricted, often requiring time-consuming analyses of account balances and specific transactions. Cost accounting by organization, activity, function, or other classification is limited or nonexistent.

Nature of Fiscal Systems

Before the widespread availability of computers for financial applications, the emphasis had to be merely on processing the large volume of details. The single entry of data serving multiple management and analytic purposes was not possible. Not unlike the approaches taken by industrial counterparts to adopting computerized techniques, the initial approaches taken by the government were predicated on automating the manual process, essentially processing the same data faster.

Exhibit 8.1 provides an overview of the process of an input-oriented, possibly manual system. The routinization of processing and need for clerical efficiency, and certainly the unavailability of electronic data processing equipment, contributed much to the nature of the accounting that was possible.

Exhibit 8.1 **OVERVIEW OF AGENCY FISCAL ACCOUNTING SYSTEM**

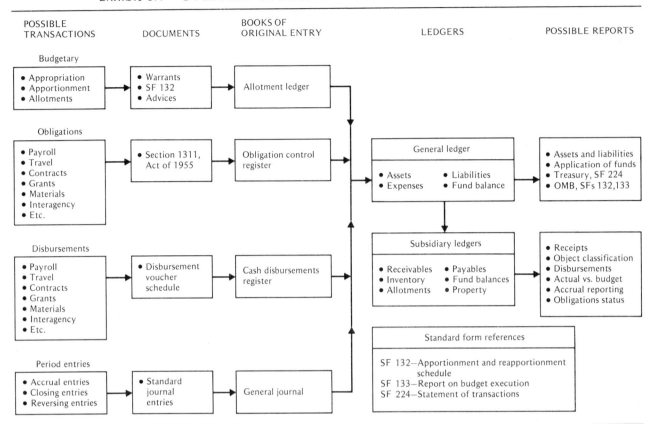

Documentation

Standard forms exist, and in some instances are required by law, for the documenting of the government's normal transactions, such as payroll, travel, contracts, interagency transactions, transportation. Disbursements are scheduled on forms acceptable to the Treasury, supportive of the central system of accounts maintained by that agency.

Many of the documents, which are carefully controlled, contained authorizations, approvals, and certifications of various levels of government executives necessary to establish or fix fiscal responsibility.

Standard journal entries, extensions of the standard forms, provided for the conversion of cash-basis accounting to a hybrid-accrual reporting basis. The systems required the reversal of earlier accrual entries to return the accounts to a cash basis for the succeeding accounting period. Throughout the fiscal period, the cash disbursement system of accounting was prevalent.

Books of Original Entry and Ledgers

Certain books of original entry (e.g., the cash receipts and cash disbursements registers and general journal) were similar to those used in industry. Considerable bookkeeping was required to maintain the records related to the fiscal and budgetary accounting of an agency. In many agencies, the focus of management was on the rate at which the agency's appropriation was being obligated or committed and on the concern that controls existed to ensure no overobligation occurred, violating a public law on that matter. Two of the more critical records of such systems were the allotment ledger and the obligation control register.

The general and subsidiary ledgers provided, to a degree, financial control over the assets, liabilities, and other resources of the agency. Subsidiary ledgers were designed to primarily address the fiscal responsibilities related to items as receivables, payables, inventories, fixed assets, and fund availability.

Reporting

Input-oriented systems typically have difficulty providing for the spectrum of reporting required of agency management to properly control and monitor operations, activities, and performance. Priority was given to developing the status of funds and disbursement-related reports required by the Office of Management and Budget and the Treasury. The systems of many agencies, though, were capable of reporting cost to a limited degree, budgeted in comparison to actual financial status, obligations by defined object classification, and other financially related data.

REQUIREMENTS OF GOVERNMENT AGENCY

Through the impetus of Congress, the GAO, the OMB, and needs of agency management to monitor more complex governmental programs, agencies have developed or are developing integrated systems capable of satisfying both accounting and broader financial management requirements.

Complete accounting is required for individual appropriations. Agencies with multiple appropriations or funding sources must ensure that the segregated accounting exists. Additionally, the system must provide for the accumulation of financial data and reporting by other dimensions that may require the accumulation of data from several funding sources in order to show total agency resources. Several of these requirements are summarized in succeeding paragraphs.

Proprietary Accounting

Depending on the nature of the appropriation or fund, an agency must establish a chart of accounts, typically double entry, which will include provision for accounting for the assets, liabilities, fund balance, revenues, and expenses. The agency must also ensure that the system is capable of providing an overall accumulation or reporting for all funds in its possession or for which it is responsible.

Budgetary Accounting

A unique characteristic of federal accounting, in contrast to commercially oriented accounting, is budgetary accounting. This requirement is directed toward fiscal or stewardship aspects of appropriation or fund management. For each appropriation or fund or budget authority, an agency is required to account for individual transactions throughout the cycle—from allotment through succeeding steps as such obligations, expenditures, payables, costs and expenses, and disbursements.

Accrual Accounting

A full accrual basis of accounting is the preferred and required basis for governmental accounting. Accrual accounting is essential to the requirement that agencies systems provide for the development of cost-based budgets and an accounting on the basis of costs or resources consumed.

Program and Responsibility Accounting

For most agencies, the Congress favors a system of funding by appropriations but the related legal accounting requirements of an appropriation are of limited utility to a financial manager. Often agency managers are responsible for programs and activities supported by numerous funding sources. Additionally, activities may be conducted and monitored in a manner that will not permit scrutiny on a single funding basis. In such instances, financial information must be aggregated by program activities or responsibilities if management is to exercise control.

Cost Accounting

The cost of government activities or services has received increased attention in recent years. Many agencies can now provide detailed costing for their programs, sometimes even in relation to a unit of measurement or achievement. The agencies, like industrial organizations, are often able to distinguish between direct materials, labor and overhead, and other support costs. As mentioned in Chapter 5, the restrictions imposed by Congress on appropriations and the reporting procedures mandated by the Treasury at times impede full costing by funding sources.

Property Accounting

The General Accounting Office requires that property and other physical resources be under financial as well as physical controls. Such an accounting requirement often can be accomplished only by rather elaborate subsidiary systems because of the extensiveness of the assets (e.g., land, buildings, machinery, equipment, furniture, and inventories) to be controlled. A truly integrated property system that provides both physical and fiscal general ledger and property controls requires considerable discipline and integration of property and fiscal control procedures.

Capital and Current Operation Accounting

Regardless of funding sources or other criteria, agencies must distinguish or describe every transaction between capital expenditures or current operation expenditures or expenses. Capital transactions would benefit more than one fiscal year whereas current expenditures would relate to the present fiscal year.

Multiyear Accounting

In addition to the integration of proprietary with budgetary accounting and the requirement that the agency's financial system be responsive both to accounting and to management needs, the federal agency's system must provide this matrix accounting for several years. By law, all appropriations and other budget authority are recorded and monitored in the agency's accounting system for at least three years—the current year, and two immediate past years. Multiyear appropriations require an accounting for longer time periods. Obligated balances for expired appropriations of earlier years are merged or transferred to the "M" accounts maintained by the Treasury.

**INTEGRATED
FINANCIAL SYSTEMS**
These accounting and other financially related requirements have dictated that agencies design systems directed more toward purposes to be served, required reports, and other management needs and away from systems of the input type.

Output Systems

Output-oriented systems give precedence to the purpose or objectives of information and the reasons for which data are accumulated, summarized, and reported. Initially, the integration related to only the myriad of financially related requirements. In recent years integrated systems have been defined and designed in a manner that provides accountants and program managers with both financial and operating information.

Nature of Integrated Systems

Continual refinements of electronic data processing equipment and computer programming techniques have permitted the development of innovative and efficient financial systems. In accounting, such systems generally use a transaction or basic data element or building block concept by which data are uniformly collected, stored, aggregated, and generated or reported, possibly to a variety of users.

Often a fiscal occurrence or other event initiates the transaction that is recorded to reflect an action. The value and other data for this item or unit is entered into the data processing system in which it is related to supporting documents and classified or coded. Often transactions entered into the system will generate other transactions automatically to complete an accounting cycle or action. The coding could be laborious—it is not uncommon to require over 100 digits to provide for the processing of a single entry of a transaction to serve a multitude of purposes. Alternatively, system designers have opted for the development of "pseudo" or "self-generating" transaction codes, that in themselves are meaningless, but that activate or are responsible for generating a series of additional codings. By so doing, the codes relieve personnel of the input burden and avoid the inevitable errors associated with extensive codings and data entry.

Exhibit 8.2 outlines, conceptually, the nature of information and uses that could be met by some of the more sophisticated financial systems. Note that accounting is only one of many requirements being satisfied from the single database. The integrated nature of these systems has changed the form, uses, and reporting of accounting information. Earlier records, registers, journals, and ledgers no longer exist. Hardcopy reports are often not required. More specific and timely information is available through obtaining a visual display of the facts on a terminal. Data must no longer be processed once for accounting uses and possibly two or more times for management and other purposes. In many automated systems, entire series of records are updated simultaneously, resulting in a considerable reduction or elimination of time-consuming reconciliations.

In addition to the apparent efficiency of these systems, the consistency of the financial data used by both agency financial managers and operating managers is enhanced. With the existence of interactive remote terminals, the increasing popularity of minicomputers, and the interfacing ability of terminals and computers, the development of such integrated systems will continue.

ELEMENTS OF INTEGRATED FINANCIAL SYSTEMS

System Considerations

The determination of financial requirements for the more advanced governmental accounting and management information systems requires considerable investment of agency resources. System designers, as well as agency top management, must participate in the system development process to define, with a high degree of specificity, the system that will best meet agencies' needs and those imposed by legislation and external sources.

Conceptually, an agency with a single appropriation has minimal problems designing and implementing an integrated system to meet the myriad requirements imposed by law or sound business prudence. More common, though, are the problems encountered by Congress providing funds to support an agency's programs in the form of several appropriations. Each appropriation requires a separate accounting—a requirement continually confirmed by Congress. Additionally, Congress, the public, the President, the OMB, and others are not restricted to the appropriation orientation when making inquiries about the manner in which an agency has discharged its responsibilities. It is not unusual (in fact it is common) for agency managers to provide auditable financial information that accumulates data not only by the original appropriations but also by political jurisdiction, agency organization, program activity, agencywide functions, special projects, and object classification of expenditures—to mention just a few.

As mentioned above, this type of data must be maintained in the agency's records for several years.

Exhibit 8.2   OVERVIEW OF AGENCY FINANCIAL AND INFORMATION SYSTEM

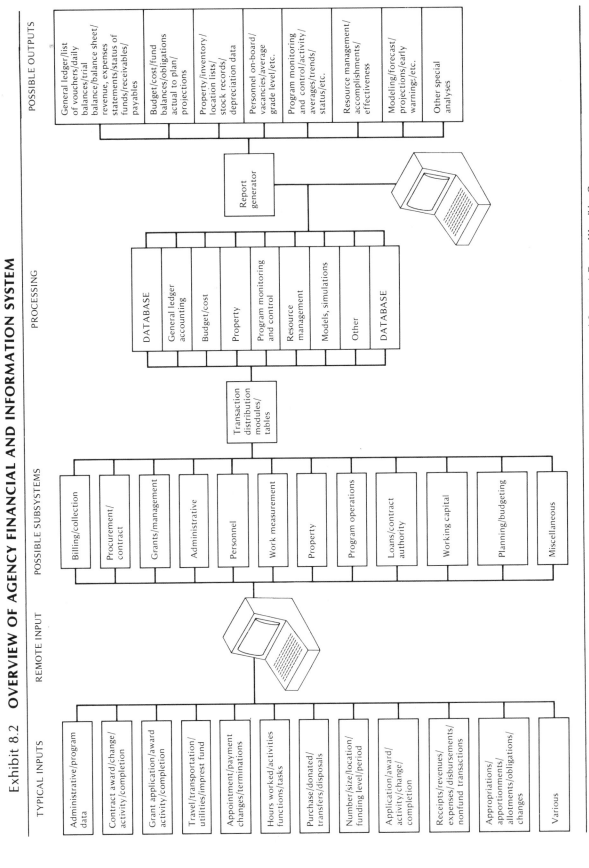

Source: Adapted from "More Effective Systems in the Governmental Sector: A Better Way," by Cornelius E. Tierney, *The Government Accountants Journal*, Fall 1977, The Association of Government Accountants, Arlington, Virginia.

Accounting Control
Considerations

Accounting control considerations are integral to the design and the implementation of systems. There are several legally mandated accounting procedures that must be incorporated into an agency's system. As one example, the appropriation-apportionment-allotment-obligation process imposes significant structural concerns for government system designers. As mentioned in earlier chapters, the disbursing function may not be uniformly executed in the government. Although most agencies utilize the disbursing capabilities of the Treasury, several agencies have their own disbursing officers, many of whom may be geographically dispersed. Some agencies have the accounting function centralized, others have the accounting performed at several locations, requiring supporting records, data, and evidence of authentication for transactions to be transmitted from the originating source to these accounting offices.

The structure of the general ledger must be capable of providing the fiscal and financial details for both internal and external requirements. Implicit in this requirement is a transaction and account coding structure that is sufficiently detailed to provide for full cash accounting for the Treasury; inventory, property, and fixed asset accounting required by the General Accounting Office; and current and operating obligation and expenditure accounting required by the Office of Management and Budget.

To the extent the agency must, by law, participate in interagency allocations, transfers or reimbursement of appropriation funds, the process is further complicated. Each of these interagency transactions must be separately recorded, accumulated, distributed to the appropriate accounts, and reported to others.

To be effective, the budgetary accounting requires a fund allocation or distribution process for providing allotments of monies to various program and agency officials. The fund allotments made pursuant to this process must be incorporated into the agency's general ledger to provide at all times a comparison of budgeted or planned activity to actual obligations, expenditures, costs, and disbursements. The funding process within an agency is not static; changes are continually required to reflect varying program priorities.

Financial Management
Considerations

In addition to the accounting control considerations, more complex relationships must be analyzed and decisions made to meet the financial needs of management and others. While by no means exhaustive, nor indicative of any single agency's system, the following are examples of system requirements or components for which an accounting may have to be provided by an agency.

▲ Appropriation
▲ Location
▲ Organization
▲ Function
▲ System
▲ Accounting control

▲ Mission
▲ Object classification
▲ Program
▲ Special projects
▲ Responsibility center

The general purpose for which such information is required and the uses that agency management could make of the information provided by the accounting dimensions above are highlighted in Exhibit 8.3. Examples of the accounting components above are discussed further in the following paragraphs.

Appropriations

Appropriations, as defined earlier, are the budgetary authority provided in law by Congress. Each appropriation must be separately accounted for, must generally contain specific fiscal criteria for which compliance is required, and the appropriation becomes the limitation on agency expenditures. Agency heads and officials are required to manage and report by appropriation or funding sources, providing a comparison of planned as well as actual expenditures by separate appropriations.

Location

Agencies are continually called upon by Congress, by the OMB, and, many times, by the public to provide a reporting of agency expenditures by geographic location. The location reporting requirement often has two aspects: (1) the various locations of the agency itself, and (2) political subdivisions, such as Congressional districts or standard metropolitan statistical areas, in which the agency's funds are spent.

While the accumulation of financial data by agency location is critical to management monitoring, the accounting for expenditure data by other geographical dimensions is generally done for external reporting purposes. In either event, agencies have opted to have systems accumulate this information to minimize the repeated analyses that have to be made to meet the continual requests for this type of information.

When compiled, such data provide the cost, by location, of agency activities, permit the comparison of several dispersed operating units, and give some insight into differing levels of performance by organizations.

Exhibit 8.3 **TYPES, PURPOSES, AND USES OF INFORMATION REQUIRED BY AGENCY MANAGEMENT**

TYPE OF INFORMATION	PURPOSE	USES
Appropriation	Identify legal fund entity appropriated by Congress	▲ Budget formulation ▲ Budget justification ▲ Initial distribution of funds ▲ Monitoring obligation rates ▲ Reprogramming decisions ▲ Prevention of "3679" violations
Location	Identify the expenditure of agency resources by geographic location	▲ Isolate geographically the utilization of agency resources ▲ Support planning and management control processes
Organization	Identify an agency organization responsible for the execution of missions, programs, activities, etc.	▲ Identify responsibility for the execution of activities and operating results ▲ Provide management evaluation and control
Functions	Identify specific activities or tasks during the execution of assigned responsibilities	▲ Segregate tasks and duties common to all agency activities ▲ Provide management planning, evaluating, and control ▲ Support integrated PPBS ▲ Develop comparisons between activities ▲ Provide function-unique detail
System	Identify physical and technological resources and related costs	▲ Provide additional information on functions ▲ Identify acquisition of resources ▲ Capture certain life cycle costs
Mission	Identify the purpose for which resources are being utilized or spent	▲ Identify direct agency mission costs ▲ Provide agencywide data for evaluating accomplishment of goals or missions
Object class	Identify the nature of costs incurred	▲ Meet requirements of OMB and Treasury reporting ▲ Provide management control and evaluation
Program	Identify resources by specific programs	▲ Meet agency reporting requirements ▲ Provide program managers with planning and control information
Special projects	Satisfy critical information requirements not accommodated by other components	▲ Provide Congressional visibility ▲ Permit changes during year ▲ Identify unforeseen events ▲ Monitor special projects
Responsibility center	Identify specific areas of responsibility	▲ Provide reports by responsibility center
Accounting control	Provide required accounting control information	▲ Control funds ▲ Identify funds ▲ Identify organizations ▲ Control report balances

Organization

Accounting by organization is common. It is necessary for agency management to relate the activities for which they are responsible to the activities of the several organizations charged with the execution. Typically such an accounting is closely related to the organization chart of the agency. The assigned codes will follow a hierarchical structure that permits the "rolling-up" or summarization of expenditures or cost by the various organizational levels of the agency. Employee numbers could be assigned to organizations relating the organization to personnel performing work for specific units. Other transactions might be similarly coded to the unit incurring the expenditure or cost.

Functions

A common requirement for government agencies is that of reporting expenditures or cost by functions. While each agency will have its own definition of functions, the activities involved relate to resources devoted to maintenance, repairs, supply, procurement, grants, training, personnel, and research and development. It is reasonable to assume that an agency with multiple appropriations will have an increasingly complex system. While a single appropriation could support or be relatable to a single function, the converse condition is probably more common: a function must support the requirements of several appropriations. Thus management must have a financial perspective that crosses appropriations.

System Costing

Some agencies must have multiyear, multiappropriation costing of major agency investments. These investments could be represented by long-term (measured in years) construction projects, research and development programs, weapons systems (in the Defense Department, for example). At times, the accounting requirements for these investments have been referred to as "life-cycle costing." Such an accounting requirement necessitates the accumulation of expenditure and cost data by the end product or finished product. Fiscal data, relating to personnel, material, and other costs, initially authorized by many appropriations over a long period of time, are coded and compiled by these major systems or investments.

Note that the sum of all life-cycle costs will not equal the total of all appropriations for which the agency was responsible over the years. The reason is that not all appropriation expenditures are related solely to these systems.

Mission

The term mission in governmental accounting refers to the agency's expressed goals and objectives. Like other management considerations, mission reporting requires a matrix-accounting viewpoint. The achievement of the agency mission often will require the integration of funds from many appropriations and the economic performance of many functions by numerous organizations, possibly dispersed throughout several geographical locations.

Object Classification

As described in more detail later in this book, the OMB has imposed a type of reporting, by appropriation, upon the government that is referred to as object classification. An object class of obligation or expenditure is the most basic level of fiscal data typically accumulated by some agencies. This relates to the purpose for which funds are used (i.e., salaries, travel, and supplies). These expenditures must be further segregated by those for capital (i.e., those benefiting future periods) and operating (i.e., relating to current period) expenditures.

This type of data must be related to individual appropriations. Management monitors data closely to ensure that no dollar limitations are violated through an overobligation or overexpenditure of appropriated funds.

Program

Although more prominent during the years of Programming, Planning, and Budgeting Systems (PPBS) and much discussed at that time, the monitoring of expenditures and costs by agency program still continues to be important. An agency program might be defined as the combination or integration of agency organizations, functions, and materials and other resources in a manner directed toward achieving one or more of the agency's goals and objectives. Programs, like other financial components, could require the financial resources drawn from several appropriations and impose a matrix-accounting requirement on the agency similar to the process for life-cycle costing, described earlier.

Even in agencies in which references are seldom made to PPBS, a program orientation or view by management is necessary. Different terms, with slightly varying emphasis, might be used to describe the process by which resources from many sources are marshalled to meet agency goals and objectives.

Special Projects

In all agencies, possibly several times a year, the need arises for management to accumulate expenditure and cost data by projects or specific jobs or activities. Systems capable of meeting this management need will contribute to a more efficient and effective utilization of agency funds. Several examples that might be viewed as special projects of activities requiring temporary or specific costing include

▲ Short-time information needs, not warranting changes to existing accounts or transactions coding structures,

▲ Information needs that arise after the start of a fiscal year may be imposed by Congress or management to provide an additional reporting,

▲ Events occurring during the year requiring a need to know cost, possibly an unanticipated interagency transaction that requires the accumulation of cost to ensure that the involved appropriations are properly charged.

There are many instances of financial reporting needs that do not span fiscal years or have a permanency of reporting that warrants the integration of the requirement into the formal account and transaction coding process of the agency. While it is not possible to anticipate all needs, provision for special project costing is an invaluable dimension for any financial system.

Responsibility Center

The responsibility center costing is closely related to performance accounting. Such a requirement has been espoused by the General Accounting Office for years. Several agencies have developed their systems to permit this level of costing. Others, as newer systems are being designed, have been requiring this capability. While financial reporting by responsibility center is similar in some respects to cost reported by organization, there could be significant differences, particularly if the responsibility center costing procedures permit loaned personnel, interagency uses of resources, and accounting on a consumption-of-resources basis.

A structuring of these various requirements in a somewhat hierarchical fashion, as shown in Exhibit 8.4, illustrates again the interrelationships or matrix considerations of agency financial information and reporting.

Other Factors

Systems supporting such accounting and reporting are structured on a "building-block" or "modular" basis that permits the combination of data

Exhibit 8.4 **INTERRELATIONSHIP OF FINANCIAL SYSTEM REQUIREMENTS**

REQUIREMENTS	APPROPRIATION	LOCATION	ORGANIZATION	FUNCTION	SYSTEM	MISSION	OBJECT CLASS
Agency program	▲ Identifies appropriation funding required to execute program	▲ Identifies programs being executed within a given location	▲ Identifies organizations involved in program execution ▲ Provides additional level of detail ▲ Identifies program for organization related elements	▲ Identifies specific tasks required to support Program Execution ▲ Provides additional level of detail ▲ Identifies program element for function-related program elements	▲ Identifies material acquired supported or used by each program ▲ Identifies program element for system related cost	▲ Identifies agency objectives supported by programs	▲ Identifies resources or services employed in execution programs
Object class	▲ Identifies specific resources (e.g., personnel/equipment) or services (e.g., contracting, travel) acquired with each appropriation	▲ Identifies resources and services employed by a facility	▲ Identifies resources or services used by the organization	▲ Identifies resources or services used in the performance of a function	▲ Identifies resources or services related to the system ▲ Determines whether transaction is acquisition, capital expenditures or operating cost	▲ Identifies specific resources or services used in executing or accomplishing agency objectives	
Mission	▲ Identifies how specific agency objectives are funded	▲ Identifies agency objectives supported by activities taking place at the facility	▲ Identifies agency objectives executed or supported by the the organization	▲ Identifies agency objectives supported/accomplished through performance of a function	▲ Identifies agency objectives		
System	▲ Provides life-cycle funding by appropriation systems	▲ Identifies material purchased by a facility and/or system-related activities at a facility	▲ Identifies material purchased and/or system-related activities by an organization	▲ Identifies material acquired in support of a function ▲ Identifies systems supported by the facilities			
Function	▲ Identifies function financed by each appropriation ▲ Identifies funds and sources of funds required to finance specific tasks (functions)	▲ Identifies all functions (including facility support) being performed at each location	▲ Identifies the tasks performed by the organization				
Organization	▲ Identifies individuals responsible for budget execution ▲ Identifies sources of funds that support the organization	▲ Identifies all organization supported by a given facility ▲ Identifies the geographic distribution of a given organization					
Location	▲ Provides total costs and sources of funding of a given agency facility						

to provide a variety of meaningful displays of information. To ensure consistency of data being recorded between fiscal period, minimize mechanical recording errors, and monitor uniformity of data classified by several appropriations within a single agency, the more advanced systems are designed to permit a transaction to be entered once. Predetermined, precoded procedures and table generated transactions then provide the operating guidance to the computer necessary to perform the entry recording, accumulation, display, and reporting functions. As may be apparent, not all of the data for each of the requirements above will necessarily have to be or are able to be transaction-related. For example, data relating to appropriation, organization, functions, object class are specifically related to individual transactions. But other requirements, such as program and mission, could be derived by summing other requirements.

To provide a perspective of the magnitude of effort required to design and implement an agency accounting and financial system, one might consider the several system phases, each of which could take, minimally, months or even years to perform.

▲ Define and determine scope.
▲ Identify and determine system input, processing, and output requirements.
▲ Construct the conceptual system design and, possibly, define an implementation plan.
▲ Develop the general and detailed system design.
▲ Construct the system programming specifications.
▲ Perform programming activities and other implementation efforts.
▲ Test and validate specifications, programming, and system operations.
▲ Install and operate the system.
▲ Conduct postimplementation quality assurance reviews.

While the phases above might be referred to by other descriptors, similar efforts, by any name, must be performed, It is not unusual, in fact it is more the rule, that a federal agency could devote three to five years from the inception to completion of an integrated accounting system. The costs, whether performed by federal personnel or under contract to a private firm, will be in the millions of dollars. At times, the number of staff may approach 100. General system specifications and guidance exist within the federal government to assist in the design and implementation of such systems. In many agencies, detailed systems' development methodologies and procedures have also been refined to a considerable degree.

BUDGETARY
ACCOUNTING
PROCEDURES
PART III **AND PRACTICES**

Appropriations, Allocations, and Apportionments

chapter 9

INTRODUCTION Appropriations are laws passed by Congress under which various agencies are assigned funds for operating government programs. To ensure that the rate of expenditures is consistent with the President's overall financial plan and budget, the Office of Management and Budget maintains a system of apportioning the appropriated funds to the agencies.

Appropriations, in addition to being the Congressional authority to incur obligations and expend federal monies, are public law. Penalties, including personal fines and imprisonment, could be imposed on those who violate appropriation laws. Federal agencies have elaborate systems of internal checks and controls to ensure that funds are obligated only for authorized purposes, for the proper amount, and within the appropriate time period. Once the funds are obligated, detailed accounting procedures are enforced to determine that subsequent obligations and expenditures do not exceed the total of the appropriation.

DEFINITION OF TERMS Most of the terms used in reference to appropriation or obligation accounting are unique to the federal government. The following definitions are used by the General Accounting Office. With slight variation, all departments and agencies have applied these definitions and have similar kinds of controls.

Appropriation

Appropriations are budgetary authority granted by Congress, both to incur obligations and make expenditures in a definite, specified amount. The actual disbursements will be made out of the Treasury. The term appropriation also includes the authority to enter into contracts before the actual appropriation of funds is made by Congress. In these instances, Congress has generally approved *contract budget authority* for which a subsequent appropriation is to be approved to meet the obligations incurred by an agency operating under contract authority.

Apportionments

An *apportionment* is a distribution by the Office of Management and Budget to agencies of amounts available for obligation and expenditure from an appropriation or fund account into amounts available generally by time period. An OMB apportionment limits the obligations that an agency can incur or, in some instances, the expenditures it may accrue, regardless of the amount appearing in the Congressional appropriation.

Allocations

An *allocation* is a transfer of obligational authority from one agency to another to carry out the purpose of the parent appropriation. The agency receiving the allocation is responsible for complying with the appropriation law and reporting the status of the allocated balances to the agency responsible for the parent appropriation. An allocation of funds is not permissible at the convenience of an agency. Congressional approval and OMB concurrence are necessary to permit the allocation of appropriated funds.

As described in the following sections of this chapter, conditions and circumstances have caused certain controls and procedures to be implemented to monitor an appropriation throughout its life cycle. The phases above of the cycle, appropriations, and apportionments are actions of organizations (the Congress and OMB, respectively) that are external to the operating executive agency.

NATURE OF APPROPRIATIONS

Authorization of Funds

It is important to remember that the appropriation of funds by Congress is a two-step process. As outlined in Chapter 3, Federal Budget Process, Controls, and Monitoring, two sets of Congressional hearings are required: one to authorize the program, the second to appropriate funds to establish the operating level of the program. The mere Congressional authorization, as further defined by GAO, does not authorize an agency to incur obligations or make expenditures unless the Congressional authorization specifically states that an appropriation of federal funds had been made.

The wording of authorization legislation is precise. For example, as illustrated in Exhibit 9.1, reference is made in the authorization act that

▲   There are authorized to be appropriated such sums as may be necessary for the fiscal year ending June 30, 1974, and for each of the three succeeding fiscal years for carrying out the provision of this Act.

Several sections of this Act, in Exhibit 9.1, are typical and contain various provisions and conditions that Congress desires to be implemented.

Availability of Appropriations

Before obligations or expenditures are incurred, an appropriation must be available. *Availability* is defined to mean (1) that an appropriation must exist for the purpose for which the obligations or expenditures are incurred and (2) that there must be a current or unexpired appropriation for the period during which the obligations or expenditures are to be incurred.

The GAO has held that appropriated funds cannot be made available by means of a transfer to a working fund or another appropriation for purposes for which such funds would not be available under the original appropriation from which the transfer was made. Working capital or funds of the revolving type cannot operate to divest appropriated funds of their identity or from the requirement that the funds be expended solely for the purpose for which they were originally made available by Congress (26 Comp. Gen. 545, 548).

Additionally, the use of a specific appropriation to pay obligations under another appropriation during a temporary exhaustion of funds is in contravention of the 31 United States Code 628, even though the repayment is contemplated after the supplemental appropriations are made. (36 Comp. Gen. 386)

Exhibit 9.1 **ILLUSTRATION OF AN AUTHORIZATION ACT—COMPREHENSIVE EMPLOYMENT AND TRAINING ACT OF 1973**

Public Law 93-203
93rd Congress, S. 1559
December 28, 1973

An Act

87 STAT. 839

To assure opportunities for employment and training to unemployed and under-employed persons.

Be it enacted by the Senate and House of Representatives of the United States of America in Congress assembled, That this Act may be cited as the "Comprehensive Employment and Training Act of 1973".

Comprehensive Employment and Training Act of 1973.

STATEMENT OF PURPOSE

SEC. 2. It is the purpose of this Act to provide job training and employment opportunities for economically disadvantaged, unemployed, and underemployed persons, and to assure that training and other services lead to maximum employment opportunities and enhance self-sufficiency by establishing a flexible and decentralized system of Federal, State, and local programs.

TRANSITIONAL PROVISIONS

SEC. 3. (a) To the extent necessary to provide for the orderly transition of supporting job training programs, and to provide continued financial assistance for such programs, prior to July 1, 1974, the Secretary is authorized to provide financial assistance in the same manner and on the same conditions as provided in the Manpower Development and Training Act of 1962, as in effect prior to June 30, 1973, title I of the Economic Opportunity Act of 1964, and the Emergency Employment Act of 1971, as in effect prior to June 30, 1973, from funds appropriated pursuant to this Act.

76 Stat. 23.
42 USC 2571 note.
78 Stat. 508.
42 USC 2701 note.
85 Stat. 146.
42 USC 4871 note.

(b) The authority contained in this section shall not be construed to postpone or impede the prompt designation of prime sponsors and the implementation of other provisions of this Act.

(c) Notwithstanding any other provision of this Act other than the provisions of section 4(d)(1), the Secretary is authorized from appropriations available under this Act for fiscal year 1974 to provide financial assistance for the program described in section 304(a)(3) during the period June 1, 1974, through October 1, 1974, in the same manner and on the same conditions as provided pursuant to the Manpower Development and Training Act of 1962, as in effect prior to June 30, 1973, and title I of the Economic Opportunity Act of 1964, as in effect prior to repeal by this Act.

Post, p. 859.

AUTHORIZATION OF APPROPRIATIONS

SEC. 4. (a) There are authorized to be appropriated such sums as may be necessary for the fiscal year ending June 30, 1974, and for each of the three succeeding fiscal years for carrying out the provisions of this Act.

(b) Notwithstanding any other provision of law, unless enacted in specific limitation of the provisions of this subsection, any funds appropriated to carry out this Act which are not obligated prior to the end of the fiscal year for which such funds were appropriated shall remain available for obligation during the succeeding fiscal year, and

Source: Public Law 93-203, United States Congress, Washington, D.C.

Exhibit 9.2 **ILLUSTRATION OF AN APPROPRIATION ACT—PROVIDING FUNDING FOR LABOR; HEALTH, EDUCATION, AND WELFARE; AND RELATED AGENCIES**

Public Law 95–480
95th Congress

92 STAT. 1567

An Act

Making appropriations for the Departments of Labor, and Health, Education, and Welfare, and related agencies, for the fiscal year ending September 30, 1979, and for other purposes.

Oct. 18, 1978
[H.R. 12929]

Be it enacted by the Senate and House of Representatives of the United States of America in Congress assembled, That the following sums are appropriated, out of any money in the Treasury not otherwise appropriated, for the Departments of Labor, and Health, Education, and Welfare, and related agencies for the fiscal year ending September 30, 1979, and for other purposes, namely:

Departments of Labor and Health, Education, and Welfare Appropriations Act, 1978. Department of Labor Appropriation Act, 1979.

TITLE I—DEPARTMENT OF LABOR

EMPLOYMENT AND TRAINING ADMINISTRATION

FEDERAL UNEMPLOYMENT BENEFITS AND ALLOWANCES

For payments during the current fiscal year of benefits and allowances to unemployed Federal employees and ex-servicemen, as authorized by title 5, chapter 85 of the United States Code, of benefits and payments as authorized by title II of Public Law 95–250, of trade adjustment benefit payments and allowances, as provided by law (19 U.S.C. 1941–1944 and 1952; part I, subchapter B, chapter 2, title II of the Trade Act of 1974), and for reimbursement to States for unemployment benefits paid on the basis of public service employment as authorized by title II of the Emergency Jobs and Unemployment Assistance Act of 1974, as amended, and for reimbursements as authorized by Section 121 of P.L. 94–566, $950,000,000, together with such amounts as may be necessary to be charged to the subsequent appropriation for payments for any period subsequent to September 15 of the current year: *Provided,* That, in addition, there shall be transferred from the Postal Service Fund to this appropriation such sums as the Secretary of Labor determines to be the cost of benefits for ex-Postal Service employees: *Provided further,* That amounts received during the current fiscal year from the Postal Service or recovered from the States pursuant to 5 U.S.C. 8505(d) shall be available for such payments during the year: *Provided further,* That amounts received or recovered pursuant to section 208(e) of Public Law 95–250 shall be available for payments.

5 USC 8501 *et seq.*
Ante, p. 172.

19 USC 2291.

26 USC 3304 note.

Ante, p. 180.

GRANTS TO STATES FOR UNEMPLOYMENT INSURANCE AND
EMPLOYMENT SERVICES

For grants for activities authorized by the Act of June 6, 1933, as amended (29 U.S.C. 49–49n; 39 U.S.C. 3202(a)(1)(E)); Veterans' Employment and Readjustment Act of 1972, as amended (38 U.S.C. 2001–2013); title III of the Social Security Act, as amended (42 U.S.C. 501–503); sections 312 (e) and (g) of the Comprehensive Employment and Training Act of 1973, as amended; and necessary administrative expenses for carrying out 5 U.S.C. 8501–8523, 19 U.S.C. 1941–1944, 1952, and chapter 2, title II, of the Trade Act of 1974,

29 USC 882.

19 USC 2271.

Source: Public Law 95-480, United States Congress, October 18, 1978, Washington, D. C.

Exhibit 9.2 is the face sheet of an appropriation act of Congress for

▲ Making appropriations for the Departments of Labor, and Health, Education and Welfare, and related agencies, for fiscal year ending September 30, 1979, and for other purposes.

Other sections of this appropriation act contain limitations on purposes for which funds may be expended, time periods for which the appropriation is available for obligation and expenditure, and the dollar amount of funds appropriated.

Types of Appropriations

Several types of appropriations exist. Unfortunately, the titles or descriptors are not uniformly applied governmentwide. Additionally, the descriptors are not mutually exclusive. Exhibit 9.3 lists and contains brief definitions for various types of appropriations and obligational authority that are preferred by the GAO.

The *unexpired* or *current* appropriation is an open or valid authorization for an agency to incur obligations or make payments. Appropriations would remain current until either of the following conditions occur: (1) the purpose intended by the Congress has been achieved, or (2) the total amount of the appropriation has been obligated or expended, depending on the terms of the appropriation act, or (3) the time period for which the appropriation was available has passed.

If one of the conditions above has occurred, the appropriation is said to have *expired* or *lapsed*. An expired or lapsed appropriation is no longer available for obligation. Amounts obligated prior to expiration, generally, remain available to the agency to pay for related liabilities that will accrue. On occasion, the appropriation act will contain restrictive language concerning the time period during which all expenditures must be made as well.

Other terms used in reference to appropriations are *definite* and *indefinite* appropriations. A *definite* appropriation contains a specified level of funding, although the duration of the appropriation could be for a varying time period. An agency might receive a definite appropriation to pay staff or support program operations. In contrast, the *indefinite* appropriation would not have a specified level of funding, but would be dependent upon a particular receipts or source of funds identified by Congress.

Additional examples of budget authority that may be available to some agencies are described in Chapter 3.

Exhibit 9.3 **TYPES OF APPROPRIATIONS AND OTHER FEDERAL OBLIGATIONAL AUTHORITY**

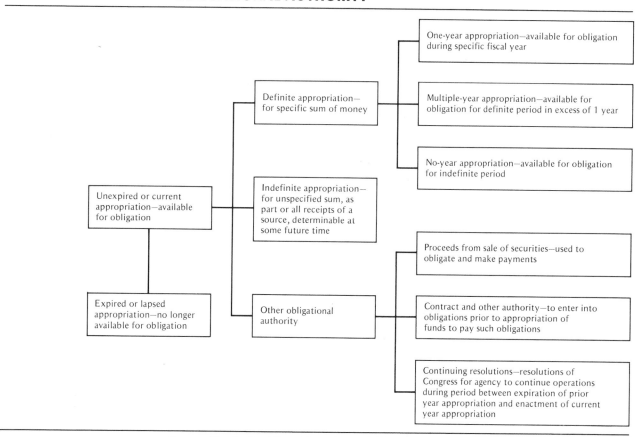

Source: *Standardized Fiscal Procedures*, GAO Manual for Guidance of Federal Agencies, Title 7, pages 7-8 to 7-10, 1967.

OVERVIEW OF PROCESS

Passage of Appropriation Act

As mentioned, an appropriation cannot exist without a prior authorization by Congress. The authorization is, itself, a separate law. In many instances, an agency's program will not have to be "authorized" annually. Generally, though, the agency must appear before the appropriation committee yearly, if for no other reason but to make a reporting. The appropriation act is often an extremely brief document, possibly describing in a single sentence the purpose of the appropriation, the amount appropriated, and the period for which the appropriation is available.

Exhibit 9.4 **DEPARTMENT OF THE TREASURY APPROPRIATION WARRANT**

(TFRM Volume I, Part II, Chapter 2000)

Warrant No. _____414-80-11-10_____

Accounting Date _____November 20, 1979_____

The Congress having, by the Acts hereon stated, made the appropriations hereunder specified, the amounts thereof are directed to be established in the general and detailed appropriation accounts, totaling in all $ 2,272,157,000.00 _____ and for so doing this shall be the warrant.

The Secretary of the Treasury

By _____

DEC 05 1979
_____
(Date Signed)

Comptroller General of the United States

By _____

06 DEC 1979
_____
(Date Countersigned)

Executive Office of the President – Agency for International Development
_____
APPROPRIATION

SYMBOL	TITLE	AMOUNT

JOINT RESOLUTION

Making further continuing appropriations for
the fiscal year 1980, and for other purposes

Public Law 96-123, 96th Congress   Approved November 20, 1979

1101021	Development Assistance Program, Economic Assistance, Executive, 1980	$ 690,520,000.00
1101036	Payment to the Foreign Service Retirement and Disability Fund, Executive, 1980	19,257,000.00

See letter from the Department of State, Agency
for International Development, dated November 29,
1979.

Issuance of an Appropriation Warrant

Appropriated funds are made available to executive agencies by the Treasury. By the issuance of a formal warrant, showing the amount to be credited to the appropriation account on behalf of an agency, the Treasury officially initiates the federal financial process. The warrant becomes the supporting record for entry of the appropriation into the central accounts of the Treasury as well as in the reciprocal accounts of the executive agency.

Exhibit 9.4 illustrates a Treasury Appropriation Warrant issued to an executive agency establishing the amount of the appropriated funds available for apportionment.

Apportionment of Appropriation

Until an appropriation has been apportioned by the OMB, an agency has no authority to obligate or expend funds. Under the apportionment process, the executive agency formally requests that its appropriation be apportioned. Apportionments will not be made for periods of longer than a fiscal year, even when the appropriation is a "no-year" or "multiple-year" appropriation. In these instances, the OMB apportionment is still for the anticipated financial requirements of the current fiscal year.

ACCOUNTING FOR APPROPRIATIONS
Entries of a preliminary nature are necessary to record the appropriation and the amount of the appropriation that is available to the agency for obligation and expenditure. Exhibit 9.5 summarizes the accounting entries for the appropriation events discussed in the following paragraphs.

Recording the Appropriation

The Treasury Appropriation Warrant is the authorizing or supporting document for the initial accounting entry to record a Congressional appropriation in an agency's accounts. The entry to record the appropriation is:

DEBIT: Fund balance with the Treasury
CREDIT: Unapportioned appropriation

The "fund balance with the Treasury" account is a government agency's equivalent of a corporate cash account. This account is increased for the amount of the appropriated funds. With few exceptions, agencies do not have a cash account nor do they disburse funds directly. Rather, the agencies use the Treasury as the disbursing agent. The "fund balance" account is increased at the time an appropriation becomes available to an agency.

The "unapportioned appropriation" account, which is the offsetting credit, is one of several budgetary accounts comprising the investment of the United States government in that agency's programs.

Exhibit 9.5 **ILLUSTRATION OF ACCOUNTING FOR APPROPRIATION APPORTIONMENT, AND ALLOCATIONS**

EVENT	ENTRY NUMBER	ENTRIES	DEBIT	CREDIT
Receipt of the Treasury Warrant, recording of appropriation	(1)	Fund balance with the Treasury Unapportioned appropriation To record Congressional appropriation.	$ 900,000	$ 900,000
Apportionment of appropriation by OMB	(2)	Unapportioned appropriation Unallotted apportionments To record a partial apportionment of appropriation.	800,000	800,000
Allocation of appropriated and apportioned funds	(3)	Unallotted apportionments Appropriations allocated to other agencies To record partial allocation of appropriation to another agency. — also —	50,000	50,000
Receivable due from another agency	(4)	Advances to other agencies Fund balance with the Treasury To establish the receivable due related to allocated funds	50,000	50,000
		TOTALS	$1,800,000	$1,800,000

STATEMENT OF ASSETS, LIABILITIES, AND INVESTMENT OF THE GOVERNMENT

ASSETS		LIABILITIES	
Fund balance with the Treasury	$850,000	None	$ —0—
Advances to other agency	50,000	**INVESTMENT OF GOVERNMENT**	
		Unapportioned appropriation	$100,000
		Appropriations allocated to other agencies	50,000
		Unallotted apportionment	750,000
TOTAL ASSETS	$900,000	**TOTAL LIABILITIES AND INVESTMENT OF GOVERNMENT**	$900,000

Accounting for Apportionments

The apportionment actions of OMB divide the Congressional appropriation by specific time periods (generally quarterly), activities, projects, objects, or a combination thereof. Reapportionments are made when earlier apportionments are no longer appropriate or there is a change in the amounts available for obligation. The Apportionment and Reapportionment Schedule (SF 132) is the authorizing or supporting document for the apportionment entry, which is

DEBIT: Unapportioned appropriation
    CREDIT: Unallotted apportionments

The credit balance in the Unallotted Apportionment account represents the funding that the agency is currently permitted to obligate and expend. Should the Congress require an allocation of the appropriation to another agency, the OMB must first apportion such funds before either the transferring or the receiving agency can act.

Allocating Funds to Other Agencies

At times, the parent appropriation must allocate a portion of its appropriation to another agency, thus transferring the authority to obligate and expend a portion of the appropriation. In these circumstances, both the allocating agency and the receiving agency must maintain reciprocal accounts to ensure the full accountability for the appropriation. The allocating agency continues to be responsible for monitoring the overall parent appropriation and making the necessary reports to the Treasury, the OMB, and Congress. The entry to allocate a portion of an appropriation to another agency is

DEBIT: Unallotted apportionments
    CREDIT: Appropriations allocated to other agencies

        plus

DEBIT: Advances to government agencies
    CREDIT: Fund balance with the Treasury

Two entries are necessary (1) to reduce the amount of apportioned funds that are now available to the agency responsible for the parent appropriation, and (2) to establish an "accounts receivable" from another agency. This receivable will be reduced as the receiving agency obligates, expends, and reports on the status of the allocated funds. The receiving agency would correspondingly increase its fund balance with the Treasury, record a liability due to the allocating agency to account for the advance of funds.

The entries above have affected only balance sheet accounts; the effect of these transactions and the financial status of the appropriation, apportionment, and allocation actions are illustrated in Exhibit 9.5.

REPORTING ON APPORTIONMENTS AND BUDGET EXECUTION

OMB Circular A-34, *Instructions on Budget Execution*, provides the guidance to government agencies with respect to apportionments and reports on budget execution. To monitor the apportionment process and receive continued assurance that the agencies systems of administrative controls are functioning properly, OMB requires that two basic forms be submitted periodically by the agencies for each appropriation or fund account for which the agency is responsible.

Apportionment and Reapportionment Schedule

SF 132, the Apportionment and Reapportionment Schedule, requires the agency to identify the sources of the budgetary authority and the application of requested apportionment of the authority. As mentioned above, no apportionment will be made for periods longer than one fiscal year. For no-year or multiple-year accounts, apportionments will cover anticipated financial requirements for the current year.

The initial apportionment schedules are submitted to OMB by late August, for the fiscal year beginning the following October 1. By law, where the budgetary authority results from current Congressional action, the apportionment schedules must be submitted to OMB within ten days after the approval of the appropriation or substantive acts providing the budget authority or by August 21, whichever is later.

SF 132 is to be used to request apportionment or reapportionment of each appropriation or fund account, subject to apportionment procedures. The form is divided into two general sections: (1) Budgetary Resources and (2) Application of Budgetary Resources. Exhibit 9.6 is an example of SF 132 showing the original request by an agency. The first section requires that the agency identify its sources of budgetary authority. In the second section, the agency requests the apportionment schedule it desires for its programs. The appropriation may be apportioned by fiscal quarters or "Category A" apportionments or by another method, referred to as "Category B" apportionments. A "Category B" apportionment would be a restriction imposed by activity or project or on some bases other than fiscal quarters.

Exhibit 9.6 **APPORTIONMENT AND REAPPORTIONMENT SCHEDULE.**
One-year appropriation—original apportionment

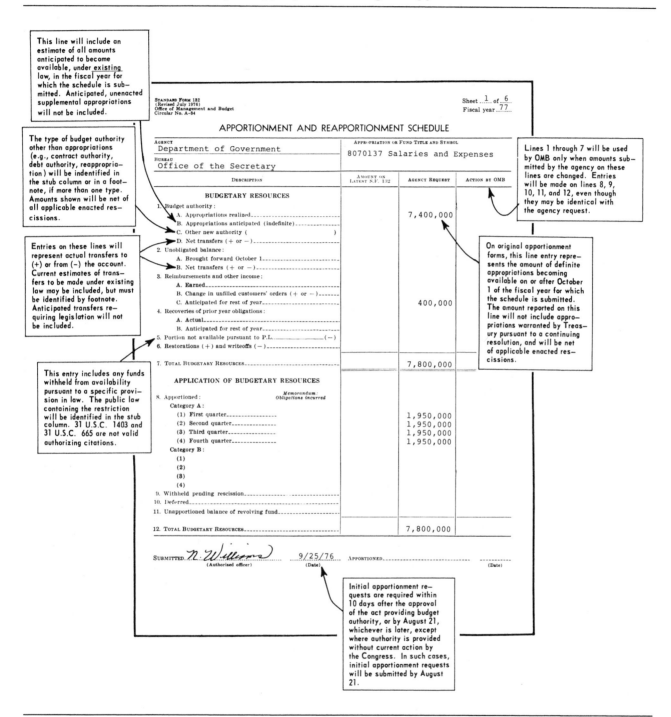

This line will include an estimate of all amounts anticipated to become available, under _existing_ law, in the fiscal year for which the schedule is submitted. Anticipated, unenacted supplemental appropriations will not be included.

The type of budget authority other than appropriations (e.g., contract authority, debt authority, reapportiontion) will be indentified in the stub column or in a footnote, if more than one type. Amounts shown will be net of all applicable enacted rescissions.

Entries on these lines will represent actual transfers to (+) or from (−) the account. Current estimates of transfers to be made under existing law may be included, but must be identified by footnote. Anticipated transfers requiring legislation will not be included.

This entry includes any funds withheld from availability pursuant to a specific provision in law. The public law containing the restriction will be identified in the stub column. 31 U.S.C. 1403 and 31 U.S.C. 665 are not valid authorizing citations.

STANDARD FORM 132
(Revised July 1976)
Office of Management and Budget
Circular No. A-34

Sheet 1 of 6
Fiscal year 77

APPORTIONMENT AND REAPPORTIONMENT SCHEDULE

AGENCY
Department of Government

BUREAU
Office of the Secretary

APPROPRIATION OR FUND TITLE AND SYMBOL
8070137 Salaries and Expenses

DESCRIPTION	AMOUNT ON LATEST N.F. 132	AGENCY REQUEST	ACTION BY OMB
BUDGETARY RESOURCES			
1. Budget authority:			
A. Appropriations realized		7,400,000	
B. Appropriations anticipated (indefinite)			
C. Other new authority ( )			
D. Net transfers (+ or −)			
2. Unobligated balance:			
A. Brought forward October 1			
B. Net transfers (+ or −)			
3. Reimbursements and other income:			
A. Earned			
B. Change in unfilled customers' orders (+ or −)			
C. Anticipated for rest of year		400,000	
4. Recoveries of prior year obligations:			
A. Actual			
B. Anticipated for rest of year			
5. Portion not available pursuant to P.L. (−)			
6. Restorations (+) and writeoffs (−)			
7. TOTAL BUDGETARY RESOURCES		7,800,000	
APPLICATION OF BUDGETARY RESOURCES			
8. Apportioned: _Memorandum: Obligations incurred_			
Category A:			
(1) First quarter		1,950,000	
(2) Second quarter		1,950,000	
(3) Third quarter		1,950,000	
(4) Fourth quarter		1,950,000	
Category B:			
(1)			
(2)			
(3)			
(4)			
9. Withheld pending rescission			
10. Deferred			
11. Unapportioned balance of revolving fund			
12. TOTAL BUDGETARY RESOURCES		7,800,000	

SUBMITTED _N. Williams_   9/25/76   APPORTIONED _____
(Authorized officer)   (Date)   (Date)

Lines 1 through 7 will be used by OMB only when amounts submitted by the agency on these lines are changed. Entries will be made on lines 8, 9, 10, 11, and 12, even though they may be identical with the agency request.

On original apportionment forms, this line entry represents the amount of definite appropriations becoming available on or after October 1 of the fiscal year for which the schedule is submitted. The amount reported on this line will not include appropriations warranted by Treasury pursuant to a continuing resolution, and will be net of applicable enacted rescissions.

Initial apportionment requests are required within 10 days after the approval of the act providing budget authority, or by August 21, whichever is later, except where authority is provided without current action by the Congress. In such cases, initial apportionment requests will be submitted by August 21.

Source: Office of Management and Budget Circular, A-34, "Instructions on Budget Execution," Washington, D. C.

Exhibit 9.7 **REPORT ON BUDGET EXECUTION**
One-year account — monthly report

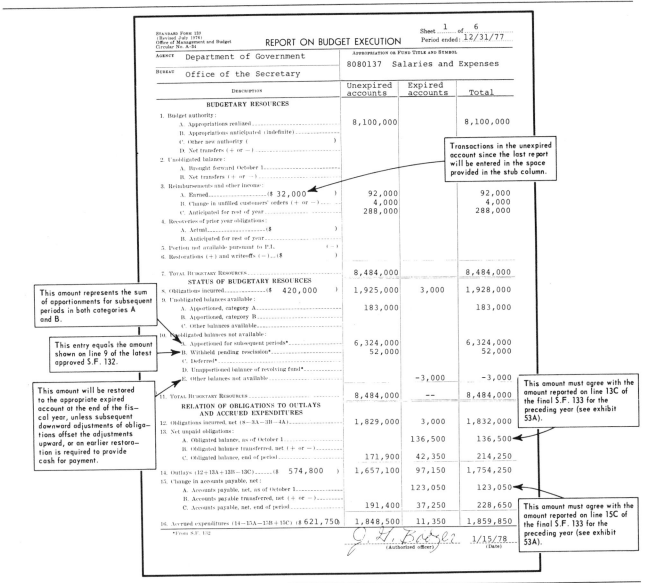

Source: Office of Management and Budget Circular, A-34, "Instructions on Budget Execution," Washington, D. C.

Report of Budget Execution

SF 133, the Report on Budget Execution, is prepared by all agencies to provide current data to OMB on the status of each appropriation or open account (except for deposit funds), whether or not the account has been apportioned. Where an apportionment has been made, the reports will have the same coverage or elements reported as were identified in the apportionment schedule (e.g., by fiscal quarter, or one of the "B" category apportionments). Any expired appropriations are included on the same report as the unexpired accounts of the same title.

Where allocations have been made to transfer appropriation accounts, a consolidated SF 133 covering both the parent account and the related transfer account will be submitted by the agency with the parent account. The report on budget execution must be submitted by each agency within 20 days after the close of each calendar month. In addition to the September 30 report, due to OMB October 20, the final report for a fiscal year must be submitted to OMB no later than November 30.

The report is divided into three general sections: (1) Budgetary Resources, (2) Status of Budgetary Resources, and (3) Relation of Obligations to Outlays and Accrued Expenditures. Generally, the first column is used for the unexpired account; the second column is used for consolidated amounts of all expired accounts, including merged or "M" accounts. For reports with both unexpired and expired amounts, the third column is used as a total column on the last report of each quarter and for the final report of the year.

Exhibit 9.7 illustrates a sample of a Report on Budget Execution showing the report for a one-year appropriation.

chapter 10 Allotments and Obligations

INTRODUCTION A distinguishing feature of a federal agency's accounting system is the integration of budgetary accounting with accounting of the proprietary type. The latter is more common in the private sector. Since the founding of the country, there has been concern with government officials committing the government to liabilities beyond those intended by the Congress. Several laws, including the Constitution, make reference to the overriding authority of Congress with respect to expenditures and set forth restrictions and penalties for violating the appropriation acts of Congress. Within government agencies, considerable personnel and financial resources are devoted to accounting for the amount and rate of obligations and expenditures. In past years, budgetary accounting may have been overemphasized to the exclusion of adequate cost accounting for an agency's appropriation.

DEFINITION OF TERMS To comply with the provisions of the Antideficiency Act, an agency must have a system of subdividing apportioned appropriations among its operating units, with the objective of maintaining control at the highest practical level in the agency. Throughout the government, this system provides for an accounting and reporting of fiscal balances as allotments, obligations, and expenditures of the agency.

Allotment

The General Accounting Office has defined an *allotment* as a subdivision or delegation of an OMB apportionment by the head of an agency to the head of an operating unit for purpose of establishing budgetary control, consistent with assigned responsibilities in the agency. The allotment is the delegated authority to enter into obligations and make expenditures on behalf of the agency.

Allowances

In some agencies, there exists a procedure for further subdividing an apportionment below the allotment level. This delegation of fiscal responsibilities is often referred to as *allowances*. In this case, the allowance is the delegated authority to enter into obligations and make expenditures on behalf of the agency.

Obligations

The Office of Management and Budget has defined *obligations* as the amount of orders placed, contracts awarded, services received, and similar transactions entered into during a given period that will require payments during the same or a future fiscal period.

The term *obligation* legally refers to the incurrence of a commitment of government funds and a possible liability that the government may ultimately pay. From an accounting view, an obligation is an event that must be recorded in the official records of the agency. As explained in earlier chapters, obligations must take a specific form to be valid.

Expenditures

The term *expenditures* or *accrued expenditures* is defined by GAO as charges incurred that require the provision of funds for goods or tangible property received, services performed, or accounts becoming owed by the government under programs for which no performance or current services are required. (Chapter 11 provides additional details on expenditures.)

LEGAL CRITERIA AND RESTRAINTS Two acts are particularly important with respect to obligating and expending federal funds: the Antideficiency Act of 1870 (as amended) and the Supplemental Act of 1955 (as amended).

Limitation on Obligations and Expenditures

Several important provisions of the Antideficiency Act of 1870, are discussed in Chapter 2, which outlines some of the general financial management policies of the government. The cited provisions prohibit the obligation or expenditure of federal funds in excess of an OMB apportionment. Additionally, the head of the agency is directed to establish a system of controls that permits the fixing of responsibility should a violation occur.

The Antideficiency Act contains several prohibitions concerning obligations and expenditures. By that act, no officer or employee of the United States shall

▲ Make or authorize an expenditure from or create or authorize an obligation under an appropriation or fund in excess of the amount available in that appropriation or fund;

▲ Involve the government in any contract or other obligation, for the payment of money for any purpose in advance of an appropriation being made for that purpose, unless such contract or obligation is authorized by law;

▲ Accept voluntary service for the government or employ personal service in excess of that authorized by law, except in cases of emergency involving safety of human life or the protection of property;

▲ Authorize or create an obligation or make an expenditure in excess of an apportionment or amounts permitted by regulations.

In addition to other penalties that might exist for violations, the Antideficiency Act states that any officer or employee violating the act shall be subject to appropriate administrative discipline, including, when warranted, suspension without pay or removal from office. An officer or employee knowingly and willfully violating the act shall, if convicted, be fined not more than $5,000 or be imprisoned for not more than two years or both.

Within the federal government, violations of the Antideficiency Act are referred to as "3679 violations;" the Antideficiency Act is more popularly known as the "3679 Statutes."

Formal Obligations of Agencies

There are precise legal formats of what constitutes a valid obligation set forth in the Supplemental Appropriation Act of 1955. Each of the object classifications mentioned later must be supported by one of the following documents to be appropriately recorded in the accounts of a government agency as an obligation.

▲ A binding agreement in writing between the parties
▲ A valid loan agreement
▲ An order required by law
▲ An order issued pursuant to law to meet a public exigency or for perishable subsistence supplies
▲ A grant or subsidy
▲ A liability resulting from pending litigation
▲ Employment or services of persons or expenses of travel and services by public utilities
▲ Other legal liabilities of the government.

Chapter 7, Accounting Concepts in the Federal Government, contains more detailed definitions of the types of transactions that constitute valid obligations of the government. The general accounting process of obligations is described in this chapter.

ACCOUNTING FOR ALLOTMENTS AND OBLIGATIONS The process of allotting and obligating appropriated funds is internal to a federal agency. The controls governing the subdivision and reservation of apportioned appropriations are an integral part of the agency's system of administrative internal controls.

Allotment of Funds

The allotment, pursuant to guidance provided by the General Accounting Office, should be established at the highest practical management level in the agency, consistent with assignments of responsibility and effective control.

Allotment of funds to allottee or program directors and other agency organizations is documented by a form or "advice of allotment" issued by the head of the agency or a person having delegated authority. The advice of allotment provides formal notice of the dollar amount, purpose, and time period or other limitations affecting the funds to be expended by the allottee. Some agencies have attempted to assign prohibitions to allotments that are similar to those contained in the Antideficiency Act relative to overobligating or overexpending an appropriation. Exceeding an allotment level, though, is a violation of an agency-imposed administrative requirement unless the sum of all allotment violations exceeds the total of the applicable apportionment or appropriation for which the agency is accountable.

Exhibit 10.1 is an illustration of one agency's advice of allotment form. No standard form exists; agencies have designed advice forms to meet their program requirements. Note that in many ways the illustrated advice contains information similar to that found on the apportionment form. The advice form also puts the allottee, or recipient, of this delegated authority on notice.

You are hereby authorized to incur, or to authorize the incurrence of, obligations within the indicated amounts and time periods for the purposes and under the conditions indicated on this advice. This authority is to be exercised in accordance with applicable orders, regulations and other directives, including those delegating or assigning authority to execute documents resulting in obligations of funds.

As mentioned above, the advices of allotment are delegations of obligational and expenditure authority from the head of the agency to program officials and office heads within that agency.

Obligation of Funds

The allottee is generally the agency official having the delegated authority, from the agency head, to formally obligate funds within the ceilings and other limitations set forth in the advice of allotment. As mentioned, to be valid, the obligation must take a specified form, in compliance with the Supplemental Appropriation Act of 1955.

Within the federal government uniform definitions exist for obligations that must be incorporated in the accounting structure of all agencies. The uniform definitions are referred to as the *object classification* of obligations and expenditures established by the Office of Management and Budget in its Circular A-12, entitled *Object Classification*.

Exhibit 10.1 **ILLUSTRATION OF AN ADVICE OF AN ALLOTMENT**

AID-7-158
(2-63)

AGENCY FOR INTERNATIONAL DEVELOPMENT
WASHINGTON, D. C. 20523

REQUEST FOR AND ADVICE OF ALLOTMENT

1. ALLOTTEE Assistant Administrator	2. COUNTRY Regional
3. FISCAL YEAR 1979	4. NUMBER 12
5. APPROPRIATION SYMBOL 72-1191021.6	6. ALLOTMENT SYMBOL 946-65-598-00-69-91 PVO/OPG a/

7. FUNCTION AND PURPOSE   Selected Development Activities - Grants

8. REFERENCES   Memo dated May 23, 1979

9. Previous Total _____ $3,150,000.00

10. Change _____ $ 63,000.00

11. New Total _____ $3,213,000.00

12. LIMITATIONS

13. REMARKS

Project Name and Number		Previously Approved	Change	New Total
Program Development and Support	598-0000	$ 38,000.00	None	$ 38,000.00
Consultants and Seminars	598-0044	437,000.00	$63,000.00	500,000.00
Partners of the Americas (NAPA)	598-0436	500,000.00	None	500,000.00
Science and Technical Information Transfers	598-0572	250,000.00	None	250,000.00
OPGS	598-0577	90,000.00	None	90,000.00
SOLIDARIOS	598-0587	1,000,000.00	None	1,000,000.00
Human Rights	598-0591	300,000.00	None	300,000.00
Development of Environment Management System	598-0602	535,000.00	None	535,000.00
TOTAL		$3,150,000.00	$63,000.00	$3,213,000.00

IT IS REQUESTED THAT THE ALLOTMENT ACTION REQUESTED ABOVE BE AUTHORIZED

(Signature) _____   (title) _____ **Controller**

5/23/79

APPROVAL

You are hereby authorized to incur, or to authorize the incurrence, of obligations within the indicated amounts and time periods for the purposes and under the conditions indicated on this advice. This authority is to be exercised in accordance with applicable orders, regulations and other directives. Including those delegating or assigning authority to execute documents resulting in obligations of funds.

BY AUTHORITY OF THE ADMINISTRATOR, AID:

(Signature) _____

CHIEF, FUNDS CONTROL DIVISION

Date Authorized: _____

The purpose of the standard object classification is to provide a method of recording financial transactions in terms of the nature of the services or articles for which obligations are initially incurred, rather than the purpose served or program benefitted.

These classifications must be used in the preparation of the agency's object classification schedule for submission of budget estimates to OMB. OMB expects that an agency's accounting system will be designed and maintained to provide the necessary object classification data. Object classification data are also maintained by agencies in terms of accrued expenditures. Where this is done, appropriate subtotals and adjusting entries are used to show the distinction between these additional details and the recorded obligations.

OBJECT CLASSIFICATION CODES AND DEFINITIONS

There are five major categories of object classification in the federal government.

▲ Personal services and benefits
▲ Contractual services and supplies
▲ Acquisition of capital assets
▲ Grants and fixed charges
▲ Other

However, the OMB and the agencies generally communicate in terms of the subcategories. Exhibit 10.2 identifies the principal subcategories and titles of the object classifications. The definitions of the object classification in the following sections have been established by OMB in its Circular A-12.

Personal Services and Benefits

The more detailed object classification relates to personal services and benefits that include obligations related to salaries, wages, benefits, and other allowances to be paid to current and former civilian and military personnel.

The principal subcategories of this object class are

▲ Personnel compensation
▲ Personnel benefits
▲ Benefits for former personnel

Exhibit 10.2 **SUMMARY OF OBJECT CLASSIFICATIONS**

10 PERSONAL SERVICES AND BENEFITS

11 Personal Compensation

11.1 Permanent positions

11.3 Positions other than permanent

11.5 Other personnel compensation

11.7 Military personnel

11.8 Special personal services payments

12 Personnel Benefits

12.1 Civilian personnel

12.2 Military personnel

13.0 Benefits

20 CONTRACTUAL SERVICES AND SUPPLIES

21 Travel and Transportation of Persons

22 Transportation of Things

23 Rent, Communications, and Utilities

23.1 Standard level user charges

23.2 Communications, utilities, and other rent

24 Printing and Reproduction

25 Other Services

26 Supplies and Materials

30 ACQUISITION OF CAPITAL ASSETS

31 Equipment

32 Lands and Structures

33 Investments and Loans

40 GRANTS AND FIXED CHARGES

41 Grants, Subsidies, and Contributions

42 Insurance Claims and Indemnities

43 Interest and Dividends

44 Refunds

90 OTHER

91 Unvouchered

92 Undistributed

93 Administrative or Nonadministrative Expenses

94 Changes in Selected Resources

99 Total Obligations

Source: Office of Management and Budget Circular, A-12, Subject: *Object Classification.*

Personnel Compensation

Personnel compensation is the gross compensation to be paid for personal services, including amounts such as the employee's share of retirement, insurance contributions, and income taxes withheld and creditable to other accounts.

The details required for this subcategory include an accounting for charges such as

11.1 *Permanent positions*

11.3 *Positions other than permanent,* such as temporary employment, part-time employment, intermittent employment

11.5 *Other personnel compensation,* such as overtime, holiday pay, Sunday pay, nightwork differential, hazardous duty pay, post differentials, other payments above basic rates

11.7 *Military personnel*

11.8 *Special personal services payments,* such as compensation to persons not reportable as regular federal employees, payments for reimbursable details, agency reimbursement to Civil Service retirement, and disability fund for reemployed annuitants, annual leave.

In the case of a revolving fund, annual leave (vacation) is obligated as earned as part of subcategory 11.8 (e.g., funded annual leave). Leave earned but not taken is reported as a positive amount; when leave earned is less than leave taken, a negative amount is reported. Terminal leave payments are classified as subcategory 11.1.

Personnel Benefits

Personal benefits are the cash allowances to be paid for personnel benefits and payments to other funds for currently employed civilian and military personnel.

For civilian personnel these payments would include quarters and uniform allowances, incentive awards, payments for services outside the United States, expenses incurred in connection with official relocation, and payments to other funds for life insurance, health insurance, retirement, and accident compensation.

For military personnel these payments include uniform allowances, reenlistment bonuses, cost of living allowances, (allowance for subsistence and quarters are recorded in subcategory 11.7), FICA taxes, and Servicemen's Group Life Insurance premiums. This would exclude types of hazardous duty pay, which is classified under subcategory 11.7.

Benefits for Former Personnel

The benefit payments are to be made for pensions, annuities, and other benefits to former employees or their survivors, and are based in part on length of time in government service. Such amounts would include retirement benefits, severance pay, and other benefits such as unemployment compensation and government payments to former employees and annuitants.

Contractual Services and Supplies

This category of object classifications includes a variety of charges, incurred by both federal employees and public carriers and contractors. Also included are the charges for many types of services provided to the government. The principal subcategories of this object classification are

▲ Travel and transportation of persons
▲ Transportation of things
▲ Rent, communications, and utilities
▲ Printing and reproduction
▲ Other services
▲ Supplies and materials.

Travel and Transportation of Persons

This object class includes the charges incurred for transportation of employees, per diem allowances, and other incidental travel expenses to be paid directly by the government or to be reimbursed to the employee. The object class includes both travel away from the official duty station and local transportation, rental, or lease of passenger motor vehicles from motor pools.

Transportation of Things

This object class includes the contractual charges for transportation and care of things while in transport, as well as postage, rental of trucks, reimbursements to employees for movement of household goods or house trailers, and freight and express payments to common carrier and contract carriers.

Rent, Communications, and Utilities

This object class includes the standard level user charges (SLUC) assessed by General Services Administration and other rental of space and other services such as communication services, utility services, and other rent for land, structures, or equipment.

Printing and Reproduction

Printing and reproduction include charges incurred for contractual printing and reproduction, related composition, and binding performed by the government or commercial printers.

Other Services

Other services include charges for contractual services not classified under another object classification. Within this subcategory would be charges for items such as repairs and alterations, storage and maintenance, subsistence and support of contractors personnel, stenographic services, publication and advertising, tuition, operations of facilities, other service contracts, and research and development contracts.

Supplies and Materials

Supplies and materials include charges for commodities acquired by formal contract or other form of purchase that are

▲ Ordinarily consumed or expended within one year after being put into use
▲ Converted in the process of construction or manufacture, or
▲ Used to form a minor part of equipment or fixed property.

Examples of supplies and materials would include office supplies, computer supplies, subscriptions, pamphlets and documents, chemicals and medical supplies, fuel, clothing, provisions, materials and parts used in construction, repair or production of equipment, machinery, buildings, and other structures.

Acquisition of Capital Assets

The capital assets object classification includes the charges incurred for durable assets such as equipment, land, structures, and investment and loans.

Equipment

The equipment object class includes charges for personal property expected to have a service period of a year or more. Included are charges for initial installation. The subcategory may consist of both capitalized and noncapitalized equipment. Agencies may maintain such distinctions in their records. Several examples of charges to be included within the subcategory are transportation equipment, furniture and fixtures, books for permanent collections, tools and implements, machinery, instruments, ADP equipment when purchased, and armaments (tanks, tractors, missiles, machine guns).

Lands and Structures

This object class includes charges for land and interest in land, buildings and other structures, additions to buildings and fixed equipment, easements, and rights of way.

Investment and Loans

This object class includes charges for purchase of stocks, bonds, notes, and other securities (except par value of government securities of wholly owned government enterprises), and loans to foreign governments, states, political subdivisions and to corporations, associations, and individuals.

Grants and Fixed Charges

A variety of charges are included within the object classification of grants and fixed charges. The primary subcategories are

▲   Grants, subsidies, and contributions
▲   Insurance claims and indemnities
▲   Interest and dividends
▲   Refunds

Grants, Subsidies, Contributions

This object class includes charges for grants (including revenue sharing), subsidies, gratuities, and other aid for which cash payments are made to states and political subdivisions, corporations, associations, and individuals. Also included within this subcategory are contributions to international societies, contributions fixed by treaty, grants to foreign countries, taxes when the federal government has consented to taxation. Readjustment and other benefits to veterans, other than indemnities for death or disability, would also be recorded in this object classification.

Obligations under grant programs involving furnishing services, supplies, and materials rather than cash are not charged to this object class but rather to the object class representing the nature of services, or articles that are purchased.

Insurance Claims and Indemnities

This object class includes charges for payments of claims on insurance policies (life, marine, flood, crop), annuities paid from trust funds of former employees, indemnities for destruction or injury of persons or property, and payment for other losses.

Interest and Dividends

Interest and dividends include charges for payments for the use of money loaned, deposited, or overpaid, and the distribution of earnings to owners of trust or other funds. The subcategory would be charged with interest payments under lease-purchase contracts for construction of buildings. However, interest due to a contractor for delayed payments under the contract are to be recorded under the same object class as the original contract.

Refunds

Refunds include payments from an appropriation or fund account to refund amounts previously received by the government, to correct errors, or to make adjustments.

Other Object Classes

The "other" or "90" series of object classification is to be used by agencies in preparing agency budget submissions to OMB. The subcategories are used principally to delineate further the year-end status of agency funds. OMB Circular A-12 provides the following definitions.

▲ *Unvouchered*—charges lawfully incurred for confidential purposes, not subject to detailed vouchering or reporting

▲ *Undistributed*—charges that cannot be distributed to other object classifications

▲ *Administrative or nonadministrative expenses*—used for adjusting revolving and trust fund budget schedules if there is a limitation on administrative or nonadministrative expenses

▲ *Changes in selected resources*—an adjusting entry to reconcile total obligations to detailed object class data reported on accrued expenditure or applied costs bases

▲ *Total obligations*—the sum of total charges to the object classifications recorded

CONTROL PROCEDURES

Although there is no governmentwide uniformity, there is a general consistency to the accounting and control procedures followed in allotting and obligating governmental funds. The purpose of these procedures is to ensure that

▲ Funds are used for authorized purposes
▲ Funds are economically and efficiently used
▲ Obligations and later disbursements do not exceed amounts authorized.

Usually, the control procedures include the following practices.

Allotment

Allotment advices are issued in terms of an allottee's obligational authority, and the allotted amounts are formally entered into the accounting records (described later). The agency's transaction and account coding structure provides for a continual matching of obligations incurred to the allotment.

Periodically, usually monthly, the obligations applicable to each allotment are reported. Toward the end of a fiscal period, the status of obligations in relation to allotments could be reported on a daily basis. Allotments may not be made in excess of the amounts apportioned by OMB through the end of the current period. For example, if the appropriation has been apportioned on a quarterly basis, advices of allotment, in total, may not exceed the cumulative quarterly apportionments.

For conservatism in fund control practices, allotments should not be made on the basis of anticipated receipts, reimbursements, or transfers until after the execution of written agreements or other valid arrangements. Further, even when such amounts have been apportioned by OMB, amounts for anticipated receipts, reimbursements, and transfers should not be allotted for obligation or expenditure unless one of the following conditions prevails.

▲ Goods or services have been furnished and the agency is entitled to receive funds.

▲ Valid orders have been received by the agency.

▲ An advance of funds have been received for orders outside the government.

Adherence to the practices above is necessary because the failure to realize anticipated receipts does not relieve the certifying officer from the responsibility of complying with the limitations of the allotment.

Obligations

The controls relating to obligations are considerably more detailed. The following control procedures are common among government agencies.

▲ *Prevalidation of obligations* involves procedures requiring a formal acknowledgment by the official in charge of the allotment that unobligated funds remaining in the allotment balance are sufficient to equal the intended obligation.

Often the document that contains the request to obligate and on which an annotation is made as to the availability of funds is referred to as a purchase or procurement request (in the case of a contract), a travel authorization (in the case of anticipated transportation needs), or a grant authorization (for intended grant fundings).

▲ *Commitment of funds,* if used, could require the formal recording of the intended obligation. A commitment procedure is particularly useful when there will be a significant delay between the initial prevalidation and the later actual obligation of funds.

The amount of the commitment must be adjusted to the amount ultimately obligated; committed funds in excess of the actual obligated amount would revert to an uncommitted or unobligated status.

▲ *Obligation of funds* is the formal recognition of a potential liability of the government. It is an event that must be recorded in an agency's accounting system.

The several documents that would, when properly executed by the agency, constitute a valid and legal binding obligation of the government were identified earlier in this chapter.

▲ *Liquidation of obligations* refers to the procedures for reducing or adjusting amounts previously obligated.

Accounting Records

Prior to the advent of the application of computers to an agency's fiscal and financial functions, the accounting related to alloting, obligating, liquidating, and reporting of allotments and obligations required extensive resources. Often the time required merely to accumulate and report on appropriation funds' balances precluded extensive analyses and detailed cost accounting of programs and activities.

While some automation may have been present, the systems required the maintenance of detailed manual ledgers (often described as allotment ledgers, obligation ledgers, or accrued expenditure ledgers) and a system of multiple journals to permit the expeditious summarization of data for reporting purposes. With many agencies the maintenance of accounts on a cash basis necessitated the posting of end-of-period standard adjusting, closing, and reversing entries to provide an accounting on an accrual basis.

Computers now permit the multiple coding of the basic obligations (and in some agencies, the commitment) by the agency's programs, activities, functions, organizations, and object classifications. A single entry often identifies the obligation in terms of the ultimate expense or asset category. The prestructuring of an appropriate chart of general ledger and subsidiary ledger accounts provides information to meet the several reporting bases required of an agency. Identifying obligations in terms of an expense (cost) or asset category to be charged on an accrued expenditure basis considerably reduces the required bookkeeping and maintains the obligation and accrual accounting in balance.

Often the computerized accounting is streamlined further through the use of pseudocodes that themselves are representative of prestructured tables of accounting entries. Considerable time is saved and increased accuracy of input is obtained by coding the reduced pseudocode to activate the much more detailed transaction codes to perform the actual accumulation and accounting. Transactions simultaneously recorded as accrued expenditures and obligation are coded and posted or input to the system once. Obligations earlier recorded as goods or services on order can later be recorded as accrued expenditures, by machine accounting without recoding the total data for each transaction as required under the earlier manual, or semiautomated accounting processes.

ACCOUNTING PROCESS The accounting within the agency for allotments and obligations is a continuation of the budgetary accounting process. Exhibit 10.3 illustrates the nature of the accounting performed for allotments and obligations.

Exhibit 10.3 **ILLUSTRATION OF ACCOUNTING FOR ALLOTMENTS AND OBLIGATIONS**

EVENT	ENTRY	ENTRIES	DEBIT	CREDIT
Receipt of appropriation, apportionment by OMB	*	Fund balance with the Treasury Unapportioned appropriation	$ 900,000	$ 900,000
	*	Unapportioned appropriation Unallotted apportionments	800,000	800,000
Issuance of advice of allotments	(1)	Unallotted apportionments Unobligated allotments To record allotments of apportioned funds and reflect unobligated balance	600,000	600,000
Incurrence of obligations through issuance of contracts, grants, travel authorizations, recording payrolls, etc.	(2)	Unobligated allotments Unliquidated obligations To record reduction in unobligated allotment balance and show the amounts of obligations	500,000	500,000

Reduction in outstanding obligations and recognition of capital and operating expenditures	(3)	Unliquidated obligations
		    Expended appropriation—
		      capital
		    Expended appropriation—
		      operating
		To record realization of amounts previously recorded as obligations.
			300,000	100,000
				
				200,000

Receipt of goods or services affecting proprietary accounts	(4)	Assets Inventory Expenses Accounts payable—others To record capital and operating events or items received for which future payment is required.	50,000 50,000 200,000	300,000
		TOTAL	$2,800,000	$2,800,000

Note: The effect of the transactions above are shown in Exhibit 10.4.
* Discussed in Chapter 9.

Allotments

The advice of allotments is the authorizing or supporting document for the accounting entry to record the release of apportioned funds to an allottee and thereby provide authorization to obligate funds. The entry to record the allotment is

DEBIT: Unallotted apportionment
CREDIT: Unobligated allotments — program A
     Unobligated allotments — program B
     Unobligated allotments — program C
     Unobligated allotments — administration

The allotment entry is required to record the initial allotment of funds or the issuance of any recisions or modifications of initial allotments. Advices of allotments are generally issued for each fiscal quarter to coincide with the OMB apportionments. The agency records must maintain a segregation of accounting by each appropriation and by each allotment within the separate appropriations.

Obligations

Throughout the period, allottees will incur obligations against their allotment. These obligations may be related to several object classifications (such as salaries, travel, contracts, grants). Each obligation must be recorded, and supporting documents must take one of the eight forms set forth in the Supplemental Appropriation Act of 1955 to be valid. The entry to record an obligation is

DEBIT: Unobligated allotments — program A
CREDIT: Unliquidated obligations — program A
     — salaries
     — contracts
     — grants

The obligation entry reduces the balance of allotments available for future obligation and establishes "unliquidated" obligations representing possible future claim on the funds of the agency.

An obligation will be "liquidated" or realized or expended by one or a combination of actions including (1) complete or partial cancellation of the obligation, (2) receipt of goods or services in full or partial satisfaction of the obligation, or (3) the accrual of an expenditure for which a prior obligation had not been established. The entry to record the liquidation of the obligation would be

DEBIT: Unliquidated obligations — program A

           — salaries

           — contracts

           — grants

    CREDIT: Expended appropriation — capital — program A

           Expended appropriation — operating — program A

                —plus—

DEBIT: Fixed assets — program A

           Inventory — program A

           Expenses — program A

    CREDIT: Accounts payable — program A

The liquidation entry reduces the outstanding and unliquidated obligation and recognizes the actual value of the expenditure accrued in relation to the earlier obligation. To the extent that the accrued expenditure is more or less than the earlier obligated amount, the balance of the unobligated allotments account should be further reduced or restored. Amounts restored to the unobligated allotments account generally are available to meet other authorized obligations, providing the appropriation under which the funds are being obligated is still current and available for further obligation and expenditure.

Note that the allotment and obligation entries affect only the budgetary accounts. Parallel entries are necessary to reflect the effect of the accrued expenditures in proprietary accounts. The effect of the transactions above and the financial status of the appropriation, apportionment, allotment and obligations are illustrated in Exhibit 10.4.

Reporting of Obligations

Uniform, governmentwide reporting requirements have been established by the OMB with respect to an agency's obligations and accrued expenditures.

Reporting of Actual Transactions

Monthly throughout the fiscal year and at the year's end, federal agencies must report to the OMB the obligations incurred, the unobligated balances available, the unapportioned appropriation balance, the obligations incurred, and the accrued expenditures. This reporting on the budget execution is made on SF133, illustrated in Exhibit 9.7.

Exhibit 10.4 **ILLUSTRATION OF EFFECT OF ALLOTMENT AND OBLIGATION ENTRIES**

a) LEDGER ACCOUNTS

Assets		Liabilities	
Fund balance with the Treasury		**Accounts payable—others**	
$900,000			(4) $300,000

Assets		Investment of the government	
Assets		**Unapportioned appropriation**	
(4) 50,000		800,000	900,000
Inventory		**Unallotted apportionments**	
(4) 50,000		(1) 600,000	800,000

Expenses			
		Unobligated allotments	
Expenses		(2) 500,000	(1) 600,000
(4) 200,000		**Unliquidated obligations**	
		(3) 300,000	(2) 500,000
		Expended appropriation—capital	
			(3) 100,000
		Expended appropriation—operating	
			(3) 200,000

b) BALANCE SHEET: STATEMENT OF ASSETS, LIABILITIES AND INVESTMENT OF THE GOVERNMENT

Assets		Liabilities	
Fund balance with the Treasury	$ 900,000	Accounts payable—others	$ 300,000
Assets	50,000	**Investment of the government**	
Inventory	50,000	Unapportioned appropriation	100,000
		Unallotted apportionments	200,000
		Unobligated allotments	100,000
		Unliquidated obligations	200,000
		Expended appropriation—capital	100,000
		Expended appropriation—operating	200,000
		Invested capital*	(200,000)
		Total liabilities and investment	
Total assets	$1,000,000	**of the government**	$1,000,000

* As described in Chapter 23, receipts, expenditures, and expenses are closed to an invested capital account at the end of the fiscal period.

Reporting of Budget Estimates

In the fall of each year, agencies, with few exceptions, must prepare and submit reports and schedules of budget estimates. The reporting of estimates is defined by the OMB in its Circular A-11, entitled *Preparation and Submission of Budget Estimates*. (The definitions of object classes are as detailed in the OMB Circular A-12, referred to in an earlier section of this chapter.)

Pursuant to Circular A-11, an object classification schedule must be prepared for transactions in each agency program and financing schedule. The object classification data must be submitted for three fiscal years: past fiscal year (PY), current fiscal year (CY), and budget fiscal year (BY).

The following phrases or descriptors are used in describing the several fiscal years for which an agency will submit a variety of financial and other information.

▲ *Past year* (PY)—the fiscal year immediately preceding the current year; the last complete fiscal year

▲ *Current year* (CY)—the fiscal year immediately preceding the budget year

▲ *Budget year* (BY)—the next fiscal year for which estimates are being submitted

▲ *Budget year + 1* (BY + 1)—the first fiscal year following the budget year

▲ *Budget year + 2* (BY + 2)—the second fiscal year following the budget year

For the 1980 budget process, a multiyear planning system was instituted by OMB to expand the planning horizon. Budget authority and outlays of agencies were required to be reported to OMB for four years beyond the budget year (i.e., BY + 4).

chapter 11 Expenditures and Applied Costs

INTRODUCTION   The accounting for expenditures and cost within the federal government, essentially accrual accounting, is increasingly becoming the basis for recording and reporting of financial information by agencies. It is doubtful that any accounting concept has been the subject of more review, discussion, study, or debate than the application of accrual accounting in federal financial management.

Accrual accounting has been addressed by many over the last several decades. The subject was researched and debated in depth by the Second Hoover Commission. Congress enacted public laws on the subject and reaffirmed its views in later laws relating to budgeting and reporting by federal agencies. Presidents have issued directives and executive orders extolling the virtues of accrual accounting and establishing the concept as policy of the government. The central accounting agencies (the General Accounting Office, Treasury, and Office of Management and Budget) have published innumerable directives, statements, instructions, and regulations on the subject. Yet federal agencies have been slow to embrace the accrual concept as a basis of accounting as well as management.

According to GAO, the *accrual basis of accounting* consists of recognizing in the books of account the significant and accountable aspects of financial transactions or events as they occur.

Chapter 7 describes several concepts prevalent in federal accounting, including accrual accounting.

DEFINITION OF TERMS

Within the federal government, references to accrual accounting mean either accrued expenditures, accrued costs, or both. Further, the concept of federal accrual accounting varies from the application common in the private sector. The GAO has established the following definitions for purposes of accounting and reporting.

Accrued Expenditures

Accrued expenditures are charges incurred during a period requiring provisions of funds for

▲ Goods and other tangible property received
▲ Services performed by employees, contractors, grantees, lessors, and other payees
▲ Amounts becoming owed under programs for which no performance or current services are required (e.g., annuities, insurance claims, other benefit payments, and some cash grant).

Expenditures accrue regardless of when cash payments are made, when invoices are received, or when property is physically delivered to the agency.

Unless the operating statements are prepared on the expenditure basis rather than on the expense or cost basis, conversions must be made to obtain the financial status of the appropriation and the progress of the program. Monies are provided by the Congress to meet the planned expenditure needs of an agency. *Expenditures*, at the federal level, have been defined to include both capital and operating transactions. Agency managers and executives in the Treasury as well as OMB, not to mention Congress, are concerned with the stewardship as well as the economy, efficiency, and effectiveness of program operations. Thus in the early years of the life of a government program, the concern is over the expenditure level. Reports prepared and submitted on the expense basis will have extremely limited value, if any, because expense information may not be known until years after expenditures have been reported.

Expenses or Costs

A distinction must be made between expenditures and expenses. In federal accounting, the terms are descriptive of two different phases in the accounting cycle of a transaction.

Thus although extremely important to a corporate executive, the reporting of only cost or expense, has limited value to a federal financial analyst. Reports on an expense basis must be reconciled to expenditures, eliminating expenses like depreciation and unfunded vacation expenses and possibly including capital expenditures to provide an accounting of what happened to the money provided by the Congress. Expense reporting becomes more significant as programs mature and continue on a relatively permanent basis. The utility of costs or expense data to a federal manager is discussed also in Chapter 8.

There are many instances, of course, in which expense accounting not only is valuable but is the *only* appropriate method of reporting. Many activities in the federal government have been established to provide a service or perform a function that is "sold" to other programs of the agency or to other agencies. In these cases, the providing activity must maintain close control over its expenses and continually ensure that its pricing policies result in a full return of all costs. Exhibit 7.1 illustrates this distinction, which is one of timing or recognition of certain events in the life cycle of a transaction.

GAO defines the terms *cost, accrued costs,* or *applied costs* as the financial measure of resources consumed in accomplishing a specified purpose (e.g., performing a service, carrying out an activity, completing a unit of work). This definition is in slight variance with another GAO requirement that the accounting system should classify costs according to (1) acquisition of assets and (2) current expenses. Generally, "costs" in relation to assets have been defined as the application or consumption of the asset, i.e., by use, depreciation, amortization, etc. Thus costs are the same as expenses—both refer to the application of resources to current operations.

In practice, the application of applied costs, in connection with reporting on budget execution to the Office of Management and Budget, varies from the definition above. In its Circular A-34, OMB defines "applied costs" as value (purchase price) of goods and services used, consumed, given away, or lost within a given period of time, and offers the following examples, some of which are at slight variance with GAO.

▲ For operating programs, applied costs represent the value of resources consumed or used. (The same definition used by GAO).

▲ For procurement and manufacturing programs, applied costs represent the value of material received or produced.

▲ For capital outlay programs, applied costs for public works equal the value of work put in place.

▲ For loan activities, applied costs represent assets acquired even though no resources have been consumed.

▲ For appropriations essentially operating in nature, equipment is to be included in costs when it is placed into use.

▲ For all programs, when data are provided in the accounting system, accrued annual leave will be included under costs when earned, rather than when taken, even though it may be unfunded at the time. Depreciation costs and other unfunded costs will be included when appropriate.

Other OMB definitions are cited later in this chapter in connection with reporting of applied costs.

Cash Expenditures

The term *cash expenditure* may still, inappropriately, be used by some agencies. When used, the term refers to cash disbursements or checks issued. Although accrual accounting and cost-based budgets have been federal policy for many years, agencies often will give considerable emphasis to the cash basis of reporting principally because of the importance of this data to the Treasury and OMB.

The requirement for accrual accounting appears in legislation enacted about 1950 and in the requirements later issued by the General Accounting Office and the Office of Management and Budget.

LEGAL CRITERIA AND REQUIREMENTS

Budget and Accounting Procedures Act Act of 1950

The Budget and Accounting Procedures Act of 1950 amended the Budget and Accounting Act of 1921 and contained a legal requirement that accrual accounting be implemented by federal agencies. The accounting requirement is described in the act (as amended by 84 Public Law 863) in Section 113 (c), as follows:

> As soon as practicable after the date of enactment of this subsection, the head of each executive agency shall, in accordance with principles and standards prescribed by the Comptroller General, cause the accounts of such agency to be maintained on an accrual basis to show the resources,

liabilities, and costs of operations on such agency with a view of facilitating the preparation of cost-based budgets as required by section 216 of the Budget and Accounting Act, 1921, as amended. . . .

An earlier section of the act (Section 112(a))required that the Comptroller General of the United States (the GAO) provide accounting guidance to federal agencies. Section 112(a) states in part that

> The Comptroller General . . . shall prescribe the principles, standards, and related requirements for accounting to be observed by each executive agency, including requirements for suitable integration between the accounting processes of each executive agency and the accounting of the Treasury Department. . . .

GAO Principles and Standards

Pursuant to the Act of 1950, the Comptrollers General have issued or refined the accounting principles and standards required to be implemented by executive agencies. The specific requirements are stated in the GAO *Policy and Procedures Manual for Guidance of Federal Agencies,* which contain several references to accrual accounting.

▲ The maintenance of accounts on the accrual basis is a basic requirement for federal agencies.

▲ The accrual basis of accounting consists of recognizing in the books and records of account the significant and accountable aspects of financial transactions or events as they occur.

▲ Agency accounting systems that provide financial information primarily in terms of obligations and disbursements are incomplete if they cannot also produce the data needed to disclose properly information on financial and property resources, liabilities, revenues and expenditures, and costs of operations by major areas of responsibility or activity. (2 GAO 14, 15; 1978)

The same manual contains GAO policy (2 GAO 44, 45, 45: 1978) with respect to cost accounting and the support required for cost-based budgets.

OMB Requirements

OMB, in its budget guidance, defines reports on budget execution by executive agencies and requires that these reports be based on the concepts of accrued expenditures and applied costs. Its Circular OMB A-34, *Instructions on Budget Execution,* has defined the concept as one in which

▲ Accrued expenditures are charges in an account during a given period that are equal to liabilities incurred and reflect the need to make payment.

▲ Except for loan payments, expenditures accrue regardless of when cash payments are made, whether invoices are received, and, in some cases, whether tangible goods have been received.

▲ Accrued but unpaid expenditures are liabilities.

▲ Payments for which expenditures have not accrued (advances and prepayments) are assets until accrual of the expenditure.

The accrued expenditures will normally be recorded and reported to OMB at the appropriation or fund level. OMB will not normally require accrued expenditure data below this level although agencies may maintain such detail.

Applied Cost Reporting

Executive agencies, also pursuant to OMB Circular A-34, must make reports on the basis of applied costs. OMB guidance requires that applied costs be associated with program outputs so that such costs become the financial measures of resources consumed or applied in accomplishing a specific purpose. OMB views applied costs as the same as accrued expenditures except as adjusted for the following transactions.

▲ Accrued expenditures reported to OMB will be net of income earned and recoveries. (Applied costs will not be reported net of such amounts.)

▲ Applied costs will include amounts for depreciation and unfunded liabilities (e.g., accrued annual leave) when such amounts are provided in the accounts of the agency.

▲ A net increase in inventories will be an accrued expenditure but not an applied cost; conversely, a net decrease in inventories will be an applied cost but not an accrued expenditure.

▲ For investment in securities involving a premium, applied cost will be amortized over the time the investment is held; the entire premium, though, must be recorded as an accrued expenditure.

▲ Severance pay becomes a reportable obligation on a period basis, but the total amount of the severance pay is an applied cost when an employee is separated under eligible circumstances.

Congressional Budget Impoundment Control Act of 1974

In 1974, with the passage of the Budget and Impoundment Act, Congress required the Comptroller General to develop, establish, and maintain standardized data processing and information systems (Section 201). Section 302 of the act directed the Comptroller General to develop, establish, maintain, and publish standard terminology, definitions, classifications, and codes for federal fiscal, budgetary, and program-related data and information. This authority included, but was not to be limited to, data and information pertaining to federal fiscal policy, revenues, receipts, expenditures, functions, programs, projects, and activities. These standard terms, definitions, classifications, and codes must be used by federal agencies in supplying fiscal, budgetary, and program-related data and information to Congress.

METHODS FOR DETERMINING ACCRUED EXPENDITURES

Over the years, methods of determining accruals have varied although with the advent of computers the full, continual accrual of transactions is more expeditious and provides significantly increased controls over alternative methods. For this reason, as more agencies automate systems, the distinctions and differences are being minimized.

Forecasting Accruals

By the *forecasting method,* an agency makes accounting entries at the beginning of the accounting period for the total forecasted liability to be incurred. Cash payments of the accounting period are then recorded against these amounts. The unpaid estimate liabilities at the end of the period are reported as the accrued liabilities. An example is to record the year's personnel budget as an estimated liability at the start of the year. As payrolls are met, the estimated liability is reduced; the balance of the estimated liability account is considered as the accrued liability.

One disadvantage of this method was its assumption that period activities (e.g., obligations, services received or performance rendered, and receipts and disbursements) were fixed and predictable, an unlikely situation. Also, the method also failed to meet the intent or criteria of GAO's accrued expenditure concept of accounting. Further, agency management is provided with no meaningful data to monitor performance or make cost-based decisions.

Inventory Accruals

A more desirable, but still less than ideal method of determining accruals is *inventorying* receivables, payables, advances, liabilities, and expenditures at the end of the reporting periods. Between inventories, the accounts are maintained on a cash disbursement or "checks issued" basis.

In describing this method, GAO (in 2-GAO-4550) outlines alternatives of (1) posting the end-of-period inventory amounts to the accounts in gross or total, or (2) posting only the net changes in the inventory amounts from one month to the next. If totals are posted, the same entry must be reversed at the beginning of the succeeding accounting period to return the accounting records to the cash basis of accounting. Although the method is expenditious in certain circumstances, the GAO recognizes the method's major disadvantages.

▲ The exact unobligated balance of allotments is determinable with accuracy only at the end of the period.

▲ The maximum benefit and currency of information for managing are available under the inventory method only with the maintenance of auxiliary records.

▲ The inventory method is not designed for and should not be considered in the maintenance of detailed cost accounts.

Exhibit 11.1 is an example by the GAO illustrating the application of the inventory method. From this exhibit, the relationships of cash disbursements to obligations incurred can be demonstrated.

▲ Cash disbursements reflect the checks issued by the Treasury on behalf of a federal agency.

▲ Cash disbursements plus the net increase or minus the decrease of the ending in relation to the beginning balance of accounts payable equal accrued expenditures.

▲ Accrued expenditures plus the net increase or minus the decrease of the ending in relation to the beginning balance of unliquidated obligation equals obligations incurred.

Full Accruals

The preferred method of accrual accounting requires continual accounting for all receivables, payables, and other changes in assets, obligations, liabilities, and accrued expenditures. Under a full accrual or continual accrual method, transactions are processed, recorded, accounted, and reported throughout the accounting period and not merely at the end of the period. Transactions are recognized in the period in which the events occur, throughout the life cycle of the transaction. The financial status reflected by such an accounting is enhanced because the method requires disciplined procedures for the approval, flow, control, safekeeping, ac-

Exhibit 11.1 **INVENTORY METHOD OF DETERMINING ACCRUED EXPENDITURES AND OBLIGATIONS INCURRED**

ITEM	MONTH OF OCTOBER	LAST 11 MONTHS OF FISCAL YEAR	TOTAL FOR FISCAL YEAR
(1) Total cash disbursements during current period	$41,250	$787,750	$829,000
(2) Increase or decrease of ending over beginning balance of accounts payable, determined by inventories of unpaid invoices and other liability documents:			
(a) Accounts payable, per ending inventory	$ 350	$ 1,000	$ 1,000
(b) Accounts payable, per beginning inventory	—	350	—
(c) Increase (or decrease)	$ 350	$ 650	$ 1,000
(3) Accrued expenditures, or liabilities incurred during the current period for assets and expenses (see Journal Entries 2 and 3)	$41,600	$788,400	$830,000
(4) Increase or decrease of ending over beginning balance of unliquidated obligations, determined by inventories of purchase orders, contracts, and other obligating documents:			
(a) Unliquidated obligations per ending inventory	$35,000	$110,000	$110,000
(b) Unliquidated obligations, per beginning inventory	—	35,000	—
(c) Increase (or decrease)	$35,000	$ 75,000	$110,000
(5) Obligations incurred, or purchase orders and contracts placed, and other obligating documents issued during the current period (see Journal Entry 1)	$76,600	$863,400	$940,000

Journal entries:

(1) Unobligated allotments	$76,600		$863,400	
Unliquidated obligations (See item 5 above)		$76,600		$863,400

(continued)

Exhibit 11.1 *(continued)*

ITEM	MONTH OF OCTOBER	LAST 11 MONTHS OF FISCAL YEAR	TOTAL FOR FISCAL YEAR
(2) Unliquidated obligations	41,600	788,400	
Expended appropriations			
(See item 3 above)	41,600		788,400
(3) Assets and expenses	41,600	788,400	
Fund balances with United States Treasury		41,250	787,750
Accounts payable		350	650
(See items 3, 1, and 2c)			

Source: United States General Accounting Office, *Policy and Procedures Manual for Guidance of Federal Agencies.*

counting, and reporting of all transactions. Management is continually aware of the full financial status of all funds.

Practical Considerations in Accruing Expenditures

GAO requires the accrual basis of accounting to recognize the significant and accountable aspects of financial transactions or events in the accounts as they occur. Similarly, the OMB, in its Circular OMB A-34, states that accrued expenditure data should be reasonably reliable, possibly using best estimates where appropriate.

Recording an obligation, accruing the expenditure, costing a resource used, and disbursing cash differ in timing and recognition of events in the life cycle of a transaction. There will be circumstances in which this distinction is either insignificant or immaterial. The recognition of the separable events is not significant when the obligation, expenditure, costing, and disbursement occur almost simultaneously. Such would be the case when a payment is made for personal services, possibly for travel and other object classes of expenditures. Additionally, the amount of the transactions might not be material. Under Circular A-34, the OMB states that reported obligations, accrued expenditures, and applied cost will be based on amounts recorded in the official accounts of an agency. The best estimate may be used in the accounts and reports if the amount is not known and cannot be feasibly determined.

The following criteria apply to the calculation of a "best estimate."

▲ Arbitrary prorations of estimates or similar formula approaches should be avoided.

▲ The best estimate should be based on a sensitive reflection of the transactions and performance that actually occurred.

▲ Estimates, using statistical approaches, may be appropriate when such procedures will eliminate the need for large numbers of reports, but such methods must be subjected to verification and validation of results obtained.

Circular A-34 recognizes that absolute precision is not possible for all types of transactions and that some data must be subjected to later adjustment as invoices are received, examined, and paid or settled. The following criteria have been established by OMB in effecting end-of-period adjustments.

▲ Adjustments for accrued expenditures will be made in the month the adjustment becomes known.

▲ Accounts for prior months will not be reopened to make such adjustments.

▲ At the end of the fiscal year, accounts will be held open to record accruals, cancelations, and adjustments before final September 30 reporting is made by agencies.

With respect to both accrued expenditures and applied cost, claims adjudicated and determined to be payable should be included in the accounting and reporting of an agency.

Basis for Estimating End of Period Accruals

Regardless of the accrual method employed, generally estimates for end-of-period accruals are required for some types of expenditures. In this event, careful, reasonable approximations of transpired events should be made. Examples of bases, suggested by GAO and used by agencies, for estimating the accruals for several transactions include

▲ For accrued liabilities, unpaid invoices from vendors covering shipments received should be inventoried

▲ Reports showing quantities received and whether a given shipment is complete or partial if the invoice has not been received may be used to accrue expenditures

▲ The accruals for payroll, payroll taxes, travel, transportation, and other period cost may be supported by vouchers prepared but not yet paid

▲ Estimates of personal services for the days between the close of the latest payroll period and the end of the accounting period based on experience and other factors, such as overtime

▲ The obligated amount may be estimated when an obligation is recorded covering expenditures accrued in the accounting period

▲ For fixed price contracts extending beyond one accounting period and covering goods manufactured to government specifications, a statement from the contractor estimating the percentage of completion, including work performed by any subcontractors is acceptable to support the accrual

▲ For cost of certain contracts, monthly reports from the contractors showing the unbilled portion of performance to the end of the accounting period, including any work performed by subcontractors may be used to estimate the accrual

▲ To estimate accruals under grants for accrued expenditures monthly performance reports from grantees may be used

▲ Progress under contracts or grants may be estimated by project managers or operating officials familiar with contract status

▲ When there is a large number of small dollar-value transactions or when sound correlations can be made, sampling or statistical methods may be used

▲ For utility services an estimate of the liability for the interval between the data of last billing and the end of the accounting period may be used

▲ For cost-of-lease, estimates based upon the pro rata use of the facility or time elapsed during the accounting period may be used

▲ Previous billings for costs of rentals based on usage provided usage does not fluctuate significantly; in that event, meter readings or usage estimates priced according to a schedule of charges

DETERMINING APPLIED COSTS As mentioned, applied costs and expenses refer to dollar amounts of goods and services used or consumed in carrying out an operation or function. In fact, GAO has taken the position that any unqualified representation of "cost" implies that all significant elements of cost (financial, property, personnel resources) consumed in carrying out a given purpose are included in the amount reported as total costs.

GAO Requirements for Accounting for Costs

In its principles and standards, GAO has established several requirements that must be considered by agencies in defining their systems of accounting and reporting of costs. Agency accounting systems should meet these criteria.

▲ The system accumulates cost information by major organization segments, budget activities, functions, cost centers, program structures, and possibly object classification.

▲ Information on all significant elements of costs is accumulated.

▲ Cost reports disclose the nature and estimated amounts of omissions and the reasons for them.

▲ Cost data provided to management and Congress is reasonably reliable for valid evaluations or decision making.

▲ Unnecessary or undue precision and refinement of data is avoided.

▲ Cost reports, prepared for internal management control purposes, are carefully designed to disclose cost information that is consistent with assignments of responsibility for those costs.

▲ Allocation of indirect cost carefully avoids producing cost data that obscure the total costs for which a manager should be held accountable.

▲ Cost assigned to a given organization or purpose is not limited to only the costs financed by appropriations of the agency.

▲ Costs financed by the agency's appropriations are distinguished from costs financed by other funds.

With respect to the last two considerations when cost is paid or financed through other funds or agencies, provision should be made to include estimates of all such costs. The consideration above should prevail regardless of differences in (1) financing the resources used, (2) requirements in obtaining reimbursement, (3) method of establishing prices for sales of goods or services, or (4) the administrative policies relating to accounting, budgeting, or reporting. GAO has stated that none of these conditions or circumstances constitutes a valid basis for excluding items of costs that are otherwise applicable to the determination of cost.

Maximum accountability requires that the accounting system of an agency classify costs according to (1) acquisition of assets and (2) current expenses. The amount of detail will depend on requirements imposed on an agency or determined by its management to permit planning, controlling, and appraising of performance. Exhibit 11.2 highlights several types of data required to account fully for a government agency's stewardship.

Methods of Cost Determination

Costs, as defined by GAO, may be determined by alternate methods: cost accounting or cost finding. Both methods are acceptable, depending on

Exhibit 11.2 **DATA REQUIRED TO ACCOUNT FOR AGENCY RESOURCES**

PLANNING AND EXECUTING A PROGRAM FOR COST TYPE BUDGETS
(All programs are based on the work or service to be accomplished and what that work will cost.)

THE TERMS USED (Measured in dollars)	HOW THE PROGRAM IS SET UP	PROGRAM CONTROLS
Transactions for Control Purposes	FIRST COST OF THE WORK + or — Changes in inventories + or — Changes in other available resources — Goods and services received without charge	ESTIMATES AND OPERATING BUDGETS Control the *scope* of the activity.
OBLIGATIONS Goods and services *ordered* regardless of when received, paid or used.		CONGRESS Through *appropriations* controls the maximum *amount of allotments* that can be made (on an obligation basis)
ACCRUED EXPENDITURES Goods and services *received* regardless of when ordered, paid or used.	SECOND ACCRUED EXPENDITURES + Increases in undelivered orders — Decreases in undelivered orders	APPORTIONMENTS Control maximum amount of *allotments* that can be made and the *rate* at which *obligations* can be incurred
COSTS Goods and services *used* regardless of when ordered, received, or paid. DISBURSEMENTS Bills *paid*, regardless of when ordered, received, or used.		
Available Resources	THIRD OBLIGATIONS — Reimbursements and funds contributed by others — Unobligated funds on hand	ALLOTMENTS *At broad levels* control the *amount of obligations* that can be incurred
APPROPRIATIONS Funds made available by Congress		OPERATING BUDGETS Control the *costs* that can be incurred
INVENTORIES Goods in stock and available for future use.		
OTHER AVAILABLE RESOURCES Things for future use, such as items in process for use, cost in suspense, and other undistributed expenditures.	FOURTH NEW APPROPRIATION REQUIRED	REPORTS Of results reflect variations in the *estimates* and furnish a basis for control of *operating budgets*

Source: United States General Accounting Office. *Policy and Procedures Manual for Guidance of Federal Agencies. Title 2—Accounting.*

the circumstances and conditions requiring an accounting. In federal agencies, cost finding is viewed as an extension of accounting in which the emphasis has historically been services and cash disbursements. In cost accounting, the emphasis is on the use of the goods or services rather than receipt.

Cost Accounting

GAO has defined *cost accounting* as a method of accounting that provides for assembling and recording all elements of cost incurred to accomplish an objective (e.g., purpose, activity, operation, unit of work, or job). Under a cost accounting system, certain costs are classified and assigned directly to the unit being costed; other costs are grouped for subsequent allocation to the unit.

A cost accounting system should use units of measurement to develop unit costs. Additionally, the cost system should distinguish between direct materials, direct labor, and controllable and noncontrollable (in terms of the unit being costed) overhead, as well as various activities, functions, or processes. The cost accounting system is ordinarily integrated with the financial accounting by having the cost accounts controlled by accounts in the general ledger.

Cost Finding

In contrast, GAO described a *cost finding* system as one under which unit costs are obtained by analyzing expenditure accounts and making test counts of units at regular or irregular intervals. A cost finding system does not provide accounts for accumulating current cost data on a continuous basis and for tying these accounts to a general ledger control.

For this reason, cost finding is appropriate only in those cases in which information is needed occasionally for specific purposes. The data produced by cost finding techniques are not so precise as those that might be obtained from a cost accounting system. Because cost finding data cannot be related to the formal system of accounting, the data may not always be accepted so readily as the data produced by a continual costing system.

Cost-Based Budgets

Accounting for the cost of work performed provides support for budgets and for comparing the results of program operations to plans. Should the budget not be based on cost, operations can still be analyzed and reviewed on the basis of cost, supplemented by an analysis of the status of obligational authority.

If accounting is on a cost basis, a periodic reconciliation to the obligation basis is necessary to ensure fund control. Similarly when obligational authority is on the basis of cost incurred, it is necessary to adjust the costs to arrive at the obligations incurred. (Exhibit 11.2 illustrates a GAO example showing these relationships.)

CONTROL PROCEDURES   The accrual of an expenditure, as mentioned in an earlier chapter, is one method by which an obligation can be liquidated or eliminated. At the time of liquidation of the obligation and establishment of a liability, agencies generally perform reviews of documentation and perform other checks to determine the validity of the claim against the government. Additionally, entries to record applied costs must be initiated and supported by appropriate documentation. In summary, the control procedures often include the following examinations.

Liquidation of Obligations

The "liquidation" or adjustment or reduction of an obligation will occur for one or a combination of the following reasons.

▲ Complete or partial cancelation of the obligation

▲ Receipt of the goods or services in full or partial satisfaction of the obligation (i.e., the accrual of the expenditure)

▲ The accrual of an expenditure for which a prior obligation had not been established

Agency personnel will examine invoices, receiving documents, contract and grant payment schedules and performance, recorded payroll, and submitted travel expense vouchers and other claims against the government to determine the following.

▲ Payment had not been previously made for the goods or services billed.

▲ The services or goods received are consistent with the purpose of the earlier obligation.

▲ The period of performance complies with the terms in the obligation documents.

▲ Whether there is an existing obligation that must be liquidated.

▲ The amount of any earlier obligation is related to the value of the accrued expenditure as evidenced by the supporting documentation.

▲ Whether the amount of an earlier obligation must be adjusted or an obligation must be established.

▲ If there is compliance with any other special conditions contained in either the earlier obligation documents, the authorizing or appropriation laws, or agency policy statements.

Determination of Applied Costs

The determination of applied costs is performed with the same care as the accrual of an expenditure. Organizations, activities, functions, and other cost units must be accurately and promptly charged for costs consumed or applied in support of their mission.

In addition to the concurrent application of costs at the time of accruing an expenditure, there are other direct costs that must be considered.

For example, if supplies and materials are recorded as inventory at the time of receipt, the withdrawal documentation completed by requestors becomes the supporting record to charge the requestors' units for the cost of such services. Where appropriate, entries of applied costs for items such as annual leave (vacation), depreciation, and other unfunded costs must be controlled and charged to users as incurred or consumed.

In addition to direct costs, the cost accounting records of an agency should provide for the equitable allocation of indirect or overhead costs to consumers of these costs. Such allocation must be supported by appropriate cost allocation plans and formulas.

Not to be overlooked are the costs consumed by users that are financed by other funds or agencies. The accounting system should adequately identify these additional resources that have been applied on behalf of the agency's programs or missions.

In each of these instances, accounting entries must be processed to recognize the application or consumption of these costs.

Accounting Records

As mentioned in earlier chapters, the computerization of accounting systems has changed the form of an agency's accounting records. The recording and accounting for obligations and accrued expenditures have been coordinated to relieve a considerable bookkeeping requirement of maintaining the government's budgetary transactions and accounts.

The proper accounting for applied or consumed costs that had been earlier recorded as an asset for use in a future period requires the completion of documentation to evidence the consumption or application of the costs. Separate transactions must be coded or input to the computerized system and are subject to separate controls. The initiation of these transactions may also be automated. For example, the form to support the withdrawal of supplies from inventory may simultaneously serve as a reorder requisition resulting in a commitment, the issuance of a purchase order creating an obligation, as well as forming the basis for the costing journal entry.

ACCOUNTING PROCESS The accounting for accrued expenditures and applied costs is a continuation of the life cycle of a transaction. These entries typically follow the recording of an obligation and precede the disbursement of funds, although instances will occur in which no obligation has been previously recognized when the agency is required to make a disbursement of funds.

As mentioned in the earlier chapters, the accounting entries must be related to a specific appropriation and the allotment of funds must be recorded within each appropriation for which an agency is responsible. Obligations must be related in the accounting records to the correct allotments.

In a similar manner, the accrued expenditures, capital as well as operating expenditures, must be cross-referenced to the earlier obligations.

Exhibit 11.3 illustrates the nature of the accounting performed for expenditures and applied costs. Each of these transactions is discussed in more detail in the succeeding sections.

For Expenditures

Should the amount of an accrued expenditure be less than the earlier obligated amount, the excess obligation would be returned to the unobligated allotment status, provided such funds remain available for obligation under the appropriation act.

At the time expenditures accrue, several groups of accounts are affected. As services and goods are received, the earlier obligations are reduced or liquidated. The accruals of expenditures must be segregated between capital and operating expenditures. Additionally, it is necessary to record the assets received or expenses incurred.

If an agency program had earlier entered obligations related to salaries, travel, contracts, and grants, for example, an entry to reduce the unobligated allotment balances and record the obligations should have been made.

The entry might be

```
DEBIT:     Unobligated allotments — program A
     CREDIT:     Unliquidated obligations — program A
                      — salaries
                      — travel
                      — contracts
                      — grants
```

Expenditures accrue as goods and services are received. For illustration, assume that these obligations resulted in accrued expenditures. The concurrent entries shown at the top of page 192 would be required to reflect the events fully.

Exhibit 11.3 **ILLUSTRATION OF ACCOUNTING FOR EXPENDITURES
AND APPLIED COSTS**

EVENT	ENTRY	ENTRIES	DEBIT	CREDIT
Receipt of appro-priation, OMB apportionment, issuance of advices of allotments, par-tial obligation of allotted balances	*	Fund balance with the Treasury Unapportioned appropriation	$ 900,000	$ 900,000
	*	Unapportioned appropriation Unallotted apportionments	800,000	800,000
	*	Unallotted apportionments Unobligated allotments	600,000	600,000
	*	Unobligated allotments Unliquidated obligations	500,000	500,000

Accrued expendi-tures by object classifications and accounting for lia-bilities related to expenditures	(1)	Unliquidated obligations
		    Expended appropriation—
		       capital
		    Expended appropriation—
		       operating
			300,000	100,000
				
				200,000

		—also—		
	(2)	Fixed assets Inventory Expenses—various Accounts payable—others	50,000 50,000 200,000	300,000

Use or consumption of assets and ex-penditures incurred during earlier ac-counting period (assumed use of assets and inven-toried item)	(3)	Expenses—depreciation
		Expenses—supplies
		    Accumulated depreciation
		    Inventory
			5,000
			10,000
				5,000
				10,000

		TOTAL	$3,415,000	$3,415,000

* Discussed in earlier chapters.
Note: The effect of the transactions above are shown in Exhibit 11.4.

DEBIT: Unliquidated obligations — program A
         — salaries
         — travel
         — contracts
         — grants

    CREDIT: Accrued expenditures — capital
             Accrued expenditures — operating

                —plus—

DEBIT: Fixed assets — program A
             Inventory — program A
             Expenses — program A
         — salaries
         — travel
         — grant

    CREDIT: Accounts payable — others

The initial entry recognizes the reduction of outstanding obligations for the goods and services received and provides an overall accounting for accrued capital and operating expenditures. The second entry is necessary to reflect properly the proprietary type of entries in the agency accounts. The entry to the accounts has the same general basis used in the commercial sector: expenses represent charges to operations during the current period. In the example above, the costs or expenses related to fixed assets and inventory will be charged to future periods on an allocation or consumption basis.

For Costs or Expenses

The accounting for costs and expenses should reflect the application or consumption or use of these resources in the accounting period in which the event takes place. In the earlier illustration, although assets were acquired and inventory items were purchased and received, none of these resources had been consumed or used for operations. Once these resources are used, the following entries would be required to adjust the asset accounts in the example.

DEBIT: Expenses — program A
         — depreciation
         — supplies

    CREDIT: Accumulated depreciation — program A
             Inventory — program A

There will be instances in which the obligation, accrual of expenditures, expensing, and disbursement occur in the same fiscal period. Salaries for federal employees would be an example. In that case, the following entries would be appropriate.

DEBIT: Unobligated allotments — program A
          — salaries
    CREDIT: Expended appropriation — operating
          —plus—
DEBIT: Expenses — program A
          — salaries
    CREDIT: Accrued salaries payable

Note that it is not necessary to record and then to immediately eliminate the obligation entry. The entries above reduce the unobligated allotments and thus prevent a possible overobligation of the allotted funds. By aggregating the balances of the unliquidated obligation and the accrued expenditure accounts, the agency will be able to report the obligation of the fund at any time.

With respect to cost and expenses, the charges should be recorded on a direct basis to the appropriate organization and fund. Several bases are appropriate, depending on the nature of the cost or expense consumed or used.

ITEM	BASIS FOR COSTING
Personal services and fringe benefits	Services rendered
Travel	Unit or activity benefiting from the travel
Supplies, materials, transportation	Unit or activity ordering; or historical experience
Utilities	Space, square footage occupied
Contracts, grants	Benefiting or responsible organization or unit
Depreciation	Assignment of equipment, furniture, fixtures

Indirect costs or overhead should be distributed to users on the basis of a formal allocation plan. As mentioned, expenditures and costs or expenses affect both budgetary and proprietary accounts. Exhibit 11.4 illustrates financial statements reflecting the results of the transactions above.

Exhibit 11.4 **ILLUSTRATION OF EFFECT OF EXPENDITURE AND APPLIED COST AND EXPENSE ENTRIES**

a) LEDGER ACCOUNTS

Asset accounts

Fund balance with the Treasury

900,000	

Fixed assets

(2) 50,000	

Accumulated depreciation

	(3) 5,000

Inventory

(2) 50,000	(3) 10,000

Expenses

Expenses

(2) Various	200,000	
(3) Depreciation	5,000	
(3) Supplies	10,000	
	*215,000	

Liabilities

Accounts payable—others

	(2) 300,000

Investment of the government

Unapportioned appropriation

800,000	900,000

Unallotted apportionments

600,000	800,000

Unobligated allotments

500,000	600,000

Unliquidated obligations

(1) 300,000	500,000

Expended appropriation—capital

	(1) 100,000

Expended appropriation—operating

	(1) 200,000

Exhibit 11.4   *(continued)*

b) BALANCE SHEET: STATEMENT OF ASSETS, LIABILITIES, AND INVESTMENT OF THE GOVERNMENT

Assets		**Liabilities**	
Fund balance with the Treasury	$900,000	Accounts payable— others	$300,000
Fixed assets	50,000	**Investment of the government**	
Accumulated depreciation	(5,000)	Unapportioned appropriation	100,000
Inventory	40,000	Unallotted apportionments	200,000
		Unobligated allotments	100,000
		Unliquidated obligations	200,000
		Expended appropriations— capital	100,000
		Expended appropriations— operating	200,000
		*Invested capital	−215,000
Total Assets	$985,000	**Total liabilities and investment of the government**	$985,000

* Closed to invested capital.

Reporting on Expenditures and Costs

Uniform governmentwide reporting requirements have been established by OMB for accrued expenditures. The accrued expenditures, along with other budgetary types of financial data, must be reported to OMB on SF133, Report on Budget Execution, explained in more detail in Chapter 9. The reported applied costs relate to the agency's program and may have to be refined to reflect accrued expenditures by activity.

chapter 12 Disbursements

INTRODUCTION A system of internal controls exists within the federal government consisting of formal procedures, standard report formats, prescribed reporting, and assignment of personal responsibility. The controls and the personal responsibility evolve around a group of officers and designated employees referred to collectively as accountable officers. The accountable officers perform critical functions in the disbursing process.

Most federal agencies do not literally pay bills or issue checks. In practice, the disbursement process of the government requires that agencies provide controls over the incurrence of obligations and liabilities that will ultimately require the payment of money. Once an agency determines that an amount must be paid, a request for payment is sent to the Treasury. The Treasury, through an accountable officer, issues the check, making the actual disbursement of money and performing the necessary cash accounting in the Treasury's central accounts. The Treasury then provides a report to the agency on whose behalf it disbursed money.

ACCOUNTABLE
OFFICERS

Defined

According to the General Accounting Office (7-GAO-81-83), an *accountable officer* is an authorized disbursing officer, certifying officer, or collecting officer. An accountable officer is responsible for an "account" that must be "settled." These latter terms have specific meaning within federal financial management.

The term *account* refers to an accountable officer's records pertaining to the public funds received, disbursed, or retained by him or her. With respect to certifying officers, these persons are not required to maintain an "account," but the term is often used and refers to the vouchers and other documents approved by these officers during their tenure in office. The term *settlement* refers to the reporting by an accountable officer and the final administrative determination of amounts due or discrepancies at the end of the final reporting period for which an accountable officer is liable.

Accountability of Officers

GAO has defined the account of an accountable officer performing a collection or disbursing function as including the following.

▲ Funds on hand

▲ Funds deposited in designated depositaries, the deposits of which have been confirmed by the depositaries

▲ Funds deposited in designated depositaries, confirmation of which has not been received from the depositaries

▲ Cash and other funds advanced to government cashiers for use as imprest funds

▲ Money disbursed on incomplete vouchers or voucher-schedules

▲ Money overpaid in contravention of completed vouchers or voucher schedules

It is important to distinguish between the responsibility of an accountable disbursing officer and that of a certifying officer. The disbursing officer is not responsible for determining, prior to disbursement, the availability of appropriations or funds to cover the prospective disbursement. This is the responsibility of a certifying officer, whose responsibilities are outlined in the section after the next one.

Responsibility of Disbursing Officers

The term disbursing officer usually refers to officials or employees of the Treasury. However, employees of other federal agencies and departments may be authorized to receive money and make minor cash disbursements. Such people are called cashiers. Cashiers are not employees of the Treasury, but perform their fiscal function in accordance with Treasury direction.

Title 31 (Section 82) of the United States Code lists these responsibilities of a disbursing officer.

▲ To disburse monies only upon and in strict accordance with vouchers duly certified by the head of the department, establishment, or agency concerned, or by an officer or employees thereof duly authorized in writing by such head to certify such vouchers

▲ To make such examination of vouchers as may be necessary to ascertain whether they are in proper form, duly certified and approved, and correctly computed on the basis of the facts certified

▲ To be held accountable accordingly

One indication of the extensiveness of the disbursing system of the federal government is the numbers of people in certifying and disbursing officers roles. According to a recent report entitled *Study on Roles and Responsibilities of Certifying and Disbursing Officers* (published by the Joint Financial Management Improvement Program), there are over 14,000 certifying officers in civilian agencies and 850 disbursing officers in the Department of Defense, accountable for about one trillion dollars in payments made annually by the government.

Responsibility of Certifying Officers

The certification of vouchers, upon which a disbursing officer may rely in making a disbursement, is an administrative action and a responsibility of the individual agencies and departments. The agency must comply with the governmentwide regulations governing disbursements; specific legislation may contain additional criteria that must be considered by the certifying officer of an agency.

Title 31 (Section 82) of the United States Code states

▲ A certifying officer shall be held responsible for the existence and correctness of the facts cited in the certificate or otherwise stated on the voucher and its supporting papers and for the legality of the proposed payment under the appropriation or fund involved. Disbursing officers shall not be held accountable for the correctness of such computations.

▲ A certifying officer must be bonded with sufficient surety, approved by the Secretary of the Treasury, in an amount determined by the agency head pursuant to Treasury standards.

▲ The certifying officer is held accountable for and required to make restitution to the government for any illegal, improper, or incorrect payment resulting from any false, inaccurate, or misleading certificate as well as any payment prohibited by law that does not represent a legal obligation under the appropriation or fund involved.

Imprest Fund Cashiers

It is a general practice of agencies to establish imprest funds and to designate employees as cashiers and alternate cashiers. Typically, the fund is instituted by the agency receiving an advance for the fund from the Treasury. As disbursements are made from the imprest fund, the specific costs and expenses are recorded against the agency's appropriation; and the imprest fund is replenished from the agency's appropriation for the amount of the expenditures.

The amount of such funds is minimal, consistent with the need for an expedited system of disbursements. The imprest fund controls are established by the Treasury and the fund disbursements are generally limited to such disbursements as minor vendor payments, advances to employees, and reimbursements to employees for authorized expenditures.

LEGAL DECISIONS OF GAO Accounting officers, disbursing officers, certifying officers, and cashiers may obtain advance decisions as to the legality of anticipated obligations or disbursements from the General Accounting Office. The Comptroller General is required by law to provide decisions in advance of obligating or disbursing actions when requested by agency accountable officers. The GAO's Office of General Counsel is responsible for preparing these decisions, which are final and conclusive on executive branch agencies. The decisions are not binding upon actions of the Congress or the judiciary or contractors, vendors, grantees, or others having a claim against the government. These decisions are published individually as issued and annually in bound form.

PERSONAL LIABILITY The existence and functioning of the controls above are important to ensure compliance with the funding intent of Congress. Personal liability exists for those accountable officers violating the terms of Congressional appropriation and funding limitations. Considerable resources are devoted by the government to the monitoring of fiscal practices to ensure compliance with the provisions of the Antideficiency Act. Specifically, agencies are concerned with avoiding violations of Section 3679 of the Revised Statutes.

As mentioned in an earlier chapter, the several prohibitions contained in these Revised Statutes are that no officer or employee of the United States shall

▲ Make or authorize an expenditure from or create or authorize an obligation under any appropriation or fund in excess of the amount available therein

▲ Involve the government in any contract or obligation for the payment of money for any purpose in advance of appropriations made for that purpose unless such contract or obligation is authorized by law

▲ Accept voluntary service for the United States or employ personal service in excess of that authorized by law except in cases of emergency involving the safety of human life or the protection of property

▲ Authorize or create any obligation or make any expenditure in excess of an apportionment or reapportionment or in excess of the amount permitted by agency regulations prescribed and approved pursuant to the act.

Violations of any of the prohibitions above of the statute require that the officer or employee be subject to appropriate administrative discipline, including suspension without pay or removal from office. Where the violation is willfull or knowingly committed, an officer or employee, upon conviction, shall be fined not more than $5,000 or imprisoned for not more than two years or both.

REPORTING BY ACCOUNTABLE OFFICERS Accountable officers of the government usually must maintain appropriate supporting documentation to provide an accounting of their stewardship and additionally must periodically make a reporting of the account or the funds received, disbursed, or retained. The reporting responsibility is accomplished by a statement of accountability and a statement of transactions.

Statement of Accountability

The statement of accountability (SF 1219) is prepared monthly by the disbursing accountable officer, regardless of whether there are any transactions to be reported for the period. Generally, the statement will be retained, along with all supporting documentation, by the agency. In some instances though, the report must be submitted to the General Accounting Office.

An accountable officer must submit the final statement as of the close of the last business day of his or her appointment as an accountable officer for a specific location. The initial statement of accountability by the successor accountable officer must be rendered at the end of the first month in which the successor is appointed. The successor's opening balance must be the same as the closing balance of the predecessor accountable officer.

Exhibit 12.1 is an illustration of the Statement of Accountability.

Statement of Transactions

The statement of transactions (SF 1220) is prepared monthly and submitted to the Treasury by an accountable officer. This report forms the basis of the Treasury's central accounting and reporting on a governmentwide basis. The statement shows the classification of collections and disbursements by appropriation, receipt, and fund accounts, and related summary totals for the month.

When consolidated statements of transactions are prepared, an audit trail must be maintained by the submitting agency from the consolidated report to the respective accountable officers' statements and supporting documents.

Exhibit 12.2 is an illustration of the Statement of Transactions.

GAO Settlement Audits

The General Accounting Office is required to perform settlement or closeout audits of each accountable officer's account. This settlement or audit must be made within three years of the GAO's receipt of the final statement of accountability from an officer. Law requires that this settle-

Exhibit 12.1   **PART I: FRONT SIDE OF DOCUMENT.**

Standard Form 1219
May 1970
2 Treasury FRM 3100

STATEMENT OF ACCOUNTABILITY

NAME OF DISBURSING OFFICER	LOCATION OF DISBURSING OFFICER *(Mailing address)*
NAME OF AGENCY	
PERIOD OF ACCOUNT	OFFICE NUMBER *(Show main check symbol number)*
FROM: THROUGH:	

SECTION I.—GENERAL STATEMENT OF ACCOUNT

PART A.—TRANSACTIONS DURING PERIOD AFFECTING ACCOUNTABILITY

1.0	TOTAL ACCOUNTABILITY BEGINNING OF PERIOD		$
2.0	INCREASES IN ACCOUNTABILITY		
2.1	CHECKS ISSUED ON TREASURER, U.S.	$	
2.2	COLLECTIONS		
2.3	OTHER TRANSACTIONS		
2.9	TOTAL INCREASES IN ACCOUNTABILITY		$
3.0	SUBTOTAL		$
4.0	DECREASES IN ACCOUNTABILITY		
4.1	GROSS DISBURSEMENTS	$	
4.2	CONFIRMED DEPOSITS WITH TREASURER, U.S.		
4.2 1	CONFIRMED DEPOSITS TO CHECKING ACCOUNT WITH TREASURER, U.S. *(Funded checking accounts only)*		
4.2 2	CONFIRMED DEPOSITS WITH TREASURER, U.S., OF UNAVAILABLE RECEIPTS *(Funded checking accounts only)*		
4.3	OTHER TRANSACTIONS		
4.9	TOTAL DECREASES IN ACCOUNTABILITY		$
5.0	TOTAL ACCOUNTABILITY CLOSE OF PERIOD		$

PART B.—ANALYSIS OF INCUMBENT OFFICER'S ACCOUNTABILITY

	CASH ON DEPOSIT IN DESIGNATED DEPOSITARY	
6.1	_____ *(Name and location of depositary)*	$
6.2	CASH ON HAND	
6.3	CASH—UNDEPOSITED COLLECTIONS	
6.4	CASH—UNCONFIRMED DEPOSITS	
6.5	CASH IN CUSTODY OF GOVERNMENT CASHIERS	
6.6		
6.7		
6.8		
6.9		
7.1	DEFERRED CHARGES—VOUCHERED ITEMS	
7.2	RECEIVABLES—CHECK OVERDRAFTS	
7.3	LOSSES OF FUNDS	
7.4	RECEIVABLES—DISHONORED CHECKS	
7.5		
7.6		
7.7		
7.8		
7.9		
8.0	TOTAL OF MY ACCOUNTABILITY	$

(continued)

Exhibit 12.1 **PART I** (continued)

PART C.—ANALYSIS OF PREDECESSOR OFFICERS' ACCOUNTABILITY

9.2	RECEIVABLES—CHECK OVERDRAFTS	$
9.3	LOSSES OF FUNDS	
9.4	OTHER ACCOUNTABILITY	
10.0	**TOTAL PREDECESSOR OFFICERS' ACCOUNTABILITY**	$
11.0	**TOTAL DISBURSING OFFICE ACCOUNTABILITY** (Same as line 5.0 above)	$

PART D.—TREASURY FUNDING TRANSACTIONS (FORMS 593)

12.0	FUNDING INCREASES TO CHECKING ACCOUNT(S)	$
13.0	FUNDING DECREASES TO CHECKING ACCOUNT(S)	$

I certify that this is a true and correct statement of accountability for the period stated at the office referred to above.

DATE	TITLE	SIGNATURE

1219–105 (OVER)

Exhibit 12.1 **PART II: REVERSE SIDE OF DOCUMENT.**

SECTION II.—SUMMARY BY SYMBOL OF CHECK AND DEPOSIT TRANSACTIONS WITH TREASURER, U.S.

PART A.—CHECKS ISSUED AND ADJUSTMENTS FOR PRIOR PERIODS *

CHECK SYMBOL	AMOUNT OF CHECKS ISSUED THIS PERIOD	ADJUSTMENTS FOR PRIOR MONTHS' ISSUES (+ or −)				TOTAL CHECKS ISSUED † (Column 2 ±3 and ±4)
		By Forms TD 5206		Other		
		ISSUE (Month and year)	AMOUNT	ISSUE (Month and year)	AMOUNT	
(1)	**(2)**	**(3)**		**(4)**		**(5)**
TOTALS ‡						

(continued)

Exhibit 12.1 **PART II** (continued)

PART B.—SUMMARY OF DEPOSITS CONFIRMED (Lines 4.2 or 4.2 2 only)

DEPOSIT SYMBOL	DEPOSITS CONFIRMED THIS MONTH (Per supporting list)	DEPOSITS CONFIRMED IN PRIOR MONTHS BUT RECORDED IN ACCOUNTS THIS MONTH (Per supporting list)		TOTAL DEPOSITS CONFIRMED (Column 2+4)
		MONTH CONFIRMED	AMOUNT	
(1)	(2)	(3)	(4)	(5)
TOTALS ‡				

* The totals reported in these columns must be in agreement with the corresponding amounts reported on SF 1179.
† The total reported in this column must be in agreement with the total shown on line 2.1 on the face of this statement.
‡ For use only if more than one (1) symbol is listed.

U. S.GPO:1975-0-565-475

ment be made by GAO in this time period if officers are to be held personally liable for any deficiencies. In cases of fraud or criminality, the period limitation does not apply. Historically, the GAO, upon completion of the settlement audit, rendered a certification of settlement to the accountable officer involved.

DISBURSEMENTS DEFINED

Disbursements in the federal government are simply payments by check or cash for operations, activities, and other obligations of the federal government. Advances by government agencies will also be considered as disbursements. In other words, disbursements are "checks issued" or "cash paid" or letter of credit "drawdowns."

Until relatively recently, possibly as late as the early 1960s, a cash-based accounting predominated. Expenditures were not defined as accrued expenditures, but rather as "cash expenditures" or "checks issued." Few agencies maintain accounting records solely on a cash basis today. After many years, the consensus and the stated basis now set forth in many legislative acts are that accounts and reporting should be on the accrual basis as described and illustrated in earlier chapters.

Exhibit 12.2

Standard Form 1220
May 1970
2 Treasury FRM 3100

STATEMENT OF TRANSACTIONS
ACCORDING TO APPROPRIATIONS, FUNDS, AND RECEIPT ACCOUNTS

OF

LOCATION

PERIOD

DEPT. OR AGENCY

BUREAU

OFFICE OR STATION

APPROPRIATION, FUND, OR RECEIPT SYMBOL (1)	RECEIPTS (2)	REPAYMENTS (3)	GROSS DISBURSEMENTS (4)
TOTALS			

DATE

SIGNATURE AND TITLE

1220–105

206

LEGAL CRITERIA AND REQUIREMENTS

By law (act of December 29, 1941, 31 U.S.C. 82b), disbursing officers in the executive branch disburse money pursuant only to vouchers received from agencies. These vouchers must be certified by that agency, and the disbursing officer must make an examination to determine that the vouchers are proper in format, properly certified and approved, and accurately computed.

The Treasury is responsible for and prescribes the standard disbursement forms used by almost all agencies in the government. The standard forms supporting the disbursement are not required if the invoices or bills present all of the required information. In this instance, these documents may be used in lieu of the forms. Generally though, the standard forms are used by agencies. The required information to support each disbursement must include an identification or reference to

▲ The items purchased or services received

▲ The quantity of units received

▲ An acceptance by the government of the items or services

▲ Applicable contracts, grants, or other agreements

▲ The party to whom the amount is owed

▲ The amount of the debt or payment due

▲ The account, including appropriation, to be charged

By law the Comptroller General may relieve certifying officers of liabilities for payments if

▲ Certification was based on official records that the certifying officer did not know and facts that reasonable diligence and inquiry could not have ascertained

▲ The obligation was incurred in good faith, payment was not contrary to any statutory provision specifically prohibiting payments of the character involved, and the government has received value for such payment.

As highlighted in a 1980 report on certifying and disbursing officers published by the Joint Financial Management Improvement Program, the Comptroller General is authorized to relieve accountable officers when losses are caused by a subordinate and not as a result of the accountable officers' negligence in the discharge of their duties. Further, the application of statistical sampling of low dollar disbursement items is permitted, with accountable officers not being responsible for improper payment not falling within the sampled population. Under certain conditions, agencies may compromise or settle claims against accountable officers up to $20,000. Such actions relieve these accountable officers for the accounts so compromised or settled.

DISBURSEMENT OF FUNDS

With the exception of the Department of Defense, selected offices of the government, and government corporations, the Treasury Department disburses the vast majority of funds for executive agencies and departments. These exempted organizations disburse their own funds.

Disbursing Process

By a network of disbursing centers and regional offices throughout the country, disbursing officers disburse funds in their own name. Minor cash disbursements are made by cashiers who are located in almost every agency. Payments are made from an imprest fund or cash balance, initially provided by a disbursing office. The imprest fund is replenished as reimbursement vouchers representing fund disbursements are submitted to the disbursing office and reported in the agency accounts.

Tens of millions of payments are authorized by agencies and disbursed by the Treasury monthly. Many payments are by check, but considerable amounts are transferred between agencies accounts by "paper transfer."

Government checks are the most common form of payment, with disbursing officers issuing about 700 million checks annually. While almost all agencies do make payments directly, these are typically for small amounts paid from an imprest fund.

There are three methods of "paper transfer" that are alternatives to the check payment system in connection with federal interagency transactions. These methods are referred to as:

▲   The *SF 1081 System* (which takes its name from SF 1081, an interagency Voucher and Schedule of Withdrawals and Credits) transfers funds from one government account to another. The system is limited to transactions between agencies for which the Treasury disburses. The 1081 form, which is processed by the proper disbursing center, serves as the record of payment, thus eliminating the need for a separate payment and reconciliation of a check in the transfer of funds.

▲   The *Simplified Intragovernmental Billing and Collection System* (SIBAC) enables simultaneous billing and collection of funds between government agencies. The decision to use the SIBAC system is made by the billing agency. SIBAC has been used by billing agencies with a high volume of interagency transactions for certain types of transactions. For example, the General Services Administration and the Office of Personnel Management are users of this system.

▲   The *Journal Voucher System* is another "paper transfer" system, developed and used by the Office of Personnel Management for the conduct of its interagency transactions.

Another method of payment, involving nonfederal organizations, is the *letters of credit* system. Letters of credit are used to make payments to public and private organizations. Under this method, the recipient organization draws cash against a letter of credit on file with either a federal reserve bank or a Treasury disbursing center (the Regional Disbursing Office system). Additionally, the recipient agency or organization must make a reporting of funds withdrawn and the expenditures incurred or costs for which the withdrawal was made.

In addition to the methods above, two "electronic funds transfer" systems are in operation:

▲ The *Treasury Financial Communication System* (TFCS)—a computer-to-computer link between the Treasury and the Federal Reserve System permitting automatic transmission of payment and deposit messages between the public and the federal government. This system is used primarily for large, nonrecurring payments as transfer of the federal contribution to state unemployment compensation and certain contributions to International Monetary Fund programs.

▲ The *Direct Deposit/Electronic Funds Transfer Program*—used by the government to transfer certain types of benefit payments (social security, civil service, railroad retirement annuities, etc.) directly to the beneficiary's account in a commercial bank or other financial organization through the Federal Reserve System. These transfers are made by magnetic tape rather than by the issuance of a check to individuals.

The accounts of disbursing officers must support payments of vouchers duly certified by the requesting administrative or executive agency having primary control over the appropriation under which the funds are being disbursed. The agency requesting payment, not the Treasury, is solely responsible for ensuring that vouchers are not certified for amounts in excess of available funds. The disbursing officers are accountable only for the transactions they consummate.

CONTROLS OVER DISBURSEMENTS

Agencies have generally established procedures to ensure that requests for Treasury check disbursements are for authorized and proper amounts only and that sufficient funds are available from the agency's appropriation to meet the requested disbursement. Additionally, much earlier in the life of a transaction, another system of control exists that requires the review of each anticipated obligation. The objective of this earlier review is to determine that obligations will not be entered into until after a decision has been made that unobligated appropriations exist to meet the anticipated commitment.

DISBURSEMENTS

Preaudit of Disbursement Vouchers

An important aspect of the internal controls of government organizations is the examination and approval of vouchers and related supporting documents prior to certification and transmission to the Treasury for payment. The GAO, in its prescribed fiscal procedures for agencies (7-GAO-24), states that the objectives of the preaudit of vouchers is to determine

▲ Whether the required administrative authorizations for procurement and approvals for the payment were obtained

▲ Whether the payment is permitted by law and is in accordance with the terms of the applicable agreement

▲ Whether the amount of the payment and the name of the payee are correct

▲ Whether the payment will be a duplicate payment

▲ Whether the goods received or the services performed were in accordance with the agreement

▲ Whether the quantities, prices, and amounts are accurate

▲ Whether all cash, trade, quantity, or other discounts have been taken and, if not, whether the reasons are shown on the appropriate document

▲ Whether all applicable deductions were made and credited to the proper account in the corrected amount

▲ Whether the appropriation or fund from which the payment will be made is available for that purpose

▲ Whether proper forms of documentation were used

▲ Whether special certificates were furnished if required.

Other Controls

At the time the agency requests the Treasury to make a disbursement, other procedures should exist to avoid duplicate or erroneous payments.

Of concern to an agency is the possibility of duplicate payment. Vouchers, voucher schedules forwarded to the Treasury, and all supporting documentation must be mutilated or conspicuously marked to prevent submission or processing for duplicate payment. GAO has pointed out to agencies that duplication is particularly possible when one of the following conditions exists:

▲ Payments have been delayed for extended periods after due date and duplicate copies of invoices are received from vendors as follow-up claims.

▲ Invoices or bills are submitted by the vendors to more than one agency for payment

▲ Adjusted invoices are received after payments have been made.

Care is generally taken to record disbursements promptly in the proper accounts and make timely reports to the Treasury. Today all documentation in support of a disbursement is retained by the originating agency for subsequent reference, analysis, and often audit by the agency's internal audit staff or the GAO or both. This documentation would include all vouchers, contracts, grants, payment schedules, invoices, payroll records, utility billings, and other authorization for disbursements.

The functions of maintaining accounting records, entering data into automated systems, and preparing forms authorizing disbursements should not be performed by the same individual. When a segregation of the records and disbursing functions is not possible, additional checks should exist to ensure the integrity of the disbursing process. With the increased reliance on computers, particular care should be taken to ensure that system's input machinery is not located in the fiscal or accounting sections, regardless of the case made for efficiency and effectiveness. According to GAO a partial listing of operations that should be segregated include

▲ Purchasing of goods and services

▲ Recording receipt of goods and services

▲ Examining invoices

▲ Preparing vouchers

▲ Authorizing or hiring of employees

▲ Keeping time records

▲ Preparing payrolls

▲ Maintaining voucher records and similar records

▲ Additionally, other tasks could be added to the list such as

Certifying the availability of funds for disbursement

Receiving cash or other valuables

Approving vouchers for payment

Conduct of the preaudit activities described above

Authority to incur obligations

Additionally agencies' controls, with few exceptions, must require that all disbursements be in the form of a check. Cash disbursements are generally not made by agency personnel.

Certification of Fund Availability

Agencies have established systems of controls that require the examination of appropriation fund balances prior to obligating funds. This action precedes the preaudit above and is often referred to as the reservation of funds. Certifying officials are required to acknowledge formally in writing the appropriateness of the intended obligation. The approval by a certifying officer signifies that the purpose, amount, and anticipated time period of the intended obligation are consistent with the terms of the appropriation.

The reservation of funds is generally an estimate of the intended obligation. Adjustments are often required, once the precise amount of the obligation is known. For programs, (such as some grant and contract programs) that require prolonged periods to obligate funds, a "commitment" could be formally recorded in the agency's accounting records. Once the obligation is known, the earlier commitment is reversed and the formal obligation recorded. The fund control process generally takes the form of a manual or computerized fund reservation or allotment-allowance registers. These records are structured to show cumulative amounts of commitments, obligations, and uncommitted or unobligated funds.

The more common reservation documents and actions, supporting the transactions included in these registers, relate to

▲ *Contracts and purchases*—Procurement requests or purchase orders must often be approved by the appropriate official before formal contracts are issued to obligate agency funds formally.

▲ *Grants*—Funding authorization documents must generally be completed by appropriate officials for amounts anticipated for grant agreements.

▲ *Travel*—Anticipated obligations for travel must be preceded by the completion of a travel order, containing an indication of the period, amount, and purpose of the travel. For employees with extensive travel, a "blanket" travel order containing an estimate of the anticipated travel cost for the reporting period may be used. With the blanket travel order, the employee is not required to complete individual orders for each trip. However, frequent reporting of travel expenses is often required.

▲ *Salaries*—As an expeditious practice, funds might be reserved for the personnel costs for employees on the payroll at the beginning of an accounting period; changes or additional commitments are supported by documents authorizing appointment, transfer, promotion, or other change in employees' status.

▲ *Other Reservations*—Other commitments (such as interagency transactions) must be reserved pursuant to specific agreements or legislation or regulation to ensure that funds are available for financing intragovernmental commitments.

ACCOUNTING PROCESS **Disbursement Entries**

Historically, the disbursement or payment of a debt was viewed as the culmination of an accounting transaction. Today with the emphasis on applied cost, the accounting for an event may extend beyond the disbursement phase particularly if the disbursement is for an asset or inventoriable item that will be amortized or consumed over future accounting periods. For many transactions though, particularly for all transactions for services or goods ordered, received, consumed, and paid for within a single fiscal period, the disbursement is the final event to be recognized in the accounting records.

Payment of Earlier Obligations

For many transactions, such as those related to contracts, grants, travel, and transportation, an obligation has been recorded earlier. The goods or services, in most instances, have been received. At the time of receipt, the items will be accounted for as assets (fixed or inventoriable) benefiting the current as well as future periods or as expenses of the current period.

The payment of such obligations is initiated by identifying the appropriate payee on Schedule and Voucher of Payments (SF 1166) that is transmitted to the Treasury and serves as the authorization for issuing checks. At the time of transmittal, the agency recognizes the disbursement by the following entry.

DEBIT: Accounts payable or expenses
CREDIT: Fund balance with the Treasury

This entry recognizes the payment of a liability or a current expense as appropriate. The fund balance, or cash account, of the agency is reduced for the amounts appearing on the SF 1166.

Payment of Advances

Under certain conditions, no obligations have been recorded nor have any services or goods been received. Such would be the case when the government made an advance of funds. Advances are made to many parties (employees, contractors, and grantees, for instance), pursuant to agency regulations and administrative procedures.

Such disbursements are treated not as expenditures or expenses, but rather as advances of funds for which a later accounting will be made when the advance is reduced or liquidated in total. The accounting for an advance would be

DEBIT: Advances (identified by the group of payees)
CREDIT: Fund balance with the Treasury

Advances may also be made by the federal government under a procedure known as a letter of credit. A letter of credit (discussed in more detail in the chapters on contracts and grants) is a commercial bank account opened for the recipient of federal funds. By presenting the proper documentation, the recipient may withdraw money from the commercial bank. The withdrawn amount may not exceed the amount obligated by the agency. In this instance, the accounting entry for the advance is slightly delayed because the withdrawal of the advance must be reported through the Federal Reserve System before the advancing agency is aware of the amount of the specific transactions. Advances by letters of credit are generally reduced or liquidated by contractors, grantees, or other recipients presenting the proper expenditure reporting to the agency advancing the funds.

Imprest Fund Payments

Minor disbursements may be made from imprest funds authorized and funded by the Treasury. Once approved, the Treasury advances funds to establish the imprest fund. The receipt of funds must be segregated from the agency's appropriated funds and a liability must be formally recognized for the amount of the imprest fund's corpus. This might be done by the following entry.

DEBIT: Imprest fund balance
CREDIT: Payable due to the Treasury—imprest advance

Cash is disbursed from the imprest fund and receipts and other supporting records are accumulated and properly coded for the posting to the agency's appropriation accounts. Periodically, the imprest fund is replenished when the fund custodian submits the disbursement records to the agency for payment. At that time the agency records the expenses paid by the fund and pays the fund for disbursements made on its behalf. It is important to remember that disbursements from an imprest fund will not have been previously obligated nor will the expenditures have been recorded. In the following entries, the obligation expenditure and disbursement of funds must be recorded against the correct appropriation:

The entry to record the obligation and expenditure for expenses paid from the imprest fund is

DEBIT: Unobligated allotments
     CREDIT: Expended appropriations—operating

A parallel entry is now required to reflect expenses and the replenishment payment of cash to the imprest fund. For example

DEBIT: Expenses
     CREDIT: Fund balance with the Treasury

The credit entry above will reduce the appropriated funds for the expenses paid by the imprest fund. The cash disbursement will be made to the order of the imprest fund thus returning the imprest funds corpus to the original amount advanced by the Treasury. Unless the imprest fund is increased, reduced, or eliminated, the entry establishing the fund will not be affected for the life of the fund.

Payees entitled to receive advances would be identified on the standard form 1166 that is transmitted to the Treasury in the same manner as for other disbursements. While other documentation might be used, agencies, for the most part, use SF 1166. On this form is recorded the following information.

▲   Name, location, and agency station number for the agency requesting that checks be issued

▲   Name, address, invoice, or other identifying number of the payee to whom the check should be addressed by the Treasury

▲   Amount of the check desired

▲   Certification by the appropriate agency official that the information contained on the form is correct and proper for payment from the designated appropriations

After payment is made, the Treasury disbursing officer records the check number for each disbursement made for the agency on SF 1166. Such information is then used for reporting and reconciliations required to be performed between the individual agencies and the Treasury.

Agencies must make a monthly reporting of receipts and disbursements to the Treasury. The reporting is made on the statement of transactions (SF 224) that displays cash receipts and disbursements for the month by each appropriation for which the agency is responsible.

Payments by Letters of Credit

As mentioned earlier, considerable sums of money are disbursed to nonfederal organizations by the federal government through various letters of credit methods. Under a letter of credit the recipient of a government contract or grant may be authorized by the federal agency to withdraw cash against a limitation set forth in the letter of credit. The letter of credit may either be with a Federal Reserve Bank or a Treasury Disbursing Center. The various letters of credit methods may be differentiated by the following characteristics.

▲ *A Regional Disbursing Office Letter of Credit* is used when permission has been obtained from a Commissioner of the Treasury and the total annual cash advances to the recipient organization exceeds $120,000. Under this method, the recipient organization may request letter of credit payments each time it makes a disbursement, but not more than once a day nor, in most cases, for amounts of less than $5,000 or more than $5,000,000. As illustrated in Exhibit 12.3, the process is relatively streamlined. Organizations authorizd to draw down funds can obtain needed cash expeditiously, but at the same time the Treasury is conserving funds and saving interest costs by eliminating the need for the recipients to have to maintain large balances of federal cash. This method allows recipients to request payment by check directly from the Treasury disbursing centers.

▲ *A Federal Reserve Board Letter of Credit* is used under conditions similar to the RDO letter of credit and has the same dollar limitations on annual cash advances and withdrawals. As illustrated in Exhibit 12.4, the FRB process varies from the RDO process outlined above. Federal agencies must provide for FRB payments in agreements with the nonfederal recipients. Such payments would be withdrawals from the federal Treasury, but the payment is through a Federal Reserve bank or branch.

▲ *A Treasury Financial Communications System Letter of Credit* is a more recent method for processing letters of credit payments. As in the earlier methods, the agreements with the nonfederal organizations must provide for payment under this method. As shown in Exhibit 12.5, recipients authorized to use this method may request payment by electronic funds transfer directly from the recipients' commercial bank. While recipients may request letter of credit payment each time they make a disbursement, not more than one request a day is to be made.

When a federal agency receives evidence of withdrawals under a letter of credit, an accounts receivable must be established and an entry made to record the disbursement of cash. That entry might be similar to the following.

DEBIT: Advances to grantees—letter of credit drawdown
　　CREDIT: Fund balance with the Treasury

Exhibit 12.3 **LETTER OF CREDIT—REGIONAL DISBURSING OFFICE SYSTEM**

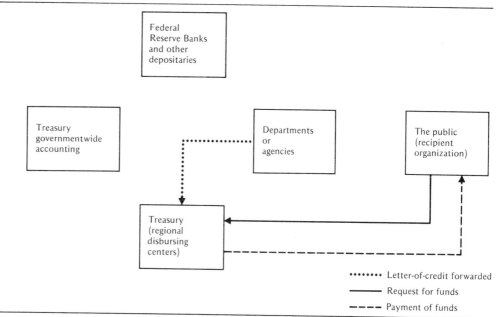

Source: *Federal Financial Transactions*, United States Treasury, Washington, D. C., June 1980, p. 33.

Exhibit 12.4 **LETTER OF CREDIT—FEDERAL RESERVE BANK SYSTEM**

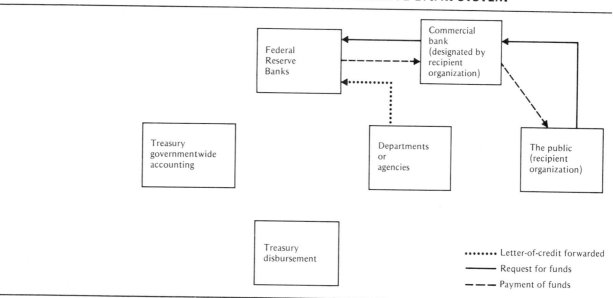

Source: *Federal Financial Transactions*, United States Treasury, Washington, D.C., June 1980, p. 35.

Exhibit 12.5 **LETTER OF CREDIT—TREASURY FINANCIAL COMMUNICATIONS SYSTEM**

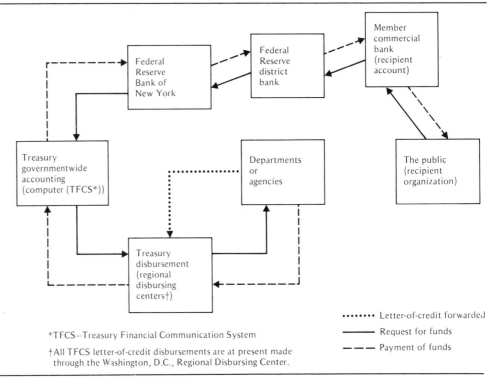

*TFCS—Treasury Financial Communication System

†All TFCS letter-of-credit disbursements are at present made through the Washington, D.C., Regional Disbursing Center.

········ Letter-of-credit forwarded

———— Request for funds

– – – – Payment of funds

Source: *Federal Financial Transactions*, United States Treasury, Washington, D.C., June 1980, p. 37.

As in the case of other advances, generally no budgetary accounts have been affected because no further agency funds have been committed or obligated. Under the letter of credit, funds have merely been advanced to a nonfederal organization. The federal organization could, in many circumstances, demand full refund prior to the time services have been rendered.

The advances under letters of credit will be reduced as reports are received from federal recipients detailing the extent of expenditures made under the contract, grant, or other agreement. At that time, entries, similar to the following, are required to eliminate the advance and record the expenditure or cost incurred.

    DEBIT: Expense accounts—by program
        CREDIT: Accounts payable—grantee (if a net amount is due)
                     Advances to grantees—letter of credit drawdown

Additionally, the following entry is required to maintain the appropriate balances in the budgetary accounts.

DEBIT: Unliquidated obligations
    CREDIT: Accrued expenditures—operating

The preceding entry would reduce the amount of the earlier obligation related to the grant and record the accrued expenditures under the grant program.

As mentioned earlier, GAO has stated that where no performance is required or when payments are scheduled to correspond approximately with performance, cash payments shall be concurrently accounted for by (1) liquidating the earlier obligation and (2) recording the payment as a cost chargeable to the appropriate program. Under such conditions, the receivable for advances due to the federal agency would not be recorded.

PART IV

ACCOUNTING FOR FEDERAL EXPENDITURES AND RECEIPTS

chapter 13 Pay, Leave, and Allowances

INTRODUCTION
In many agencies, expenditures for payroll or personal services, leave, allowances, and related benefits are the most significant cost. Considerable concern and interest is devoted to the accounting and payment of personal services in the government. In many instances, the total staffing, levels of compensation, amounts for meritorious performance and promotions, benefits, annual and sick leave, and retirement payments are predetermined by law or the administrative regulations of other government agencies. The role delegated to the operating agencies is one of effective management and administration of the cost of personnel within these myriad requirements.

DEFINITIONS
Payroll and related expenditures of a government agency include several specific elements, each of which has been defined in greater detail in Chapter 10, Allotment and Obligation of Funds. In that chapter, the object classifications established by the Office of Management and Budget are defined. Pay, leave, and allowances are included in object classification 10,

"Personal Services and Benefits," comprising Personal Compensation (subcategory 11) and Personnel Benefits (subcategory 12).

Personnel Compensation

Personnel compensation represents the gross compensation due to employees for personal services including

- ▲ Total salary
- ▲ Employee's share of retirement
- ▲ Employee's share of insurance contribution
- ▲ Income taxes

Expenditures for personnel compensation must be accounted separately for permanent positions, positions other than permanent, other compensation (such as overtime and night work), military personnel, and special personnel services payments (such as retirement and disability fund payments for reemployed annuitants, and annual leave).

Personnel Benefits

Personnel benefits are amounts to be paid for authorized benefits to currently employed civilian and military personnel. Examples of such benefits would include living quarters, uniform allowances, incentive awards, expenses in connection with relocation, and payments to funds for life insurance, health insurance, and retirement. A subcategory within personnel benefits is "Benefits to Former Personnel" that represents payments for pensions, annuities, and other benefits to former employees. Normally, this element applies only to the Office of Personnel Management (OPM).

The definitions above are applied governmentwide and appear as a part of the OMB Circular A-12, entitled *Object Classification.* As mentioned in Chapter 10, the prescribed object classifications have been incorporated into agency account structures and serve as the subsidiary obligation and expenditure accounts.

RESPONSIBILITIES OF VARIOUS ORGANIZATIONS The Congress and several agencies as well have issued criteria that govern the number of employees and other types of personnel that an agency may employ and the nature of the benefits that such personnel should receive.

An operating agency must ensure that its payroll system complies with these requirements. Some of the general responsibilities of these other agencies are outlined in following paragraphs.

Congressional Responsibilities

The Congress, in both the authorization as well as in the appropriation legislative process, may and has established personnel ceilings for individual agencies and governmentwide. Additionally, levels of compensation for civilian and military personnel, benefits, leave payments, and other related remunerations are set forth in law by the Congress.

Office of Personnel Management

By the Reorganization Plan No. 2 of 1978, the Office of Personnel Management was created to provide guidance on personnel matters to federal agencies. Additionally, the OPM has the responsibility to conduct evaluations and audits to ensure compliance with laws and its rules, regulations, and instructions.

The basic guide, published by OPM and its predecessor, the Civil Service Commission, is the *Federal Personnel Manual* that includes policies, principles, standards, and criteria for implementing various laws and executive orders and other rules and regulations relating to the management of federal personnel. Additionally, OPM is responsible for administering four federal personnel programs (1) retirement, (2) life insurance, (3) health benefits, and (4) a grants program to strengthen personnel resources of state and local governments. Under these programs, OPM has varied and broad responsibilities such as control and overseeing of recruiting, examining of personnel for competitive civil service positions, developing and maintaining qualification and job-rating standards, managing the Senior Executive Service (for managers at the General Service Grade 16 through Level IV positions in the executive branch of government).

Office of Management and Budget

By specific legislation and the exercise of its responsibilities as the budget agency and advisor to the President, the OMB monitors the direct and indirect cost of personnel, and thus the pay, leave, and allowances of agencies. OMB, and its predecessor, the Bureau of the Budget, has the continuing authority and responsibility to correlate, revise, reduce, or increase agency requests for appropriations. Additionally, OMB must monitor the level of expenditures being incurred by the government under existing appropriations to permit required reports to be made to the Congress. Several forms, comprising an agency's budget submission, require the detailing of past, present, and forecasted levels of expenditures for personnel and related costs. Agency employee ceilings, average number of personnel employed during the year, and the end-of-year number of employees are known by OMB for all agencies of the government.

From time to time, to achieve specific purposes, meet policy requirements, and, in particular, to comply with the law, OMB will provide specific guidance to individual or all agencies concerning levels of personnel and rates of expenditures.

General Accounting Office

By the Budget and Accounting Procedures Act of 1950 and other legislation, the General Accounting Office is required to prescribe principles, standards, and related requirements for accounting to be observed by each federal agency, including the accounting for payrolls and related leave and allowances. The standards, control requirements, forms, responsibility, and other requirements relating to civilian and military pay and allowances are set forth by the GAO in its *Manual for Guidance of Federal Agencies*, Title 6, "Payroll, Leave, and Allowances." Additionally, because of the technical complexity of administering a governmentwide payroll system, GAO has also published a *Civilian Pay Manual* containing information of various statutes, regulations, and decisions by the Comptroller General of the United States relating to the payment of compensation and allowances, and matters such as promotions, demotions, separations, employee rights, conflicts, and other subjects related to the expenditures of appropriated money for matters of a personnel type.

Operating Agency Responsibility

By the Budget and Accounting Procedures Act of 1950, the head of each executive agency is responsible for establishing and maintaining an adequate payroll system covering pay, leave, and allowances as part of the required accounting and controls system. This system must meet the principles and standards published by the GAO.

226

CONTROL PROCEDURES An agency's payroll system should be an integral part of its overall accounting system, containing both detailed and summary ledger accounts, supported by cost accounting or labor distribution procedures designed to provide payroll cost data by program, organization, function, activity, and other categories to permit a full accounting of these personnel expenditures. As a part of the system, the GAO requires that several control procedures be in existence.

▲ Suitable control records, detailed payroll forms and source documentation must be maintained and controlled to provide evidence of approval and accuracy of computed payrolls.

▲ Procedures to control the accurate processing of the payroll must be incorporated into the accounting system, ensuring that all data are considered in processing and that no unauthorized alterations are made to transactions or records during processing.

▲ Payroll vouchers, representing the authority for coding and paying a payroll, must be certified prior to payment by a certifying officer who must examine the basic facts underlying the payroll voucher, considering the internal controls to assure the correctness and validity of the payments made.

▲ All departments and agencies are directed to make payroll disbursements by check unless there are compelling reasons for cash payments.

▲ For cost effectiveness purposes, regular employees of the government shall not be paid more often than every two weeks, unless permitted or required by law.

▲ To permit the accurate preparation of a payroll, a sufficient lag must exist between the end of the pay period and the actual payment of the payroll, but the lag may not exceed 12 days.

In addition to prescribing accounting principles and the control features above, the GAO has also published a guide, *Review Guide for Federal Agency Payroll System Designs*, for use by federal agencies in developing payroll systems and documentation to support the payroll process. GAO uses this same guide in considering and reviewing designs of payroll systems submitted to GAO for approval.

OMB OBLIGATION, ACCRUAL, AND COSTING CRITERIA The General Accounting Office has prescribed the accounting principles for payroll. However, the Office of Management and Budget in its Circular A-34 has prescribed the criteria for recognizing obligations, accrued expenditures, and applied cost concepts for reporting transactions relating to personal services and benefits. Except when precluded by law, agencies are required to report obligations and applied costs in accordance with these concepts, which are set forth in OMB Circular A-34.

▲ Uniform allowances and incentive awards—when payable to the employee

▲ Severance pay—an obligation of the pay period when disbursed on a pay period basis

▲ Authorized reimbursable expenses—an obligation when orders are issued to the employee

▲ Annual leave—an obligation when due and payable as terminal leave, except when (1) for funded annual leave for revolving funds and (2) for other cases authorized by law. In the case of revolving funds, funded annual leave is reported as obligations when earned.

Accrued Expenditures

Generally, the reporting of accrued expenditures for personal services and benefits is consistent with the criteria established for obligating similar type transactions. The exception is that authorized reimbursement for real estate, temporary subsistence, and other dislocation expenses are reported as accrued expenditures on the basis of amounts earned by and payable to the employee rather than when the travel or other orders are issued.

Applied Costs

The reporting of applied costs related to personal services and benefits is similar to accrued expenditures, with the following exceptions.

▲ When the data are provided in the accounting system (1) accrued leave will be included as an applied cost when earned, rather than when taken, even though unfunded, and (2) the pro rata share of other leave (sick, administrative) anticipated to be taken and employee benefits that accrue in periods when leave is taken will be included as applied costs.

▲ The estimated amount of severance pay is reported as applied costs when an employee is separated under circumstances making him or her eligible for such pay.

ACCOUNTING FOR PAY, LEAVE, AND ALLOWANCES

Overview of Payroll Process

Within established agencies, accounting and processing a payroll are systematized and done either on the positive or the exception basis. Unless an exception is made known, by a notation on or by processing an appropriate form, an employee will be paid for the full regular work period.

Exhibit 13.1 OVERVIEW OF PAYROLL PROCESS

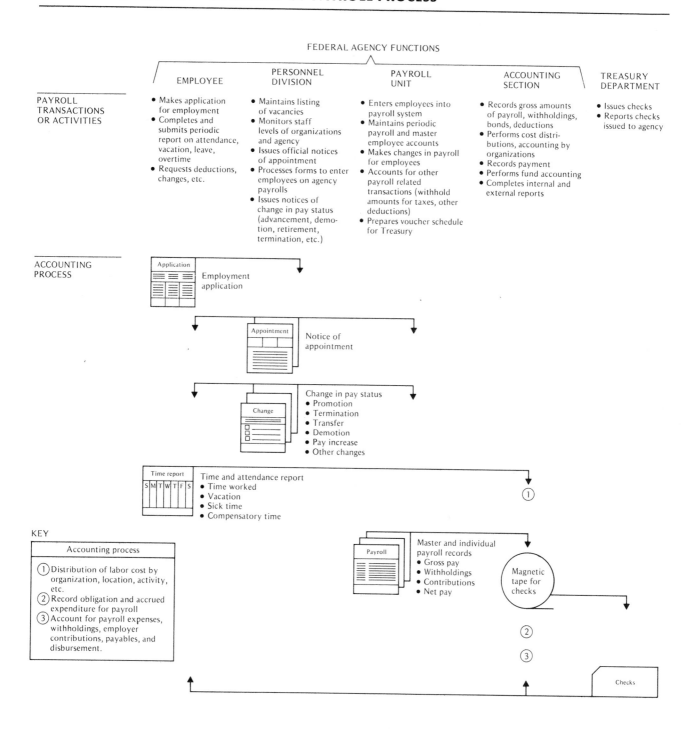

FEDERAL AGENCY FUNCTIONS

	EMPLOYEE	PERSONNEL DIVISION	PAYROLL UNIT	ACCOUNTING SECTION	TREASURY DEPARTMENT
PAYROLL TRANSACTIONS OR ACTIVITIES	• Makes application for employment • Completes and submits periodic report on attendance, vacation, leave, overtime • Requests deductions, changes, etc.	• Maintains listing of vacancies • Monitors staff levels of organizations and agency • Issues official notices of appointment • Processes forms to enter employees on agency payrolls • Issues notices of change in pay status (advancement, demotion, retirement, termination, etc.)	• Enters employees into payroll system • Maintains periodic payroll and master employee accounts • Makes changes in payroll for employees • Accounts for other payroll related transactions (withhold amounts for taxes, other deductions) • Prepares voucher schedule for Treasury	• Records gross amounts of payroll, withholdings, bonds, deductions • Performs cost distributions, accounting by organizations • Records payment • Performs fund accounting • Completes internal and external reports	• Issues checks • Reports checks issued to agency

ACCOUNTING PROCESS

Application — Employment application

Appointment — Notice of appointment

Change — Change in pay status
• Promotion
• Termination
• Transfer
• Demotion
• Pay increase
• Other changes

Time report — S M T W T F S — Time and attendance report
• Time worked
• Vacation
• Sick time
• Compensatory time

①

Payroll — Master and individual payroll records
• Gross pay
• Withholdings
• Contributions
• Net pay

Magnetic tape for checks

②

③

Checks

KEY

Accounting process

① Distribution of labor cost by organization, location, activity, etc.
② Record obligation and accrued expenditure for payroll
③ Account for payroll expenses, withholdings, employer contributions, payables, and disbursement.

Source: Adapted from Cornelius E. Tierney, 1979, *Government Auditing*, Chicago: Commerce Clearing House, p. 284.

The exception documentation often requires a special payroll, or at least a special processing procedure. Although agencies may have unique processing steps and controls to ensure compliance with specific conditions or operations, Exhibit 13.1 illustrates, in general, the basic forms and payroll process.

The employment application is carefully examined by the agency to assess the prospective employee's qualifications. If found acceptable and the appropriate vacancy exists in the agency's staffing table, a notice of appointment is prepared and approved by responsible agency officials, placing the person on the payroll. Periodically, (usually every two weeks), the employee or the supervisor must submit an attendance report showing an accounting for the employee's time. Presuming that an employee worked the full pay period or, if absent, had sufficient vacation or sick leave or was on other authorized leave that still qualified the employee for the full pay, the payroll is prepared for the agency. Incorporated into the payroll must be all changes authorized by the employee, required by law, or to meet other circumstances. These changes could affect the "normal" pay that would have been disbursed to the employee. Individual and master payroll earnings records are maintained by each agency displaying the "gross to net" pay history of employees. Upon the receipt of a properly certified payroll voucher from an agency, the Treasury issues a payroll check on behalf of the individual employee.

Payroll Forms and Records

The forms and records related to processing a payment for pay, leave, and allowances are controlled by several organizations in an agency. These actions must be closely coordinated or either the individual employee or the agency could suffer from an improper disbursement. Generally, the forms may be grouped as (1) personnel forms, (2) payroll forms, and (3) accounting records.

Personnel Forms

Personnel functions of agencies are responsible for compliance with the general requirements of the *Federal Personnel Manual* and adherence to any other requirements applicable to the appointments or employees of the agency. The personnel function utilizes a set of forms to document and monitor the appointment, promotion, demotion, and transfer or termination of personnel. In every instance in which such a change will affect the compensation level of an employee, the personnel function is responsible for making the change known to the payroll function. To be accepted for a change in the payroll, each personnel form must provide for full identification of the employee, the reason or basis for the change in compensation, and the amount of the change or the new salary authorized.

In some instances, the personnel function will initiate the pay status change, as for example when an employee is due a pay increase for satisfactory performance over a given time period. Alternatively, the employee by completing and processing a change to a health benefit plan, a savings bond deduction, or a desired withholding could affect the amount of net pay due each pay period. In either event, the change form must be examined and signed by the authorized agency executive to be accepted as a valid request for change in pay status.

Payroll Forms

The payroll forms are required to support the processing of a payroll entry and ultimately the issuance of a check on behalf of an employee. Payroll forms are several in number. While all are similar, variations occur among agencies. The more common forms include

▲ *Time Distribution Sheets*—These are records of work performed by or for organizations, activities, units, or jobs that for the most part are maintained by the individual employee. These sheets show productive time, overhead or unassigned time, status of various types of leave, and personal identification data (such as employee name, number, and organization), plus the beginning and ending dates of the pay period. When time distribution sheets are required, these forms may also serve as the Time and Attendance report. Also, if a time and distribution sheet is required, the supervisor might summarize the total hourly data on a composite T&A for the group.

▲ *Time and Attendance Reports*—These reports are summary records of attendance and any approved absences and overtime worked. They are prepared by an authorized person who is knowledgeable about the presence of the employee.

▲ *Individual and Master Payroll Records*—These payroll records provide a full accounting of gross wages-to-net wages paid to individuals and in total for all employees on the payroll for both the current pay period and cumulative totals for the current fiscal year. The records show the total authorized compensation, mandatory deductions (such as taxes, and retirement), voluntary deductions and allotments, and the net amount paid or to be paid an employee.

▲ *Summary Payroll Vouchers*—Summary forms showing the total amount of the payroll, supported by details identifying the individual employee and amount due that comprise the total. They exist in either hardcopy records or magnetic tape or other form of telecommunication forwarded to the Treasury to permit the printing of checks on behalf of the employees. This record documents the amounts entered into the general and other summary accounts of the agency for payroll and related disbursements.

Accounting Forms

The accounting forms vary among agencies, being designed to address governmentwide and unique accounting requirements applicable to a particular agency. However, while the format and title vary, the purpose of the documentation is rather uniform. Examples of records related to accounting for pay, leave, and allowances include

▲ *Payroll Distribution Journal or Run.* This form is a record summarizing the payroll charges by the identifying organizations, activities, units or jobs cited on the time distribution sheets. The journal, when summarized, shows the total resources consumed by the benefiting entity or job for the pay period. The summary data in the journal will also form the basis for settling amounts for labor due under revolving fund or reimbursable agreements.

▲ *Accruals, Adjusting, and Closing Entries.* Standard or predetermined journal entries often exist to permit the accurate reflection of other costs, in addition to the cash disbursements, in the accounting records for the fiscal period. Typically, the general and subsidiary ledger accounts are debited or credited for end-of-period accrual, adjusting, and closing entries. In the case of computer systems, the entries are preprogrammed and require only the calculation and insertion of a dollar value for the entry to be made.

▲ *Payments to Others.* Various standard and special forms exist that must be completed by an agency when making payments to other organizations for amounts withheld from employees salaries. Withholdings are held in trust by agencies and deposited periodically with the Treasury or the Office of Personnel and Management for taxes, bonds, and retirement payments.

▲ *Subsidiary Accounts.* As part of its responsibility to maintain an adequate system of accounting and control, an agency must design and utilize an integrated account structure that will permit the accounting for its resources consumed, and cost of performance, including the cost of pay, leave, and allowances by appropriation, organizational segments, budget activities, program structures and, preferably, operating units or cost centers.

▲ *General Ledger Accounts.* Each agency is required to design that structure of general ledger accounts that best permits it to control and account adequately for all resources for which it has stewardship responsibility. The structure must include appropriate general ledger payroll accounts.

Accounting Transactions

Recording Payroll Costs

Because the elapsed time between the calculation of the obligation for compensation and the payment of this obligation is generally minimal, the practice has been to generally process the accounting entry for both the obligation and the liability for compensation simultaneously.

DEBIT: Unobligated allotments
    CREDIT: Expended appropriation—operating

The dollar amount of this entry would be equal to the total or gross compensation due to employees for the pay period. The gross amount of the payroll should be recorded, including any amounts that must be withheld for taxes, retirement, or special deductions authorized by the employee.

The following entry must also be made in parallel with the preceding entry in order to record payroll and related costs in the proprietary accounts:

DEBIT: Payroll costs or expenses
    CREDIT: Salaries payable
            Payable to other agencies:
                Withheld — FICA
                Withheld — Retirement
                Withheld — Bonds
                Withheld — Insurance

In practice, agencies with cost accounting procedures would distribute the total payroll costs to various subsidiary accounts, structured by organization, activity, function, or cost centers, to provide a reporting of the resources consumed by each operation in the accounting period. Amounts withheld by law or on behalf of employees represent money to be held in trust by the employing agency to be paid to another government agency or other organization at a specific time. In some instances, the agency is required to match the withheld amounts and provide a payment, combining the amount withheld from the employee and the employer's contribution to a designated agency.

Recording Personnel Benefits

Like the payroll costs, related personnel benefits are recorded for the period incurred. The obligation or restriction of the unexpended appropriation must be recorded as well as the cost to the agency of the personnel benefits.

Again, there must also be a parallel entry to record the costs in the proprietary accounts.

DEBIT: Personnel benefits
    CREDIT: Payable to other agencies

Employer's share—FICA
Employer's share—Retirement
Employer's share—Insurance

The agency's cost of personnel benefits must be distributed by subsidiary accounting to the various organizations, activities, functions and cost centers to provide a full accounting of resources consumed by each operation in the accounting period.

Payment of Compensation and Benefits

Separate entries are processed to record the payment of compensation due employees and to record any payments made to designated depositaries by the agency. The entries to record payments resulting from the above transactions include

DEBIT: Salaries payable
     CREDIT: Fund balance with the Treasury

The entry above is necessary to record payment of personnel compensation due employees and reduce the available cash or fund balance with the Treasury.

In a similar manner, the following entry is necessary to record payment to the Internal Revenue Service for amounts withheld and agency matching share and reduce available fund balance with the Treasury.

DEBIT: Payable to other agencies:
          Withheld—FICA
          Employer's share—FICA
     CREDIT: Fund balance with the Treasury

Other withheld amounts and employer matching contributions must be recorded. The following type entry is needed to record payment to Office of Personnel Management, the designated depositary, of amounts withheld and agency matching share and reduce available fund balance with the Treasury.

DEBIT: Payable to other agencies:
          Withheld—Retirement
          Employer's share—Retirement

Withheld—Insurance

Employer's share—Insurance

CREDIT: Fund balance with the Treasury

Accrual, Adjusting, and Closing Entries

Adjusting entries, often related to correcting earlier erroneous entries, may be made to accounts at any time during the period. Such entries generally relate to adjusting of incorrect amounts or redistribution to other, more appropriate, accounts.

Accrual and closing entries are typically processed at the end of a reporting period and the end of a fiscal year. Accrual entries are necessary to provide for a full accounting of the resources consumed in the period. For example, in the case of personnel costs, the government's practice is to pay every two weeks. This payment cycle will not always coincide with the end of a month or the fiscal year. If payment is made with two workdays remaining in the period, an accrual for this additional personnel cost, not yet paid, must be recorded to provide the full cost of operations for the period.

An accrual entry may be processed as of the last day of a reporting period, for example, a month within the fiscal year. The accrual entry could remain on the books and be treated as part of the payment entry for the next payroll. An alternative is to reverse the accrual entry at the beginning of the next month; thereby returning the cost and expense accounts to the equivalent of the cash basis. The reversal permits the full recognition of the total payroll at the next pay period.

At the end of the fiscal year, an agency is required to account for the accrual to provide a proper accounting cutoff, close the cost accounts and recognize the unliquidated obligation that must be met in the following fiscal year. At year end, the entries would be as follows.

DEBIT: Unobligated allotments

CREDIT: Expended appropriation—operating

This entry records the obligation related to accrued but unpaid salaries and wages and related personnel benefits at the end of the fiscal year.

The following companion entry is necessary to record the related accrued but unpaid cost related to personnel compensation and agency's share of personnel benefits.

Exhibit 13.2 ACCOUNTING TRANSACTIONS: PAY, LEAVE, AND ALLOWANCES

BUDGETARY ENTRIES	DR	CR	PROPRIETARY ENTRIES	DR	CR
Record Payroll					
Unobligated allotments	x		Payroll costs or expenses	x	
Expended appropriation—			Salaries payable—employees		x
operating		x	Payables to others		x
Recording Benefits					
Unobligated allotments	x		Personnel benefits	x	
Expended appropriation—			Payables to others		x
operating		x			
Payment of Compensation and Benefits					
None			Salaries payable	x	
			Payables to others	x	
			Fund balance with the Treasury		x
Accrual Entries					
Unobligated allotments	x		Payroll costs or expenses	x	
			Personnel benefits	x	
Expended appropriation—			Accrued salaries payable		x
operating		x	Payables to others		x
Closing Entries					
Expended appropriation—			Invested capital	x	
operating	x		Payroll costs or expenses		x
Invested capital		x	Personnel benefits		x
Reversal Entries					
Expended appropriation—			Accrued salaries payable	x	
operating	x		Payables to others	x	
Unobligated allotments		x	Payroll costs or expenses		x
			Personnel benefits		x

Legend: DR = Debit entry
CR = Credit entry

DEBIT: Payroll costs or expenses
Personnel benefits
CREDIT: Accrued salaries and wages
Accrued benefits

To close cost or expense accounts of a fiscal year to the invested capital account, the following entry is needed.

DEBIT: Invested capital

Accrued expenditures—operating

CREDIT: Payroll costs or expenses

Invested capital

Note that a reversal entry is made but, at year end, the cost or expenses are closed to the invested capital account (an account including the year-end balances transferred from general and special fund accounts for receipts, expenditures, income, costs, or expenses).

Accrued Annual Leave

Most government agencies do not include an amount for annual leave as part of the end-of-period accrued expenditure even though it is a cost of the current accounting period. For nearly all appropriations, accrued annual leave is an unfunded liability until taken or paid, for example, when an employee terminates services. The exception is when accounting for a cost-reimbursable activity. In this instance, the servicing agency must recover full cost of the period from all benefiting organizations. Under these conditions (revolving funds, stock funds, reimbursable services) accrued annual leave is accounted for as a funded liability and reported as part of the end-of-period accrued expenditure and expense balance.

The several accounting entries discussed in the preceding sections have been highlighted in Exhibit 13.2.

chapter 14 Travel and Transportation

INTRODUCTION

Travel and transportation costs are closely monitored by all federal agencies for several reasons. There is continual concern that such costs represent the opportunity for personal abuse. Probably more important, though, is the fact that such funds represent one of very few sources of discretionary funds available to most agencies. As was noted in the earlier chapter many external criteria and limitations are imposed on an agency with respect to personnel. Thus agencies are more administrators than managers of personnel compensation funds. Travel and transportation funds are not as closely controlled. The rate and purpose of expenditure of funds budgeted for travel and transportation are generally within the discretion of agency management.

DEFINITIONS

Travel and transportation expenditures include costs of lodging, meals, and movement required to perform the business of government. Prior to May 1973 (Executive Order No. 11717), the Office of Management and Budget had the responsibility for prescribing uniform, governmentwide regulations for travel and transportation. These regulations were set forth in the OMB

Circular A-7, Standardized Government Travel Regulations (SGTR). After that date, the General Services Administration assumed these responsibilities. OMB Circular A-7 was rescinded (August 31, 1973) and replaced by the GSA's Federal Personnel Management Regulations 101-7. Generally, though, the definitions of the travel and transportation expenditures have remained constant.

Travel and Transportation of Persons

Expenditures related to *travel and transportation of persons* include

▲ *Transportation* of government employees and others;

▲ Their related *per diem allowances* (i.e., lodging costs and meal allowances), and

▲ Other *incidental expenses* incurred either away from their duty station or for local travel; also

▲ *Contractual services for carrying persons* from place to place (on land, sea, or in the air), and

▲ *Costs for commercial or private carriers, vehicles,* or *conveyances.*

Agencies may establish their own policies and procedures governing the allowances for the expenditures above and the nature of approvals and authorizations that are required to incur such costs. However, no agency may exceed the rates or allowances set forth in SGTR.

Transportation of Things

Transportation of things has been defined in applicable regulations as including contractual costs for transporting employees' household effects, freight, and mail. OMB Circular A-12 includes within this object classification.

> . . . contractual charges for transportation and care of things while in transport, including postage, rental of trucks, reimbursements to employees for movement of household goods or house trailers and freight and express payments to common carriers and contract carriers.

RESPONSIBILITIES OF VARIOUS ORGANIZATIONS

Congress

Congress has generally recognized the need to place responsibility for control of travel and transportation expenditures in agency management, with the requirement that there be conformance with governmentwide guidelines as set forth by OMB or GSA.

239

Office of Management and Budget

Historically, OMB was responsible for prescribing uniform, government-wide guidelines related to travel and transportation expenditures. These guidelines provided for maximum per diem rates to reimburse employees in travel status for costs incurred for lodging and meals while away from their official duty station. Rates were also established to pay for or reimburse employees for transportation costs incurred on behalf of the government.

At present, OMB is concerned with the budgeted levels of such expenditures and the rate at which such expenditures are being incurred by an agency during budget execution phases.

General Services Administration

At this time, the GSA is responsible for prescribing the governmentwide regulations and allowances for travel and transportation. In recent years, inflation and the significantly disparate costs of lodging and meals between urban and suburban and rural locations has complicated this responsibility. For the most part, uniform daily dollar allowances do not exist. Allowances for lodging and subsistence have been established for many individual cities in the country, significantly complicating the accounting for these types of expenditures.

Agencies may have administrative regulations defining alternative allowances, but in no event may such administrative determinations exceed those established by GSA.

Additionally, GSA is responsible for the development and execution of federal government's program concerned with transportation and traffic management and auditing all government transportation bills and processing of transportation claims by and against the government.

Operating Agency Responsibility

Inherent in the responsibility placed with the head of each agency by the Budget and Accounting Procedures Act of 1950 to establish and maintain an adequate system of accounting and internal controls, is the responsibility to establish appropriate controls over travel and transportation expenditures. Such controls must provide for advance authorization by proper officials and, often, include a procedure for prepayment audit of employee travel vouchers and claims. The agency procedures must conform to the standards and principles established by the GAO for accounting for expenditures and costs.

Travel and Transportation Expenditures

Travel and transportation expenditures are closely monitored by most government agencies. The controls often require conformance to pretravel and posttravel procedures in order for employees to be expeditiously reimbursed or paid for these costs. These procedures often include

▲ The submission of a request to travel for approval in advance of commencing travel, identifying the duration of travel, itinerary, lodging and subsistence costs, and other related expenses and transportation costs;

▲ The maintenance of a register to ensure the availability of unobligated appropriations equal to the estimated cost of the travel or transportation;

▲ The close control and continuous monitoring of requests for payment of and settlement of advances mode to travelers;

▲ Formal certification as to the availability of funds prior to the commencement of travel;

▲ A detailed accounting by the traveler of all expenses of travel and transportation within a timely period after incurring these costs, requiring review and approval by an authorized and knowledgeable person;

▲ Prepayment audit of the submitted travel voucher or other expense form claiming payment, settlement or an outstanding advance, or reimbursement for the costs incurred; and

▲ The use of prenumbered, controlled forms relating to the authorization, any advances, and expense vouchers.

Use of Transportation Requests

To minimize cash transactions and provide increased control over payments for transportation services, the government requires employees to use *transportation request* forms in place of cash. Because transportation request forms are highly negotiable, agencies closely monitor their use and have established systems of personal accountability for these forms. These forms are accepted in much the same manner as a check by public or common carriers in payment for transportation services. The carriers must later claim reimbursement for all honored transportation requests from the agency.

Government Bills of Lading

With respect to the transportation of things, standard forms must be submitted by common carriers to receive payment. Bills of lading must be properly completed, receiving reports must exist, and appropriate officials must signify receipt of the services or goods. Detailed prepayment audits are made of claims. Bills of lading are serially numbered and controlled with fixed accountability because the forms are negotiable when completed. Standard forms exist for billing freight and express transportation charges to government agencies.

ACCOUNTING FOR TRAVEL AND TRANSPORTATION

The authorizing, accounting, and payment of travel costs are tedious processes in many agencies, involving many internal checks and controls.

Invariably, travelers must have travel approved in advance. They must also obtain formal certification of fund availability, and submit precise itineraries should they require an advance of money to perform the travel. Designated officials must approve the initial travel request, the request for travel advance, and review and approve the subsequent voucher claiming cost of travel. Formal reservations of funds before performing the travel is required; advances of funds must be recorded; and contemplated itineraries are preaudited for reasonableness of estimated costs, followed by a posttravel audit of costs claimed.

Exhibit 14.1 illustrates, in summary, the nature of the forms and the process that an agency might require to ensure that travel funds are properly expended, documented, and recorded.

Travel and Transportation Forms—Persons

Travel Request and Authorization

Each agency has its version of a travel request and authorization form that must be completed by the employee in advance of travel. The form provides for

▲ Full identification of the employee including organization, position, official duty station, and phone number;

▲ Description of the itinerary including origination and destination, intermediate stopovers, beginning and end date of travel, and the purpose of the travel;

▲ Estimated cost of the travel including the per diem rate for lodging and subsistence, local travel cost, and common carrier transportation costs;

Exhibit 14.1 OVERVIEW OF TRAVEL AND TRANSPORTATION PROCESS

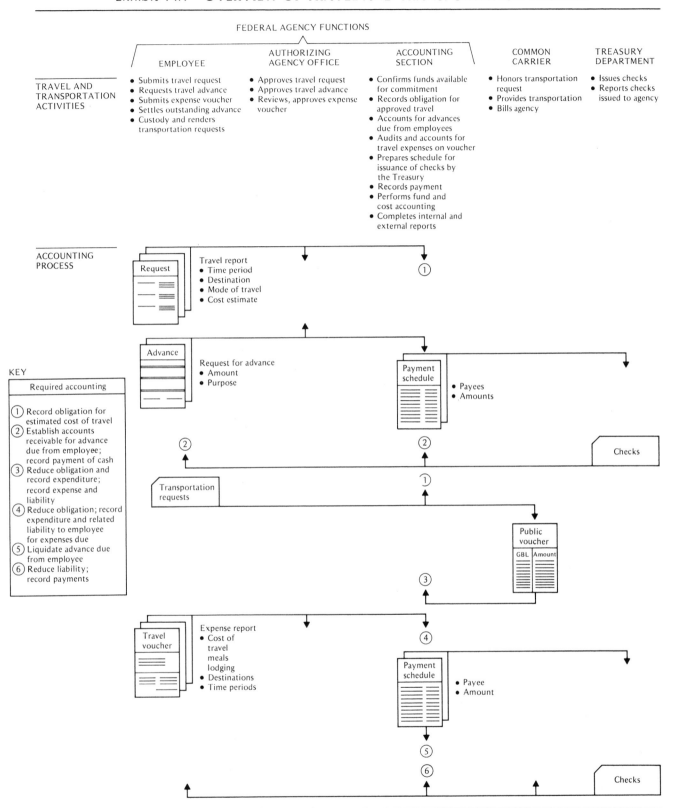

Source: Adapted from Cornelius E. Tierney, 1979, *Governmental Auditing*, Chicago: Commerce Clearing House, p. 288.

- ▲ Mode of travel, e.g., common carrier, air or other, private vehicle, rented vehicles, and government-owned vehicles;
- ▲ Approval and certification to fund availability (typically the form requires signatures from an approving officer and authorizing official, plus fiscal personnel who identify accounting and appropriation accounts to be charged and certify to the availability of unobligated funds to meet the anticipated travel cost).

The request and authorization form constitutes the documentation to support the formal obligation of appropriated fund. In some instances, the same form will provide for approval of a cash advance and the use of government transportation requests to pay for common carrier costs.

Request for Travel Advance

The receipt of a travel advance often requires the traveler to complete and obtain approval on a separate form, which becomes the supporting documentation maintained by fiscal personnel responsible for monitoring accounts receivable or advances in possession of officials and employees. Once funds are advanced, the employee must make a cash refund or payment or submit a travel expense voucher claiming an amount equal to or in excess of the advance in order to liquidate or eliminate the advance.

Travel Voucher

A travel voucher is submitted by the traveler upon the completion of the itinerary. (For most government agencies, use is made of SF 1012, entitled simply Travel Voucher.) On the form the traveler must enter

- ▲ Identifying information, similar to the employee information entered on the request and authorization form;
- ▲ References to the original request and authorization;
- ▲ Specific identification of all transportation requests used;
- ▲ Actual itinerary (including origination and destination and intermediate stopovers, beginning and end dates);
- ▲ Actual mode of travel used, with a daily accounting of costs incurred while in travel status; and
- ▲ A certification that the amounts claimed are correct and proper for payment.

Considerable personnel penalties accrue to the traveler in the event a fraudulent claim is submitted (e.g., forfeiture of the amounts claimed, a fine of up to $10,000 or five years' imprisonment, or both).

The travel voucher is the support documentation to liquidate the earlier obligation and record the actual costs of travel. If disbursement is not immediate, a payable may be due to the traveler for any amounts owed. Also, the agency must await the presentation of the transportation requests from the common carrier; thus a payable should be established for these transportation costs as well.

Voucher and Schedule of Payments

Payments or disbursements are initiated by an agency requesting that the Treasury issue a check for a specific amount to a payee identified by the agency. The form used throughout the government to make such request to the agency is the Voucher and Schedule of Payments, SF 1166. If a check is required to be issued for the travel advance or for an amount due the traveler for travel costs incurred, the agency, after completing the required fiscal reviews, lists the name and other information about the traveler and the amount due on a voucher and schedule of payments being submitted to the Treasury.

This form represents the support documentation of an agency for the entry to reflect funds disbursed. The activity on these schedules are closely monitored by both the agency and the Treasury on a monthly basis. The form contains the necessary appropriation identifiers, account coding, and a certifying signature by an agency official that the amounts on the schedule are correct and proper for payment from the designated appropriation.

Public Vouchers for Transportation of Passengers

Common carriers who have honored transportation requests and provided transportation to government employees still have the task of obtaining payment for their services. The carrier must bill the agency cited on the transportation request. The scheduling of transportation requests for which payment is requested and the formal record for submitting such claims is the Public Voucher for Transportation (SF 1171).

Upon receipt of this form, agency fiscal personnel make a review of the costs claimed to information submitted by the traveler and reconcile any differences. Once the costs claimed are approved for payment, the carriers claim constitutes supporting documentation for authorizing a disbursement of funds by the Treasury by the formal submission of the voucher and schedule of payments to the Treasury.

Transportation Forms — Things

For many government agencies, minimal costs are incurred relating to the transportation of things. Possibly the only transactions within this object classification are those incurred in the movement of employees' household goods at times of changes in duty stations. Other types of transportation costs could be incurred for services rendered by rail, highway, water, or air common carriers. Such costs may also be incurred by a contractor of an agency on behalf of the agency.

As illustrated in Exhibit 14.2, the forms and process for monitoring the costs related to the transportation of things is simpler than the employee travel and transportation. Carriers are generally aware of the government's requirements.

Travel Request and Authorization

An agency might use the same travel request and authorization for the movement of employee's household effects as was used to authorize the travel of the employee. The employee must then provide an estimate of moving expenses on the form. Typically, the estimate is prepared by the employee obtaining a quotation from a carrier/mover.

Accounting Forms

The accounting forms and records vary by agency, being designed to address the general as well as the unique accounting requirements of the particular agency. The purpose of the documentation is uniform — to provide for full disclosure of activities. The forms used in practice will include subsidiary accounts, general ledger accounts, and provisions for accrual, adjusting, and closing entries.

Subsidiary Accounts

As part of the responsibility to maintain an adequate system of accounting and controls, agencies must design and utilize an integrated account structure to permit full accounting for resources consumed and cost of performance. This requires the coding, accounting, and reporting of travel and transportation transactions by appropriation, organization, budget activities, program structures, operating units, and cost centers.

Exhibit 14.2 **OVERVIEW OF TRANSPORTATION**

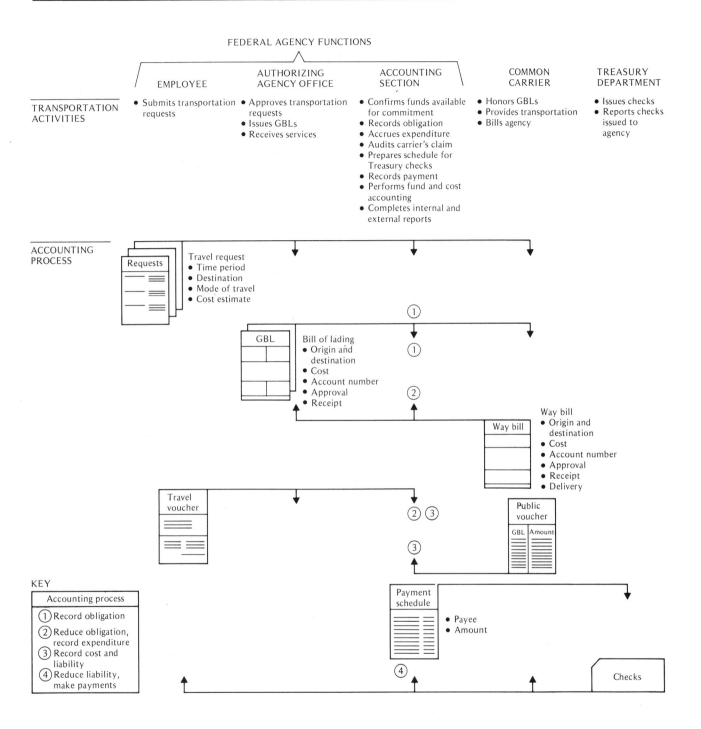

FEDERAL AGENCY FUNCTIONS

	EMPLOYEE	AUTHORIZING AGENCY OFFICE	ACCOUNTING SECTION	COMMON CARRIER	TREASURY DEPARTMENT
TRANSPORTATION ACTIVITIES	• Submits transportation requests	• Approves transportation requests • Issues GBLs • Receives services	• Confirms funds available for commitment • Records obligation • Accrues expenditure • Audits carrier's claim • Prepares schedule for Treasury checks • Records payment • Performs fund and cost accounting • Completes internal and external reports	• Honors GBLs • Provides transportation • Bills agency	• Issues checks • Reports checks issued to agency

ACCOUNTING PROCESS

Requests

Travel request
• Time period
• Destination
• Mode of travel
• Cost estimate

①

GBL

Bill of lading
• Origin and destination
• Cost
• Account number
• Approval
• Receipt

①

②

Way bill

Way bill
• Origin and destination
• Cost
• Account number
• Approval
• Receipt
• Delivery

Travel voucher

② ③

③

Public voucher

GBL	Amount

KEY

Accounting process
① Record obligation
② Reduce obligation, record expenditure
③ Record cost and liability
④ Reduce liability, make payments

Payment schedule

• Payee
• Amount

④

Checks

Source: Adapted from Cornelius E. Tierney, 1979, *Governmental Auditing*, Chicago: Commerce Clearing House.

General Ledger Accounts

Each agency is required to design a general ledger account structure to best control and account for all resources for which it has stewardship responsibility. Ideally, the account structure is in sufficient detail to permit the preparation of all required reports from control or subsidiary account balances without the need for further analysis or allocation of data.

Accrual, Adjusting, and Closing Entries

Standard or predetermined journal entries often exist to permit the accurate reflection of cost in the records, in addition to cash disbursements, at the end of the period. Typically, the end of period accrual, adjustment, or closing entries exist in a preprinted form—in the case of computerized systems, preprogrammed entries. In these instances, only the calculation of the dollar value is required to complete the accounting.

Government Bills of Lading (GBL)

The government bill of lading (SF 1103) is prescribed for the procurement of freight or express transportation services by all modes of common carriers. The form, serially numbered and controlled, comprises several parts.

▲ The original bill of lading containing terms and conditions of the transportation, identification of items to be shipped, evidence of delivery, shipment costs, and appropriation to be charged;

▲ The shipping order, retained by the carrier's agent;

▲ The freight-way bill that accompanies the shipment to destination; and

▲ Extra copies of the bill of lading.

The bill of lading represents the incurrence of the obligation for freight or express transportation services. In instances in which the time lag between issuance of the bill of lading and the performance of services is short, the obligation and cost of the transaction are recorded simultaneously. When the lag time is significant, the amount of the bill of lading should be obligated and an adjustment made to actual cost, if required, at the later date of delivery.

Public Voucher for Transportation Charges

The public voucher for transportation charges (SF 1113) is used by the common carrier to bill government agencies for services provided and requires the listing of each bill of lading on the voucher by serial number and amount. The review and approval of properly completed SF 1113s provide the documentation to support the recognition of an account payable and the liquidation of the earlier obligation.

Voucher and Schedule of Payments

As mentioned earlier, the voucher and schedule of payments is the formal request by an agency to the Treasury to issue checks for specific amounts to identified payees. Payments due to carriers will be listed on the schedule along with other types of requested disbursements and be forwarded to the Treasury for payment. The schedule represents the documentation in support of the cash disbursement.

OMB OBLIGATION, ACCRUAL, AND COSTING CRITERIA

The Office of Management and Budget prescribes the criteria for the obligation, accrued expenditure, and applied cost concepts for reporting transactions relating to travel and transportation. Except where precluded by law, agencies are required to report obligations and applied costs in accordance with the concepts set forth in OMB Circular A-34.

Obligations Incurred

Obligations incurred for travel and transportation include transactions related to transportation requisitions and government bills of lading issued to commercial carriers, commercial contracts, and intragovernmental orders for specific transportation services. Also included are travel orders for employee per diem allowances, incidental travel expenses, and expenses for use of motor vehicles.

The agency's obligations must be recorded on the basis of individual travel orders or on the basis of the total estimated travel to be performed during the month, provided that such estimate is recorded at the beginning of the month. When travel obligations cannot be reasonably estimated, OMB permits amounts to be reported on the basis of reimbursements earned by the employee. Other specific accounting and reporting procedures relating to the obligation of funds exist with respect to the following travel-related transactions.

▲ Obligations for reimbursements to employees for transportation of household effects are based on amounts estimated to be paid under authorized orders issued to employees.

▲ For transportation requests and bills of lading, the estimated amount for travel or transportation not yet commenced shall be eliminated from the reported obligations.

▲ For reimbursements on a commuted basis for movement of household effects, reported obligations at year end should be reduced for reimbursements not yet earned.

In the last two cases, the amounts eliminated as obligations of the current year should be recorded as an obligation of the succeeding fiscal year, if the travel, transportation, or reimbursement is still expected to be made.

Accrued Expenditures and Applied Costs

With respect to accrued expenditures and applied costs for travel and transactions, OMB, in A-34, requires that the following reporting criteria be used.

▲ For transportation requests, related expenditures and costs will be reported when earned by the carriers.

▲ For government bills of lading, commercial contracts, and intragovernmental orders for transportation, related expenditures and costs will be reported when earned.

▲ For reimbursements to employees for transportation of household effects, related expenditures and costs will be reported when earned.

If the unperformed transportation at the end of the period is not material, OMB permits the entire transaction to be reported at the time the transportation commences as both an accrued expenditure and a cost of the current period.

It can be seen that the OMB reporting criteria above may not be totally consistent with the OMB and GAO definitions relating to accrued expenditures (i.e., services received) or applied costs (i.e., services consumed). However, such disparities, in the case of travel and transportation, are not likely to have a material dollar significance in an agency's reported data.

Accounting for Transactions

Recording Travel and Transportation of Persons

Typically, a time period elapses between the authorization of travel expenditures, performance of the travel, and the submission of an accounting for travel expenses by a government traveler. For this reason, an agency must record several entries to properly reflect the status of its funds relating to travel and transportation during fiscal periods.

Obligation of Funds

The initial accounting entry must restrict a portion of the unobligated allotment balance for the contemplated travel. The entry to record that obligation of funds for imminent travel and transportation is

DEBIT: Unobligated allotments
    CREDIT: Unliquidated obligations

The dollar amount of this entry is the amount shown on the authorized and approved travel request and authorization submitted by an employee, generally in advance of performing travel or incurring transportation costs.

Travel Advances

If the authorizing official approves the advance of cash to an employee for the purpose of travel, an entry must be made to record the disbursement of cash and establish an account receivable due from the employee. The entry would be

DEBIT: Receivable due—employee travel advances
    CREDIT: Fund balance with the Treasury

Note that the advance of cash to the employee is not recorded as either an obligation of agency funds or an expenditure at this time. This entry is supported by an approved request for travel advance, generally for an amount that does not exceed the amount obligated.

Liquidation of Obligation
and Advances

Upon completion of travel, an employee will complete and submit a full accounting of expenses of travel or transportation. This information is provided on a travel voucher form. The entries to adjust or liquidate the earlier obligation, settle or adjust the travel advance, and record the cost of travel or transportation require that parallel accounting be performed by recording the events in both the budgetary and proprietary accounts. The following entry is made to the budgetary accounts.

DEBIT: Unliquidated obligations
    CREDIT: Expended appropriation—operating

Unless the amount of the travel expenses equals the earlier amount obligated, an adjustment will be required to the earlier obligation.

The parallel entry to reduce the advance and record the travel expense in the agency's proprietary accounts is

DEBIT: Travel expense

          Transportation expense

    CREDIT: Receivable due—employee travel advances

          Accounts payable—employees

The cost accounting system of the agency provides for a distribution of the expenses above to various subsidiary accounts, organizations, activities, and functions. The payable due to the employee is generally equal to the amount claimed on the travel voucher less the amount of the earlier travel advance.

For employees in continual travel status, the advance may not be liquidated upon submission of periodic travel vouchers. Rather, the employee may be reimbursed for a part or the full amount claimed on the voucher. This reimbursement replenishes the travel advance. Under such procedures, the traveler must settle the travel advance in total, on a regular basis. Typically, such advances are paid and a new one requested at the end and beginning of a fiscal year. The document supporting this type of travel arrangement is referred to as a blanket travel authorization or order.

The entry to pay the traveler for any amounts due for travel in excess of the advance received or to replenish the traveler for the travel advance expended is

DEBIT: Accounts payable—employees

    CREDIT: Fund balance with the Treasury

This disbursement of funds is recorded on the voucher and schedule of payments forwarded to the Treasury for payment.

Transportation Requests

As described earlier, the federal employee may purchase transportation services through the use of a negotiable transportation request, which is provided to the common carrier at the time transportation is provided. The obligation of agency funds for estimated common carrier costs is recorded along with other estimates of travel costs, which are initially shown on the travel request and authorization form. The rendering of an expense voucher does not liquidate the amount obligated for transportation if a transportation request is used. The liquidation of the transportation obligation is recorded upon the receipt of a public voucher for transportation of passengers submitted at a later date by the common carrier to obtain payment for services provided. the entry to account for services received is

> DEBIT: Unliquidated obligations
>   CREDIT: Expended appropriation—operating

This entry reduces the amounts earlier obligated and is supported by submitted copies of public vouchers for transportation of passengers. This is a schedule listing information submitted by the carrier identifying the several transportation requests under which the carrier provided services.

The entry to record cost of transportation services and related parallel payment is

> DEBIT: Transportation expenses
>   CREDIT: Accounts payable—others

The supporting documents for this entry are the same as those provided for the entry above. The debit for transportation expenses is distributed to the several cost centers, as appropriate, by an agency's cost accounting system.

> DEBIT: Accounts payable—others
>   CREDIT: Fund balance with the Treasury

The entry above would record payment to the carrier for services rendered and billed to the agency. The amounts to be paid are listed on the schedule of voucher and payments. This is the standard form submitted to the Treasury listing payees for whom the Treasury is requested to issue checks.

Recording Transportation of Things

Obligating Funds

The accounting for the transportation of things requires slightly different entries. The obligation for the procurement of freight or express transportation services is initiated by the issuance of a government bill of lading by the agency, containing an estimate of the cost of services to be provided by the common carrier and results in the following entry in the agency's records.

TRAVEL AND TRANSPORTATION

    DEBIT: Unobligated allotments
       CREDIT: Unliquidated obligations

This entry reduces the allotment balances and establishes an obligation that remains until the agency obtains notice that the services had been received.

Liquidating Obligation

Receipt of services is noted by the appropriate officials evidencing that goods have been received in the quality and quantity stated on the initial bill of lading. If the agency's system of controls is sufficiently refined to permit this distinction, the accrued expenditure and the cost of services performed should be recorded upon receipt of goods, without waiting for the carrier to render an invoice. The entry to liquidate the obligation and record the accrued expenditure is

    DEBIT: Unliquidated obligation
       CREDIT: Expended appropriation—operating

The parallel entry required to record the cost of services and the related liability is

    DEBIT: Transportation expenses
       CREDIT: Accounts payable—others

The public voucher for transportation charges is the document supporting the entry above. There may be instances in which the bill of lading and the services will be performed within the accounting period or the time lag between ordering and receiving the transportation services is short. Under these conditions, agencies have recorded the obligation and cost of the transaction concurrently.

Payment of Liability. Payment for services rendered by common carriers would require the same disbursement entry as required for other payments.

    DEBIT: Accounts payable—others
       CREDIT: Fund balance with the Treasury

Exhibit 14.3 **ACCOUNTING FOR TRANSACTIONS: TRAVEL AND TRANSPORTATION**

BUDGETARY ENTRIES	DR	CR	PROPRIETARY ENTRIES	DR	CR
Approval of Travel or Transportation Requests					
Unobligated allotments	x		None		
Unliquidated obligations		x			
Travel Advance					
None			Receivable due—advances	x	
			Fund balance with the Treasury		x
Receipt of Employee Travel or Expense Voucher					
Unliquidated obligations	x		Travel expenses	x	
Expended appropriation—operating		x	Transportation expenses	x	
			Receivable due—advances		x
			Accounts payable—employees		x
Payment for Amounts Due in Excess of Earlier Advances					
None			Accounts payable—employees	x	
			Fund balance with the Treasury		x

Legend: DR = Debit entry
CR = Credit entry

This entry is supported by amounts being listed on the schedule of voucher and payments submitted to the Treasury to request that a check be issued to the designated payees.

The several accounting entries discussed in the preceding sections are highlighted in Exhibit 14.3.

chapter 15 Contracts

INTRODUCTION For many agencies, expenditures by contracts are minimal. However, in other agencies, the funds for contracts to purchase a wide variety of services, equipment, property, and program support greatly exceeds all other expenditures in the agency's budget. Contracting and procurement personnel must have detailed working knowledge of the applicable procurement regulations, OMB circulars, and public laws governing or relating to the award and administration of contracts. The accounting records must reflect the amount of the financial obligation or liability at any given time. The dollar magnitude of contracts in relation to many other agency transactions make it necessary to have controls that provide for the prompt accounting and settlement of contractual expenditures in order that the accounting records reflect the financial position of the agency at any point in time.

DEFINITIONS *Contracts* are commitments of the government, generally in writing, obligating the government to an expenditure of money upon delivery of goods or performance of services. Contracts may be issued by agencies for procurement of a variety of services or products, such as transportation, printing and reproduction, supplies and materials, equipment, and other capital items. Often contracts are the preferred form to provide support to nongovernment organizations for the conduct or performance of program activities.

There are various contract formats in use. The contract form selected for a particular procurement will depend on the scope of work to be performed and the nature of the risk that will be shared between the agency and the contractor. Exhibit 15.1 summarizes several types of contracts used by federal agencies. Generally, these contracts fall into two groups: cost-reimbursable contracts and fixed-price types of contracts.

The *cost-reimbursable contracts* are used when the agency and contractor are not able to define the required scope of work in definite terms or when there is no valid basis for predicting results or performance. Under such contracts, the contractor is reimbursed for allowable costs and a fixed or incentive fee.

Conversely, when desired results of performance can be predicted and a definite price can be negotiated for the services, a *fixed-price contract* will be negotiated. Any costs in excess of the fixed price must be borne by the contractor, provided the scope of work has remained as defined in the contract. If performance is rendered for less cost than the fixed price, the contractor is entitled to the full contract amount. As illustrated in Exhibit 15.1, differing versions of fixed-price contracts exist.

RESPONSIBILITIES OF VARIOUS ORGANIZATIONS

Several organizations share the responsibility for the award, administration, and settlement of contracts. The following paragraphs outline the nature of guidance or control exercised by the various organizations with respect to government contracts.

Congressional Responsibilities

Congress, through its authorization and appropriation committees, has the ultimate authority and responsibility for procurement policy. This authority and responsibility are exercised in separate legislation having governmentwide applicability to all federal agencies. Additionally, Congress may deem it necessary to provide specific guidance to individual agencies. In these instances, the legislation applicable to the separate agencies contains directions concerning the award and administration of contracts by that agency.

Exhibit 15.1 **TYPES OF FEDERAL CONTRACTS**

TYPES OF CONTRACTS	DESCRIPTIONS
Cost Reimbursable Contracts	
Cost plus fixed fee	Reimburses contractor for allowable costs, plus negotiated fee. Maximum risk for cost with agency; scope of work difficult to define.
Cost plus incentive fee	Reimburses contractor for allowable costs, plus variable fee if contract is completed for various target cost levels. Scope of work is uncertain at time of negotiation.
Cost and cost sharing	Reimburses contractor for allowable costs. No fee or profit, since contractor anticipates a mutual benefit from performing scope of work.
Time and materials	Reimburses contractor for labor and cost of materials in form of a negotiated rate for each hour of labor; rate must include direct cost labor, overhead, and profit factors.
Labor-hour	Similar to time and materials types of contracts. Reimbursement is made to the contractor on the basis of a fixed labor rate, which includes a factor for cost of labor, overhead, and profit. The only variable is the number of hours provided under contract.
Fixed Price Contracts	
Firm fixed price	Reimburses contractor for full amount of contract for completion of scope of work. The contractor assumes the risk for price and performance.
Fixed-price incentive	An alternative to a firm fixed-price contract when parties agree on scope of work, but can not agree on specific price. Contractor and agency share in cost savings or underruns and overruns.
Fixed-price escalation	Reimburses contractor for full amount of contract and effect of certain financial risks beyond the contractor's control. Escalation clauses generally are based on a predetermined price or cost index, providing for the adjustment of material and labor costs.
Purchase Orders	
Purchase orders	For fixed price, made effective by the vendor or the supplier's acceptance or performance. For amounts not in excess of $10,000 when (1) supplies are readily available in local area, (2) one delivery and one payment will be made, and (3) this form is more economical and efficient than other methods.

Source: Cornelius E. Tierney and Robert D. Hoffman, 1976, *Federal Financial Management: Accounting and Auditing Practices*, New York: AICPA.

Cost Accounting Standards Board

The Cost Accounting Standards Board was established in 1970 by Congress to be an independent organization in the legislative branch. The role of CASB was to issue cost accounting standards to achieve uniformity and consistency in the cost accounting principles followed by defense contractors and subcontractors under federal contracts. The promulgated standards were to be used by contractors in pricing, estimating, accumulating, and reporting costs in connection with defense contracts and subcontracts in excess of $100,000. The CASB standards were later made applicable to contractors and subcontractors doing business with nondefense agencies. Unless acted upon by Congress within 60 days of issuance, proposed standards of the CASB automatically became effective on federal contractors and subcontractors.

On September 30, 1980, CASB's appropriation to support an existence as a separate agency was not renewed by Congress. The general responsibilities and functions were assumed by OMB until a final resolution of CASB's role is determined by Congress.

General Accounting Office

Under various legislation, the General Accounting Office is required or authorized to audit the expenditures of federal monies spent under contracts and other instruments. In the exercise of this responsibility, GAO will review the agencies' systems of accounting and internal controls relating to the award and administration of contracts and other procurements. This review is made both at the agency and at contractor locations. Additionally, the GAO renders advance decisions binding upon federal agencies relating to the propriety of a prospective procurement action. Agencies and private organizations may solicit GAO to review decisions relating to procurement actions and contract awards. GAO decisions are fully binding on the agency. However, the contractor has the option of further pursuing a remedy in the courts.

Over the years, the GAO has issued considerable guidance to assist agencies in the award, administration, and accounting for government contracts.

General Services Administration

For many years, the General Services Administration has been responsible for publishing and overseeing the federal procurement regulations. The FPR's are the rules and regulations applicable to nondefense agencies. These regulations have been renamed and restructured and are now known as the Procurement Acquisition Regulations (PARs). The PARs appear in Chapter I of Title 41, *Public Contracts,* of the Code of Federal Regulations issued by the Federal Supply Service. The administrator of GSA issued the procurement regulations under authority provided by the Federal Property and Administrative Services Act of 1949.

These regulations were applicable to all federal agencies except those specifically exempted by the Congress. Examples of the latter class of agencies include the Department of Defense and the National Aeronautics and Space Administration, each of which issued its own procurement regulations that parallel those of the FPR in many respects.

Office of Management and Budget

The Office of Management and Budget and its predecessor, the Bureau of Budget, have also issued important regulations relating to government procurements. Most notable are those regulations outlining allowable costs under government contracts. These include

▲ OMB Circular A-21 (also known as FMC 73-8), setting forth the cost principles for contracts with educational institutions

▲ OMB Circular A-87 (formerly known as FMC 74-4), setting forth cost principles applicable to state and local governments

▲ OMB Circular A-122 setting forth the cost principles for nonprofit organizations

Additionally, by the Federal Procurement Policy Act (PL 93-400), an Office of Federal Procurement Policy was established within the OMB to provide governmentwide procurement policy for federal agencies. The responsibility of the office included establishing a system of uniform procurement regulations, monitoring and revising policies relating to reliance on either the private or public sector to furnish property or services, establishing a governmentwide procurement data system. OMB was prohibited from interfering with the determination of need for property or services or in specific actions in the award or administration of procurement contracts.

Operating Agency Responsibility

The Budget and Accounting Procedures Act of 1950 required the head of each agency to establish and maintain an adequate system of accounting and internal controls. Pursuant to that act and other legislation, agencies have designed procedures relating to the solicitation and evaluation of proposals, negotiation, award, and administration of contracts, and the full accounting for all phases of contract performance. It is critical that the accounting system of the agency be sufficiently precise to be used to monitor the obligation, liquidation of obligations, costing, and paying of funds relating to performance or service received under a contract. The controls relating to procurement by contract generally require the coordination among numerous functional organizations of the agency.

CONTROL PROCEDURES Many organizations, as outlined above, have authority and responsibility to issue and require adherence to their policies and regulations relating to contracts. The design of a system of controls to meet the criteria of these agencies and to protect the government adequately in procurements is the sole responsibility of the operating agency. While the specific steps or details vary, most agencies have established procedures requiring

▲ The preparation and approval of a procurement request or authorization, approved by the responsible program official and annotated to show that unobligated funds exist to meet the estimated amount of the intended procurement;

▲ Procurements to be competitively awarded, whether the contract is ultimately awarded through advertising or negotiation. (Competition may be obtained by the solicitation of more than one source or publication in the *Commerce Business Daily,* a newsletter of the Department of Commerce listing agency requests for proposals and notifications of earlier contract awards.)

▲ A formal review process for objectively evaluating all proposals received by the agency, both solicited and unsolicited;

▲ The adherence to prescribed negotiation practices precedent to the execution and award of a contract;

▲ The execution and issuance of the contract, with the timely notification to the fiscal function for the prompt obligation of funds in an amount equal to the funded value of the contract;

▲ Reporting, on a periodic basis, of the rate of expenditures by the contractor as well as performance or deliveries being provided;

▲ Positive assertion of the receipt and satisfaction of service or performance received by the agency;

▲ Conduct of a prepayment audit of all invoices received to ensure that amounts, deliveries, and compliance with contract terms are consistent with those negotiated between the agency and contractor;

▲ Prompt and accurate payment of all invoices rendered by the contractor and the timely processing of all accounting entries;

▲ Settlement of any advances of money and inventories of property in a manner consistent with agency policy or contract conditions;

▲ Assessing the extent to which the purpose or objective of the contract is being or has been achieved;

▲ Conducting a survey or review of the recipient's accounting and management control systems by conducting on-site examinations and consulting with other federal agencies with whom the recipient has done business in the past;

▲ Specific conditions governing bank accounts and contributions of any required matching or cost-sharing contributions by the recipients;

▲ Evaluation of the recipient's management personnel, personnel practices, and intent to comply with various federal laws;

▲ Timely settlement of contract debts and prompt closeout and final acounting and reporting at the conclusion of the contract;

▲ A final audit of the recipient, with the federal agency retaining the right to recover appropriate amounts after fully considering audit recommendations and any disallowed costs identified during the audit.

OMB OBLIGATION, ACCRUAL, AND COSTING CRITERIA

The Office of Management and Budget has prescribed certain criteria for the obligation, accrued expenditure, and applied cost of contract transactions relating to the acquisition of services such as

▲ Printing
▲ Reproduction
▲ Other contractual services
▲ Supplies and materials
▲ Equipment

Except when precluded by law, agencies are required to report obligations, expenditures, and applied costs in accordance with these concepts, which are set forth in OMB Circular A-34.

Obligations Incurred

The reporting of obligations incurred for printing, reproduction, other contractual services, supplies and materials, and equipment must include orders placed and contracts awarded. Section 1311 of the Supplemental Appropriation Act establishes the required documents to evidence the existence of a valid obligation. For these transactions, Section 1311 requires evidence of binding agreements, orders, or other legal liabilities prior to the recording and reporting of an obligation. The OMB has further established criteria for recognizing obligations by specific types of contracts and orders.

▲ *For cost plus fixed fee and other contracts without a fixed price,* include as obligations the total estimated costs of contracts (including fixed fee). This amount is to be reported for the month during which the contract is awarded.

▲ *Fixed-price contracts with escalation, price redetermination, and incentive provisions* include as obligations an amount equal to the fixed price stated in the contract or the target or billing price in the case of an incentive contract.

▲ *Continuing contracts, subject to availability of appropriations* include as an obligation the appropriation amount made known to the contractor.

▲ *Letters of intent* include as an obligation the maximum liability indicated in the letters.

▲ *Contracts for variable quantity* include as an obligation only the amounts for the quantity specified for delivery, exclusive of permitted variations.

▲ *Purchase orders* include as obligations orders under which the government assumes a specific obligation for material or services.

▲ *Orders required by law to be placed with another agency* include as obligations the amount of such orders at the time the order is issued.

▲ *Orders involving deliveries of stock from other appropriations or funds* should be included as an obligation amounts related to the capacity in which the supplying activity functions. For example,

> For standard stock items, which the supplying activity has on hand or on order for prompt delivery at published prices, the obligation is incurred at the time the order is placed by the requisitioning activity.

> For stock items, except those mentioned above, the obligation is incurred at the time of issuance of the formal notification from the supplying activity that the items are on hand or on order and will be released for prompt delivery.

> When a specific contract must be executed, the obligation is incurred by the requisitioning agency at the time the contract is entered into by the supplying activity. For agencies electing to record obligation at the time the order is placed with the supplying agency, adjustments must be made at year end to conform with this principle.

▲ *Other intragovernmental orders,* include as obligations amounts withdrawn and credited pursuant to section 601 of the Economy Act that are available for obligation only for the same period as the account from which the amounts are withdrawn.

With respect to the last point, an agency may not change congressional restrictions over its monies through the medium of placing orders or issuing contracts to other parties or other agencies. With respect to an agency's administrative commitments, i.e., requisitions within an agency, invitation to bids, or any action short of binding contract, order or agreement, OMB has stated that these actions will not be included in amounts reported as obligations.

Accrued Expenditures

Expenditures for printing and reproduction, contractual services, supplies and materials, and equipment will accrue when a contractor, vendor, or other party performs the service or incurs costs. The tests of performance may be physical receipt, passing of title, or constructive delivery, when the accounts of the agency provide such information.

CONTRACTS

Applied Costs

The reporting of applied costs related to contracts, orders, and agreements are similar to the reporting of accrued expenditures with the following exceptions.

▲ Applied costs include depreciation and unfunded liabilities when such amounts are provided in the accounts of the agency.

▲ A net increase in inventories is an accrued expenditure, but not an applied cost. Conversely, a net decrease in inventories is an applied cost, but not an accrued expenditure.

▲ For operating programs, a change in capital assets is not an applied cost even though it is an accrued expenditure; the use of consumption (by depreciation) is the cost of a capital asset.

ACCOUNTING FOR CONTRACTS Note that not all of the controls above are resident within a single organization. For example, the completion of a procurement requires coordination between the program office desiring the services, the fiscal function having current knowledge of the status of unobligated funds, and the procurement personnel having information of sources that might be solicited for the services. Procurement personnel attend to the administrative compliance with contract conditions (reporting, delivery, submission of invoices, etc.) Program officials must provide the information concerning the acceptability of the quantity and quality of service or performance rendered. The financial personnel must ensure that any advance payments or inventories of properties be properly disposed of and that the records of the agency provide for a full accounting of the financial transactions for each contract.

Exhibit 15.2 illustrates, in summary form, the nature of the procurement process and the forms required to contract within a federal agency.

Procurement Forms

The several forms required to fully account for a contract generally include

▲ Procurement request or authorization
▲ Request for proposal
▲ Proposal
▲ Contract document
▲ Financial expenditure reports and invoices

264

Exhibit 15.2 **OVERVIEW OF PROCUREMENT PROCESS**

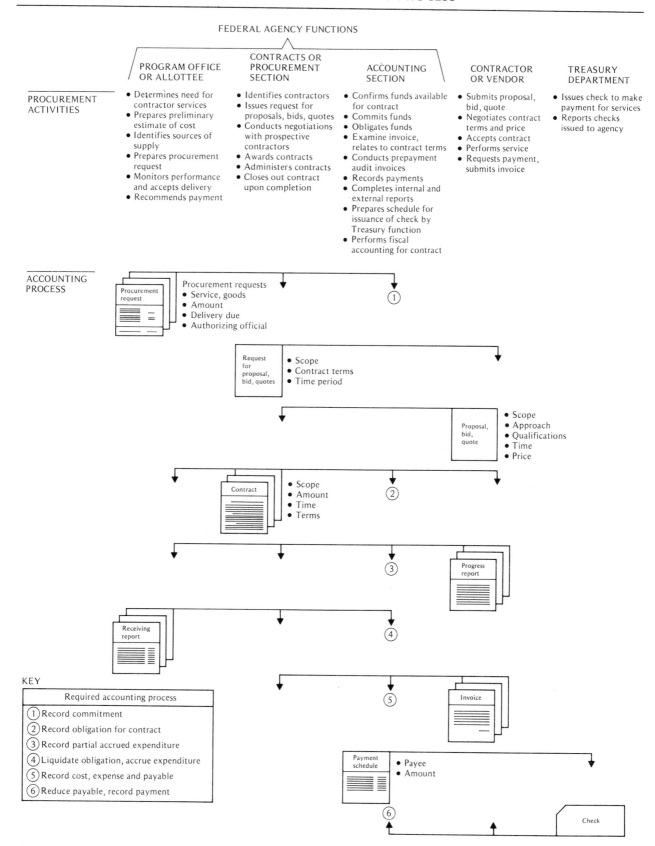

FEDERAL AGENCY FUNCTIONS

PROGRAM OFFICE OR ALLOTTEE	CONTRACTS OR PROCUREMENT SECTION	ACCOUNTING SECTION	CONTRACTOR OR VENDOR	TREASURY DEPARTMENT

PROCUREMENT ACTIVITIES

PROGRAM OFFICE OR ALLOTTEE
- Determines need for contractor services
- Prepares preliminary estimate of cost
- Identifies sources of supply
- Prepares procurement request
- Monitors performance and accepts delivery
- Recommends payment

CONTRACTS OR PROCUREMENT SECTION
- Identifies contractors
- Issues request for proposals, bids, quotes
- Conducts negotiations with prospective contractors
- Awards contracts
- Administers contracts
- Closes out contract upon completion

ACCOUNTING SECTION
- Confirms funds available for contract
- Commits funds
- Obligates funds
- Examine invoice, relates to contract terms
- Conducts prepayment audit invoices
- Records payments
- Completes internal and external reports
- Prepares schedule for issuance of check by Treasury function
- Performs fiscal accounting for contract

CONTRACTOR OR VENDOR
- Submits proposal, bid, quote
- Negotiates contract terms and price
- Accepts contract
- Performs service
- Requests payment, submits invoice

TREASURY DEPARTMENT
- Issues check to make payment for services
- Reports checks issued to agency

ACCOUNTING PROCESS

Procurement request

Procurement requests
- Service, goods
- Amount
- Delivery due
- Authorizing official

①

Request for proposal, bid, quotes
- Scope
- Contract terms
- Time period

Proposal, bid, quote
- Scope
- Approach
- Qualifications
- Time
- Price

Contract
- Scope
- Amount
- Time
- Terms

②

③

Progress report

Receiving report

④

⑤

Invoice

Payment schedule
- Payee
- Amount

⑥

Check

KEY

Required accounting process
① Record commitment
② Record obligation for contract
③ Record partial accrued expenditure
④ Liquidate obligation, accrue expenditure
⑤ Record cost, expense and payable
⑥ Reduce payable, record payment

Source: Adapted from Cornelius E. Tierney, 1979, *Governmental Auditing*, Chicago: Commerce Clearing House, p. 294.

Procurement Request and Authorization

The procurement request or authorization (the PRs) represent the initiating document for a procurement. This record is completed by the program office determining that a need exists that cannot be met with agency resources. The form often provides for

▲ A description of the services desired, the time period during which the services will be provided, and, often, an estimate of the amount of the budget that the program official is willing to spend for the services

▲ An approval of the described services, time period, and funding by the responsible program official

▲ A certification by the program allottee that sufficient unobligated funds exist to meet the cost of the procurement

▲ A recording of the amount on the PR as a commitment or preliminary reservation of the balance of unobligated funds to avoid a duplication or overobligation of funds

The last step is often required when there is a long delay between the commitment of funds and the actual negotiation and award of the contract. Some agencies will formalize the commitment by an accounting entry.

The procurement request is an internal document and generally is not made available to persons external to the agency.

Request for Proposal (RFP)

The request for proposal represents the specification of the scope of work desired by the procuring program office. The form and content vary among agencies but, as a minimum, the RFP should contain (1) the scope of work, (2) the period of performance, (3) the estimated level of resources required to conduct or perform the scope of work, (4) the type of contract to be awarded, (5) the special and general conditions to be applicable to the contract, and (6) on some occasions, the estimated budget of the agency. The RFP is then distributed to interested organizations believed to have the skills required to perform the work. (Numerous RFPs or procurement invitations of the federal government are published in the *Commerce Business Daily*, issued by the Department of Commerce.)

No accounting entry results from the preparation or issuance of an RFP. Although in the development of the RFP the scope of work may be better defined, causing an evaluation to be made of the amount estimated earlier on the "PR." Any variance should be reflected by modifying the amount committed.

Proposals

Interested organizations respond to the RFP by submitting proposals describing how they would undertake to solve the problem or perform the scope of work, the type of resources that would be required to complete the work satisfactorily in the desired time period, and the amount of money for which services will be rendered. Through a review and evaluation process, a firm will emerge as the winner or contractor. No accounting entry results from this phase of the contractual process.

Contract Document

The execution and award of the contract constitutes the incurrence of a legal obligation. The contract, signed by the contractor and agency, contains the scope of work, time period, description of special and general terms and conditions, the amount of the contract, and the amount funded. The last two points are important from an accounting view. The *amount* of the contract could be significantly in excess of the *amount funded* or obligated by the agency. In such instances, the contract is said to be *incrementally funded;* the government agency may limit its liability to the amount funded by stating that full funding is conditional upon the later availability of additional funds.

The accounting entry to record the obligation related to the contract is for the amount cited in the contract as being funded, which may be less than the full amount of the contract.

Financial Expenditure Report or Invoice

Most agencies provide for progress or partial payments through the duration of the contract unless the contract is small. The amount of the payment could be dependent on expenditures shown on periodic financial reports submitted by the contractor. Additionally, invoices for work performed or cost incurred are submitted by contractor organizations to the agency for payment. These organizations are said to be on a reimbursement basis because costs and expenses have been incurred before any reporting or billing is made to the government.

These documents are subjected to a prepayment audit and support an accounting entry to liquidate the earlier obligation and record the accrued expenditure.

Advances

Certain contractor organizations (usually nonprofit organizations and nonfederal government entities) are permitted to receive an advance of funds by which the government finances the work of the contract. Advances could be in two forms: (1) a lump-sum advance may be given to the contractor to cover operations for a specified time period, such as 30 or 60 days, and (2) a letter-of-credit drawdown.

The lump-sum advance is often provided to the contractor at the time of contract award. Throughout the period of performance, the advance is replenished as financial reports or invoices are submitted and is liquidated at the conclusion of the contract.

The letter-of-credit process requires the existence of certain forms such as

▲ An *authorized signature card* identifying the contractor's certifying officer, which is placed on file with the Treasury and the contractor's commercial bank or other designated disbursing organization;

▲ A *letter of credit* completed by the government agency and forwarded to the Treasury identifying the Federal Reserve Bank or Treasury disbursing agent, that identifies the contractor, establishes the total amount of the letter of credit, the periodic withdrawal limits, and the time period for which the letter of credit will be available;

▲ A *request for payment on letter of credit* prepared by the contractor, consistent with the letter of credit, to withdraw funds to finance the contract scope of work. The form requires the reconciliation of balances, withdrawals, and other letter-of-credit transactions and an identification of the program for which funds are being withdrawn.

The issuance of an advance at the time of contract award or the release of funds pursuant to the submission of a request for payment on a letter of credit constitutes a disbursement of funds that must be posted, as an accounts receivable and a reduction in the agency's fund balance with the Treasury.

Schedule and Voucher
of Payments

As described in other chapters, the voucher and schedule of payments is the formal request by an agency to the Treasury to issue checks for specific amounts to identified payees. The Treasury makes no distinction between checks issued for services or for advances. This accounting is a responsibility of the individual agency. The schedule represents the documentation in support of an agency's cash disbursements.

Accounting Forms

The accounting forms and records vary by agency. They are designed to address the general as well as the unique accounting requirements of a particular agency. The purpose of the documentation is uniform—to provide for full disclosure of activities. The forms used in practice include subsidiary accounts, general ledger accounts, and provisions for accrual, adjusting, and closing entries.

Subsidiary Accounts

As part of the responsibility to maintain an adequate system of accounting and controls, agencies must design and utilize an integrated account structure to permit full accounting for resources consumed and cost of performance. This requires the coding, accounting, and reporting of contract transactions by appropriation, organization, budget activities, program structures, operating units, cost centers, and object classification.

General Ledger Accounts

Each agency is required to design a general ledger account structure to best control and account for all resources for which it has stewardship responsibility. Ideally, the account structure is sufficiently detailed to permit the preparation of all required reports from control or subsidiary account balances without the need for further analyses or allocations of data.

Accrual, Adjusting, and Closing Entries

Standard or predetermined journal entries often exist to pemit the accurate reflection of cost in the records, in addition to cash disbursements at the end of the period. Typically, the end-of-period accruals, adjustments, or closing entries exist in a preprinted form or, in the case of computerized systems, in preprogrammed entries. In these instances, only the calculation of the dollar value is required to complete the accounting.

Accounting for Transactions

The accounting for a contract requires the processing of several transactions to reflect the progress or performance of the contractor throughout

Exhibit 15.3 **ACCOUNTING TRANSACTIONS: GOVERNMENT CONTRACTS**

BUDGETARY ENTRIES	DR	CR	PROPRIETARY ENTRIES	DR	CR
Award of Contract			None		
Unobligated allotments	x				
Unliquidated obligations		x			
Advance of Funds					
None			Advances outstanding—contractors	x	
			Fund balance with Treasury		x
Receipt of Expenditure Report or Invoice					
Unliquidated obligations	x		Asset accounts	x	
Expended appropriation—capital		x	Expense accounts	x	
			Accounts payable—contractors		x
Expended appropriation—operating		x			
Letter-of-Credit Withdrawals					
None			Advances outstanding—letter-of-credit withrawals	x	
			Fund balance with the Treasury		x
Payment or Reimbursement of Contractor					
None			Accounts payable—contractors	x	
			Fund balance with the Treasury		x

Legend: DR = Debit entry
CR = Credit entry

the contract period. The several transactions have been highlighted in Exhibit 15.3. The events that must be identified in the accounting records are discussed in the following sections.

Commitment of Funds

All agencies keep memorandum registers or files on the dollar value of procurement requests or authorizations approved in various stages of the contracting process. But most agencies do not record a formal accounting entry for these PRs in their financial records. At times, particularly when there is a long delay between the issuance of the PR and the award of the contract, a formal entry may be made. However, it should be noted that the procurement request does not conform to the documents defined by the Supplemental Appropriation Act of 1955 as constituting an obligation.

Contract Obligation

The award of a contract constitutes a legal obligation of the government and must be formally recorded in the accounts. A budgetary entry is necessary to reduce the unobligated allotment balance and establish an obligation that will be liquidated in the future through delivery of goods or performance of services. If the contract has been incrementally funded, this entry would be for an amount less than the full amount of the contract. Later, as additional funds are allocated to the contract, the same entry must be made for the additional obligation. No proprietary entry is necessary at this time as no performance has been received under the contract.

Advance of Funds

Should the contract qualify for an advance of funds and the advance be made, an entry is required to establish an accounts receivable from the contractor and to record the disbursement of cash.

No entry is made to the budgetary accounts at this time because no funds have been legally committed. In effect, the advance constitutes an interest-free loan to the contractor.

Receipt of Expenditure Report or Invoice

The receipt of an expenditure report, an invoice, or other information that recognizes that goods have been delivered or that services have been performed under the contract constitutes the basis to liquidate part or all of the earlier obligation, whether or not payment has been made. Depending on the terms of the contract, advances may be reduced by reimbursing the contractor for less than the full amounts reported on the submitted expenditure reports or final settlement of advances could be made at the end of the contract.

An entry must be made to the budgetary accounts to reduce or liquidate the earlier obligation for the amount of performance and recognize the expenditure of funds. At the same time, an entry is required to record the asset received or expenses incurred and the accounts payable due to the contractor.

Letter-of-credit Withdrawals

As information is received concerning withdrawals under letters of credit, an accounts receivable must be established and an entry made to reflect the disbursement of cash.

As in the case of the advance, no budgetary accounts have been affected because the agency has not legally committed any funds; it has merely advanced money for which it could, if it so desired, demand a full refund prior to the time services have been rendered.

Payment of the Contractor

Payments to contractors require the reduction of the accounts payable amount due to the contractor and a reduction in the "cash" account of the agency. No budgetary accounts are affected at this time; this entry is necessary to reflect the cash paid to the contractor.

At the end of the reporting period or a fiscal year, it will be necessary to calculate the amounts of expenditures that have accrued, but which as yet have not been reflected in the form of documentation. Such a condition would exist when the end of the period occurred between reporting and invoicing the dates. In this event, an estimate of performance is required. The following general guides are appropriate for estimating accruals for contracts.

▲ For fixed price contracts extending beyond one accounting period and covering goods manufactured to government specifications, a statement from the contractor estimating the percentage of completion, including work performed by subcontractors, could be used to determine the accrued amount.

▲ For cost contracts, monthly reports from the contractors showing the unbilled portion of performance to the end of the accounting period, including any unbilled performance of subcontractors, could be used to determine the accrued amount.

▲ Estimates by government project officers or operating officials familiar with progress under the contracts may be used in lieu of or as a check on information received from a contractor.

▲ In some instances in which the obligation covers the expenditures accrued in the accounting period, the obligation may, itself, be the best estimate of the expenditure.

Accounting for the end of period accrual requires that two entries be made. A budgetary entry is necessary to record the liquidated or reduced obligation that has now, by performance, been transformed into an accrued expenditure. In the proprietary accounts, it is necessary to show concurrently the ownership in an asset or the cost of services performed and the amount due to but not yet billed by the contractor.

Reversal Entries

Once the necessary end-of-period reporting has been completed, it is necessary to return the accounts to the status they held prior to the entering of the accrual information. This procedure will minimize the risk of duplicating transactions and amounts when the formal documentation is later received or the precise amounts of expenditures become known in the later accounting period. Without the reversal entry, there is a risk that the partial liquidation of obligations for the end-of-period accrual will not be properly treated in the accounting records and that information on the documentation submitted by the contractor will be processed for the full amounts reported. Should this happen, the balance in the accounts would be overstated by the amount of the earlier accrual.

chapter 16 Grants

INTRODUCTION
The amount of money expended by the federal government through grants, subsidies, contributions, revenue sharing and other forms of assistance entitlements to state and local governmental units, educational and other organizations exceeded 90 billions of dollars during fiscal year 1981, representing a very significant growth over the amounts expended under similar agreements during the 1970s and 1960s. Increased attention is being given by several federal organizations to improved accounting, reporting, and utilization of federal funds in the hands of grantees. Grants (and the fiscal and other management procedures relating to these types of instruments) have received greater attention from Congress, as evidenced by the increasing legislational activity on the subject. The General Accounting Office, Office of Management and Budget, and several federal grantors have issued regulations concerning the award, performance, stewardship, and auditing of grants during the past few years.

DEFINITIONS
The GAO and OMB have defined grants variously, depending on the nature of the activity or the objective of the grant.

By GAO

In its revision to Title 2, Accounting, of its *Principles and Standards for Federal Agencies* (1978), GAO has defined *grants* as

> Payments in cash or in kind made to provide assistance for specified purposes, the acceptance of which creates a legal duty on the part of the grantee to use the funds or property made available in accordance with the conditions of the grant.

By OMB

OMB, in its Circular A-12, *Object Classification,* defines *grants* as including

> Revenue sharing payments, subsidies, gratuities, and other aid for which cash payments are made to states and political subdivisions, corporations, associations and individuals, including contributions to international societies, contributions fixed by treaty, grants for foreign countries, taxes where the federal government has consented to taxation, readjustment and other benefits to veterans.

OMB, in Circular A-12, excludes from the grant definition obligations involving the acquisition of furnishings, services, supplies, and materials for the federal government, which OMB states should be charged under the object classification best representing the nature of the services or property purchased.

It is important to note that the definition above is at slight variance with OMB's definition of the term, provided in its Circular A-102, *Uniform Administrative Requirements for Grants-in-aid to State and Local Governments.* Under that directive, *grants* or *grants-in-aid* are defined as

> Money or property provided in lieu of money, paid or furnished by the federal government to a state or local government under programs that provide financial assistance through grant or contractual arrangements.

Circular A-102 excludes from the definition technical assistance programs or other assistance in the form of revenue sharing, loans, loan guarantees, or insurance.

For federal accounting, agencies generally adhere to the definition in Circular A-12.

Types of Grants

The types of grants vary considerably. Instruments considered as contracts by one agency may be accounted for as grants by another. Similarly, a variety of descriptors is applied to grants; no uniform terminology exists at this time. The more common classifications have included

▲ *Formula grants*, which by law have a mandated funding level for which only identified types of grantees are eligible, with little or no discretion being exercised by the federal grantor

▲ *Project grants*, which resemble contracts because the grantor agrees to pay the grantee for services, performance, or the completion of a project

▲ *Construction grants*, which are awarded only for construction of permanent facilities, often with the federal grantor and the grantee agreeing to share in the total cost of the program

▲ *Categorical grants*, which are awarded by grantors for a specified objective or purpose

▲ *Block grants*, which are intended to consolidate the funds for broad purposes into a single funding action, typically issued to governments with minimal expenditure restrictions

▲ *Noncompetitive grants*, which may be awarded to all applicants meeting specified legal or other criteria

▲ *Competitive grants*, which may be awarded to a selected number of grantees having similar qualifying characteristics after an evaluation of proposals, in a manner similar to that used for competitive contract awards

The definitions above should not be viewed as mutually exclusive. In practice, a grant award could conceivably fall within two or more of the categories above.

RESPONSIBILITIES OF VARIOUS ORGANIZATIONS

Congress

As with all federal expenditures, Congress by the Constitution has the sole mandate to authorize and appropriate money for grant expenditures. Over the years, this responsibility has been exercised in many ways. The more common form of Congressional direction is to include specific provisions in an agency's enabling legislation setting forth criteria and conditions relating to any grant-making authority conferred on the grantor agency. Often, though, entire laws may be directed to programs of the grant type. The involvement of Congress may vary from general overseeing provisions to monitoring rather specific conditions imposing directed guidance of expenditure of funds, accounting requirements, audit conditions, manner of obligating funds, and other matters.

General Accounting Office

The General Accounting Office, by several laws, is required or authorized to audit the expenditure of federal funds under grants and to prescribe the accounting principles and procedures relating to grants. The exercise of this responsibility generally takes two forms: (1) GAO monitors the accounting and controls existing within the federal grantor agency to ensure that the appropriate checks and balances exist and that grants funds are being properly applied and expended, and (2) GAO will conduct numerous reviews, audits, and examinations of programs operated by grantees' organizations, themselves. Over the years, GAO has increased its involvement with respect to grant programs and has issued numerous documents

Exhibit 16.1 **OMB CIRCULARS APPLICABLE TO GRANTS UNDER FEDERALLY ASSISTED PROGRAMS**

OMB CIRCULARS	SUBJECT
A-102	Uniform administrative requirements for grants-in-aid to state and local governments
A-87	Cost principles applicable to grants and contracts with state and local governments
A-110	Uniform administrative requirements for grants and other agreements with institutions of higher education, hospitals, and other nonprofit organizations
A-21	Cost principles for educational institutions
A-88	Coordinating indirect cost rates, audit, and audit follow up at educational institutions
FMC-73-7*	Administration of college and university research grants
A-100	Cost sharing on federal research
A-73	Audit of federal operations and programs
A-111	Jointly funded assistance to state and local governments and nonprofit organizations
A-122	Cost principles for nonprofit organizations

*Executive Order No. 11893, December 31, 1975, transferred responsibility for certain Federal Management Circulars from General Services Administration to OMB. These are the FMCs applicable to grants.

Sources: *Financial Management of Federal Assistance Programs* and *OMB Circulars, Tables of Contents*, Office of Management and Budget, Washington, D.C., 1980.

setting forth policy and procedural guidance for government agencies as well as for grantees.

Office of Management and Budget

The Office of Management and Budget and its predecessor, the Bureau of Budget, have issued several circulars relating to grants and practices of federal grantees. Exhibit 16.1 lists several circulars (applicable to grants) that contain cost principles and uniform administrative requirements for grants and contracts and other agreements between the federal grantors and (1) state and local governmental units and (2) other nonprofit organizations.

Additionally, OMB exerts considerable influence over federal grantor agencies in its role as the reviewer of agency budgets and expenditures and through the exercise of its apportionment authority by controlling the rate and purpose of expenditures by grantors.

Grantor Agency

The Budget and Accounting Procedures Act of 1950 required the head of each grantor agency to establish and maintain an adequate system of accounting and internal controls. Implicit in this responsibility is the design of procedures relating to the receipt and evaluation of grant proposals and the negotiation and the administration of grants. Like the controls relating to contracts, grant controls must be sufficient to monitor the obligation, liquidation of obligations, costing, and payments of funds granted to nonfederal organizations. The proper execution of accounting and these controls requires coordination among several functional organizations in the grantor organization.

CONTROL PROCEDURES It is the responsibility of the grantor agency to establish the accounting and internal controls to discharge properly its stewardship responsibilities for funds being expended under the agency's grants. Although the specific steps or details vary, grantor agencies have generally established procedures requiring

▲ A formal review process to assess and evaluate objectively grant proposals received by the agency

▲ The adherence to prescribed negotiation practices precedent to the award and execution of a grant

▲ The preparation and approval of a preaward or commitment form to document the existence of and reservation of previously unobligated funds equal to the estimated amount of the grant

▲ The execution and issuance of the grant with timely notification to the fiscal function for prompt obligation of funds in an amount equal to the funded value of the grant

▲ An assessment of the extent to which the purpose or objective of the grant is being or has been achieved

▲ The conduct of a survey or review of the recipient's accounting and management control systems through on-site examinations and consultations with other federal agencies with which the recipient has done business in the past

▲ Specific conditions governing bank accounts and contributions of any required matching or cost-sharing contributions by the recipients

▲ An evaluation of the recipient's management personnel, personnel practices, and intent to comply with various federal laws

▲ The periodic report of the rate of expenditures by the grantee as well as of performance or deliveries being provided by the grantee

▲ The conduct of a prepayment audit, if the grantee is on a reimbursement basis, to ensure that expended funds are consistent with the grant conditions

▲ Prompt and accurate payment of all invoices submitted by grantees

▲ Settlement of any advances of money and inventories of property in a manner consistent with agency policy and grant conditions

▲ A final audit of the recipient, with the federal agency retaining the right to recover appropriate amounts after fully considering audit recommendations and any disallowed costs identified during the audit

▲ Timely settlement of grant debts and prompt close-out and final accounting and reporting at the conclusion of the grant program

OMB OBLIGATION, ACCRUAL, AND COSTING CRITERIA

The OMB has prescribed the application of the obligation, accrued expenditure and applied cost concepts for reporting transactions relating to grants and taxes payable to state and local governments. Except when precluded by law, agencies are required to report to OMB their obligations and applied costs in accordance with these concepts.

Obligations Incurred

The amounts to be reported as obligations for grant-in-aid programs, shared revenues, and taxes payable to state and local governments will be determined in accordance with the following criteria set forth in OMB Circular A-34, *Instructions on Budget Execution.*

▲ For grants with no administrative determinations and which are automatically fixed by formula or specified by law, the reported obligation will be the amount determined by the application of the legal formula or the amount appropriated, whichever is smaller, at the time the amount so determined becomes available to the grantee.

▲ For grants based upon approved financial programs, the reported obligation will cover the time period for which financial requirements have been established and approved, and for which it has been determined that funds are to be paid to the grantee.

▲ For construction grants and related projects, the reported obligation will be the federal share of the project at the time of federal approval.

▲ For other grants requiring administrative approval, the reported obligation will be the amount approved for payment.

▲ For payments in lieu of taxes, the reported obligation will be the amount of taxes due.

▲ For taxes and assessments based on property valuations, the reported obligation will be the amount involved at the time payment is due unless further action is required by Congress to authorize payment. For a revolving fund, taxes will be recorded as accrued.

Obligations for grants administered through a letter-of-credit financing mechanism will be determined on the bases outlined above. It is important to note that drawdowns under letters-of-credit are not ordinarily concurrent with incurring obligations. Obligations should be recorded before such drawdowns. The drawdown of funds is actually an advance of funds to the grantee.

According to the OMB, the requirement that recipients of federal funds provide matching contributions does not affect the federal government's obligations. When it is determined that future payments should be modified or discontinued, the earlier reported obligation should be adjusted.

The reported obligations for grants, subsidies, and contributions, other than those cited above, must conform to other OMB Circular A-34 criteria, as follow.

▲ Amounts for grant agreements will be recorded at the time the agreement is consummated.

▲ Amounts paid in accordance with treaties will be recorded at the beginning of the period for which the money is appropriated.

▲ All other amounts for grants, subsidies, and contributions will be recorded at the time payment is made.

Accrued Expenditures and Applied Costs

Accrued expenditures and applied costs will be recorded as amounts become legally due to grantees for performance rendered or when approved by the federal agency for payment if no performance is required. As mentioned, treaties will be recorded at the beginning of the period for which the money is appropriated.

Taxes, assessments, and payments in lieu of taxes will be reported at the same time as obligations are incurred. Note that advance payments, when performance is required, remain assets (receivables due to the agency) until the money is earned by the grantee, at which time the advance outstanding is reduced and the accrued expenditure recognized.

ACCOUNTING FOR GRANTS

An agency's accounting for grants must be on the basis of each grant awarded and must cover the full period of the grant from the time of the preaward commitment of funds to the final close-out and liquidation of any remaining obligated funds. The GAO, in its revised Title 2, *Accounting, Principles, and Standards for Federal Agencies,* requires that this accounting include (1) the formal recognition of the approval of the grant application, (2) the award or execution of a grant agreement obligating agency funds, (3) the disbursement of federal money, and (4) the reporting and final settlement. GAO also requires that advances to grantees be shown as receivables until the grantee provides evidence of performance.

The actual award of a grant requires close coordination among program officials responsible for the grants, fiscal personnel providing the accounting and reporting, and grant recipients. Exhibit 16.2 summarizes the nature of the grant process used by federal grantors to account for grants.

Grant Forms

The federal grantors have developed rather similar practices for monitoring grant programs. In each agency, certain events or transactions are recognized in the accounts of the grantor. Typically, formal approvals are required for each step in the grant transaction although the specific forms and content vary by agency. The several forms often include documents for

▲ Commitment of funds
▲ Grant agreement

Exhibit 16.2

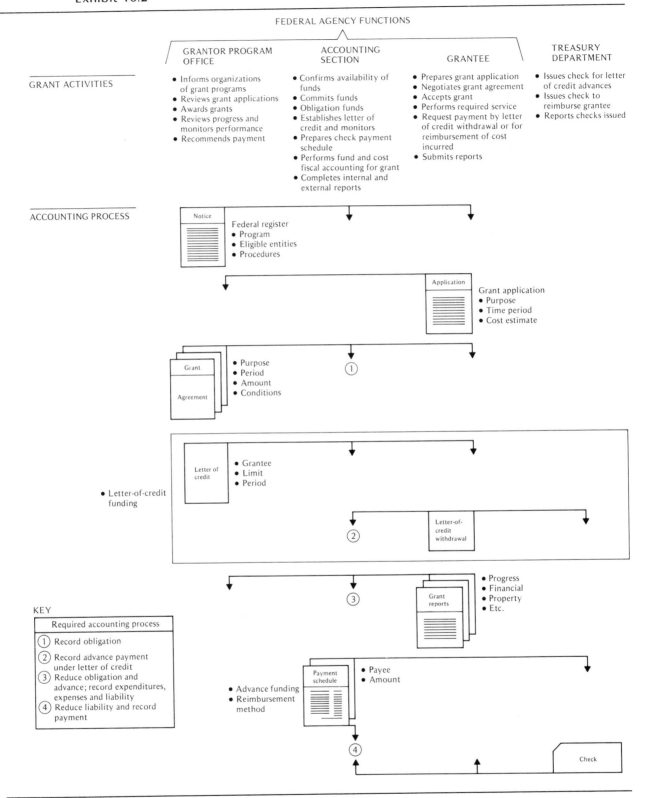

- ▲ Financial expenditure reports or invoices
- ▲ Advances
- ▲ Schedule and voucher of payments
- ▲ Accounting forms

Commitment of Funds

The initial fiscal action is generally related to the approval of a grant application or similar document that contains

- ▲ The purpose of the request for grant
- ▲ A grant budget for estimate or request for grant funds
- ▲ A description of the intended grant program
- ▲ Obligations and conditions of the parties to the grant
- ▲ Approval by the responsible grantor official
- ▲ The formal or informal commitment or reservation of unobligated funds to meet the anticipated grant program expenditures

In most agencies, the commitment of funds to meet future grant expenditures is not formally recognized in the accounts. Typically, a register or other internal record is maintained, which is not usually made available to persons external to the agency.

Grant Agreement

The execution and award of a grant constitute a formal obligation of agency funds pursuant to Section 1311 of the Supplemental Appropriation Act of 1955. In Title 2, cited above, GAO states that this action obligates and binds the government to disburse grant funds either unconditionally or conditionally. The GAO also prescribed the following accounting treatment.

- ▲ Advance payments to grantees for work to be performed shall be accounted for as advances by the grantor agency until evidence of performance has been received from grantees.
- ▲ Payments to reimburse grantees for work performed or cost incurred shall be accounted for as reductions in liabilities of grantors to pay for such work or cost.
- ▲ Payments to grantees, when no performance or reporting is required or when payments are scheduled to correspond approximately with performance, shall be accounted for at the time of payment as liquidations of obligations or as cost incurred.

The executed grant agreement is generally signed by both the grantor and the grantee and contains such information as (1) the scope of the grant program, (2) the time period of the grant, (3) a description of special and general terms and conditions, (4) the amount of the grant, and (5) the amount of the grant funded at time of award.

The last two items are important from an accounting view-point. The amount of the grant could be significantly in excess of the amount funded or obligated by the grantor. In such instances, the grant is said to be *incrementally funded:* the government generally limits its liability to the amount funded by stating that the full funding is conditional upon the later availability of additional funds.

The accounting entry to record the obligation related to the grant should be for the amount cited in the grant agreement as being funded even though a larger value may be cited as the amount of the grant.

Financial Expenditure Reports or Invoices

Certain grantees may be required to submit periodic expenditure reports and possibly invoices to request reimbursement by the grantor of grant funds expended. These documents are subjected to a prepayment audit or review before being approved for payment.

Once grant funds have been approved by the grantor, GAO requires that the reports be used as the basis for liquidating earlier obligations, reducing any advance accounts pursuant to the grant agreement, recording the liability for cost incurred, and making charges to appropriate cost and property records.

Advances

Certain grantee organizations are permitted to receive advances of funds by which the grantor finances the grant program. Advances may be in two forms: (1) A lump-sum advance to cover operations for a specified time period, such as 30 or 60 days, and (2) letters-of-credit drawdown.

A lump-sum advance may be provided to the grantee at the time of the grant award. Throughout the grant period, the advance is replenished as financial reports or invoices are submitted and is eliminated at the conclusion of the grant.

The letter-of-credit process is more complicated and requires the existence of certain forms.

▲ *An authorized signature card* identifying the grantee's certifying officer, which is placed on file with the Treasury and the grantee's commercial bank or other designated disbursing organization

▲ A *letter-of-credit*, completed by the government grantor, forwarded to the Treasury, and identifying the Federal Reserve Bank or the Treasury disbursing agency, the grantee, the periodic withdrawal amount, and the time period for which the letter of credit will be available

▲ A *request for payment on letter of credit*, prepared by the grantee, consistent with the letter of credit, to withdraw funds to perform the scope of the grant program. The form requires the reconciliation of balances, withdrawals, and other letter-of-credit transactions and an identification of the program for which funds are being withdrawn.

In addition to this method, the Federal Reserve Bank method, there are two other letters-of-credit systems: (1) the Regional Disbursing Office system and (2) the Treasury Financial Communications system. The three systems are described and illustrated in more detail in Chapter 12.

Voucher and Schedule of Payments

As described in other chapters, the voucher and schedule of payments is the formal request by an agency to the Treasury to issue checks for specific amounts to identified payees. The Treasury makes no distinction between checks issued for services performed or for advances.

The schedule represents the documentation to support a cash disbursement. The accounting for cash disbursed and the necessary reconciliations between the agency records and the Treasury are the agency's responsibilities.

Accounting Forms

Accounting forms and records vary by agency and are designed to address the general as well as the unique accounting requirements of the agency. However, the uniform purpose of the documentation is to provide for full disclosure of agency activities. The forms and records used in practice will include subsidiary accounts, general ledger accounts, and provisions for accrual, adjusting, and closing entries.

Subsidiary Accounts

As part of the grantor's responsibility to maintain an adequate system of accounting and controls, agencies must design and utilize an integrated account structure to permit full accounting for resources consumed and cost of performance. This system will require coding, accounting, and reporting of grant transactions by appropriation, organization, budget activities, program structures, operating units, and object classification.

General Ledger Accounts

All grantors must design a general ledger account structure to best control and account for all resources for which it has stewardship responsibility. The structure should be sufficiently detailed to permit the preparation of required reports from control or subsidiary account balances without the need for further analysis or allocation of data.

Accrual, Adjusting, and Closing Entries

Standard or predetermined journal entries often exist to permit the accurate reflection of cost in the records, in addition to cash disbursement at the end of the period. Typically, end-of-period accruals, adjustments, or closing entries exist in preprinted form or, in the case of computerized systems, preprogrammed entries. In these instances, only the calculation of the dollar value may be required to complete the accounting.

Accounting Transactions

Accounting for grants requires the processing of several transactions that have been highlighted in Exhibit 16.3. The events that must be formally identified and recorded in the accounting records are discussed in the following sections.

Commitment of Funds

Federal grantors maintain a register or file identifying approved grant applications and other pertinent information, including the amount to be funded by the grantor. In some agencies, a formal entry is made to record this event. However, neither the approved grant application nor the funds committed to approved applications satisfy the criteria for a valid obligation under the Supplemental Appropriation Act of 1955. The approval of a grant application is not viewed as an obligation or future liability of the agency.

Exhibit 16.3   **ACCOUNTING TRANSACTIONS: GOVERNMENT GRANTS**

BUDGETARY ENTRIES	DR	CR	PROPRIETARY ENTRIES	DR	CR
Award of Grant			None		
Unobligated allotments	x				
Unliquidated obligations		x			
Advance of Funds					
None			Advances outstanding—grantees	x	
			Fund balance with the Treasury		x
Receipt of Grant Expenditure Report/Invoice					
Unliquidated obligations	x		Expense accounts	x	
Expended appropriation— operating		x	Accounts payable—grantees		x
Letter-of-Credit Withdrawal					
None			Advances outstanding— letter-of-credit withdrawal	x	
			Fund balance with the Treasury		x
Payment/Reimbursement of Grantee					
None			Accounts payable—grantees	x	
			Fund balance with the Treasury		x
Accrual Entries					
Unliquidated obligations	x		Expense accounts—accrued	x	
Expended appropriation— operating		x	Accounts payable—accrued		x
Closing Entry					
Expended appropriation— operating	x		Invested capital	x	
Invested capital		x	Expense accounts		x
			Expense accounts—accrued		x
Reversal Entries					
Expended appropriations— operating	x		Accounts payable—accrued	x	
Unliquidated obligations		x	Expense accounts—accrued		x

Legend: DR = Debit entry
CR = Credit entry

Grant Obligation

The formal execution and award of a grant agreement constitute the consummation of an obligation that must be recognized in the accounting records of the grantor. The amount of funds obligated vary depending on the specific terms of the grant. For example, a grant for three years could possibly be funded in three one-year increments. Similarly, the total amount of the grant may include a required sharing or contribution by the grantee. In this instance, the grantor is obligated only for the federal share. When the amount of the grant is more than the amount obligated by the grantor, the grant is said to be *incrementally funded*. In future periods, additional funds may be obligated up to the full amount of the grant.

At the time of the grant award, a formal accounting entry is made for each grant to reduce a portion of the unobligated allotment balance and to establish an obligated balance for each grant that will be liquidated in the future by the grantee performance.

The grant award does not require an entry in the proprietary accounts because no performance or services have been rendered by the grantee.

Advance of Funds

The grantee may be eligible to receive an advance of funds to assist in financing the grant program. For qualifying grantees, the principal types of advances available would be

▲ An advance of funds equal to the total amount of the grant when the time period is relatively short or the grant is for a relatively small amount

▲ A cash advance for a specified period of grant operations, possibly 30 to 45 days, the advance being replenished periodically as the grantee submits financial expenditure reports

▲ An advance under a letter of credit, when an advance drawdown would be permitted against the established account balance to cover specified time periods or operations, though in some instances, the letter of credit is established with a zero-balance bank account condition.

If funds are advanced by the grantor under any of the conditions above, an accounting entry is required to recognize the accounts receivable due to the agency and to record the disbursement of cash to the grantee. No entry is made to budgetary accounts because the advance has no effect on the amount of funds legally obligated by the agency. The advance represents merely an interest-free loan to the grantee organization.

Performance by the Grantee

As services are rendered or activities of the grant are performed, grantees are required to submit financial expenditure reports, or in some cases invoices, evidencing the expenditures made during the accounting period. Once these documents are examined and approved, an accounting entry must be made for each grant for which such documents have been received. The reports and invoices are viewed as the authority to reduce or liquidate a portion of the earlier obligations and possibly earlier advances pursuant to the grant agreement.

This event is recognized by an accounting entry made to the budgetary accounts to reduce the earlier obligation and to recognize the amount of the accrued expenditure, equal to the expenses reported or claimed. Additionally, a proprietary entry is required to reflect formally the grant expenses incurred and an accounts payable due to the grantee.

Withdrawals under Letters of Credit

When evidence is received by the grantor of withdrawals by a grantee under a letter of credit, an accounts receivable must be established and an entry made to record the disbursement of cash. As in the case of other advances, generally no budgetary accounts have been affected because no further agency funds have been legally committed. Funds have merely been advanced to the grantee, and the grantor could, if desired, demand full refund prior to the time grant services have been performed. However, as mentioned earlier, GAO has stated that when no performance is required or when payments are scheduled to correspond approximately with performance, payments shall be concurrently accounted for as liquidating the earlier obligation and as costs to be charged to the program.

Payments to Grantees

Disbursements to grantees require an entry to reduce the account payable due to the grantees and record the disbursement of cash. No budgetary accounting entry is necessary at this time. This entry reflects the payment of the liability resulting from the liquidation of an earlier obligation. The amount of the disbursement entry could vary depending on whether funds must be retained by the grantor to settle an earlier advance.

Accrual Entries

At the end of a reporting period or fiscal year, the grantor must determine the amount of grant expenditures that have accrued, but which have not been reflected in the form of documentation from the grantee. Such a condition would exist when the end of the period occurred between reporting dates. In this event, an estimate of the grantee's performance or an accrual is necessary.

Grant accruals may be estimated in the following way.

▲ The rate of grant expenditures, as evidenced by earlier expenditure reports, may be used as a basis for estimating the amount of accrued performance since the last reporting.

▲ If more reliable or current, estimates by government officials familiar with the grantee's progress would suffice.

▲ When no performance is required for entitlement to grant funds, the earlier obligated amount may be the best estimate of the accrued expenditure.

The end-of-period accrual entry required that two entries be made: (1) A budgetary entry to record the liquidated or reduced obligation which by performance has now been transformed into an accrued expenditure, and (2) a proprietary entry to record the grant expense and the amount due, but not yet billed by the grantee at the end of the period.

Reversal Entries

Once the necessary end-of-period reporting has been completed, it may be necessary to return the budgetary and proprietary accounts to the status they held prior to entering the accrual information. This procedure will minimize the risk of duplicating transaction and amounts when the formal documentation is received or the precise amount of accrued grant expenditures becomes known at a later time.

Without the reversal entry there is the risk that the partial liquidation resulting from the end-of-period accrual will be treated improperly in the accounting records and that the documentation later submitted by the grantee will be processed for the full amounts shown. Should this error happen, a duplicate accounting will occur and account balances would be overstated by the amount of the earlier accrual.

COOPERATIVE AGREEMENTS   *Cooperative agreement transactions* and grants are accounted for in similar manners. This instrument was defined by the Congress in the Federal Grants and Cooperative Agreement Act of 1977. Under that legislation, Congress distinguished among contracts, grants, and cooperative agreements by identifying the conditions under which each instrument was to be used.

▲ A *contract* is to be used whenever the principal purpose of the instrument is the acquisition, by purchase, lease, or barter, of property or services for the direct benefit of the government; or whenever an executive agency determines that the use of a contract is appropriate.

▲   A *grant* is to be used whenever the purpose of the relationship is to transfer money, property, services, or anything of value to accomplish a public purpose of support or stimulation authorized by federal statute and no substantial involvement is anticipated between the executive agency and the recipient during the performance of the contemplated activity.

▲   A *cooperative agreement* is to be used whenever the purpose of the relationship is the transfer of money, property, services, or anything of value to accomplish a public purpose of support or stimulation authorized by federal statute and substantial involvement is anticipated between the executive agency and the recipient during performance of the contemplated activity.

▲   The cooperative agreement, while still in the experimental phase, has a contract format. Often agencies use the standard general contract conditions, modified to the circumstances. However, the accounting for a cooperative agreement is similar to that performed for a grant agreement.

chapter 17 Selected Interagency Transactions and Other Expenditures

INTRODUCTION By law or for other reasons government agencies may obtain goods and services from other government agencies. Additionally, all agencies will incur costs for types of housekeeping expenditures such as rents, communications, and utilities that may require a prescribed accounting rather than an accounting in accord with generally accepted principles. Depending on the enabling legislation of an agency, certain expenditures may require special or unique accounting and reporting. Examples of such expenditures include payments for interest and dividends, investments, loans, and possibly guarantees.

DEFINITIONS **Interagency Orders**

An *interagency order* or contract is an agreement entered into between two or more agencies under which there is a requirement by one agency to obtain goods and services from another agency. Often the goods or services provided by another agency could, in

292

other circumstances, be provided directly by a commercial firm. At the federal level, however, laws require that needs for certain goods or services be met by procurement from another government agency. Payment for the goods or services provided by another agency may be by a cash disbursement or by an interagency transfer of funds, in much the same manner as payment is made to a commercial supplier.

Housekeeping Expenditures

An agency must incur several types of housekeeping expenditures to support its programs. Such expenditures may be payable to commercial organizations, utilities, or other agencies, depending on the nature of the services. The more common housekeeping expenditures have been defined by the Office of Management and Budget in its Circular A-12, *Object Classification*, as rent, communications, utilities (which include the standard level user charges (SLUC) assessed by the GSA), other services, and other rent for land, structures, or equipment. Printing and reproduction costs would also be included in this general category.

Other Expenditures

Depending on an agency's mission or purpose, other obligations and expenditures might be incurred for which specific accounting is prescribed. Some of these expenditures, discussed in this chapter, include those for interest and dividends, investments, loans, and governmental guarantees.

RESPONSIBILITIES OF OTHER AGENCIES

As mentioned, several public laws direct that certain goods and services be procured by government agencies from other government agencies. The following are examples of some of the legally mandated government sources and the related legislation.

General Services Administration

The General Services Administration is the housekeeping agency of the government. The Federal Property and Administrative Services Act of 1949, as amended, governs the procurement and management of the property. The same act established the GSA to provide many of these services including the procurement and supply of personal property and nonpersonal services (e.g., motor pool transportation, public utility services, procurement of goods, repair and maintenance, and establishment of forms and procedures), utilization and preservation of available government property, disposal of surplus property, and management of records, as well as other supportive activities.

Government Printing Office

The expenditures for printing and reproduction by federal government agencies is under the continual surveillance of the Congress. In fact, the Joint Committee on Printing, one of the oldest committees of the Congress, was established in 1846 to monitor these types of expenditures. Pursuant to law, the primary source of printing and reproduction services to an agency is required to be the Government Printing Office. With certain exceptions, all printing, binding, and reproduction must be done by the GPO. In practice, because of the limited capacity of the GPO, these types of services are performed by commercial sources by contractors approved by the GPO. (63 Stat. 405; 44 USC 111)

Federal Prison Industries

Limited manufacturing and repair and maintenance services are performed by the Federal Prison Industries. Government agencies are legally directed to consider the FPI as a preferred source of supply for the level and nature of supplies that can be met by the FPI. (18 U.S.C. 4124)

Other Agencies

The degree of direction and monitoring provided by the General Accounting Office and the Office of Management and Budget with respect to interagency services is less than the surveillance given to procurement from nongovernment sources. The primary concern of interagency procurements is to ensure that agencies are procuring from the preferred source if one is designated. However, the GAO and OMB promulgations relating to accounting and fiscal procedures and financial reporting are as applicable to interagency transactions as to other types of expenditures.

CONTROL **Nature of Agency Controls**
PROCEDURES

An agency must establish procedures to control interagency and housekeeping expenditures in much the same manner as it establishes procedures to control other types of expenditures. In some instances, unique controls will be required because the prescribed accounting may dictate that an agency's funds are simultaneously obligated, expended, and possibly disbursed at the time an order is placed with another agency.

The control procedures relating to interagency transaction and housekeeping expenditures will often include such procedures and practices as

- ▲ A written agreement between the agencies involved, properly approved and executed, specifying the legal and fiscal liabilities of the agencies, and the appropriations from which the expenditure will be made
- ▲ Executing, monitoring, and controlling the performance required under the interagency agreement in the same manner as for other procurements
- ▲ A system of prepayment or prefund transfer audit (to the extent possible) to determine the reasonableness of the requested payment or fund transfer in relation to performance rendered or services received
- ▲ Formal processing of housekeeping (rent, utility, communication) expenditures and monitoring receipt of services where appropriate
- ▲ Protection of and regular accounting for assets and any inventories
- ▲ Ensuring the accuracy and completeness of records to support the full transaction accounting cycle from initial obligation, accrual of expenditure, recording of assets or expenses, and ultimate payment or fund transfer

Concerns over Interagency Transactions

In many respects, the control procedures for interagency transactions cannot be any less than those exercised for nongovernmental expenditures. Often increased care must be exercised because the value of individual transactions may be considerably greater. To be unaware of the intragovernment controls and accounting procedures could subject an agency to the possibility of an overobligation or overexpenditure of an appropriation, in violation of law.

In practice, interagency transactions may not be fully obligated or closely controlled. These relaxed conditions are possibly due to the inherent belief that transactions between agencies are not subject to the same risk as those with a nongovernment, third-party organization. However, there is a real possibility that interagency transactions and liabilities will be overlooked by a debtor agency until a bill is rendered for the services. Because such funds may be paid immediately through an automatic interagency fund transfer, the benefiting government agency may find itself in an overobligated or overexpended condition and yet have received no interagency bill. An overexpended appropriation for an inter-agency item carries the same reporting and personal liability as a viola-tion related to any other transction.

OMB OBLIGATION, ACCRUAL, AND COSTING CRITERIA

The Office of Management and Budget has prescribed obligation, accrued expenditure, and applied cost concepts for reporting interagency and housekeeping transactions such as communication, utility services, and rent transactions. Except when prescribed by law, agencies are required to report obligations and applied costs in accordance with these concepts.

Obligations Incurred

The following criteria for reporting obligations incurred for communica-tion, utility services, and rents have been established by OMB in Circular A-34.

▲ The reported obligation by an agency to OMB shall include amounts for ser-vices received or amounts owed for use of property during the period.

▲ When bills are rendered for a period beginning in one month and ending in another, the services received after the latest billing date need not be in-cluded. (Such a practice would omit the cost accrued at the end of the reporting period.)

▲ If the accrued liability for communication and utility services performed for the portion of the month between the end of the billing period and the end of the month is material, provision should be made for recording the obliga-tion.

▲ Money spent for postage, stamps, and "franked" mail dispatched during the reporting period should be reported as obligations. (Agencies often refer to franked mail as "penalty mail.")

▲ For contracts within or beyond the fiscal year for recurring services, the amounts for services not yet performed will be excluded from the reported obligations even though the contract is definite. (Such a practice will result in an understatement of the obligation balance.)

▲ There are two exceptions to the rule for contracts.

For GSA rental space, obligations reported will include the amount of Standard Level User Charges (SLUC) payments owed, earned, and advanced on the basis of bills rendered to agencies by GSA pursuant to regulation.

With respect to leasing of ADP equipment on a contractual basis without a purchase option, obligations are incurred when contracts are consummated—not as services are rendered.

▲ For fixed-term contracts, the total amount of the contract is to be included as an obligation. For contracts with renewal options the amount to be reported as the obligations to OMB include the amount required for the basis period and any penalty charges for failure to exercise options.

Accrued Expenditures and Applied Costs

The reporting of accrued expenditures and applied costs related to communication, utility services, and rents are similar to obligations incurred, with the following exceptions.

▲ Amounts earned under contracts and recorded by the procuring agency accounts for rental of ADP equipment and rental space furnished by the GSA will be based on the SLUC payments.

▲ For postage, agencies may rely on any practical modification of the accrual concept; those using a consumption method are encouraged to continue such an approach.

Other Transactions

The Office of Management and Budget has also prescribed the application of obligation, accrued expenditure, and applied cost concepts for the reporting of transactions relating to

▲ Pensions, annuities, insurance claims, refund, awards, and indemnities
▲ Interest and dividends
▲ Investments
▲ Loans
▲ Guarantees

Except when precluded by law, agencies are required to report obligations and applied costs in accordance with the concepts outlined in the following paragraphs. These criteria are set forth in OMB Circular A-34. It should be noted that many agencies will not be involved with these activities.

Pensions, Annuities, Insurance
Claims, Refunds, Awards, and
Indemnities

The reported obligations for transactions of these types will include an amount determined administratively or judicially to be due and payable when no further action is required by Congress to authorize payment. Accrued expenditures and applied costs should be reported on the same basis as the obligations incurred. In many instances, all of these accounting events will occur simultaneously.

Interest and Dividends

The reported obligation for interest or dividends (other than dividends payable from a government-owned fund to the Treasury) would be the interest owed and the dividends declared during the reporting period. For ordinary interest, the accrued expenditure and applied cost would be reported on the same basis as the obligations incurred.

Investments

Amounts reported as obligations for investments would include the purchase price of securities (if other than the par value of United States government securities) and other investments made during the period. The recorded accrued expenditures and applied costs would be the cash disbursed or outlays made for securities and other investment.

Loans

Amounts reported as obligations for loans will include amounts of loan agreements entered into or loan payments made that were not preceded by loan agreements. The obligation for loans is not to be reduced by any agency collections on loans. Further, funds collected in loans may not be available to the agency for making additional loans unless specific authority has been given by Congress. The accrued expenditures and applied costs reported for loans will include the amount of all outlays or loan payments made in the reporting period.

Guarantees

Some government agencies are required by law to promote public sector investments by guaranteeing loans awarded by lending institutions. Unless the agency is required to establish a reserve for future liability, there is no fund reservation or costing to reflect the contingent liability for the guarantee in the accounts. However, the potential liability is required by OMB to be reported in the following manner.

The reported obligations for guarantees must include the amounts of potential liability undertaken by the government except

▲ When partial funding is authorized by law (e.g., 25 percent of the potential liability is set aside in a guaranty reserve), only the appropriate amount specified will be included as the reported obligation; or

▲ When there is specified authority in law to issue guarantees without prior funding, an obligation is to be recorded only for the amount of each claim adjudicated and determined to be payable.

The accrued expenditures and applied costs for guarantees will include only amounts of claims adjudicated and determined to be payable. Thus there is typically no formal agency accounting for the guaranty liability of the government.

Foreign Currency

While not a transaction common to many agencies, the accounting for foreign currency requires compliance with OMB, Treasury, and GAO requirements.

Foreign currency is defined, in OMB Circular A-34, as a fund established to record foreign currencies that are acquired without payment of dollars abroad and that may be expended with or without charge to dollar appropriations.

"Foreign currency accounts" are not the same as "Special foreign currency program appropriation accounts." The appropriation accounts are general fund accounts whose obligations and other transactions *are* chargeable to dollar appropriations, but whose payments to recipients must be in excess foreign currencies rather than in United States dollars.

Cash resources in the form of foreign currencies, whether purchased with appropriated funds or acquired directly under a foreign program operations, are subject to the same GAO accounting principles and standards that are applicable to domestic cash resources. The Treasury, pursuant to responsibilities assigned by the Foreign Assistance Act of 1961, prescribes procedures relating to the administration, accounting, and reporting of all foreign currency assets. By this law the Secretary of the Treasury has the authority to prescribe exchange rates at which foreign currencies or credits are to be reported by government agencies.

GAO has prescribed the following accounting for the foreign currencies exceeding the needs of the Treasury.

▲ When approved by OMB, the excess foreign currency may be allocated to agencies for use in programs, becoming a part of the agency's fund balance maintained by the Treasury similar to an appropriation from the Congress, or

▲ For accountability, the foreign currency is to be included as part of the fund balances and investment of the government, with a footnote that the currencies are not available for payment of general obligations of the agency.

ACCOUNTING FOR INTERAGENCY AND OTHER EXPENDITURES

Interagency transactions and the other expenditures described in this chapter should be subjected to the same controls as those described in earlier chapters. Funds must be appropriated by Congress, apportioned by OMB, allotted by the agency head, and certified by an accountable officer prior to obligation and disbursement.

Difficulty arises because the nature of the interagency and housekeeping transactions causes the cost of the services to be overlooked in the allocation of agency funding. To avoid embarrassment that would arise from a funding deficiency, agencies have made it a practice to obligate at the beginning of the fiscal year an amount of funds equal to the full year's estimated cost of these transactions. While such a practice will preclude the possible overrun or overexpenditure of funds, the budgeted funds and accounting results will not reflect operations at any time during the year.

Accounting Forms

Standard forms exist to permit the uniform, governmentwide accounting of some interagency transactions. However, many significant services are provided to an agency under unique, specifically negotiated agreements. The agreement or order would form the basis for recording an obligation. Examples of the type of forms used to record obligations, expenditures, disbursement and fund transfers for several interagency and housekeeping transactions are described in the following paragraphs.

Interagency Transactions

Agencies often require that a "letter of agreement" be executed with contractor agencies for each contract entered into. There may be instances in which a standard form will suffice for the contractural letter agreement. Implicit in such agreements is the requirement to account for "billings" and "payments" between agencies.

With the exception of the Simplified Intragovernmental Billing and Collection system, which provides for checkless, simultaneous billing and collection of funds transferred from one agency to another, payments between agencies generally are made on the basis of billing documents issued by the agency providing the goods or services.

For those agencies for which the Treasury does the disbursing, the billing and paying agency many settle amounts due by using standard form 1081—Voucher and Schedule of Withdrawals and Credits. The SF 1081 is, itself, a payment schedule. Thus it is not necessary to list agency payees on the checks disbursement form (which is the Voucher and Schedule of Payments, SF 1166).

There are agencies that do their own disbursing and report to the Treasury on different forms. If either the billing or paying agency is not serviced by the Treasury's disbursing function, interagency billings are made on SF 1080—Voucher for Transfers between Appropriations and/or Funds.

When SF 1081 is used, payment is made by the Treasury disbursing center through a simultaneous charge and credit to the accounts of the agencies involved. In the case of SF 1080, payment is made by a check actually being issued by the paying agency's disbursing office. The billing agency is responsible for initiating the appropriate form. The paying agency has the responsibility for certifying to the appropriateness of the amounts appearing on the forms and forwarding the billing forms to the Treasury disbursing center where (1) an interagency debit and credit entry is made to the involved agencies' accounts or (2) a check is issued in settlement of the obligations.

The fact that certain transactions are made between agencies does not relieve agencies from examining billings for propriety of amounts, quantities, delivery sites, quality, etc., prior to processing for payment. These intragovernmental billing forms are evidence supporting the liquidation of earlier obligations and accrual of expenditures.

Printing

A specific example of an interagency transaction is the receipt of printing services from GSA or the Government Printing Office. An agency desiring such services from GSA or the GPO would requisition services from GSA or GPO; this requisition should be recognized as the incurrence of the obligation. If the printing services were received through the GSA, the GSA might render a billing—the GSA form 789—Schedule of Withdrawals and Credits—which is an order upon the Treasury to withdraw agency funds and credit the billed amount to GSA. If services are provided by GPO, an invoice is forwarded to the benefiting agency. If the invoice is examined and found to be accurate, the approved invoice would be the basis for liquidating the earlier obligation and recording the accrued expenditure. Payment might then be made to the GPO by listing the GPO invoice and pertinent data on a Voucher and Schedule of Payments for forwarding along with a copy of the GPO invoice to the Treasury for payment.

Postage

Accounting for postage costs differs from accounting for printing costs. The obligation should be recorded monthly on the basis of the estimated billing received from the Postal Service. Adjustments for the costs of actual services rendered may be made at a later date. When an advance payment is required by the postal service for franked or "penalty" mail, the amount of the advance payment is shown as the obligated amount.

Telephone

The accounting for commercial telephone bills follows a pattern similar to that of accounting for postage. For example, as agencies incur costs for services, or make long-distance calls, records are maintained by GSA of services provided. Periodically (generally monthly), a billing is made to benefiting agencies on which GSA provides details of telephone-related services provided and the cost of services. The billing could be made on a Schedule of Withdrawals and Credits form, which is audited and forwarded to the Treasury. Because the form is a payment schedule, there is no need to list it on the Voucher and Schedule of Payments that is required when checks are to be issued by the Treasury. The receipt of the billing from GSA will, unless obligated earlier, constitute the obligation as well as the accrual of expenditures for communications. The forwarding of the GSA invoice or Schedule of Withdrawals and Credits constitutes an automatic disbursement or transfer of funds.

Rent

The forms for accounting for rent are similar to those used in accounting for telephone costs. Agencies will generally be assigned space by the GSA. Periodically (usually quarterly), the GSA will present the benefiting agency an invoice for rent, along with a Voucher for Transfer between Appropriations and/or Funds (SF 1080). If an earlier obligation has not been established, the agency's unobligated appropriations balance must be reduced and an accrued expenditure recorded for the amount of rental costs billed. Additionally, upon review and approval, a notice of the GSA invoice will be sent to the Treasury and a "disbursement" or transfer of agency funds recorded.

Accounting Transactions

The accounting for a variety of interagency and housekeeping transactions is generally similar to other expenditures of a government agency. Obligations must be established as soon as they are known, expenditures must be accrued for evidence of delivery of goods or performance of services, and disbursements and transfers from an agency's appropriation balance must be promptly recorded. With respect to the disbursement of agency funds, controls must be established to ensure that the agency's appropriation is not overobligated or overexpended because of failure to recognize certain peculiarities of interagency transactions.

It is important to maintain a distinction between the types of disbursements that can be made with respect to these transactions: (1) A cash disbursement or (2) an automatic and immediate transfer of funds to the agency providing the service.

Interagency Cash Transactions

An interagency cash transaction would be identified by the necessity to prepare a Voucher and Schedule of Payments requesting the Treasury to issue a check to another agency for services rendered to the paying agency. The general sequence of the accounting process would comprise entries similar to the following.

Obligation of Funds. For many types of services, an agency would execute an interagency letter of agreement setting forth the performance required, the period of performance, and the rate or amount of funds that will be required to pay for the services. Payment is then, typically, made by the benefiting agency to the performing agency. The performing agency generally is reimbursed for the services of its personnel or possibly for the cost of services or goods that it may have contracted to perform for the benefiting agency.

The following entry is required to reflect the agreement.

> DEBIT: Unobligated allotments
> CREDIT: Unliquidated obligations

This entry records the obligation of agency funds pursuant to the letter of agreement. The funds obligated should be equal to the contemplated, ultimate liability that will be owed to the performing agency. However, like other procurements, the transaction may be only partially or "incrementally" funded. Unless the level of funding is specifically mentioned in the letter of agreement, the performing agency has a reasonable basis to assume that funds sufficient to cover the full scope of services have been obligated. An incrementally funded agreement should never be recorded without providing formal notification to the contractor agency.

Performance of Services. In many instances, the first notification of the interagency services rendered might be the receipt of SF 1081— Voucher and Schedule of Withdrawals and Credits, which is a payment schedule. If this is so, there is no need to prepare the Voucher and Schedule of Payments that is typically submitted to the Treasury requesting that a check be issued to identified payees.

If a letter agreement existed, an earlier obligation would be recorded in the manner mentioned above. If an earlier obligation had not been established, such an omission must be rectified and the unobligated allotment account balance must be reduced by the amount of the obligation for services performed. In this latter condition, at the time the billing or credit notice was received, the entries would be

DEBIT: Unobligated allotments
  CREDIT: Expended appropriation—operating
          plus
DEBIT: Expense—personnel, reimbursable detail
     Expense—supplies and material
     Expense—printing
  CREDIT: Fund balance with the Treasury

The first entry reduces the unobligated allotment balance and recognizes the accrued expenditures for services performed by the contractor agency. The second entry is necessary to record cost of assistance and services furnished by contractor agency and the payment of agency funds pursuant to submitted schedules of withdrawals and credits.

Advance Funding of Interagency Transactions. Certain agencies, for example, the General Services Administration and Government Printing Office, may have the funding to provide services and may then bill benefiting agencies. Other agencies may have no such authority or funding. Their appropriations may be sufficient only to support their own programs. In the latter instances, the benefiting agency must advance funds to the performing agency. These advances are accounted for as appropriation transfers by the following entries, which would precede any of the entries above relating to service performed.

> DEBIT: Unallotted apportionments
> CREDIT: Allocation to other agencies (investment account)

The entry above records the allocation of funds apportioned by the OMB to provide an advance of funds to another agency for services to be performed pursuant to the letter of agreement.

If a cash advance was provided to the performing agency, an accounts receivable due for advanced funds must be shown. Also the disbursement of appropriated agency funds, relating to the allocation of apportioned funds to contractor agencies, must be reflected.

> DEBIT: Advances to other government agencies (receivable account)
> CREDIT: Fund balance with the Treasury

Performance of Services.   As services are performed, the contractor agency will bill for its costs, pursuant to the conditions outlined in the letter of agreement. A billing requiring a cash settlement may be made by rendering copies of the SF 1080, the Voucher for Transfers between Appropriations and/or Funds to the benefiting or customer agency. Upon receipt by the benefiting agency, the information on these documents is audited in much the same manner as an invoice received from a nongovernment source is audited. The required entries are:

> DEBIT: Unliquidated obligations
> CREDIT: Expended appropriation—operating
>
> plus
>
> DEBIT: Expense—personnel, reimbursable detail
> Expense—supplies and materials
> CREDIT: Accounts payable—government agencies

The first entry liquidates the earlier obligation and recognizes the accrued expenditures for services performed by the contractor agency. A parallel entry is necessary to record cost of personnel assistance and goods furnished by the contractor agency and reflect the liability due to this agency.

Payment for Services.   In many instances a payment will actually be made by the Treasury to settle the amounts owed between agencies. Several SF 1080s may be listed on the Voucher and Schedule of Payments

(SF 1166), the formal request to the Treasury to issue checks to the identified payees. The payment entry would be

DEBIT: Accounts payable—government agencies
       CREDIT: Fund balance with the Treasury

This entry records payment of interagency services billed on SF 1080s, which were listed on accompanying Voucher and Schedule of Payments by the benefiting agency.

If funds had been advanced, the following entries would then be required by the benefiting agency when notified of services performed.

DEBIT: Allocation to other agencies (investment account)
       CREDIT: Expended appropriation—operating
                       plus
DEBIT: Expense—supplies and materials
       CREDIT: Advances to other government agencies (receivable account)

The first entry records the accrued expenditures for services received pursuant to letter of agreement and reduces the earlier allocation of funds. The second entry records the cost of work performed by another agency and reduces the amount of the earlier advance to the contractor agency.

The contractor agency receiving the advance would have an increase in its resources and a liability to the ordering agency until the advance is earned or liquidated. The contractor agency would be required to treat the advance allocation of funds in a manner similar to an appropriation or other restricted fund, which cannot be exceeded. The cost of the services performed by the contractor agency would be subjected to the same accounting and other controls as exist for its own activities.

Interagency Transactions of
the Credit Type

Another category of interagency transactions requires the simultaneous billing and "payment" of services provided by one agency to another. In this instance, the interagency billing system results in a withdrawal or credit of one agency's funds for the benefit of the agency performing services.

These types of transactions can be identified by the existence of a withdrawal and credit form received from the performing agency. Examples of services billed and paid under the no-cash transfer of funds might include printing and telephone services received through the GSA.

The risk to a customer agency is that there may not always be timely notification by the performing agency that the customer agency's appropriation is being reduced for the amount of billed services. Further, with respect to interagency services, the practice requires that these billings be paid before conducting a prepayment audit to determine that the billed services have been received in the stated quality and quantity.

Under these conditions, it is possible that the customer agency did not anticipate the funding necessary to "pay" for these interagency services and, to that extent, the obligations of the customer agency are understated. Further, if services result in a higher-than-budgeted cost, the customer may have unknowingly committed to an overexpenditure of its appropriation equal to the difference between the budgeted amount and the amount ultimately billed by the performing agency.

chapter 18 Receipts, Transfers, Reimbursements, and Refunds

INTRODUCTION By authority of Congress, certain agencies have responsibility for collecting receipts. Additionally, other agencies may have a level of funding for expenditures that is greater than their appropriated funds. This additional funding results from the advances or allocations or transfers of funds from other agencies for whom services must be performed.

Reimbursements and refunds have the effect of reinstating or replenishing agency funds. That is, reimbursements and refunds become available for reobligation and expenditure, provided a current appropriation continues to exist.

All agencies must be authorized by specific legislation to use receipts as appropriations available for agency expenditures. Receipts of an agency may be unavailable for expenditure by the collecting agency for several reasons: (1) Congress has provided no authorization or appropriation related to the receipts; (2) additional action may be required by Congress prior to funds being available for obligation and expenditure; or (3) the receipts have been earmarked or dedicated to activities other than those of the collecting agency.

Exhibit 18.1 **EXAMPLES OF RECEIPTS ACCOUNTS**

RECEIPT ACCOUNTS	DEFINITIONS
Special and Trust Fund Accounts	For recording only those receipts that are required to be deposited in the Treasury and that are available for appropriations, or amounts equal will be appropriated for specific purposes
General Fund Receipts Accounts	For recording receipts not dedicated to specific purposes
Special Fund Receipt and Appropriation Expenditure Accounts	Separate receipt and appropriation expenditure accounts to record receipt and later disbursement of government funds earmarked by law or where equivalent amounts are earmarked by law for specific purposes
Trust Fund Receipt and Expenditure Fund Accounts	For recording receipts held in trust to carry out specific purposes and programs according to statute or agreement, generally consisting of separate receipt and expenditure accounts
Trust Revolving Accounts	For recording a fund entity when the trust's corpus is dedicated to a business type of operation, which uses a combined receipt and expenditure account
Deposit Fund Accounts	For recording receipts temporarily held in suspense pending payment for refund or payment to another government account or for receipts held as custodian or trustee pending payment by direction of the depositor
Revolving Fund Accounts	Authorized by law for recording transactions of a continuing cycle of operations; receipts available in entirety for use by the fund
Receipt Clearing Accounts	For recording general, special, or trust-fund receipts pending credit to applicable receipt accounts

Source: Excerpted from *Manual for Guidance of Federal Agencies*, Title 7—Standardized Fiscal Procedures, United States General Accounting Office, Washington, D.C., pp. 7-10 to 7-13.

For example, taxes collected by the Internal Revenue Service and duties collected by the Bureau of Customs, two organizations within the Treasury, constitute the predominant sources and amounts of receipts of the federal government. These receipts are generally not available for obligation and expenditure by these agencies, but must be deposited in the central Treasury for governmentwide financing. The freedom of agencies to use receipts will vary by the authorized nature of the agency's activities.

Typically receipts will include proceeds from sale of property, fees, rents, royalties, fines and penalties, interest, and gifts and donations.

DEFINITIONS The terms receipts, transfers, reimbursements, and refunds have definite connotations within federal financial management and should not be viewed as interchangeable or synonymous.

The definitions in the several following paragraphs have been established by the General Accounting Office in its *Accounting Principles and Standards and Internal Audit Guidelines,* (Title 2) for federal agencies.

Receipts

Receipts are collections by government agencies, including gifts and donations, which may or may not, depending on enabling legislation by Congress, be available for general or specific use by the collecting agency. If made available by Congress, receipts are immediately usable, in whole or part, as appropriations for the agency to expend without further action by the Congress.

Several examples of receipts accounts are defined in Exhibit 18.1. When collections by government agencies are either appropriated or available for appropriation for specific purposes, the receipts are generally credited to special or trust fund accounts. Again, receipts, in some instances, may be used for supporting fund or agency activities; but in each such instance, there must be prior existing legislation.

Transfers

A *transfer* is an allocation of an appropriation, in whole or part, pursuant to Section 601 of the Economy Act, between government agencies.

The Office of Management and Budget, in Circular A-34, *Instructions on Budget Execution,* further defines a transfer between appropriation accounts as

> A transaction that, pursuant to law, withdraws budget authority or balances from one appropriation account for credit to another. Payments to other accounts for goods or services received or to be received are not transfers but rather are outlay transactions of the paying appropriation.

Thus OMB has defined a *transfer appropriation account* to be a separate account established to

▲ Receive and subsequently obligate and expend allocations from an appropriation of another organization

▲ Carry symbols identified with the original appropriation

▲ Identify allocations that are neither outlays of the parent account nor receipts in the transfer appropriation account

When funds are allocated to transfer appropriation accounts, the allocation transaction creates neither an expenditure nor a reimbursement to the receiving agency. The effect of the transfer merely conveys authority to the receiving agency to obligate and expend the funds transferred for the purposes stated in the original appropriation. Ultimately all assets or expenses must be reflected on the books of the parent agency from whose appropriation the transfer was made, which is referred to as the parent account.

Reimbursements

Reimbursements are defined by OMB, in its Circular A-34, as

▲ Amounts earned for which payments are required to be credited to an appropriation or fund account for commodities, work, or services furnished to an individual, firm, corporation, state or local government, or another account of the federal government

▲ Orders accepted from another account of the government for which an obligation is reportable by that account and the collection is creditable to an appropriation or fund, including amounts advanced or collected from the public that are not yet earned by the account or fund.

In its Title 2, GAO points out that reimbursements are not corrections or adjustments of earlier expenditures. Instead a reimbursement would be a restoration of the appropriation. Appropriation reimbursements do not automatically become available to the agency for reobligation or expenditure. Such funds must be apportioned anew by OMB.

Appropriation reimbursements to be realized may be estimated at the outset of the year and become available for obligation, expenditure, and disbursement. However, agencies must monitor such practices closely since the agency is required to maintain its obligations below amounts realized or apportioned, whichever is lower. Optimistic estimates of reimbursements or a rate of obligation in excess of reimbursements from customer agencies could force the appropriation of the supplying agency into a deficit position.

Refunds

OMB, in Circular A-34, defines a *refund* as a recovery of excess payments that are credited to an appropriation or fund account. Refunds are not to be accounted for as reimbursements to appropriations or funds. Rather, a refund is to be reflected in the accounts as a reduction in an earlier outlay. OMB also provides that refunds could include credits to an appropriation or fund account resulting from accounting adjustments relating to obligations or outlays where such procedure is permissible by law or regulations.

A refund is a collection by an agency of an amount paid in error or a recovery of an advance. Refunds must be accounted for as a reduction of an earlier disbursement and must be related to the earlier asset or expense transaction. This reinstatement of a part of the appropriation balance need not be reapportioned.

RESPONSIBILITIES OF VARIOUS ORGANIZATIONS

Congress, the central agencies (Treasury, OMB, and GAO), and the individual operating agency have various responsibilities for the collection, reporting, and accounting for the several types of fundings that might be made by an agency.

Congress

The responsibility for collections in government must be prescribed by Congress. Additionally, the use of collected monies by agencies must be in accord with appropriations and legislation of the Congress. By its authority under the Constitution that states that no money can be drawn from the Treasury except pursuant to an appropriation made by law, the Congress sets the overall policy governing receipts and subsequent use of funds collected by government agencies. Additionally, by Section 601 of the Economy Act, Congress has authorized reimbursements to be made between appropriations of two or more agencies, thus increasing the efficiency of accounting for interagency transactions.

The Treasury

As a part of its central accounting responsibilities, the Treasury has issued regulations and guidance to account for collections of government agencies.

In the Treasury's document entitled *Receipts, Appropriations, and Other Fund Account Symbols*, groups of receipts are defined by *fund*, including several subsidiary receipt classifications. The total number of receipt accounts exceeds 1,000 governmentwide. The principal classes of receipts are grouped under the following funds.

GENERAL FUND	FUND NUMBER
Government Receipts	
Taxes	0100
Customs duties	0300
Receipts from monetary power	0600
Fees for regulatory and judicial services	0800
Fines, penalties, and forfeitures	1000
War reparations and recoveries under military occupation	1100
Gifts and contributions	1200
Clearing accounts	3800
Proprietary Receipts	
Interest	1400
Dividends and other earnings	1600
Rent	1800
Royalties	2000
Sale of products	2200
Fees and other charges for services and special benefits	2400
Sale of government property	2600
Realization upon loan and investments	2800-2999
Recoveries and refunds	3000
Special Fund	5000-5999
Trust Fund	
Department and agencies (exclusive of District of Columbia)	7000-8999
District of Columbia	9000-9999

In addition to classifying receipts by type of fund, the Treasury has defined receipts by the nature and sources of receipts. These categorizations are not mutually exclusive and all are used in practice.

When referred to by the *nature* of the receipt, the categories will include: (1) governmental, (2) proprietary, or (3) intrabudgetary.

▲ *Governmental receipts* result from the sovereign rights of government to levy and collect various taxes and duties.

▲ *Proprietary receipts* result from the businesslike operations of agencies, such as from sales of publications or licenses, or charging of fees.

▲ *Intrabudgetary receipts* of various classes result from activity between federal accounts or agencies.

If classified by *sources* of receipts, the groupings of federal receipts would be (1) internal revenue receipts, (2) alcohol and tobacco taxes, (3) custom receipts, and (4) miscellaneous receipts. The internal revenue receipts, alcohol and tobacco taxes and customs duties are collected by organizations of the Treasury. Miscellaneous receipts are collected, often, by the federal agency most closely associated with the revenue or services performed.

Office of Management and Budget

The Office of Management and Budget is legally and administratively responsible for the review and monitoring of receipts and expenditures of the federal government. OMB takes a particular interest in the income of the government and the allocation of budgetary authority among and between government agencies. Close control is maintained through the apportionment process because receipts, transfers, and reimbursements do not automatically become funds that a collecting agency may use to finance its activities and programs.

OMB in its Circular A-34 provides guidelines to agencies concerning the collection, accounting, and reporting of these funds. Additionally, more specific guidance on user-charges is provided by OMB in its Circular A-25. This circular sets forth general policy for developing systems of charges for payment for government services and property, including the description of the scope of user charges, the guidelines for executing policy, and the reporting by agencies involved with the collection of user charges. OMB policy requires that a reasonable charge should be made to identifiable recipients for measurable units or amounts of government services or property from which the party derives a special benefit. The *special benefits* would relate to a gain, advantage, or other benefit received by certain individuals beyond those which accrue to the public at large. The user charge should be imposed to recover the full cost to the government for rendering that service.

Operating Agencies

The inherent responsibilities of an operating agency to establish and maintain an adequate system of accounting and internal controls (required by the Budget and Accounting Procedures Act of 1950) apply equally to expenditures and the collections and other sources of funding and additional budget authority that may become available or be collected by an agency. Collections by agencies are subject to the same Congressional authorization and appropriation approval requirement and the OMB apportionment requirements that apply to other types of funds and budgetary authority.

CONTROL PROCEDURES
The purpose of internal controls is to assure that funds, property, assets, and other resources of an agency are properly used and safeguarded to prohibit waste, destruction, misuse, or misappropriation. Like other types of financial transactions, those related to receipts, transfers, reimbursements, and refunds, while internal to the government, require that same level of diligence to ensure that financial management is consistent with applicable laws and governmental regulations.

In addition to specific considerations, the controls over these transactions should provide for a division of duties and functions. The responsibility for authorization, approval, collection, accounting, and reporting should be assigned to several persons in a manner that the actions of one provide a check on the performance of others.

Receipts

Agencies having collection responsibilities must establish and maintain internal control procedures that provide for identifying conditions requiring the collection of revenues, monitoring of collections, and continually assessing the reasonableness of rates and fees charged.

Generally, the procedures will be designed to include controls and checks on practices such as

▲ Periodically monitoring the nature of services, commodities, or property being provided to the public to determine whether a special benefit is being conferred on recipients, for which a charge would be appropriate

▲ Determining the charge, rate, fees, or other price to be levied for the services, commodities, or property being furnished

▲ Continually monitoring the charge to ensure its overall reasonableness in relation to the benefits received by recipients

▲ Preventing the delivery of services and goods without charge or for a charge below cost

▲ Assuring that billings are rendered on time and accurately to all users or recipients of the services or goods

▲ Providing an internal check on adherence to prescribed policies and procedures and for possible detection of any irregular practices

▲ Segregating the warehousing or storing function from the billing and collection functions although the procedures of each should be designed to form a system of checks and balances over the entire operation

▲ Using prenumbered, serially controlled forms, with accountability for the entire sequence of forms used for the various functions

▲ Ensuring the timely collection, accurate recording, and immediate deposit of all monies

▲ Periodically verifying sales to collections to any physical inventories

▲ Monitoring of billing and accounts-receivable functions

The control procedures will necessarily vary depending on the reasons for which collections are being made. For example, revenues may originate from sales of commodities and property, fees for services, rents, royalties, fines, penalties, and interest. The conditions surrounding these collections will dictate the types of controls needed.

Transfers

The controls relating to transfers of appropriations do not have to be so stringent as those related to receipts. With respect to transfers, the receiving agency is liable for monitoring the available budget authority and meeting other legal and fiscal requirements. The parent or paying account or appropriation is responsible for providing the overall reporting of the stewardship by the agency to whom funds were transferred.

Reimbursements

Reimbursements to appropriation accounts must be closely monitored. Should one agency pay from its appropriation for services performed for another agency, the failure to obtain a reimbursement to its appropriation for the services performed could constitute a diversion of its appropriated funds for the benefit of another agency. Such a transaction, without the approval of Congress or apportionment by OMB, is not permitted and is illegal. Further, although the performing agency may incur obligations on the basis of anticipated reimbursements, the performing agency is liable for any obligation in excess of the actual reimbursements realized.

While reimbursement transactions are internal to the federal government, procedures should nevertheless be established to include controls or checks such as

▲ Periodic reviews of interagency agreements for services performed for other appropriation accounts or other government agencies

▲ Examination of the amount, timing, and rate of reimbursement by another appropriation or account to the performing account

▲ Frequent reconciliations of rates of obligations to amounts of estimated reimbursements

▲ Confirmation of actual reimbursements in an amount equal to obligations incurred by the performing account or agency

Reimbursement transactions must be monitored in much the same manner as other contractual arrangements of the agency. The possibility exists for the receiving agency to modify its intention, with a resultant change in its rate of reimbursement to the performing agency. Such a change could put the performing agency at risk unless its rate of obligation and expenditure can also be modified accordingly.

Refunds

Refunds represent recoveries of payments made in error or advances made to various parties. The applicable controls would be those related to the expenditure transaction itself. However, the accounting for refunds must be carefully monitored. Unless the earlier expenditure is reduced, the reobligations and expenditures of the refunded amounts will be reflected in the accounts as duplicated transactions, possibly giving the appearance of an overobligation or an overexpenditure violation if the total exceeds the amount of the original appropriation account.

ACCOUNTING FOR RECEIPTS, TRANSFERS, REIMBURSEMENTS, AND REFUNDS The accounting for receipts among agencies varies almost by types of receipts. Similarly, although procedures and some standard forms exist to account for transfers and reimbursements to agency appropriations, the underlying conditions for such transactions must be set forth in specific legislation and be subjected to review and approval by OMB.

Accounting Forms

Receipts and Revenues

Federal monies are collected through diverse processes, each being established for the type of receipt and revenue being sought.

For example, collections under internal revenue laws are based on tax returns (for income taxes, estate taxes, admissions taxes) filed by taxpayers or through the sale of stamps. The receipts are deposited by collection officers with Federal Reserve banks or general, designated depositaries for the account of the United States. Typically, commercial banks are the designated depositaries for the Federal Reserve System. In the cases of income and social security taxes on wages, the withheld amounts are deposited by employers with depositaries for the Treasury's account. The depositaries credit the Treasury's tax and loan account and report collections to the Federal Reserve bank.

Taxes relating to alcohol, tobacco, and firearms are paid under a system in which the tax returns and remittances are filed with the Internal Revenue Service. This is the second largest source of general revenue to the government.

The Customs Service, by collecting duties on imports, excise taxes, and miscellaneous receipts and receipts other than general funds (such as appropriation reimbursements and refunds, trust fund, available receipts, and collections of other agencies) is the third largest revenue-collecting agency in the government. Customs collections are deposited by district directors with the Federal Reserve or general depositaries for the account of the Treasury. For the most part, each type of revenue has its own prescribed set of forms and processing procedures.

Miscellaneous receipts (miscellaneous taxes, fees for permits and licenses, proceeds from sales of property, rents, royalties, gifts, contributions, etc.) are collected by the agency most closely associated with the source of revenue. Collections must be delivered in a timely manner to a designated depositary for the credit of the Treasury. Trust receipts, like miscellaneous receipts, are collected by many departments and government establishments. (Some of the major trust funds are the Civil Service Retirement, Federal Old-Age and Survivors Insurance, Federal Disability Insurance, Highway, Airport and Airway, Unemployment, and National Service Life Insurance trust funds.)

Transfers

For the agency receiving an allocation or appropriation transfer, the reporting for such budgetary authority is much the same as that which would exist for appropriations received directly from Congress. The forms to document the transactions related to an appropriation transfer are the same as those used for the expenditures described in earlier chapters. The performing or receiving agency must maintain the records required for incurring obligations, accruing expenditures, and making disbursements. The final accounting for assets acquired or expenses incurred are reflected on the books of the customer or transferring agency otherwise known as the parent account or appropriation.

Reimbursements

Collections, constituting reimbursements to appropriations, are generally documented to reflect the compliance with agency controls. The forms will include a record for listing and summarizing collections, deposit slips, summarizing statements of transactions, reports to and from the Treasury or its designated depositary, and to the OMB. Note that reimbursements to an appropriation do not become available automatically for reobligation and expenditure by the collecting agency, but must be subjected to the OMB apportionment process like other budgetary or appropriation authority.

Refunds

Refunds, which are collections or adjustments for errors or other circumstances, are shown as an offset or reduction to the earlier related expenditure. The refund could take the form of a personal check (in the case of an individual), a credit on an invoice to the government, or some other form of reduction of the cost to the government. The forms that document a refund are not standard.

Accounting for Collections

Receipts

As mentioned earlier, the significant receipts of the government are collected by organizations within the Treasury—the Internal Revenue Service; the Bureau of Alcohol, Tobacco, and Firearms; and the Bureau of Customs. Each of these organizations has prescribed forms for recording collections, making deposits, summarizing and reporting transactions related to the receipts monthly, quarterly, and annually.

For the most part, other government agencies have their operations financed through expenditure appropriations. When authorized by law, these agencies may have additional obligational authority resulting from such sources as appropriation reimbursements, transfers, and appropriations refunds.

Available Receipts

Generally, receipts of most agencies available for obligation relate to specific purposes previously identified by Congress. The funds may, however, still have to be subjected to the apportionment process of OMB. If the receipts are deemed available, the agency may immediately obligate and expend for authorized purposes.

The accounting for an available receipt would require the establishment of an estimate of the receipt with a corresponding anticipated increase in the investment accounts of the agency. The entry for such a transaction would be

DEBIT: Estimated appropriation receipts (receivable)
    CREDIT: Unapportioned appropriations (or unallotted apportionments)

Like estimated appropriation reimbursements, the estimated receipts are not considered realized until they are actually collected. The rate of obligations and expenditures must therefore be monitored closely to ensure that these transactions do not exceed the amounts appropriated or apportioned. When collections occur the entry would be similar to

DEBIT: Fund balance with the Treasury
    CREDIT: Estimated appropriation receipts

A separate account should be maintained for receipts estimated to be realized during the current year; unrealized balances should be reversed at the close of the fiscal year. The availability must be detemined anew for each fiscal year.

Because the funds are available to the agency as collected, the obligation, expenditures, and disbursement accounting would be the same as that performed for all other types of transactions.

Unavailable Receipts

Unavailable receipts, at the time of collection, are those receipts that are not available to the agency for obligation or expenditure. Congressional action may be required, or possibly some limitation has been placed on the use of the funds. Until appropriated or apportioned, these receipts may not be used by the agency. The entry for estimated unavailable receipts might be similar to the following.

DEBIT: Estimated appropriation receipts
    CREDIT: Unappropriated funds

The entry above the estimate of receipts and records provides for the fact that such funds, if collected, are not yet appropriated or available to the agency for further obligation or expenditure.

If collections occur, that event could be reflected by the following entry.

DEBIT: Fund balance with the Treasury
    CREDIT: Estimated appropriation receipts

If Congress were to provide an appropriation permitting the agency to obligate and expend the collected receipts, that event could be accounted for as follows.

DEBIT: Unappropriated funds
    CREDIT: Unapportioned appropriations

The entry above supports the availability of an appropriation; the funds have yet to be apportioned by OMB in order for the agency to incur obligations against this appropriation. At the end of the fiscal period, the continued availability of the collected receipts would be dependent on the conditions in the appropriation law.

Transfers

The accounting for an appropriation transfer can best be illustrated by viewing the accounting on the records of both the transferring and the receiving agency. Exhibit 18.2 highlights the entries that would be made by the individual agencies.

As outlined in Chapter 17, relating to interagency transactions, the document to support the initial transfer of appropriated funds is often a letter of agreement setting out many of the particulars to be met by the contractor agency or organization. The detailed accounting is performed on the books of the performing or contractor organization although the ultimate asset or expense is shown against the "parent" appropriation on the books of the transferring or benefiting agency.

Exhibit 18.2 **ILLUSTRATION OF ACCOUNTING FOR TRANSFERRING AND RECEIVING AGENCIES**

RECORDS OF AGENCY TRANSFERRING APPROPRIATION TRANSFER	DR	CR	RECORDS OF AGENCY RECEIVING APPROPRIATION TRANSFER	DR	CR
To Record Transfer					
Unallotted apportionments	x		Fund balance with the Treasury	x	
Appropriation allocated to other agencies		x	Advance from others		x
Advances to other agencies	x				
Fund balance with the Treasury		x			
To Record Budget Authority					
None			Appropriations allocated by others	x	
			Unallotted apportionments		x
To Record OMB Apportionment					
None			Unallotted apportionments	x	
			Unobligated allotments		x
To Record Obligation					
None			Unobligated allotments	x	
			Unliquidated obligations		x
To Record Cost of Work Performed					
None			Work-in-process—others	x	
			Accounts payable		x
To Liquidate Obligation					
None			Unliquidated obligations	x	
			Expended appropriations—operating*		x
To Record Payment of Liabilities					
None			Accounts payable	x	
			Fund balance with the Treasury		x
To Record Cost of Work Reported by Others					
Expenses or assets	x		Advances from others	x	
Advances to other agencies		x	Work-in-process—others		x
To Record Expenditures and Reimbursement					
Appropriation allocated to others	x		Invested capital	x	
Expended appropriation—operating or capital*		x	Appropriation allocated by others		x

*Closed out to invested capital account at end of fiscal period.

Payments or funds transfers may be supported by the submission of invoices or, if two government agencies are involved, by the transmittal of withdrawal and credit notices. At the end of an accounting period, appropriate accrual adjustments should be made for work performed but not shipped or reported to the parent agency at that time. The accrual entries are necessary to reflect the proper status of completion on the records of both the transferring and the receiving agency.

Appropriation Reimbursements

The earnings collected as appropriation reimbursement from the sale of services or goods are generally credited to an appropriation account. At the beginning of the fiscal period, OMB will require the agency to prepare and account formally for the estimated appropriation reimbursements that are to be available for obligation and expenditure. The estimated appropriation reimbursements are considered to be realized when the services or goods have been furnished. When collections are made, the funds are credited to the appropriation financing the cost of the services or goods delivered. Reimbursements may be received from either government or nongovernment sources or both, which must be segregated in the accounting records. The entries to record these events are shown in the following paragraphs.

To record the estimated appropriations requires establishing an asset account and recognizing the additional unapportioned appropriation authority.

DEBIT: Estimated appropriation reimbursements (an asset)
   CREDIT: Unapportioned appropriations
To record the estimated reimbursements and the related unapportioned appropriation or budget authority.

As mentioned earlier, an agency must monitor closely actual reimbursements to ensure that it maintains the level of actual obligations below either the amount collected or the amount apportioned, whichever is lower.

As sales are made, the estimated reimbursements are adjusted to reflect the actual reimbursements that could be collected. For example

DEBIT: Reimbursements to appropriations (an investment account)
   CREDIT: Estimated appropriations reimbursements
To recognize reimbursements realized through sales and to adjust earlier estimates.

Additionally, the following companion entry would be required to the proprietary accounts to reflect the revenue from the sale. As billings are made for the services rendered or goods provided, and funds are collected to reimburse the agency, the following entry would be appropriate.

DEBIT: Accounts receivable
    CREDIT: Revenues
To record the accounts receivable due from billings made for services or goods delivered and the related revenues realized from this sale.

The actual collections would be recorded in the same manner as other cash receipts.

DEBIT: Fund balance with the Treasury
    CREDIT: Accounts receivable
To record collection of cash and reduction of account receivable due the agency.

The collections would be formally recorded and reported to the Treasury and deposits made with the designated depositary. The realized reimbursements, which must ultimately be transferred to the invested capital account, must also be reflected in the reporting to OMB.

Refunds

As mentioned earlier, a refund is either a collection of an amount paid in error or the recovery of an advance. Entries are made to reflect the amount to be refunded for the error, the adjustment to the unobligated allotment balance of the agency, and the receipt of cash or other credit. These transactions are highlighted in the following paragraphs.

To reflect the amount due and to reduce the expense or asset account earlier charged in error, the entry would be

DEBIT: Accounts receivable—appropriation repayment due
    CREDIT: Expenses—reimbursable duty for another agency (or an asset account)
To record receivables due for erroneous payment and reduction in amounts recorded in either the expense or asset accounts.

Because funds have been refunded, the benefiting agency must also increase or restore the unobligated allotment balance. An increased amount is now available for reobligation. In this instance, the entry would be

DEBIT: Expended appropriation—operating (or capital)
    CREDIT: Unobligated allotments
    To reduce amount erroneously accrued for expenditures and to restore the refunded amounts to the unobligated allotment balance.

Neither of the entries above reflects the actual receipt of funds due for the refund. That entry would be recorded in the following manner.

DEBIT: Fund balance with the Treasury
    CREDIT: Accounts receivable—appropriation repayment due
    To record cash refund and eliminate accounts receivable due from another agency for refund.

PART V

ACCOUNTING FOR ASSETS, LIABILITIES, AND INVESTMENT OF THE GOVERNMENT

chapter 19 Current Assets

The placement of this discussion concerning assets is not intended to indicate a lesser importance of such accounts, but it is probably in the perspective given to these balances by federal financial managers. Discussions in an agency could lead one to conclude that the only concern was with the cash balance and the rate of obligation and expenditures.

By law and General Accounting Office standards and principles, agencies must provide an accounting for all assets, properly reflect the application or consumption of assets, fairly present program liabilities, and show the residual investment or equity of the government.

DEFINITIONS Unlike the reporting done by corporations, the segregation of an agency's assets between current and fixed- or longer-term assets has minimal reporting significance in the federal government. However, many agencies do maintain the distinction. The following paragraphs describe the more common types of assets recorded in agency accounts.

Generally, the current assets of an agency consist of

▲ Fund balance with the Treasury
▲ Imprest funds
▲ Accounts receivable
▲ Advances
▲ Inventories

Fund Balance with the Treasury

Often agencies will refer to a "cash" account or "cash in bank." Both of these are misnomers. Few agencies truly have cash accounts and even fewer have the cash in a bank. The fund balance with the Treasury represents the undisbursed balance of an agency's appropriation, which is in possession of the Treasury.

Imprest Funds

Imprest funds are advances by the Treasury to agencies for purposes of providing cash to meet official incidental, smaller expenditures of the agency. Typical imprest fund transactions include reimbursement of employees for taxi fares, nominal travel advances, and other minor expenses. The cashiers of such funds, although agency employees, act as agents of the Treasury and must comply with the requirements of that department.

Accounts Receivable

Accounts receivable represent amounts due to an agency for services rendered, possible overpayments to various parties (contractors, grantees, employees, and others), and other amounts due. The more common types of receivables could include

▲ *Repayments to appropriations*—repayments or reimbursements to an appropriation, due for services or overpayments made to other agencies, and refunds arising from erroneous payments or adjustments of amounts previously disbursed
▲ *Due from government agencies*—amounts due to agency revolving funds from other government agencies
▲ *Accounts receivable—other*—amounts due from other parties (including erroneous payments to contractors) excluding other government agencies

Advances

Advances are amounts paid to others prior to the receipt of services or performance of an activity or delivery of goods. The more common types of advances include travel advances to employees, advances to other government agencies under agreements or contracts, and advances of cash or under letters of credit to nonfederal organizations.

There will be instances in which a receivable is later determined to be uncollectible, a condition no different from that occurring in the private sector. The accurate estimating of uncollectible receivables and the continual accounting of receivables are important aspects of accrual accounting in government. An allowance should be made during each fiscal period for estimated uncollectible receivables. (Receivables determined to be finally uncollectible must be pursued and settled in accordance with government regulations.) Typical of these receivable valuation accounts would be one possibly entitled *Allowance for uncollectible accounts*. This account would be shown as a deduction from the receivable balance in the financial statement. The net amount would be the estimate of collectible balances.

Inventories

Inventories are cost incurred for materials and supplies and work in process for the agency's purposes or others and, where appropriate, finished goods.

RESPONSIBILITIES OF VARIOUS ORGANIZATIONS

As mentioned in previous chapters, several organizations in addition to the operating agency have responsibilities for assets acquired with governmental funds. The principal organizations are the Congress, Office of Management and Budget, and General Accounting Office.

Congress

By several laws, the Congress has set policy with respect to the acquisition, accounting, and safeguarding of assets acquired by the expenditure of governmental funds. Agencies such as OMB, GAO, and GSA are legally responsible for providing guiding regulations to other agencies of the government. The heads of the individual operating agencies are required by law to establish systems of accounting and controls to properly acquire, manage, preserve, protect, and dispose of assets purchased with governmental funds.

Office of Management and Budget

The legal responsibilities of OMB require a continuing accounting and reporting to it of the resources consumed or possessed by an operating agency. The reporting of fund balances, obligations, property in the possession of an agency, and other assets or property under the stewardship of the agency has been detailed in several OMB Circulars.

- ▲ OMB Circular A-11, *Preparation and Submission of Budget*
- ▲ OMB Circular A-12, *Object Classification*
- ▲ OMB Circular A-34, *Instructions on Budget Execution*
- ▲ OMB Circular A-102, *Uniform Administrative Requirements for Grants-in-aid to State and Local Governments*
- ▲ OMB Circular A-109, *Major Systems Acquisitions*
- ▲ OMB Circular A-110, *Uniform Administrative Requirements for Grants and Other Agreements with Institutions of Higher Education, Hospitals, and Other Nonprofit Organizations*

Additionally, these statutory and other requirements are supplemented by numerous executive orders, issued by the President, requiring OMB to exercise additional authority and assume responsibilities with respect to the overall accounting for the assets of the government.

General Accounting Office

The GAO, under several laws, has been made responsible by Congress for prescribing the accounting and auditing principles and standards to federal agencies to ensure the proper stewardship and management of government assets or properties. The guidance by GAO relates to the accounting, management, reporting, and preservation of all the assets of the government. Although the principal promulgation of GAO is its *Policy and Procedures Manual for Guidance of Federal Agencies,* numerous other publications exist in areas of auditing of governmental assets and properties, detection of fraud and systems of internal controls, legal decisions relating to the appropriateness of disbursements of agency funds, procedures and criteria for claims settlement and debt collection, and records management, as well as accounting for the assets of an agency.

The Treasury

The Treasury has been legally vested with the responsibility relating to the estimation of funding needs, and the receiving, keeping, and disbursing of these funds. The Treasury issues guidelines to operating agencies prescribing the uniform reporting of funds available to agencies for obligation and expenditure. Additionally, the Treasury manages the establishment and utilization of imprest and cashier's funds throughout the government. Detailed reporting of transactions affecting the balances with the Treasury are required of every agency in the government.

The principal regulation of the Treasury is *The Treasury Fiscal Requirement Manual*. This manual contains the procedures imposed on government agencies relating to fiscal matters. The procedures include central accounting requirements, disbursing procedures, accounting for advances, and other requirements.

Operating Agencies

The head of each operating agency is legally responsible for establishing and maintaining a system of accounting and controls adequate to safeguard government assets against waste, loss, or improper or unwarranted use. The operating agency must implement and incorporate into a coherent system for controlling assets the various regulations prescribed by Congress and the central agencies above.

ASSET CONTROL PROCEDURES

The head of the operating agency is responsible for establishing and maintaining a system of internal controls. The control systems related to accounting and safeguarding of assets are similar to sound controls exercised by concerned corporate officials. There are some variations, however, related primarily to the nature of the controls resident among the central agencies and the operating agencies.

Selected controls and internal checks relating to the collection of cash and negotiable items were highlighted in Chapter 18 *(Receipts, Transfers, Reimbursements, and Refunds of Appropriated Funds)*. Other controls concerned with materials and property acquired by an agency are synopsized in the several chapters describing expenditure transactions of the government. (See Chapters 13, 14, 15, 16, and 17.)

Cash

In its Title 2, *The Accounting Principles and Standards for Federal Agencies,* the GAO prescribed the following procedures with respect to accounting and controlling cash resources.

▲ The accounting for cash receipts, disbursements, and balances on hand shall be complete, accurate, and honest.

▲ Receipts must be deposited promptly and recorded immediately after receipt and not deferred until transmission to a depository

▲ Disbursements shall be promptly recorded on the basis of paid vouchers

▲ Cash transactions shall be closed monthly, with a prompt reporting of transactions consummated only during the reporting period

▲ Separate cash accounts shall be maintained for major categories of cash resources (e.g., cash on deposit in banks, fund balance with the Treasury, imprest funds, etc.), with subdivisions provided to facilitate monitoring of restrictions on availability and reporting

▲ Cash resources must be handled in strict accordance with requirements of law, executive orders, central agencies guidance, and other requirements

▲ Responsibilities for handling, accounting, reporting, disbursing, and other cash-resource-related activities shall be divided among several officials and employees

▲ Each agency must establish an effective prepayment audit and voucher approval system (sampling techniques may be used under certain conditions) as a prerequisite to disbursement of agency funds

▲ Controls must exist to prevent duplicate payments

▲ Internal, independent audit reviews shall be made of controls relating to cash resources

Receivables

The timely and accurate accounting for receivables is an integral part of an accrual system. GAO, in Title 2, has stated that receivable accounting is an important form of control over agency resources resulting in a systematic record of amounts due that must be accounted for and reported. The GAO principles and standards relating to receivables require that

▲ Receivables be recorded accurately and promptly on completion of acts entitling an agency to collect amounts owed to it

▲ Recorded receivables shall consist of amounts actually due under contractual or other arrangements governing transactions resulting in the receivable

▲ Separate accounts must be maintained for major categories of receivables to facilitate clear and full disclosure

▲ Loans to others shall be accounted for as receivables only after funds have been disbursed. (Approved, but undisbursed loans should not be reported as assets with related liabilities.)

▲ Regular, periodic estimates must be made of amounts that may not be collectible and must be recorded separately in the accounts

▲ Receivables collectible in foreign currency that are not freely convertible into United States currency are subject to the same reporting standards as restricted foreign currency

Inventories

Several laws require that operating agencies establish and maintain inventory controls and accountability systems. By law, agencies are directed to have an accounting system that contains adequate monetary property accounting records. Property accounting procedures must provide both financial and quantitative information about these assets. The property accounting procedures prescribed by GAO must include these.

▲ All acquisitions (by purchase, transfer, donation, or other means) must be recorded on the date custody is obtained

▲ The accounting must recognize the use, application, consumption (through expensing for supplies and materials), and disposal of property

▲ Keeping of physical records of quantities of property by location, including those relating to use, transfer, and disposal

▲ Periodic confirmation of inventory by physical verification shall be made to confirm quantities, weight, quality, and controls with differences between the records and physical verifications being investigated and the variances recorded in the accounts

ACCOUNTING FOR CURRENT ASSETS

Accounting for Cash Type of Resources

The Congress appropriates funds for agencies to operate programs in the manner outlined in authorization and appropriation legislation. Most agencies are not involved with handling and accounting for significant amounts of cash although most agencies do have imprest funds requiring close control.

Appropriated Fund Balances

The "cash" account in most operating agencies is represented by the "Fund balance with the Treasury" account. When an appropriation bill is signed by the President, the Treasury will issue a warrant establishing the amount of the appropriation for agency operations. Each appropriation has a unique appropriation symbol assigned by the Treasury. In most instances, however, this full appropriation symbol is not recorded in the agency's accounts; appropriations are usually identified by a single digit or much simpler descriptors.

The initial entry by an agency to record the appropriation, once the Treasury has issued an appropriation warrant, would be

DEBIT: Fund balance with the Treasury
    CREDIT: Unappropriated appropriations
    To record funds appropriated by Congress upon receipt of the Treasury appropriation warrant

Cash Receipts and Disbursements

Other details concerning the accounting for cash receipts and disbursements appear in Chapter 18 (Receipts, Transfers, Reimbursements, and Refunds of Appropriated Funds) and Chapter 12 (Disbursements), respectively.

When an agency is authorized to collect receipts or other funds are received, the "Fund balance with the Treasury" may be increased, but the unapportioned appropriation balance may remain unchanged. Under this condition, the entry would be

DEBIT: Fund balance with the Treasury
    CREDIT: Accounts receivable or revenue
    To record receipt of cash for performance of services

Some agencies have collection responsibilities; these agencies maintain an accounting for cash receipts. However, the receipts of an agency may not be available to that agency for obligation and expenditure unless separate, specific legislation permits the use of receipts by the agency.

Disbursements are generally made by the Treasury upon written direction by an operating agency. The operating agency forwards a schedule listing payees for whom it desires checks to be issued.

The entry to record disbursements might involve the following accounts.

DEBIT: Advances
        Accounts payable
        Assets
        Expenses
    CREDIT: Fund balance with the Treasury
    To record transmittal of vouchers and schedule of payments to the Treasury for issuance of checks to designated payees.

Other Fund Balance Transactions

In addition to the above, other transactions will affect the "Fund balance with the Treasury" account. Some examples include

▲ Reimbursement by an operating agency to the Treasury for payments made by it under letter-of-credit drawdowns

▲ Transfers of funds to other agencies; nonexpenditure or interagency types of financing arrangement

▲ An allocation of part of the appropriate funds to another agency

▲ Transfer of funds to another agency upon processing by the other agency of a withdrawal or credit notice in payment for services rendered.

With the exception of the last transfer, which would be payment for services or goods obtained, the other transfers require agreement with the Treasury and Congressional recognition.

Fund Accounting Structures

GAO requires that separate accounts be maintained for the major categories of cash accounts. Additionally, such a categorization is often practical because of the analysis and detailed reporting required of this account. Separate codings have been established to signify specific transactions affecting the account balance. For example, the summary account, "Fund balance with the Treasury" and all subsidiary accounts used for specific types of transactions affecting this summary account could be coded to show (1) balance of the account; (2) increases; and (3) decreases.

In the case of the "Fund balance with the Treasury," the coding might be

(0) *Summary account*
$100 \times \underline{} \ \underline{}$ = Fund balance with the Treasury

(1) *Summary account balance*
$100 \times \underline{1} \ \underline{0}$ = Balance September 30/October 1, normally debit balance

(2) *Increases or debit balance subsidiary accounts*
$100 \times \underline{2} \ \underline{0}$ = *Confirmed deposits,* an increase or debit entry
$100 \times \underline{3} \ \underline{0}$ = *In transits,* an increase or debit entry

(3) *Decreases or credit balance subsidiary accounts*
$100 \times \underline{4} \ \underline{0}$ = *Checks issued,* a decrease or credit entry
$100 \times \underline{6} \ \underline{0}$ = *Treasury reimbursement* for grantee or contractor drawdowns under letters of credit, a decrease or credit entry
$100 \times \underline{7} \ \underline{0}$ = *Transfers to other agencies* (nonexpenditure, interagency financing), a decrease or credit entry

$100 \times \underline{8} \; \underline{0}$ = *Allocations to other agencies*, a decrease or credit entry

$100 \times \underline{9} \; \underline{0}$ = *Transfer to other agencies or funds by fund withdrawal or credit notices* (e.g., GSA 789, SF 1081), a decrease or credit entry

At the end of the fiscal period, the cash details reflected in the subsidiary accounts are closed to the summary "Fund balance with the Treasury" account. During the fiscal period, however, the reporting to the Treasury and OMB is considerably facilitated by structuring a general ledger to conform as closely as possible with the recurrent reporting requirements.

As indicated during discussion of various types of expenditures, payees to whom the agency desires to have checks drawn must be listed and forwarded to the Treasury, which actually writes the check. Other reductions in this account would relate to interagency fund transfers resulting from letters-of-credit transactions or the forwarding of withdrawal and credit "invoices" between agencies.

The subdivision of a general ledger account is not restricted in practice to the account above. The technique is useful with any account that requires repeated analysis or for which unique reporting requirements exist.

Imprest Funds

The cash of an imprest fund represents an advance from the Treasury for which a periodic accounting must be made by the recipient agency. As an expenditure is made from the imprest fund, an entry is made in the agency's records for the expenditure and reimbursement payment to the imprest fund. The reimbursement payment returns the imprest fund balance to the original amount of the funds advanced by the Treasury.

The accounting for receipt of the fund and the replenishment of expended amounts would be done in the following manner.

DEBIT: Imprest fund
  CREDIT: Imprest fund advance (liability account)
  To record advance from the Treasury to establish the imprest fund

DEBIT: Advances, travel, supplies, material
  CREDIT: Fund balance with the Treasury
  To record expenditures from imprest fund and disbursement to replenish the fund

Disbursements for expenditures must also be recorded and reflected as a reduction in the unobligated appropriation balance of the agency. For example

338

DEBIT: Unobligated allotments
    CREDIT: Expended appropriation—operating
To record the purchase of supplies and material from petty cash disbursements

The entry above is necessary because imprest-fund disbursements will not have been previously recorded as an obligation. In effect, the obligation, the liquidation of the obligation, and the accruing of the expenditure are simultaneous events.

Accounts Receivable and Advances

As described earlier, receivables may arise from the disbursement of funds to others, e.g., advances made to agency employees, contractors, and grantees. Under these conditions, accounting for the receivable transaction is

DEBIT: Accounts receivable—travel advances
                  Accounts receivable—grantee advances
    CREDIT: Fund balance with the Treasury
To record funds disbursed for advances

Additionally, the receivables could represent transactions between two government agencies. This might occur when one agency advances funds to another for services to be received. In contrast, an agency may have performed services for another and is awaiting payment of a bill.
In the case of the advanced funds the accounting is

DEBIT: Advances to other agencies
    CREDIT: Fund balance with the Treasury
To record transfer of advanced funds to another agency

Additionally, if the entry above was an appropriation transfer, the following companion entry would be required to restrict the unallotted appropriation fund balance of the original agency. For example,

DEBIT: Unallotted apportionments
    CREDIT: Appropriation allocated to other agencies
To record reduction in unallotted appropriation and restriction of appropriation for amounts transferred to another agency

The account, "Appropriation allocated to other agencies," is an equity account representing a restriction of the appropriation balance that is now remaining to the agency advancing the funds.

A contrary accounting occurs if an agency receives a portion of another agency's appropriation for which it must perform a service. Under these conditions, the following events must be recorded.

▲ The receipt of the advance, which creates a liability until services are performed

▲ The increase in the receiving agency's funds available for obligation

▲ Recognition of obligations in the same manner as is done for the receiving agency's own appropriation

▲ Accounting for work performed or services rendered on behalf of another agency

▲ Payment of vendors and others for costs incurred

▲ Recording and distribution of costs to completed projects or services

▲ Liquidation or elimination of the liability for advances and recognition of income earned

▲ Balancing out the appropriation received from the other agency and recognizing the reimbursement to the performing agency's appropriation for funds

▲ Billing for services rendered and revenues earned

The entry for the last event, if no advance had been received, is

DEBIT: Account receivable—appropriation reimbursements
   CREDIT: Revenues
   To record accounts receivable due from billings made for services or goods delivered and related revenues realized from the sale

Uncollectible Receivables

Periodic reviews must be made of receivables due. Amounts owed by government as well as nongovernment organizations should be examined for collectibility. There will be instances in which a recorded receivable may be contested by the other agency. This dispute will have an effect on the amounts ultimately collected.

For financial-statement purposes, an estimate for uncollectible receivables could be based on a historical average or other supportable indices. Additionally the account balances of individual customers might be assessed. The conclusion concerning the uncollectible amount would have to be recorded in a manner similar to the following.

DEBIT: Uncollectible receivables—estimated
    CREDIT: Allowance for uncollectible accounts
    To record the estimated cost of uncollectible accounts and establish an allowance as a reduction to the reported accounts receivable balance

The entry above must be adjusted for accounts later determined to be uncollectible. A distinction must be made between estimates of uncollectible accounts and those accounts actually determined to be uncollectible. The Federal Claims Collection Act of 1966 makes agencies responsible for collecting debts due to the United States that arise as a result of the agency's activities, including amounts due resulting from illegal, improper, or incorrect payments.

The settlement, including compromising debts and amounts due the United States, requires adherence to precise, prescribed procedures, which involve the General Account Office and, in some instance, the Congress itself. GAO sets forth guidance to such transactions in Title 4— *Claim-General,* of its *Manual for Guidance of Federal Agencies.* At present, agencies may adjudicate claims for less than $600; amounts above that value must be settled by the General Accounting Office.

Inventories

Many operating agencies do not maintain asset accounting for inventories. The practice is to charge such amounts directly to expenses or operations as incurred. This method may be appropriate because the supplies and materials ordinarily included in such accounts could be relatively insignificant in comparison to other expenditures of the agency. Further, the supplies and materials may be consumed during the period of purchase.

Inventories are normally recorded (1) when the balance of such items is significant, (2) when work-in-process accounts are maintained for agency projects in progress, or (3) when agency operations involve the production of finished goods awaiting distribution to users. Under these conditions several events must be recorded.

1. Obligations are required for purchased materials and supplies.
2. Cost of work performed must be recorded.
3. Obligations must be liquidated or reduced for accrued expenditures.
4. Liabilities must be paid.
5. Cost of resources consumed must be charged to operations.

These events are reflected by the following accounting entries.

1. DEBIT: Unobligated allotments
   CREDIT: Unliquidated obligations

2. DEBIT: Work-in-process inventory
            Finished goods inventory
            Inventory—other
   CREDIT: Accounts payable

3. DEBIT: Unliquidated obligations
   CREDIT: Expended appropriation—operating

4. DEBIT: Accounts payable
   CREDIT: Fund balance with the Treasury

5. DEBIT: Expenses
   CREDIT: Work-in-process inventory
            Finished-goods inventory
            Inventory—other

METHOD OF COSTING ACTIVITIES In Title 2, *Accounting*, GAO has prescribed that materials and supplies issued for use shall be charged to the using or consuming activities on the basis of cost.

GAO permits "cost" to be determined by the simplest method that produces reasonable and useful measures of cost. Identified, acceptable methods could include

▲ Specific identification of the cost of items issued

▲ Cost determined on a first-in, first-out assumption

▲ Computed average cost

▲ Standard cost, adjusted periodically to reflect actual cost

Accordingly, agencies whose operations are supported by a general fund type of appropriation usually value inventories at cost of acquisition. Agencies involved in the manufacturing of finished goods or those operating activities of a business type must make the same valuation decision as financial managers in the private sector, within the restraints above.

REPORTING CURRENT ASSETS To assist in reporting and to minimize efforts required to perform repetitive analyses of a financial type, most agencies structure the general ledger and subsidiary ledger accounts in a manner that permits the aggregation

Exhibit 19.1 **AN AGENCY STATEMENT OF ASSETS, LIABILITIES, AND INVESTMENT ASSETS**

CURRENT ASSETS

Cash

In banks		$ x,xxx	
On hand and in transit		xxx	
Unexpended with other agencies		xx	$ x,xxx
Balances with the Treasury			
Operating funds		$xxx,xxx	
Trust and deposit funds		x,xxx	
Allocation from other agencies		xxx	xxx,xxx

Advances receivable

Travel	$xxx		
Contractors	xx		
Grantees	xxx		
Government agencies	xxx		
Other	xx	$ x,xxx	
Less allowance for uncollectibles		(xx)	x,xxx

Accounts receivable

Repayment to appropriation	$xxx		
Due from government agencies	xxx		
Contractors	xxx		
Grantees	xx		
Other	xx	$ xxx	
Less allowance for uncollectibles		(xx)	xxx

Inventories

Commodities for sale, finished goods	$xxx		
Work-in-process	xx		
Materials and supplies	x	$ xxx	
Less: allowance for loss		(xx)	xxx

Accrued interest receivable		x,xxx
Notes receivable		
Loans receivable		xxx
Total current assets		$ xxx,xxx
Fixed and long-term assets		xxx,xxx
Other assets		$ xx,xxx
TOTAL ASSETS		$x,xxx,xxx

of asset amounts by a variety of known reporting formats. One such report is the Treasury's Statement of Financial Condition (SF 220) that displays assets, liabilities, and net investments of the agency. This form is a condensed balance sheet of a government agency that is required to be submitted annually.

In addition to the central reporting to the Treasury, an agency may have more frequent reporting needs and internal requirements by management. Thus monthly an agency should produce its own balance sheet designed to permit detailed reporting of assets and, when summarized, meet governmentwide requirements. Exhibit 19.1 lists examples of the current asset accounts that could be reported on the internal balance sheet.

The total operating fund account balance comprises several ledger accounts relating to balances of amounts available to the agency in its general, special, and revolving fund accounts. The funds relating to trust and deposit funds are separately identified. In a combined balance sheet display, the accounts for the several funds and appropriations for which an agency is responsible would be aggregated. The agency, to meet the requirements of appropriation legislation, must maintain separate accounts in its ledgers for each of the appropriations or funds for which it has some type of stewardship responsibility

chapter 20 Fixed Assets and Other Assets

INTRODUCTION The accounting for fixed assets of an agency is one of the most discussed subjects among governmental financial managers. The unresolved questions relating to valuation and costing of these investments are seen by many as a real impediment to adoption of full accrual accounting in the government sector.

Questions persist with respect to the basis for valuing and reporting fixed assets, particularly those of historical significance and others having extremely long lives. The determination of useful asset lives is also perplexing to agency managers. The utility of accounting for depreciation as a current cost, for which funds were provided in a fiscal period in the distant past is continually questioned.

In practice, rather good controls may exist over the physical aspects of the asset. Possibly the property records even address location, quantity, and quality of the asset over the years. Often, though, the financial valuation and costing history have been lost, and financial and physical property records may no longer be comparable.

FIXED ASSETS AND OTHER ASSETS

DEFINITIONS *Fixed assets* include the cost of resources benefiting agency operations beyond a fiscal period or those resources not intended to be consumed by agency activities or operations during a single fiscal period. While not all agencies have these assets on their records, fixed assets may include

- ▲ Buildings
- ▲ Equipment
- ▲ Leasehold improvements
- ▲ Land

Differences appear to exist between the Office of Management and Budget and the General Accounting Office in defining fixed assets. However, the nature of the reporting is probably more responsible for any inconsistency.

OMB is concerned with the acquisition and timely reporting of current expenditures for capital assets. GAO also has interest in the proper accounting and utilization of such items. GAO's interest may continue long after expired appropriation accounts have been merged into the Treasury. Once the expired accounts have been merged with the Treasury accounts, the invested capital remaining from the expired appropriation is reflected solely by the fixed assets acquired when the appropriation was available for obligation and expenditure.

OMB Definitions

The OMB Circular A-12, *Object Classification*, includes definitions of obligations and expenditures for fixed assets such as equipment, structures, and land within the definition of capital assets. Under that circular these categories are to be reported in the following classifications.

Equipment

Equipment includes charges for personal property with a service life of a year or more and includes the cost of initial installation and transportation. The category includes such assets as equipment, furniture and fixtures, machinery, instruments, automatic data processing equipment and, when purchased, armament.

Land and Structures

Land and structures, according to OMB criteria, include charges for land and interests in land, buildings, and other structures, additions to buildings, fixed equipment, easements, and rights-of-way.

GAO Definitions

From an accounting view, the GAO has established (in its *Manual for Guidance of Federal Agencies*—Title 2, Accounting) slightly varying definitions for fixed assets. These definitions and the standards and principles set forth by GAO form the financial and accounting criteria with which an agency must comply.

Equipment

Equipment includes the cost of all machinery, equipment, furniture and fixtures, and other nonexpendable property not classified in other fixed-asset accounts. Typical examples are typewriters, copiers, and furniture.

Buildings

This account reflects the cost of government-owned buildings under the control of the agency, including the purchase costs and cost of additions or betterments after the date of acquisition, as well as permanent fixtures and equipment.

Leasehold Improvements

Leasehold improvements include the cost of improvements to any leased property, such as land, buildings, or other facilities occupied by a government agency as lessee. Of course, the cost of government-owned buildings located on leased land are improvements to be recorded in the proper fixed-asset account.

Depreciation

Full costing of an agency's activities or operations requires a determination and accounting for the consumption or utilization of assets. The General Accounting Office requires that there be an accounting for depreciation as an integral part of accrual-based accounting. Such depreciation, or amortization in the case of a leasehold, may not be a currently funded expenditure of a fiscal period, but it is still a cost consumed to support the agency's operations. The several accounts that might be involved are

▲   Accumulated depreciation—buildings
▲   Accumulated depreciation—equipment
▲   Amortization of leasehold improvements

The accounts are shown in the financial statements as deductions from the related fixed-asset accounts.

Capitalization Criteria

April 4, 1980, the GAO published the following capitalization criteria for fixed assets.

	DOLLAR AMOUNT
▲ Furniture, fixtures, office equipment	$ 300
▲ All other property	1000

Acquisition for less than the amounts above are to be recorded as expenses. An agency could adopt a lower minimum but no minimums above these amounts are to be used.

Land

This account reflects the cost of government-owned real estate under control of the agency and is debited with the purchase price, appraisal fees, clearing costs, improvements, surveys, and removal and relocation of other property purchased but not used by the agency.

RESPONSIBILITIES OF THE GENERAL SERVICES ADMINISTRATION (GSA)

In addition to OMB and GAO, the GSA has considerable legal responsibilities for property in government. The GSA, established by the Federal Property and Administrative Act in 1949, exercises a governmentwide responsibility relating to assets, property management, and the procurement of these resources. Among the several responsibilities of GSA affecting or relating to the accounting for properties by an operating agency are

▲ Planning, acquisition, custody, leasing of space, facilities, buildings, furnishing, and equipment

▲ Design, construction, alteration, remodeling, repair, and general preservation of government assets

▲ Inventory management, including agency supply operations

▲ Management, operation, and utilization of federal data processing centers providing services to other departments and agencies

▲ Promotion and coordination of purchase, lease, maintenance, operations, and utilization of computers and related equipment

While much of GSA operations are financed from direct appropriations, advances from, and user charges to, customer operating government agencies and rental proceeds and sales to other agencies are other methods of interagency payments for assets acquired by GSA for operating agencies.

CONTROL PROCEDURES It is the responsibility of each agency to establish those policies, procedures, and practices to account for and safeguard the assets for which it has accountability. The designed controls must be adequate to assure management that

▲ Only needed property is acquired in the quantity, of the quality, and for the price that is most advantageous to the government

▲ Physical property records are maintained for all acquired property, regardless of whether it was acquired by purchase, construction, transfer, donation or in other ways; records show quantity, quality, and location of property

▲ Accounting records are established and kept current to show the acquisition, use, application or consumption, or ultimate disposal of all property

▲ Periodic checks or inventories or confirmation are made of properties, and a comparison for consistency is made to the physical and the financial accounting records

▲ Accounting adjustments are made to reconcile the balances of the physical property records to the fiscal records

▲ Accounting for additions, betterments, repair, and maintenance are consistent with agency policy

▲ Property in possession of contractors and grantees of the agency is regularly reported and physically verified periodically to ensure its continued existence and proper utilization

GAO, in Title 2, requires that, where necessary, the cost of consumption should be accounted for over the property's useful life through depreciation-accounting techniques. In practice, though, some agencies have yet to integrate fully the logistical aspects of property accounting with the fiscal accounts. Thus the balances in the general ledger often may not serve as control accounts over the property-accounting activities. Also, depreciation is not a cost requiring the current commitment of funds from an active appropriation; that is, depreciation is an unfunded cost. Thus because it is an unfunded cost, less emphasis is given to its accounting.

Some agencies do, however, maintain sufficient subsidiary financial accounts to permit the ready identification of fixed assets. These control accounts are in turn supported by subsidiary ledgers and property records providing detailed information for each asset or group of items within an asset category.

Often, the subsidiary fixed asset and property records will contain such identifying information as

▲ Description or code number, part number
▲ Identification or code number
▲ Source from which acquired
▲ Purchase price or other value
▲ Date acquired
▲ Present location
▲ Responsible organization or custodian
▲ Date of inventory
▲ Information on betterment or improvements
▲ Information to permit computation of depreciation
▲ Estimates of residual values
▲ Quantity
▲ Quality

ACCOUNTING STANDARDS AND PRINCIPLES FOR FIXED ASSETS

GAO prescribes the basic standards, principles, and, in some instances, the procedures relating to the valuation, changes, and inventorying of fixed assets in the possession of agencies. Additionally, guidance has been published on depreciation practices.

Valuing Changes in Inventory of Fixed Assets

Title 2, *Accounting,* contains the standards, principles, or procedures relating to the accounting for fixed assets, which state or require that

▲ The primary basis of accounting for property is cost to the agency responsible for its management. If incurred costs are not measurable or not known, reasonable estimates or alternative bases (such as appraised values) may be used.
▲ For long-lived property, the use, application, or consumption should be accounted for as an operating cost over the property's estimated useful life by appropriate depreciation techniques.
▲ Independent checks must be made on the accuracy of accounting records through periodic physical count, weighing, or other measurement.
▲ Basic cost shall include acquisition cost, transportation, installation, and other cost to put the property in the form and place to be used or managed.

350

- ▲ Fixed assets shall be capitalized in agency accounts pursuant to criteria giving consideration to (1) length of service or useful life, (2) repetitive use, (3) frequency of replacement, (4) retention of identity when in use, (5) significance of cost, and (6) significance of changes affecting usefulness, productivity, life, and capacity.

- ▲ Capitalization criteria should consider identifiable units or groups of property; no minimum in excess of $300 for furniture, fixtures, and office equipment or $1,000 for all other property shall be established by any agency.

- ▲ Cost of constructed facilities should include all material elements of cost such as engineering and architectural and other services for designs, plans, and specifications; acquisition cost; labor, materials, supplies, and other direct charges; shares of cost of equipment and facilities used in construction; applicable indirect costs; fixed and severable equipment and cost of installation; inspection, supervision, and administration of construction contracts and work; legal fees and damage claims; fair value of donated property.

- ▲ For property produced by agencies for use within the government, the inclusion of interest in accounts or disclosure as a cost is not necessary. Interest must be disclosed when comparisons are required or if the omission would result in incomplete disclosures.

- ▲ Property should be capitalized at the time of receipt or acceptance by the government rather than at the time payment is made or when title passes to the government.

- ▲ Property acquired under lease-purchase contracts are to be capitalized when the purchase option is exercised; the amount capitalized will be the contract purchase price less cumulative allowances.

- ▲ Interagency transfers of property shall be accounted as follows

  If the transfer is made on a reimbursable basis, the receiving agency will use the transfer price as set forth in the agreement, statute, or central agency regulation but not at less than the estimated useful value.

  If the transfer is made on a nonreimbursable basis, the recorded amount shall be estimated by the receiving agency, considering condition, use, and market value, including cost of incoming transportation.

- ▲ Cost of property acquired by trading in other property shall be at the lesser of (1) the cash paid or payable, plus amounts allowed by seller on traded property, or (2) the purchase price had there been no trade-in.

- ▲ Property acquired by foreclosure shall be capitalized at the lesser of (1) the appraised or fair market value, or (2) the amount owed by borrower or debtor, plus cost incurred by the government.

- ▲ Capitalized value of property acquired by any other means shall be the estimated amount that the agency is willing to pay, considering usefulness, condition, and fair market value.

- ▲ Purchase discounts are deductions from cost; such discounts are not income.

- ▲ Cost of making changes is capitalized when changes significantly extend useful life or enhance the capacity to render service and the cost of property or features superseded or destroyed during change is removed from the property accounts.

▲ Capitalized leasehold improvements must have an estimated useful life of over one year; the cost of improvements should be depreciated over the period of occupancy or life of the improvement, whichever is less.

Conditions Requiring Depreciation

The utility of computing depreciation on government-owned assets has been discussed for years. In government, depreciation accounting is often performed more for compliance and conformance than from a belief in the utility of the concept. Invariably, practitioners conclude discussions with no resolution on the appropriate depreciation policy or method to be used.

Over the years, GAO has taken the positions (1) that depreciation is a cost, but one that does not require the current expenditure of funds and (2) that there is no way to determine precisely such costs. Additionally, GAO, in its Title 2, has stated that depreciation accounting shall be accomplished whenever the need arises for a periodic determining of the cost of all resources consumed in performing services.

The latter point by GAO is important. Often there is not a need to determine the cost of all services or functions performed by a government agency. According to GAO, there are at least four instances in which depreciation costs are required.

▲ When financial results of operations, in terms of cost of performance in relation to revenues earned, are to be fully disclosed in financial reports

▲ When amounts to be collected as reimbursement for services performed are determined on a full-cost basis, pursuant to legal or administrative policy

▲ When investment in fixed property assets used is substantial and there is a need for total cost for comparisons, evaluations, and planning purposes

▲ When cost of property constructed by an agency is needed to determine the amounts to be capitalized

Depreciation Defined

Depreciation is an estimate of the cost of a long-lived capital asset consumed, used, or rendered obsolete that benefits or supports operations or performance during the estimated useful life of the asset. Depreciation is a cost of an agency. It is somewhat difficult, at times, to estimate this cost precisely.

Depreciation Practices

The depreciation practices are not uniform among the federal agencies. Generally, agencies with activities that are supported by "selling" services to other organizations in the agency or to other agencies will carefully calculate depreciation and ensure that the "selling price" to others provides for a full return of total cost, including depreciation. There are several principles and procedures prescribed by GAO, in Title 2, that have been implemented by agencies in which the need exists to perform and use depreciation accounting.

▲ The cost of capital assets to be depreciated shall be reduced by the estimate of realizable salvage value, as in the case of land.

▲ The estimate of useful life of the asset must consider the effects of technological and economical utilization of the physical life of the facility. (The difficulty in estimating useful life is not considered by GAO as a valid reason for not accounting for depreciation.)

▲ The maximum useful life for a federal asset is 100 years.

▲ Undue precision and detail should be avoided in depreciation account.

The dollar amount to be recorded for the periodic depreciation expense is determined by allocating (or dividing) the net depreciable capital asset value by the units of service life (i.e., the straight-line method of depreciation). For example, an asset with a net depreciable value of $15 million, having a service life of ten years, would have an estimated periodic depreciation cost of $1.5 million.

Under the GAO standards, the undepreciated net capital asset value, plus the value of betterments or additions, should be depreciated over the extended useful life of the property or the enlarged capacity of the facility. In the case of leasehold improvements, these costs should be depreciated over either the period of occupancy or the life of the improvement, whichever is less.

Being public entities, not concerned with income tax liability, government agencies do not use the accelerated methods of depreciation associated with income tax determination (i.e., double declining balance or sum-of-the-years digits). An increased rate of consumption or acceleration in the utilization of the capital asset could, however, be reflected in the selection of the appropriate unit or rate of depreciation.

For capital assets placed in service, the periodic accounting entry for depreciation is

DEBIT: Depreciation
　　CREDIT: Accumulated depreciation
To record depreciation on capital assets consumed during this accounting period

No companion entry is required to adjust the obligation accounts or record an accrued expenditure. The expenditure entries were made during an earlier period when the capital asset was acquired or constructed. For this reason, the depreciation is referred to as an "unfunded" cost and must be identified in the agency reports as not affecting the current period's appropriated fund balances.

ACCOUNTING FOR FIXED ASSETS

The acquisition of fixed assets by a government agency may be by one or more of the following methods: (1) purchase from a nongovernment source; (2) construction by the agency; (3) transfer from another agency; or (4) donation. The value to be recorded will vary under each of these conditions and will accordingly affect depreciation accounting.

Purchase from a Nongovernment Source

A capital asset may be purchased directly from a nonfederal organization under a contract or other form of agreement. The value of the capital assets so acquired should be

▲　Purchase price in cash or reasonable estimates if cost is not measurable or is not known
　　　Plus: transportation-in, installation costs, and interest expense
　　　Less: value of land and purchase discounts.

Once the value of the capitalized asset is determined, the accounting includes a recognition of the formal obligation, recording of the asset acquired, providing for an estimate of depreciation or cost consumed. The specific transactions include

DEBIT: Unobligated allotment
　　CREDIT: Unliquidated obligation
To reduce the previously unobligated allotment balance and record the obligation related to the execution of a contract or agreement to acquire a capital asset

DEBIT: Unliquidated obligation
    CREDIT: Expended appropriation
    To record the liquidation obligation and the expended funds related to the acquisition of a capital asset

plus

DEBIT: Fixed asset
    CREDIT: Accounts payable
    To record the capital asset in the accounts and the liability owed

DEBIT: Accounts payable
    CREDIT: Fund balance with the Treasury
    To record payment of liability and reduction of balance with the Treasury

DEBIT: Depreciation
    CREDIT: Accumulated depreciation
    To record estimated depreciation as an expense of the current period and accumulated depreciation as a reduction in the value of the capital asset consumed

When other costs are properly includable in the capitalized cost of an asset, these costs (such as transportation, installation or other preparation costs, or interest costs) might be recorded in subsidiary capital asset accounts to permit the ready indentification between original purchase price and other costs and avoid time-consuming analyses concerning the value of recorded assets. These additional related costs must be accounted for in the same manner as the initial cost of the asset. The obligation and later accrued expenditure must be recorded as well as the accounting for the increase in the value of the capital asset.

Construction by an Agency

GAO requires that the capitalized value of constructed assets include all material elements of cost, such as

▲ Engineering, architectural and outside services for designs, plans, specifications, and surveys

▲ Acquisition of land, buildings, and other facilities

▲ Labor, materials and supplies, and other direct charges

▲ An appropriate share of equipment and facilities used in construction

▲ Applicable indirect cost

▲ Fixed and severable collateral equipment and its installation to complete the facility for its intended use

▲ Inspection, supervision, administration of construction contracts, and construction work

FIXED ASSETS AND OTHER ASSETS

▲ Legal fees and damage claims

▲ Fair value of contributed or donated land, facilities, utilities, labor, materials, supplies, services, and equipment

▲ Interest cost incurred during construction

For constructed assets, the accounting is performed through accumulating costs during construction in suspense or inventory series of accounts. Typically, agencies will use an asset account, entitled *Construction Work in Progress*.

The total value of the capital asset should be accumulated without regard to the financing or other source of benefiting resource. The sources of expenses and cost recorded in this account could be varied, having their origin in inventory drawdowns, agency labor, purchased materials, allocated overhead and indirect costs, contracted services and other work, utilization of equipment, and interest expenses. These various charges are accounted for in a manner similar to that used in accounting for all other expenditures of a federal agency. Each must initially have been the result of an obligation, and the accounting records must show the accrued expenditure.

As costs are consumed for the asset being constructed, the costs are transferred from the accounts initially charged to the construction work-in-progress account. Other expenditures will be incurred only for the asset being constructed. These types are charged directly to the work-in-progress account. Inventory items and depreciation and amortized costs have to be allocated. Expense accounts have to be relieved for indirect or overhead costs that are more appropriately a part of the constructed asset. Charges or debits to the work order subsidiary accounts would be increases as well as to the control asset account, construction work in progress. As the constructed assets are completed and placed in services, the work-in-progress account is reduced or relieved of the costs of assets placed into operation or service.

Agencies with construction activities have usually established a work order, job order, or project cost accounting system. All costs related to the construction effort are charged to a specific work order.

The several entries, in summary form, are

DEBIT: Unobligated allotments
CREDIT: Unliquidated obligations
To reduce the balance of the unobligated allotment balance and record obligations for contracts, orders, and agreements related to the acquisition of services, goods, materials, and equipment to be used in constructing a capital asset

DEBIT: Unliquidated obligations
   CREDIT: Expended appropriation—capital
                   Expended appropriation—operating
To record the liquidation of obligations and recognition of various accrued expenditures

plus

DEBIT: Inventory (asset)
                Construction work-in-progress
                Expenses
   CREDIT: Accounts payable
To record expenditures for future consumption (inventory), direct charges to the construction work-in-progress account, and other expenses of the period

DEBIT: Accounts payable
   CREDIT: Fund balance with the Treasury
To record payment of liabilities and reduction of available funds in the Treasury

DEBIT: Construction work-in-progress
   CREDIT: Accumulated depreciation
                Inventory
                Equipment
                Expense
To record resources consumed through use of other depreciable assets, withdrawn inventory, reclassification of equipment, as direct cost of construction project, reallocation of expenses (possibly indirect or overhead) to the construction project

DEBIT: Building
   CREDIT: Construction work-in-progress
To record the completion of the construction project and placement of the asset in service

Entries to the construction work-in-progress account are supported by the costs accumulated on the various work or job orders identifying specific project charged. These records are the supporting documents for any subsidiary accounts as well.

While the asset is under construction, no depreciation for the asset itself is recorded. The reason is that no service is available from the asset under construction. Depreciation will be recorded from the date the asset is placed in service and formally recognized as a fixed and operating asset of the organization. It is proper, of course, to record the depreciation of equipment and other facilities used in construction as charges to the construction work-in-progress account.

Transfer from Another Agency

The value of capital assets received from another agency depends on the nature of the interagency agreement and the useful value. According to GAO, value of a transferred capital asset shall be determined as follows.

▲ If the capital assets are acquired on a *reimbursable basis,* the value to be recorded by the receiving agency is based on the agreement, applicable statute, or regulation, but not less than the estimated useful value (presumably fair market value).

▲ If the capital assets are acquired on a *nonreimbursable* basis, the amount to be recorded is estimated by the receiving agency, considering condition, use, and market value.

The agency transferring capital assets on a nonreimbursable basis shall record the book value of the transferred asset as a reduction in the government's investment in that agency's assets. When the receiving agency's estimated amount differs from the depreciated value of the asset as reflected on the transferring agency's records, the transferring agency is notified and the reasons therefor documented in the records.

Transportation and installation costs would be appropriate additions to the capital asset account balance. It is not necessary, though, for agencies performing services for use within the government to include interest in the accounts or disclose such costs in the financial statement.

The accounting for an asset acquired on a reimbursable basis could vary, depending on whether (1) the receiving agency had earlier transferred or allocated a portion of its appropriation to another agency for the purposes of acquiring the capital asset, or (2) the receiving agency is merely reimbursing the other agency for a capital asset acquired or constructed by the other agency in the course of its normal business. In both instances, the receiving agency ultimately must use some of its appropriation balance to pay for the assets received. (The accounting for allocation of appropriations and reimbursements to appropriations is discussed in Chapter 18.)

With respect to an asset received on a nonreimbursable basis, the receiving agency must reflect an increase in the asset balance for which it is accountable and a corresponding increase in the account disclosing the investment of the government. The transaction does not affect the appropriation accounts or fund balances of the receiving agency. In this case, the effect on the accounts would be similar to the receipt of a donated or contributed asset.

OTHER ASSETS While much attention is given to the accounting for current and fixed assets, considerable efforts are also required of the government agencies to reflect properly the many transactions that are categorized as the other asset accounts.

While *other assets* may be generally defined as all assets other than current and fixed, this description does not disclose the nature of these balances. Within this category are, to mention a few, suspense accounts awaiting distribution to other accounts, prepaid supplies and materials, security deposits, and the reciprocal accounts required for controlling retirement deductions.

Suspense Accounts

Other asset accounts, for example, suspense accounts, may be established by agencies initially to record expenses and costs until final allocation or distribution is determined. Such transactions must be processed through the same obligations and expenditure processes required of all other governmental transactions.

Prepaid Supplies and Materials

On occasion, supplies and materials may be prepaid and not consumed by the end of the accounting period. Such amounts may be established by inventory and will be costed to agency operations during the next fiscal period. At reporting date, however, a resource exists that will benefit a future period.

Unless significant in relation to other asset account balances, agencies would not, however, accrue or record the prepaid expenses for supplies and materials.

Security Deposits

Under certain conditions agencies may require surety deposits as security or partial guarantee of performance. When required, the other asset account, possibly entitled *Securities deposit,* is recorded as a contra account to a liability account reflecting the amount that might be repayable to the depositor at some future date.

Retirement Reciprocal Accounts

Agencies have been required to maintain a cumulative accounting of payroll deductions for civil service retirement purposes. The amounts must be recorded formally in a series of memoranda accounts that are grouped within the other asset category.

One account, a debit balance account, entitled *Reciprocal account — Civil Service Commission,* is used to record the aggregate retirement deductions from employees from current and prior years that were deposited with the Treasury to the credit of the Retirement and Disability Fund. Two contra credit balance accounts are maintained: (1) Retirement deductions—prior periods records accumulated amounts deducted for civil service retirement in prior calendar years. (This single account is maintained for all prior period deductions regardless of appropriations or funds to which the employees' salaries were originally charged and is supported by the individual employees' retirement records.) (2) Retirement deductions—current year show the amount deducted from employees during the current calendar year. (This single account is maintained for all current year deductions regardless of appropriations or funds to which the employees' salaries were originally charged and is supported by Individual Pay Cards.) Both the debit balance and the two credit balance accounts (if displayed at all) are viewed as other asset accounts and are shown as off-setting asset accounts in a financial statement.

The accounting process for other assets would adhere to the same transaction process: obligations, accrued expenditures, payables, and disbursements.

REPORTING FIXED ASSETS AND OTHER ASSETS Many agencies will prepare monthly balance sheets showing the general and several subsidiary ledger accounts. While the total detail may not be required by external agencies such as the Treasury or the Office of Management and Budget, the monthly balance sheet provides management with pertinent information. Properly structured, the account listing will preclude numerous financial kinds of analyses. Exhibit 20.1 lists examples of how the fixed and other asset accounts could be reported on an internal balance sheet.

Exhibit 20.1 **AN AGENCY STATEMENT OF ASSETS, LIABILITIES, AND INVESTMENT ASSETS**

CURRENT ASSETS			$ xxx,xxx
FIXED- AND LONG-TERM ASSETS			
PLANT AND EQUIPMENT			
Equipment	$x,xxx,xxx		
Buildings and structure	xxx,xxx		
Construction and rehab in progress	xxx,xxx		
Excess plant and equipment	x,xxx	$x,xxx,xxx	
LEASEHOLD IMPROVEMENTS		xxx,xxx	
Less: Accumulated depreciation/ amortization		(xx,xxx)	x,xxx,xxx
LAND			xxx,xxx
OTHER ASSETS			
Suspense accounts		$ x,xxx	
Prepaid supplies and materials		x,xxx	
Security deposits		x,xxx	
Deferred charges		x,xxx	
Other		xx	x,xxx
TOTAL ASSETS			$x,xxx,xxx

In a combined balance sheet or composite reporting, as in the example above, the several funds and appropriations for which an agency may be responsible are assumed to be merged. Within the general and subsidiary ledger account structure, the illustrated asset account balances must be maintained for each separate fund and appropriation pursuant to law or applicable regulations.

chapter 21 Liabilities

INTRODUCTION In governmental accounting the concern with liabilities has historically been in connection with the unrecorded liabilities of the government. For example, until recently, few governmental agencies reflected any obligation for employees' retirement and disability plans, probably the largest of all liabilities of the government. Even today, fewer government agencies have the financial resources to fully fund these types of liabilities, although it is now the practice to disclose the extent of this unfunded liability. Additionally, contingent liabilities may not have been recognized at all. If financial debts, such as bonds, were reflected, the accounting was not done in the general funds of the government.

The federal government has established certain accounting prescriptions with respect to liabilities that require careful analysis to ascertain the true financial status of an agency. The practices relating to several types of liabilities are discussed in this chapter.

DEFINITIONS The corporate distinction between current and long-term liabilities does not have the same significance in accounting for federal agency operations. At the federal level, more appropriate might be a distinction between current and other types of liabilities and "funded" and "unfunded" liabilities.

Liability versus Obligation

In general, the term liability represents an amount owed or payable to others, generally resulting from the receipt of funds, property, or services. However, there might be circumstances in which, by law, an amount is owed to a party for which no current services have been performed.

The distinction between an "obligation" and a "liability" must be maintained in federal accounting. As discussed in Chapter 10, Obligations, the term obligation has a precise legal connotation and specific accounting considerations. A transaction may be an obligation of the federal government, but that obligation may never mature into a liability whereby an amount is owed or payable. For example, an awarded contract or grant is a legal obligation. However, if the contract or grant is terminated before any services are performed under the agreement, there will be no liability (or only a minimal one) on the part of the government.

Current liabilities generally include amounts, owed by the agency, that must be paid within a year. Within this grouping, there are several types of current liabilities, such as accounts payable, accrued liabilities, and contingent liabilities. Another categorization of current liabilities would be by "funded" and "unfunded" liabilities. The terms current, other, and funded or unfunded liabilities are not mutually exclusive.

Accounts payable are balances owed and payable to nongovernment and government organizations for services or property received that are expected to be paid within a year. Additionally, an accounts payable to another agency could result from the acceptance of an advance from that agency for which the collecting agency must perform some service within the current year. Until the service is performed and the advance becomes earned, the collecting agency must show the account payable.

Accrued liabilities are balances owed, but not yet payable, to nongovernment and government organizations for property or services received. Accrued liabilities include amounts owed but for which no billing has been rendered by the performing organization or party. Examples include such amounts owed, but not yet payable, for payroll, contractor or grantee performance, utilities, and interest expense. The balance in the account represents the estimated liability at the end of an accounting period for which a payment must be made or for which a billing is expected in the near future.

Contingent liabilities, as defined by the General Accounting Office, in its Title 2, *Accounting Principles and Standards,* is an existing condition, situation, or set of circumstances involving uncertainty as to possible gain or loss to an agency that will ultimately be resolved when one or more future events occur or fail to occur. There are conditions under which a contingent liability would not be recorded in an agency's accounts and may not be disclosed in a financial statement. Several examples, by GAO, of circumstances contributing to contingent liabilities would be

▲ Doubt concerning collectibility of receivables

▲ Risk of loss or damage to government property by fire, explosion, or other hazard

▲ Pending or threatened litigation

▲ Actual or possible claims or assessments

▲ Guarantees of indebtedness of others

▲ Agreements to repurchase receivables or related property that has been sold by the government

GAO, in Title 2, requires that an estimated loss from a contingency shall be accrued as an expense if *both* of the following conditions exist.

▲ Information available prior to publication of a financial statement indicates the probability that an asset has been impaired or a liability has been incurred as of the date of the financial statements, and

▲ The amount of the loss can be reasonably estimated.

The loss for a contingency may be recognized by recording the accrual in the accounts or by a footnote disclosure to the financial statements.

Funded and Unfunded Liabilities

Reference is made in practice to "funded" and "unfunded" liabilities. These references are at best unclear because all liabilities must be funded (either in some past fiscal period or in the current or future period) if payment is to be made and the debt settled.

A *funded* liability is an amount owed, whch may or may not be currently payable, and for which the agency's current appropriation is available for payment. Examples of funded liabilities would be amounts owed by an agency to its employees, contractors, and grantees for services performed in the current fiscal period. Additionally, amounts, which must be paid within the year, may be owed to another government agency for certain purchases.

Funded liabilities require an agency to restrict its unobligated allotment balance, record a formal obligation or restriction of its unexpended appropriation balance, and finally make a disbursement to satisfy the debt.

An *unfunded* liability is an amount owed by an agency for which no funds have been currently appropriated or for which no budget authority currently exists. The amount owed results from a cost incurred during the period. The amounts owed to federal employees for their accumulated vacation is an example of an unfunded liability. A liability has accrued and no funds are earmarked by the Congress or the agency to pay for the liability. GAO has recognized that the cost exists, a liability is owed, but has permitted an accounting under the theory that funds will be appropriated in the year in which the unused vacation is taken or in which the employee is given a lump-sum settlement.

The unfunded accrued liability for past accumulated vacation is not recognized in most of the agency's reports on current or active appropriation unless a payment must be made to an employee. Thus a segregation is maintained in many agencies between the "provided for" or funded liabilities and those liabilities that will be met in total against some future year's funds, i.e., an unfunded liability.

Other Liabilities

In addition to the liabilities above, which are more often related to current operations, an agency could incur other liabilities. These may be defined as (1) amounts owed that are not expected to be paid during the current fiscal period or (2) amounts owed that will be settled through payment of nongovernment funds.

The former category might include the unpaid balance of borrowings, funds advanced by the Treasury for imprest funds or other purposes. The latter category would include amounts held in deposit funds as security for performance, in the case of a contractor.

Deferred credits could arise, which would be reflected as another liability, when the agency has collected receipts for which the revenues will not be earned until a future period.

AGENCY RESPONSIBILITY A liability is the latter stage in the life-cycle of a transaction and can originate from a variety of activities, such as the incurrence or acquisition of personnel services, contracts, grants, capital assets, equipment, transportation, and travel. The responsibilities of an agency and others have been outlined in the separate chapters relating to these types of expenditures.

However, it is important to note that GAO, pursuant to the Budget and Accounting Act of 1921, is ultimately responsible for the settlement of claims and demands against the government. There are classes of claims that may not be paid or denied by administrative agencies, but that must be forwarded to the GAO for adjudication and final settlement. These claims and detailed procedures that exist for generally resolving claims and demands on the government have been outlined by GAO in its *Manual for Guidance of Federal Agencies,* Title 4—*Claims.*

LIABILITY CONTROL PROCEDURES

GAO accounting principles and standards notwithstanding, there exist agencies that do not maintain a full accrual system with respect to the accounting for liabilities.

Often invoices and other documents supporting claims against the government are not recorded or recognized in the agency's accounting system until the payment is to be made for the debt. At the end of reporting periods, an inventory of amounts owed or liabilities may be compiled and this estimate of payables could be reflected in the end-of-period balances. Without procedures for the prompt and consistent recording of all claims documents, there is a possibility the end-of-period inventory will omit significant payables, thus understating the amounts owed and misstating expenditures as well.

Many of the controls exercised by a corporate organization over its accounts payable, accrued liabilities, long-term liabilities, and deferred credits would be equally applicable to a government agency. Procedures should exist for ensuring that the total liability is reflected in the accounts of an agency.

▲ Amounts earned, not yet billed, by contractors and grantees should be accrued.

▲ Obligations to employees, other agencies, and others should be accumulated and reflected in the accounts of the agency.

▲ Cost incurred, but not funded and not yet payable, should be determined and recorded. (Vacation pay is one example.)

▲ Services performed by other agencies and amounts owed to other agencies, but not billed, should be determined and reflected in the accounts.

▲ Amounts owed to others, held in trust or on deposit (as security deposits from contractors), should be immediately recorded in the accounts as owing to these parties.

▲ Advance receipts, which have not been earned by the agency, should be reflected as a liability until services or performance has been rendered.

▲ Procedures should exist for disclosing all amounts owed, whether funded or unfunded, at reporting dates.

▲ Procedures should exist to provide a current reporting of any contingent liabilities affecting the agency.

Special reporting procedures must exist for agencies guaranteeing the indebtedness of others. Under such programs, for example, a loan guarantee program, the precise amount of the liability will not be known until the borrower defaults or otherwise violates a specified condition under which the loan was obtained. At this time, the government may have a debt requiring a disbursement of funds. However, at any given time, the amount disbursed may not be reflective of the imminent liability of the government as a guarantor.

PRINCIPLES AND STANDARDS

GAO, in Title 2, requires that agencies adhere to certain principles, standards, and procedures with respect to the accounting for liabilities. The accounting of an agency should provide that

▲ All liabilities shall be measured and recorded in the period incurred and removed from the accounts in the period liquidated or paid;

▲ Amounts recorded as liabilities shall represent amounts owed for goods or services to be furnished under contractual or other arrangements;

▲ Incurred liabilities shall be accounted for and reported irrespective of fund availability or authorization for payment;

▲ Separate accounts shall be maintained for major categories of liabilities for clear and full disclosure and shall provide for funded and unfunded liabilities, intragovernmental, and other liabilities;

▲ Accounting records shall include all transactions relating to liabilities of the accounting period;

▲ Liabilities requiring measurement on an actuarial basis (federal insurance, pensions, etc.) shall clearly disclose the full current cost and the estimated liability as accrued, regardless of whether funds have been appropriated or otherwise provided to make payment;

▲ Installment purchase payments that, in substance, are lease payments should be recorded as liabilities when the property is received or accepted from the contractor; and

▲ Performing agencies must show receipts paid in advance of performance by other agencies as liabilities until performance occurs.

GAO provides that a contingency may be recorded as an accrual in the accounting records and disclosed as a contingency in financial statements and reports. The contingency shall be accrued as an expense with an offsetting liability if *both* of the following conditions exist.

▲ Available information indicates that it is possible that an asset has been impaired or liability incurred at the financial statement date. That is, it is probable that one or more future events will occur confirming the loss; *and*

▲ The amount of the loss can be reasonably estimated.

If both conditions are not met, a disclosure should nevertheless be made discussing the nature of the possible loss and the dollar amount or range if possible to state.

Agencies with automated systems often find it more convenient to establish procedures for immediately recording all claims into the accounts, thus providing continual control and accounting over these liabilities. The recording of all claims made on the agency and other receipts in advance of being earned is considerably more time consuming and somewhat duplicative for agencies with manual accounting systems. In these agencies, close control is required of all documents to ensure that debts are examined and settled in an appropriate and timely manner.

ACCOUNTING FOR LIABILITIES Whether the liabilities are continually accounted for or, if unprocessed, claims are inventoried at the end of the accounting period, the balance of the liability accounts should reflect the total amounts owed by an agency. The following paragraphs illustrate the accounting generally performed for several types of liabilities.

Current Liabilities

Accounts Payable

Accounts payable accounts may reflect amounts owed to many organizations such as

▲ Contractors who may have billed for goods delivered

▲ Grantees who may have amounts owed to them for cost incurred under authorized grant programs

▲ Other government agencies to whom amounts may be due for goods and services received

The cumulative effect of such transactions was probably the result of entries similar to the following.

DEBIT: Unliquidated obligations
    CREDIT: Expended appropriation—capital
                Expended appropriation—operating

To liquidate previous obligations and record performance and deliveries received as accrued expenditures

Companion entries are required to record the actual assets received or expenses incurred and the resulting liabilities. For example

DEBIT: Capital assets
               Inventories
               Expenses
    CREDIT: Accounts payable
To record goods and services received and resulting amounts owed by agency

Advances from Other Agencies

Certain agencies are authorized or required by legislation to furnish personnel, goods, and services to other agencies. In these instances, the performing agencies may receive advances. Such advances must be shown as liabilities until performance has been completed. The accounting for these events is

DEBIT: Fund balance with the Treasury
    CREDIT: Advances from government agencies (liability)
To record transfer of an appropriation allocation for services to be performed

The performing agency, in the course of performing services or delivering goods, records obligations, makes expenditures, incurs costs and expenses, and disburses cash. Often the expenditures related to the other agency will be accumulated in a work-in-process inventory asset account. The summary accounting could be reflected in the following manner.

DEBIT: Unliquidated obligations
    CREDIT: Expended appropriation—capital
                   Expended appropriations—operating
To liquidate previous obligations and recognize expenditures for work performed for another agency

DEBIT: Work-in-process—other agencies
    CREDIT: Accounts payable
To record in inventory cost incurred in performance for another agency and related liability

also
DEBIT: Advances from government agencies
   CREDIT: Work-in-process—other agencies
To reduce earlier liability for advances received from another government agency and reduce inventory account for work performed or completed for that agency

Liability for Accrued Leave

Vacation is referred to as annual leave by the federal government. According to GAO, the costs and related liability for accrued annual leave should be disclosed in financial reports regardless of whether funds have been made available to pay for such leave or vacation. The following accounting would be required to record such expenses at the time leave is earned.

DEBIT: Expenses
   CREDIT: Liability for annual leave
To record accrued leave as an expense and record liability to employees for accumulated annual leave

The "liability for annual leave" account is increased or credited for leave earned and decreased or charged when payment is made for leave taken.

The GAO has stated that there is no requirement to accrue the cost and show the liability for other forms of leave (e.g., accrued sick leave). If the cost of other types of leave is accrued, the amount should be based on an expected-to-be-taken basis.

Because the earned, but unpaid annual leave is an unfunded cost, there is no current appropriation. Thus it would not be appropriate for an agency to restrict its unobligated allotment balance or record an obligation for the accrued leave costs at this time. The obligation would occur in the period during which payment is made for the leave. An inventory of accrued leave is generally maintained by the agency to show the balances of annual leave, sick leave, and other types of leave earned, taken, or still due the employee.

Liabilities Relating to Salaries

At the end of the period, the accrued but unpaid accounts may reflect several liability balances due to others. Depending on the nature of employment conditions (relating to whether an employee is covered by FICA or civil service retirement), an accounting similar to the following is made to record the liabilities related to payrolls.

DEBIT: Salaries and wages

Expenses—accrued leave

—Employer's share of group insurance

—Employer's share of FICA

—Employer's share of civil service retirement

CREDIT: Accounts payable—salaries and wages

Liability for accrued leave

Employee's bond deductions

Employee's tax withholdings

Employee's FICA withholdings

Employee's retirement deduction

Employee's group insurance deduction

Employer's liability for FICA

Employer's liability for group insurance

Employer's liability for civil service retirement

To record payrolls and related costs incurred, but unpaid at end of period

As payments are made to settle the various liability accounts, these balances are reduced or debited and the fund balance with the Treasury credited to reflect disbursement made. Because an obligation will not have been made earlier, a companion accounting entry is required to reduce the unobligated allotment balance and recognize the obligation for payroll to the extent appropriate. That accounting might be

DEBIT: Unobligated allotment

CREDIT: Expended appropriation—operating

To reduce the balance of allotted and appropriated funds in an amount equal to the accrued payroll for the period and reflect the accrued expenditures for the period

OTHER LIABILITIES Imprest Funds and Treasury Advances

The accounting for advances from the Treasury is the same for imprest fund or cashier fund purposes.

DEBIT: Imprest fund balance

Cashier fund balance

CREDIT: Liability for imprest fund advances

Liability as agent—cashier fund advance

To record advances of funds from the Treasury and related liabilities

A liability must be recorded for the initial advance and for any increases in the advanced amount. The liability account is debited only when the fund is returned to the Treasury.

Liability for Funds on Deposit

A fiduciary responsibility will arise in certain instances, such as when an agency accepts funds on deposit for certain purposes. Such a condition could arise when agencies are required to accept deposits from a contractor as a surety for performance. The offsetting balance is an other-asset account, surety on deposit. For example,

DEBIT: Surety on deposit

CREDIT: Liability for securities on deposit

To record receipt of surety deposit and amount due to contractor

A similar type of liability should be reflected at the end of the accounting period for amounts withheld by an agency from contractor's earnings or vouchers, pending the completion of the contract. However, few federal agencies record the latter type of liability.

Note that the surety deposit does not affect the appropriation accounts of the agency, nor must one be concerned with the obligating funds. Surety funds are not normally available to the collecting agency for obligation and expenditure purposes.

Bonds and Notes Payable

Few agencies are authorized to issue financial instruments or borrow amounts from outside the government. Where such borrowings are required or permitted, the liability must be recorded and amounts shown as due in the formal accounts of the agency. Where the funds borrowed are available to the agency for operations or other uses, the entry to record the liability would be

DEBIT: Fund balance with the Treasury

CREDIT: Bonds or notes payable

To record and reflect liability for amounts borrowed or owed

Exhibit 21.1 **AN AGENCY STATEMENT OF ASSET, LIABILITIES, AND INVESTMENT LIABILITIES**

CURRENT LIABILITIES

Accounts payable

Employees	$x,xxx		
Contractors	x,xxx		
Grantees	xxx		
Other agencies	xxx		
Others	xx	$x,xxx	

Accrued liabilities

Employees	$x,xxx		
Contractors	x,xxx		
Grantees	xxx		
Other agencies	xxx		
Others	xx	$x,xxx	

Advances from

Other agencies	$ xx		
Liability for imprest fund advance	xx	$ xx	

Trust and deposit liabilities

Security on deposit	$ xx		
Due to government agencies	xx		
Other trust and deposits	xx	$ xx	

Bonds, debentures, notes payable

Other agencies	$ xx		
Others	xx	xx	$x,xxx

Other liabilities

Deferred, undistributed credits		xx	
Annual leave		xx	xx

Total liabilities $x,xxx

REPORTING LIABILITIES As mentioned earlier, one of the reporting principles of GAO requires that separate accounts be maintained for major categories of liabilities to provide for full disclosure of all liabilities, both funded and unfunded. Additionally though, many agencies will adhere to a practice of having the greatest number of accounts to permit a ready determination of the status of various types of liabilities, thereby avoiding numerous repetitive analyses of accounts to respond to inquiries by management and others. In the monthly balance sheet of an agency, the liabilities might be shown as illustrated in Exhibit 21.1.

With respect to any of the liability accounts, the general ledger of the agency would provide considerably more detail. For example, the amounts due to other agencies relating to deposit liabilities would as a minimum be an aggregation of several ledger accounts, such as

▲ Employee's bond deductions
▲ Employee's tax withholdings
▲ Employee's FICA withholdings
▲ Employee's retirement deductions
▲ Employer's share—FICA
▲ Employer's share—insurance
▲ Employer's share—retirement

As it was in the case with assets, a combined balance sheet or composite reporting, assumes that the several funds and appropriations for which an agency is responsible have been merged. Within the general and subsidiary ledger account structure, the illustrated liability accounts must be maintained for each separate fund and appropriation pursuant to law or applicable regulations.

chapter 22 Investment of the Government

INTRODUCTION

When accounting for federal activities, it is important to remember that the accounting entity is the appropriation. An agency or department may be responsible for conducting operations supported by several appropriations. Additionally, an appropriation may be required to be spent by several agencies, with one agency being responsible to submit a consolidated accounting for expenditures.

The assets, debts, and residual equity of the government must be recorded, accounted and reported by individual appropriations. While an agency may, for various reasons, present a combined statement of financial position that is somewhat comparable to a corporate balance sheet, the combined values may have little relevance to the agency in the management of its resources. By law, agencies must provide a stewardship reporting and other types of reports on an appropriation-by-appropriation basis.

GOVERNMENT INVESTMENT AND EQUITY

There is some basis for comparing the investment of the government to the equity or net worth of a corporation during the period that the appropriation is current, active, or otherwise available for obligation. However, the analogy to the net worth of a corporation becomes strained once the appropriation has expired and particularly after the accounts have been merged into the Treasury's accounts and the agency no longer has a continuing accounting responsibility by appropriation.

Limited Life of Appropriations

Most appropriations are made for a one-year period. This is not to say that Congress has not appropriated funds for projects spanning more than one fiscal year or that Congress has not provided that an appropriation would not remain available until expended for the purposes enacted. Generally though, almost all the appropriations laws passed are of one-year duration.

Merging Appropriations

In practice, unless otherwise modified or restricted by laws, a government agency has an approved budget authority to obligate funds under an appropriation for the current fiscal year. At the end of the fiscal year, the appropriation lapses and the authority to obligate additional funds ceases. Agencies will continue to account for the expenditures related to obligations incurred during the fiscal year of the appropriation for another two years after expiration. At the end of the second year, the accounts for the appropriation are "merged" with the other expired appropriation accounts maintained by the Treasury. In essence, the books of the agency are closed with respect to the expired appropriation and, for all practical purposes, the accounting trail and costing responsibility ends. The Treasury will continue to honor all claims for expenditures that were properly obligated before the appropriation expired.

Thus within a three-year period, most accounting entities or appropriations cease to exist. In contrast, organizations in the private sector are the accounting entity and may have lives lasting many years, possibly decades. While a government agency may combine the several appropriations for which it is responsible, these funds will be in various stages of maturity, including many which may have expired and are on the books waiting to be merged into the Treasury's accounts. The presentation of the total resources of an agency has some value, but to practitioners the value is minimal in relation to the significance of the appropriation entity.

Government Investment

In lieu of the term "government investment" or "equity," a more appropriate description might result from use of the term "appropriation equity." This term relates the accounting and reporting to the appropriation corpus and possibly more clearly indicates that once the appropriation expires, no new activity can be generated. The appropriation equity would be equal to that amount required to settle outstanding obligations, plus any fixed assets that may be owned by the agency.

When an appropriation is active, the agency may incur obligations that will result in future expenditures and cash payments. The investment or equity of the government consists of the unexpended appropriation and any assets acquired, but not consumed, at the time of the reporting date. Once the appropriation has expired, the unobligated balance of the appropriation lapses. After the lapse date, the agency may no longer claim or report the unobligated balance as part of the government's investment or equity in the agency or for that appropriation. After expiration, but before the passage of two years, when appropriation accounts will be merged into the Treasury, a balance sheet of an appropriation might consist of the following.

BALANCE SHEET FOR LAPSED APPROPRIATION

ASSETS		LIABILITIES	
Balance with the Treasury (for settlement of unliquidated obligations)	$xx	Accounts payable	$xx
		INVESTMENT	
Fixed assets	xx	Unliquidated obligations	xx
Prepaid assets	xx	Invested capital	xx
TOTAL ASSETS	$xx	**TOTAL LIABILITIES AND INVESTMENT**	$xx

EXPIRED APPROPRIATIONS

Legal Requirements

Other chapters relating to receipts, expenditures, assets, and liabilities outlined the general accounting considerations required for current or active or unexpired appropriations.

The accounting for *expired appropriations* is somewhat different. An *expired appropriation*, simply defined, is an appropriation that is no longer available to an agency for obligations. Pursuant to law (31 U.S.C. 701(a) (2)), once the availability for obligation has expired

> ... the unobligated balance shall be withdrawn and, if the appropriation was derived in whole or part from the general fund, shall revert to such fund ... if ... derived solely from a special or trust fund, shall revert ... to the fund from which derived. ...

Unobligated balances of appropriations not limited to a specific time period may be withdrawn in the same manner as for expired appropriations when the purpose of the appropriation has been completed. Also (by 31 U.S.C. 706) an appropriation must be withdrawn whenever disbursements have not been made against the appropriation for two consecutive years. The *unobligated balance*, described more fully in this chapter, is the difference between the obligated balance and the total unexpended balance of an appropriation.

Obligations of Expired Appropriations

In addition to the expiration of the unobligated balance of an appropriation, agencies must be concerned with the accounting for outstanding or unliquidated obligations incurred during the period when the appropriation was current.

The *obligated balance* of an appropriation comprises the total unliquidated obligations of an appropriation less any amounts collectible as repayments to the appropriation (31 U.S.C. 701 (c)). On September 30 of the second full year after the expiration of an appropriation, these obligations are transferred to a merged appropriation account to which all unliquidated balances from other expired appropriations for the same general purposes have been transferred. Such an account is referred to as a *successor account* or merged ("M") account.

The balances transferred to such accounts must be the same balances reported to the Treasury for discontinued appropriations. The successor account serves as an appropriation account and will remain open indefinitely for payment of obligations chargeable against any expired appropriation enacted by Congress for the same general purpose. Such payments will be processed in the same manner as disbursements being made to settle obligations of current appropriations.

Restored Balances

Withdrawn appropriation or merged balances may be restored by the agency head for limited purposes pursuant to procedures of the Treasury. However, the restored amount generally may not exceed the unobligated balance of the expired appropriation. At all times, an agency must be cognizant of the prohibitions, penalties, and reporting requirements relating to violating the Antideficiency Act by overobligating or overexpending an appropriation.

EQUITY Defined

The term "investment" or "equity" must be qualified when making reference to federal finances to distinguish between the equity of the government and appropriation equity.

The *equity of the government* includes (1) the invested capital plus (2) the cumulative balances of *all* unexpended appropriations for which an agency is accountable. The *appropriation equity* relates to a *single* funding authorization by Congress and is equal to (1) the invested capital of a single appropriation plus (2) the unexpended balance of that appropriation.

Thus the appropriation equity may be viewed, simplistically, as

Equity = invested capital + unexpended balance of appropriation.

Invested Capital

The *invested capital* is the net investment of the government, related to the agency as a whole or to a single appropriation. When the term is used in reference to an appropriation account, the balance of the account reflects the residual resulting from the transfer of all receipts, expenses, and accrued expenditure transactions to this account, as would be done at the end of a reporting period. As a result of the offsetting effect of these transactions, the net invested capital account balance will often represent the undepreciated value of fixed assets and any prepaid expenses that will benefit some future accounting period. As mentioned, the invested capital for the agency as a whole is the cumulative residual assets acquired by all appropriations of past fiscal periods.

The accounting required by GAO provides that at the end of the accounting period, the agency's balance of the invested capital account will reflect the total of the net amount of balances transferred from the several general or special funds for which the agency is responsible. In summary, the invested capital will consist of the year-end balances transferred from the following general and special fund accounts.

INVESTED CAPITAL = Expended appropriation
- Funds returned to the Treasury
+ Reimbursements to appropriation
+ Donations
± Transfers of property to or from other agencies
+ Income
- Expense

The expended appropriation will include both capital and operating accrued expenditures. The reimbursements to appropriations would be an additive unless, of course, such amount had been previously closed to an accrued expenditure account, which in turn had been closed to the invested capital account.

The net balance of the transactions above generally reflect a credit balance in the invested capital account. This balance results from the difference between assets not yet consumed as expenses by the agency and the total of the accrued expenditures incurred during the period when the appropriation was current or active. As assets are costed to future periods (through depreciation in the case of fixed assets; and consumed in the case of prepaid expenses and inventories), the invested capital account will balance out to zero.

Unexpended Balance

The *unexpended balance* is the unspent portion of appropriations. Stated another way, the unexpended balance would be

Unexpended balance = total appropriations − expended appropriation.

If no expenditures have been accrued, then the unexpended balance is equal to the total value of the appropriation. Otherwise, the deduction of the accrued expenditures from the total appropriation equals the unexpended balance.

Composition of Unexpended Balance

Because of continual concern by the Office of Management and Budget, the Treasury, Congress, agency management, and others, agencies must

Exhibit 22.1 **DETERMINATION OF UNEXPENDED APPROPRIATION BALANCES**

CYCLE PHASE	FUNDING AUTHORITY to → ACTING ORGANIZATION	OMB APPROPRIATIONS[1]	AGENCY HEAD APPORTIONMENTS[2]	PROGRAM OFFICIALS ALLOTMENTS[3]	PROGRAM OFFICIALS OBLIGATIONS[4]	PROGRAM OFFICIALS EXPENDITURES[5]	FUND BALANCE WITH THE TREASURY
Appropriation phase	Congress/Treasury	$ + 10,000,000					$ + 10,000,000
Apportionment phase	OMB	$ − 5,000,000	$ + 5,000,000				
Allotment phase	Agency head		$ − 4,000,000	$ + 4,000,000			
Obligation phase	Program officials			$ − 1,500,000	$ + 1,500,000		
Expenditure phase	Program officials				$ − 1,000,000	$ + 1,000,000	
Disbursement phase	Program officials						$ − 500,000[6]
Unexpended balance		$ 5,000,000	$ 1,000,000	$ 2,500,000	$ 500,000		

1 Congress passes $10 million appropriation. Treasury issues Treasury warrant.
2 OMB apportions $5 million to agency head.
3 Agency head allots $4 million to program officials.
4 Program officials obligate $1.5 million for contracts and purchase orders.
5 Program officials receive goods and services valued at $1 million.
6 Program officials disburse $.5 million from the Treasury to pay for goods and services

closely monitor and regularly report the unexpended balance of all appropriations.

The unexpended balance comprises the ending balances of several subsidiary accounts related to the individual appropriations.

Unexpended appropriation = unapportioned appropriation
+
unallotted apportionment
+
unobligated allotment
+
unliquidated obligation.

The total of the subsidiary accounts above would be reported by an agency as the unexpended balance of an appropriation. Exhibit 22.1 illustrates the relationships of the various accounts. In this illustration the unexpended balance of a $10-million appropriation is $9 million; the undisbursed balance of the same appropriation is $9.5 million.

ACCOUNTING FOR INVESTMENT

General Fund Appropriations

The details and special considerations related to accounting for the individual transactions resulting in the balance reported by agencies as invested capital and unexpended appropriations are set forth in several chapters.

▲ Chapter 9—Appropriations and Apportionments
▲ Chapter 10—Allotment and Obligation of Funds
▲ Chapter 11—Expenditures and Applied Costs
▲ Chapter 12—Disbursements
▲ Chapter 13—Pay, Leave, and Allowances
▲ Chapter 14—Travel and Transportation
▲ Chapter 15—Contracts
▲ Chapter 16—Grants
▲ Chapter 17—Selected Interagency Transactions and Other Expenditures
▲ Chapter 18—Receipts, Transfers, Reimbursements, and Refunds of Appropriated Funds

The net effect of the accounting outlined in these several chapters will be adjustments made to the appropriations provided to the agency by Congress. The several accounts often required to determine the investment of the government and the nature of specific amounts of the appropriation balances are summarized in Exhibit 22.2. Each appropriation

Exhibit 22.2 **GOVERNMENT INVESTMENT ACCOUNTS**

ACCOUNT TITLE	DESCRIPTION	NORMAL BALANCE
Unapportioned Appropriation	Appropriated funds not yet apportioned (by fiscal quarter, amount, other basis) by OMB and other appropriated balances reserves by OMB	Credit
Appropriation Allocated to other Agencies	Reflects amounts transferred to another agency to be obligated and expended by the other agency	Credit
Appropriations Allocated by other Agencies	Reflects amounts transferred by another agency to be obligated and expended for the benefit of that agency	Debit
Unallotted Apportionments	Apportioned amounts available for allotment within the agency for programs and operations	Credit
Unobligated Allotments	Balances of alloted appropriations not yet obligated by the agency	Credit
Unliquidated Obligations	Balance of outstanding obligations or undelivered orders, services, or performance	Credit
Expended Appropriation*	Expenditures made from appropriation for current operations and capital	Credit
Reimbursements to Appropriation*	Reflects the gross reimbursements to appropriations billed or collected during fiscal period	Debit
Transfers of Cost and Property to and from Agencies*	Cost or appraised value of property transferred from agencies without reimbursement	Debit or Credit
Funds Returned to Treasury*	Total amount of general and special funds returned to the Treasury in current period (detailed by source or kind of revenue)	Debit
Invested Capital	Reflects transfer or closed balances at year end of several accounts	Credit
Appropriated Capital	Amounts appropriated by Congress to establish or increase working capital of a revolving fund	Credit
Donations*	Amount of donations or contributions in cash, services, or other property received	Credit

* Closed to invested capital account at year end.

Source: Summary account descriptions, United States General Accounting Office, Title 2, *Accounting, Manual for Guidance of Federal Agencies.*

under the stewardship of an agency must have these series of accounts, maintained by the assigned Treasury symbol and title.

To minimize continual analyses of the balance of appropriation accounts and simplify the reporting, many agencies utilize the "split-account" technique in much the same manner as was illustrated for the fund balance with the Treasury account, described in Chapter 19. For example, the balance of the unapportioned appropriations account shows the Congressional appropriations that have not been apportioned by OMB. Further, other unapportioned appropriations may exist in the form of estimated reimbursements anticipated by the agency. The available unapportioned appropriations may also have been reduced by transfers to other agencies or restricted by OMB through a reservation of a certain amount. To report on each of these events might require repeated analysis of the unapportioned appropriation account, unless the account is subdivided in a manner that highlights these events.

The "split accounts" might be

ACCOUNT NUMBER	TITLE	NORMAL BALANCE
300.00	Unapportioned appropriations—summary	Credit
300.10	Opening balance	Credit
300.20	Appropriations	Credit
300.30	Appropriation transfers—out	Debit
300.40	Appropriation transfers—in	Credit
300.50	Appropriation reimbursements	Credit
300.60	Appropriation receipts	Credit
300.70	Apportionments	Debit
300.80	Reserves	Debit

With the split-account technique, the algebraic sum of the amounts in the various subaccounts represents the total unapportioned appropriations of the agency. In summary, the accounting detail would be

▲ A new appropriation is credited to the unapportioned appropriation—300.20 account; the debit is to the asset account, fund balance with the Treasury

▲ Appropriations transferred to other agencies are debited to the account appropriations transfers—out—300.30; the credit is to the asset account, fund balance with the Treasury

▲ Appropriations transfers received from other agencies are credited to the account appropriations transfers—in—300.40; the debit is to the asset account, fund balance with the Treasury

▲ Appropriation reimbursements are estimated at the beginning of the fiscal year and are credited to the account estimated appropriation reimbursements—300.50; the debit is to estimated appropriation reimbursement (an asset account)

▲ Anticipated receipts are estimated at the beginning of the fiscal year and are credited to the account appropriation receipts—300.60; the debit is to estimated appropriation receipts (an asset account)

▲ Apportionments and appropriation reserves by the Office of Management and Budget are debited to the appropriate subaccount, either 300.70 or 300.80; the credit is to unallotted apportionments or reserved, as applicable.

The net balance of the debits and credits among the subaccounts represents the total of the unapportioned and reserved appropriations for the year. At the end of the year, the balances in the split-accounts are closed to the summary account, in this case, account 300.00. A new unapportioned appropriations account is opened the next fiscal year to permit the accounting for the new appropriation.

Trust and Special Fund Accounts

Trust and special fund investment accounts of trust and special funds have transactions of similar types. Two contra accounts related to special and trust fund receipts require slightly different treatment.

ACCOUNT	DESCRIPTION	NORMAL ACCOUNT BALANCE
Special Fund Receipts Deposited	Debited for amounts of available special fund receipts deposited during current fiscal year. (Available receipts credited to the unapportioned appropriation account; unavailable receipts credited to unappropriated funds account—pending appropriation by Congress)	Debit
Trust Fund Receipts Deposited	Debited for amounts of available trust fund receipts deposited during current fiscal year. (Available receipts credited to unallotted apportionment account; unavailable receipts credited to unappropriated funds account—pending appropriation by Congress)	Debit

Because trust funds do not ordinarily require apportionment, estimates for available trust fund receipts should be credited to the unallotted apportionments account.

A special account must be maintained for each special and trust fund. The special fund account would be closed out to an invested capital account at year end; the trust fund account would be closed to a trust capital account.

In the case of the trust capital account, this account would include, as a credit balance, the original capital at the time the trust was created and the year-end balances transferred from the following trust-related accounts.

▲   Expended funds

▲   Trust fund receipts deposited

▲   Trust fund payments to the Treasury

▲   Reimbursements to appropriations (if not previously closed to accrued expenditures account)

ILLUSTRATION OF GOVERNMENT INVESTMENT

Invested Capital Account Illustrated

Generally, the profile of an invested capital account, after the transfer or closing of several investment-type accounts might be similar to the following.

INVESTED CAPITAL

DEBITS		CREDITS	
Reimbursements to appropriations	$xxx xxx	Expended appropriation— capital	$x,xxx
Expenses	xxx	Expended appropriation— operating	xxx
Donations to other agencies	xx	Revenues	xx
Funds returned to the Treasury	xx	Donations from other agencies	xx
Transfer of property to other agencies	xx	Transfer of property from other agencies	
Total	$xxx	Total	$x,xxx
		Balance	$ xx

An analysis of the effect of the entries above shows that the balance of the invested capital account consists of the unconsumed assets. In the instance of an expired appropriation, there would no longer be a balance in the funds balance with the Treasury, the cash account. Typically, the remaining assets of an expired appropriation would be the undepreciated balance of fixed assets, the unconsumed balance of inventory and supply accounts, and the residual balance of any prepaid or deferred expense account.

Unexpended Appropriations Illustrated

For an agency financed by Congressional appropriations, the government's investment will consist of the unexpended appropriation accounts and the accounts comprising the invested capital. While the individual accounts may vary slightly, many of the accounts will be similar. Using the illustration in Exhibit 22.1 the investment section of that agency's balance sheet would be similar to the following.

AN AGENCY STATEMENT OF ASSETS, LIABILITIES, AND INVESTMENT (000's OMITTED)

ASSETS		LIABILITIES		
Current assets	$9,500	Current liabilities	$x,xxx	
Fund balance with the Treasury		Trust and deposit liabilities	xx	
Fixed assets	xxx	Bonds, debentures, notes payable	xx	
Other assets	xx	Other liabilities	xx	
		Total liabilities		$x,xxx
		GOVERNMENT INVESTMENT		
		Invested capital (for expenditures)		$ 500
		Unexpended appropriations		
		Unapportioned appropriation	$5,000	
		Unallotted apportionment	1,000	
		Unobligated allotments	2,500	

(continued)

AN AGENCY STATEMENT OF ASSETS, LIABILITIES, AND INVESTMENT (000's OMITTED) (continued)

		GOVERNMENT INVESTMENT			
		Unliquidated obligations	500	9,000	
		Total investment			9,500
TOTAL ASSETS	$x,xxx	**TOTAL LIABILITIES AND INVESTMENT**			$x,xxx

In this illustration the several funds and appropriations of the agency are assumed to be combined within the ledger accounts of the agency; the investment accounts must be maintained for each separate fund and appropriation pursuant to law or regulation.

chapter 23 Financial Reports and Statements

INTRODUCTION

Maximum disclosure is seldom effective reporting. To be effective, reporting must transform data into meaningful information. Several objectives should be considered in the design of reports to ensure that appropriate information is being reported to management. Additionally, considerable efforts are expended within agencies to meet the external, often legally required, reporting mandates. While such reports are important, the external requirements may not be precisely the same reporting most needed by agency executives to manage activities and operations properly.

When reporting requirements are properly analyzed and integrated, the transactions coding and account classifications should be segregated and distinguished to permit the accumulation of data and the preparation of reports with minimal analyses.

USERS OF GOVERNMENTAL STATEMENTS AND REPORTS

Like those in the corporate sector, reports and financial statements of government agencies have a single broad objective—to provide information to users. To achieve this objective, the reports and statements must simply and accurately either convey a financial position at the close of a specified date or show the results of operations for a specified period of time.

In this chapter, the assumption is made that the several GAO standards (outlined in Chapter 6) have been considered in the design of the transaction coding structure, the account hierarchy, and the accumulation of data for reporting and statement purposes. Additionally, it is presumed that the information reported is accurate, supported by the proper all-inclusive documentation, and has been consistently compiled from one reporting period to another.

Information on agency operations generally is compiled for two groups of users: external and internal. Prior to the emphasis on the accrual concept and cost-based budgets, agencies' financial systems were structured toward fiscal or stewardship accounting, or toward the external users. Today, possibly even more emphasis is given to internal reports, which concurrently contain information to meet external needs.

External Users

Principal among external users requiring reports and statements are the Congress, the Treasury, and the Office of Management and Budget. As a general rule, these external reports and statements provide information with respect to appropriations and budget authority. Increasingly, public interest groups and other members of the general public have shown interest in these agency documents. Much of this information, in summarized form, is also published in the Congressional hearings records by the authorization and appropriation committees before which the agency appears for funding authority.

This financial information is usually arrayed by appropriation or budget authority, which often is of only limited value to the agency's managers in operating the day-to-day activities of the agency. These macrolevel reports and statements provide no clue to the economy, efficiency, or relative effectiveness of agency operations. The primary conclusions to be obtained from the external reporting is whether or not certain spending levels or ceilings have been attained or exceeded.

Internal Users

As the operations of government have increased in complexity, so have an agency's internal information requirements. With few exceptions, users' internal reports and statements require more detailed, different, and more frequent information than appears in the external reports. This is not to leave the impression that two sets of information are compiled because this is not so. Principally, internal users are concerned more with managing the resources of the agency and controlling its operations and activities. There is real concern with costs, financial trends, variances, deficits, and surpluses.

AGENCY NEED FOR FINANCIAL DATA

Background

Historically, agency management had a lessened concern once the apportioned budget authority was obligated, so long as the obligated amounts remained below the amounts appropriated by Congress. Accrued expenditures were also monitored. The information presented in both external and internal reports were essentially the dollar values of obligated and cash-expended amounts, which many times were viewed as synonymous with cost.

Beginning in the 1950s and with increasing emphasis during the 1960s and 1970s, Congress, GAO, OMB, and agency management recognized the limitations of obligation accounting. Stewardship reporting was not sufficient to meet the full financial management needs of government. In the 1960s, Congress itself became concerned with agencies that may have obligated appropriated funds on the federal ledgers, but that were not managing the program to ensure that the rates of expenditures were consistent with program plans and desired economic thrusts, and were reflective of promised accomplishments or results. These programs found themselves subject to even more legislation: not only was a time limitation placed on the period for obligation but also Congress placed legal limitations on the time period by which the federal monies had to be expended. If both time limitations were not met, the agency funding authority lapsed.

With the Budget and Impoundment Act of 1974, Congress reemphasized the need for information other than that of the fiscal sort by requiring that budgets transmitted to Congress for fiscal year 1979, and later, contain other types of financial data presentations. That law required that a presentation of budget authority, proposed budget authority, outlays, proposed outlays, and other information be in the terms of agency missions and basic programs. In this act, Congress stated that to the extent practicable each agency was to furnish information on its mission in terms of functions, subfunctions, and mission responsibilities of component organizations. The act also required the agency to relate its programs to its mission.

Limitations of Appropriation Reporting

The Congressional requirements to report by appropriations, as mentioned above, falls considerably short of the agency's information requirements to manage its operations. Often, the concern with appropriations is an inhibiting influence on agency management and may actually be an impediment to the development of an agency's financial management information system. Some agencies have expressed satisfaction with financial systems that merely summarize the obligations by specific appropriations. These agencies show minimal concern for rates of expenditures and consumption of resources by an activity.

The restrictive nature of appropriation accountability becomes clearer when Congress elects to fund portions of operations from a variety of appropriations. Under these conditions, agency management encounters difficulty in managing programs and operations and relating the cost of resources-used to several appropriations. When an agency receives its funding from a number of appropriations, the reporting to Congress, the OMB, and the Treasury makes it appear that each funding source is separately supporting a program or operation. Such, of course, is not and cannot be the case. Agency management must conduct operations in a manner to achieve the stated goals of Congress and the administration, using a single appropriation or a multitude of appropriations to fund the required activities. The reporting by appropriation, therefore, is to a degree artificial and not reflective of the way in which the agency must manage its resources to achieve the will of Congress.

Importance of Expenditure and Expense Reporting

An issue often discussed by financial personnel is the relative importance of expenditure versus expense reporting. Of course, both are necessary. A singular importance can be placed on one only if the activities for which a person is responsible can be monitored by one type of reporting.

Expenditure data are reflective of the level of budget authority to *finance* the resources required for a particular level of activity. In contrast, expense reporting highlights the level of expenses, costs, or resources required to *sustain* a level of activity in a specific fiscal period. Not unlike accounting in the private sector, fixed assets, inventories, prepaid costs, and deferred expenses all have a value to the activities of a future period. Without such resources, the financing for the future period would have to be greater. The use of fixed assets and consumption of inventory and prepaid costs financed by expenditures of some earlier period reduces the level of budget authority necessary to sustain the activity of the current period.

Utility of Data

The utility of data is carefully analyzed by agency financial managers. Unless the data have utility, the transformation of raw data into useful information has not occurred. The utility of data is principally related to their content, structure, and timeliness.

With respect to content, the data must provide facts on the activities, organizations, functions, or other responsibilities of a manager. Typically, a requirements analysis is made to determine the nature of the monitoring to be performed, indicators of performance, and the types of decisions that are to be made by various levels of management. From this analysis, decisions are made on the content of the reporting required.

The structure or format of information is important. The practice of providing voluminous computer printouts of data to management accomplishes little. It simply consumes considerable resources. The format of data must be consistent with the manner in which management desires to examine the activities for which it is responsible. Care must be taken to ensure that reports and other forms of reporting highlight information reflective of or in response to the responsibilities that must be exercised. Exception reporting, trend analyses, variances, changes, and performance indicators are all attempts to ensure that information is structured or formatted in a manner that is most responsive to the inquiries that management is trying to answer.

Achieving timeliness has historically been a problem in public-sector reporting, particularly with respect to financial data. Often, the practice was to give financial reports a low priority. Typically, financial reports and statements were not available to agency users until the third or fourth week after the end of the prior month or fiscal period. Late reports and financial statements have limited value to management. More often, they are worthless. Reporting that is subject to long delays cannot be considered to be responsive. The lateness of the data precludes their use in the decision-making process. Flash reporting and issuance of preliminary reports and statements have improved information in many agencies.

Real-time access to databases and the increasing reliance on computer-accessible terminals have further enhanced the timeliness of reported data. The integration of state-of-the-art electronic data processing, accumulation, and display techniques may eliminate the delayed reporting of data essential to the agency.

Purpose of Reporting

Reports and financial statements within an agency are necessary for measuring the level of activity or resource consumption and for controlling the level of performance. Additionally, the use of such data in planning and budgeting operations and activities is paramount. As mentioned earlier in the chapter relating to the budget process, considerable management and agency resources are committed to the programming, planning, and budgeting of finances for as many as five years into the future. As more current data become available to agency personnel, the estimating database is continually being updated.

TYPES OF REPORTS AND STATEMENTS

A description of reports must consider the level of management or operations being reported on. Reports considered invaluable for one level of management might be of limited or of no utility to other managers. Additionally, a distinction should be made between reports related to production of data and reports on the data itself. Agency reporting may also be categorized into several groupings: system reports, operation reports, management reports, and external reports and statements.

System Reports

There are many reports, particularly for automated data processing systems that assist operators in monitoring the effectiveness of the system. Such reports provide information relating to the input of data to the system, the correctness of the data, updating of certain standard data files, and scheduling and operating the computer, to mention a few.

Exhibit 23.1 illustrates one such report. This report, a transaction listing, provides an audit trail to the transactions processed in a period, and shows the accounts affected, the nature of the expenditures, and the organization against which the expenditure should be recorded. Other data, such as the cumulative totals through the end of the prior period, will often provide reference points required during later analyses. Again, this report, although produced to permit a monitoring of the system's operations, also provides information of value in tracing the nature of

Exhibit 23.1 TRANSACTIONS LISTING OF OBLIGATIONS PROCESSED
(Week ending March 7, 19xx)

SEQUENTIAL TRANSACTION NUMBER	DOCUMENT NUMBER	ORGANIZATION		ACCOUNTS AFFECTED	
				Debit Unobligated Allotment	*Credit* Unliquidated Obligations
March 2					
1	C101	Department	B	$ xxxx	$ xxxx
2	C102		C	xxxx	xxxx
3	C104		E	xx	xx
4	C105	Administration		xxx	xxx
	C101		B	xxx	xxx
5	C105	Administration	B	xx	xx
March 5					
6	G201	Department	B	xxxx	xxxx
7	G204		E	xxx	xxx
8	G204		E	xxxx	xxxx
9	G205	Administration		xx	xx
10	G201	Department	B	xxxx	xxxx
11	T301		B	x	x
12	T302		C	x	x
13	T305	Administration		x	x
March 6					
14	P402	Department	C	xx	xx
15	P402		C	x	x
16	P405	Administration		xx	xx
17	P402	Department	C	xx	xx
18	C101		B	xxxx	xxxx
19	C104		E	xxxx	xxxx
March 7					
20	T301	Department	B	x	x
21	T301		B	x	x
Total obligations				$xxxxx	$xxxxx

appropriation number 1981/2

Legend: C = Contract G = Grant T = Travel authorization P = Purchase order transactions processed in a period or in conducting research on a particular entry.

Systems reports will be of minimal value to financial managers, but the information contained is important to the reliability of the system. Often system reports include or are referred to by such titles as the input transaction list, batch input list, error listing, files change list, and production reports. Such a report provides trails relating to the effectiveness of the system rather than to sources of information. The principal users of such reports might include the accounting personnel, the program analysts responsible for processing data into the agency's systems, and the personnel of the computer facility.

Operation Reports

Operation reports for financial personnel include those required to conduct ongoing financial activities and monitor certain types of performance. Such activities could include maintenance of receivables and payables, receipts and disbursement details, and reconciliation of data reported to such external sources as the Office of Management and Budget and the Treasury. Often these data form the basis of reports provided to higher levels of management.

An example of such reports might be a schedule of outstanding travel advances, showing the necessary detail to permit financial personnel to monitor the currency of this account. Exhibit 23.2 illustrates an operational report required to permit the financial monitoring of certain subsidiary accounts. Although the illustration relates to the outstanding travel advance account, similar types of reports are required for accounts receivables, payables, receipts, and disbursements. Other accounts, such as inventory and fixed assets, require that operational reports be produced to permit the monitoring and accountability of assets in possession of the agency.

Management Reports

The management reports of an agency are more summarized than are systems or operation reports. The objective is to provide an overview on matters such as the status of funds, the rates of obligation and expenditures, and the amounts of resources consumed to support varying levels of operations. These reports must be tailored for each agency. Often program offices within the agency will require unique report formats to ensure that the activities and operations are being financed and managed within the budgetary and other resource limits and are consistent with the legislative intent of Congress or with directives received from OMB.

Exhibit 23.2 **SCHEDULE OF OUTSTANDING AND AGED TRAVEL ADVANCES**
(For fiscal year ended September 30, 19xx)

EMPLOYEE NAME	ORGANIZATION	TRANSACTION Date	Document	TRAVEL ADVANCE	ADVANCE LIQUIDATION	DAYS SINCE LAST LIQUIDATION 0-30	31-60	61-90	Over 90
E. Jones	Department B	7-1	T525	$ x	$	$	$	$	$
		7-15	V504		x				
		8-15	V605		x		x		
H. Henry	Department C	8-15	T620	x					
		9-5	V720		x				
J. Smith	Administration	6-15	T433	xxx					
		6-30	V485		xx				
		7-10	C237		x			xxx	
V. Able	Department E	9-1	T820	xxxx					
		9-20	V788		xxxx				
			C435		xx				
B. Cate	Department E	4-23	T385	xxxx					
		5-1	V301		x				xxxx
Total advances for year (A)				$xxxx					
Total liquidations for year (B)					$xxxx				
Advances outstanding (A) − (B)				$ xxx		$	$x	$ xx	$xxxx

Legend: T = Travel authorization
V = Travel expense voucher
C = Cash or check payment

397

Exhibit 23.3 illustrates a summary status report directed toward answering the questions of concern to agency top management about the appropriations for which it is responsible. The funds status report, or a derivation thereof, is prepared by every agency to permit management to monitor the rates of obligation and expenditures of appropriated and apportioned funds. Exhibit 23.3 portrays a summary reporting of several appropriations. Other reports generally required by top management include those providing a status of the nature of the obligations and expenditures made by the agency against the various appropriations.

The OMB mandates that summary obligation and expenditure data categorized by the governmentwide object classifications be reported monthly. The OMB reporting must be supplemented in more detail to permit agency executives to ensure that funds have been expended pursuant to the apportionments. Exhibit 23.4 is an illustration of a report that provides top management with the rate of obligations and expenditures by departments, different appropriations, and the amounts of funds outstanding from a prior year's appropriation.

In practice, detailed reports are generated to answer even more specific inquiries of management and permit program personnel to monitor specific items and activities. Exhibit 23.5 is one example of a status report for a subsidary organization. Such a report is required by those officials who have been designated allottees within the agency. (Recall, the Antideficiency Act prohibits entering into obligations or making expenditures in excess of the apportionments of the OMB, which become the budget for each governmental program.)

Other officials within the same programs or departments may be more interested in the dollar value of resources consumed or required to operate a program during a particular period, regardless of the source of funding. For example, resources consumed during the current period might consist of supplies and materials acquired during a prior fiscal year. Assets could be used that were purchased from the appropriation of several years past. Additionally, there probably were unliquidated obligations outstanding at the end of the prior fiscal period. As discussed in earlier chapters, an obligation against the last year's appropriation still finances activities or results in the current period. Exhibit 23.6 is illustrative of a report that highlights the nature of the resources consumed to sustain a level of program operations.

External Reports and Statements

As discussed in earlier chapters, at the federal level a governmentwide system of standard reports exists. These reports must generally be made to the Treasury and the OMB. For the most part, these external reports

Exhibit 23.3 **AGENCYWIDE STATUS OF FUNDS REPORT**
(For the fiscal quarter ended March 31, 19xx)

MAJOR FUND OR APPN. NO.	GENERAL LEDGER ACCT.	THIS MONTH			YEAR TO DATE			BUDGET AUTHORITY REMAINING	
		Accrued Expend.	Obligation	Variance from Month Plan	Accrued Expend.	Obligation	Variance from Year Plan	Unexpend. Oblig.	Unoblig. Appn.
S&E-1982	xxxxx	$ xxxx		− 2%	$xxxxx	$	+ 5%	$	$
	xxxxx		$xxxxx	− 5%	xxxxx	xxxxx	+ 5%	xxxxxx	xxxxx
	xxxxx								
	xxxxx								
Totals this fund		$ xxxx	$xxxxx		$xxxxx	$xxxxx		$xxxxxxx	$xxxxxx
R&D-1982/3	xxxxx	$ xxxx	$	+ 4%	$ xxxx	$	+ 2%	$	$
	xxxxx		xxx	+ 8%	xxxx	xxxx	+ 3%	xxxx	xxx
	xxxxx								
	xxxxx								
Totals this fund		$ xxxx	$ xxx		$ xxxx	$ xxxx		$ xxxx	$ xxx
CAP-198x	xxxxx	$ xxx	$	− 10%	$ xxx	$	− 5%	$	$
	xxxxx		xxx	− 15%	xxx	xxx	− 8%	xxxx	xxxx
	xxxxx								
	xxxxx								
Totals this fund		$ xxx	$ xxx		$ xxx	$ xxx		$ xxxx	$ xxx
TOTALS ALL FUNDS		$xxxxx	$xxxxx		$xxxxx	$xxxxx		$xxxxxx	$xxxxx

Note: Similar reports would be produced for each program, department, and office of the agency having obligations and expenditure authority.

Exhibit 23.4 **REPORT ON OBLIGATED FUNDS—BY OBJECT CLASSIFICATION**
(For the fiscal quarter ended June 30, 19xx)

DEPARTMENT	APPROPRIATION NUMBER	OBJECT CLASS.	THIS MONTH'S BUDGET				THIS YEAR'S BUDGET				VARIANCE FROM YEAR PLAN
			Accrued Expend.	Unliq. Oblig.	Total	Plan for Month	Accrued Expend.	Unliq. Oblig.	Total	Plan for Year	
B	S&E—1982	Salaries	$xx	$ x	$xx	$xx	$xxx	$ x	$xxxx	$xxxx	−1%
		Benefits	x	x	x	x	xx	x	xx	xx	−1%
		Travel	x	x	x	x	x	x	x	x	−5%
		Other services	xx	xx	xx	xx	xxx	xx	xxx	xxx	−5%
		Grants	xx	xx	xx	xx	xxx	xxx	xxx	xxx	−8%
		Printing	x	x	x	x	x	x	x	x	−2%
		Supplies	x	x	x	x	x	x	x	x	−1%
		Equipment	xx	x	xx	xx	xxx	xxx	xxx	xxx	+5%
Total this fund			$xx	$xx	$xx	$xx	$xxx	$ xxx	$xxxx	$xxxx	−5%
Prior year fund			x	x	x	x	xx	xx	xx	xx	
Total—dept.			$xx	$xx	$xx	$xx	$xxx	$ xxx	$xxxx	$xxxx	
C	S&E—1982	Salaries	$xx	$ x	$xx	$xx	$xxx	$ x	$xxxx	$xxxx	+1%
		Benefits	x	x	x	x	xx	x	xx	xx	+1%
		Travel	x	x	x	x	x	x	x	x	+1%
		Supplies	x	x	x	x	x	x	x	x	+1%
Total this fund			$xx	$xx	$xx	$xx	$xxx	$ x	$xxxx	$xxxx	+1%
Prior year fund			x	x	x	x	x	x	x	x	
Total S&E Funds			$ x	$xx	$xx	$xx	$xxxx	$ x	$xxxx	$xxxx	
	CAP—198x	Contracts	$ x	$xx	$xx	$xx	$ xxx	$xxxxx	$xxxx	$xxxx	+1%
Total this fund			$ x	$xx	$xx	$xx	$ xxx	$xxxx	$xxxx	$xxxx	+1%
Total—dept.			$xx	$xx	$xx	$xx	$ xxx	$xxxx	$xxxx	$xxxx	
Summary Totals— All Departments											
	S&E—1982		$xx	$xx	$xx	$xx	$xxx	$ xxx	$ xxx	$ xxx	
	Prior year fund		x	x	x	x	xx	xx	xx	xx	
	CAP—198x		xx	xx	xx	xx	xxx	xxxx	xxxx	xxxx	

Exhibit 23.5   **STATUS OF FUNDS REPORT — BY DEPARTMENTS**
(For the fiscal quarter ended June 30, 19xx)

DEPARTMENT	Appropriation Allotment	AUTHORIZED RESOURCES Annual Budget	SPENT TO DATE Expended	SPENT TO DATE Unliquidated Obligations	SPENT TO DATE Total	REMAINING AVAILABLE BUDGET
B	S&E—1982	$xxxxx	$ xxxx	$xxxx	$xxxxx	$ xxx
		xxxxx	xxxx	xxx	xxxxx	xxx
		xxxxx	xxxx	xx	xxxxx	xx
Total this fund		$xxxxx	$ xxxx	$xxxxx	$xxxxx	$ xxx
	R&D—1982/3	$ xxxx	$ xxxx	$ xxx	$ xxxx	$ xxx
Total this fund		$ xxxx	$ xxxx	$ xxx	$ xxxx	$ xxx
Total department		$xxxxx	$xxxxxx	$xxxx	$xxxxx	$xxxx
C	S&E—1982	$ xxx	$ xxx	$ xxx	$ xxx	$ xxx
		xxx	xx	xxx	xxx	xx
		xxx	xxx	xx	xxx	x
Total this fund		$ xxx	$ xxx	$ xxx	$ xxx	$ x
	Capital—198x	$ xxx	$ xxx	$ xx	$ xxx	$ x
		xx	xx	x	xx	x
Total this fund		$ xxx	$ xxx	$ xx	$ xxx	$ x
Total department		$ xxx	$ xxx	$ xx	$ xxx	$ x
Summary Totals— All Departments	S&E—1982	$xxxxx	$ xxxx	$xxxx	$xxxxx	$ xxx
	R&D—1982/3	xxxx	xxxx	xxx	xxxx	xxx
	Capital—198x	xxx	xxx	xx	xxx	x
		$xxxxx	$ xxxx	$xxxx	$xxxxx	$ xxx

Exhibit 23.6 **REPORT OF RESOURCES REQUIRED BY ACTIVITY**
(For the fiscal quarter ended June 30, 19xx)

DEPARTMENT:	B			
ACTIVITIES:	PROGRAMS 1 and 2			
APPROPRIATION:	S&E; CAPITAL			

EXPENSES INCURRED IN PERIOD	TOTAL AMOUNT	FOR MONTH		
		1	2	3
Personnel	$xxx	$ xx	$xx	$xx
Benefits	x	x	x	x
Travel	xx	x	xx	x
Other services	xx	x	x	xx
Grants	xxx	xxx	x	x
Supplies, materials	xx	xx	x	x
Equipment	xxx	xxx	x	x
Total	$xxx (A)	$xxx	$xx	$xx
ADJUSTMENTS:				
LESS EXPENDITURES:				
Equipment	xxx	xxx	x	x
Supplies, materials	xx	xx	x	x
	$xxx (B)	$xxx	$ x	$ x
PLUS CONSUMED:				
Depreciation	x	x	x	x
Inventories	x	x	x	x
	$ x (C)	x	x	x
Resources for period	$xxx	$xxx	$xx	$xx

(A) − (B) + (C)

reflect the status or stewardship balances of appropriations and budget compliance for appropriations for which the agency is responsible. Because many of these reports require detailed information, particular care is taken in the system designs to ensure that required totals and subaccount balances are accumulated and maintained.

The use of the split-account techniques, highlighted in earlier chapters, and subsidiary ledger accounts are widespread to avoid repetitive data analyses. While such reports are of concern to agency management, few of these external reports provide the type of information necessary to monitor or control agency activities. Periodically (often monthly), financial managers will prepare a detailed trial balance of all ledger accounts, that might consist of a few hundred account balances, prior to summarization. A system design objective is to accumulate financial data by the level of detail that would permit the ready, possibly even computer-generated, external reports from selected account balances.

Illustrative of the detail required to be reported to the Treasury is the statement of financial condition, of which the information in Exhibit 23.7 is merely a summary. The more common external reports were discussed and several illustrated in earlier chapters. OMB has long required that agencies submit a

▲ *Report on Budget Execution*, monthly—SF 133
▲ *Report on Obligations*, monthly—SF 225

Similarly, the Treasury requires from all agencies, the following reports, which are described in greater detail in the Treasury's *Fiscal Requirements Manual.*

▲ *Statement of Transactions*, monthly—SF 224
▲ *Statement of Financial Condition*, annually—SF 220
▲ *Report of Selected Balances for Stating Budget Results on the Accrual Basis—Appropriation and Fund Accounts* (showing current assets and liability classifications affecting accrued expenditures), monthly—BA-6727
▲ *Report of Selected Balances for Stating Budget Results on the Accrual Basis—General, Special and Trust Fund Receipt Accounts* (showing current assets and liability classifications affecting accrued revenues), monthly—form BA-6728

These reports are often accompanied by several supporting schedules, providing additional information concerning account balances. Additionally, agencies, pursuant to their specific authorizing or appropriation legislation, may be required to submit special external reports periodically to the Congress or one of the central agencies.

Consolidated Reporting

During the 1970s, the federal government experimented with publishing consolidated financial statements of the United States government as a whole. In 1976 and 1977, the Secretary of the Treasury published a prototype report containing such statements.

Exhibit 23.7 **STATEMENT OF FINANCIAL CONDITION**
(September 30, 19xx)

ASSETS			LIABILITIES		
Selected Current Assets			**Selected Current Liabilities**		
Fund balance with the Treasury			Accounts payable		
Budget funds		$ xx	Government agencies		$ xx
Budget clearing accounts		x	The public		xx
Deposit funds		x	Other		x
Foreign currency funds		x	Advances from		
Allowances, foreign currency (minus)		(x)	Government agencies		xx
			The public		x
Federal security holdings, par		x	Other		x
Accounts receivable			**Total Selected Current**		
Government agencies		x	**Liabilities**		$ xx
The public		x	Deposit fund liabilities		x
Other		x	Unfunded liabilities		
Allowances (minus)		(x)	Accrued leave		x
Advances to			Other		x
Government agencies		x	Debt issued		
The public		x	Borrowed from the Treasury		xxx
Total Selected Current Assets		$ xx	Agency securities outstanding		xx
Loans receivable			Other		x
Repayable in dollars		x	Other liabilities		x
Repayable-foreign currency		x			
Allowances (minus)		(x)			
Inventories			**Total Liabilities**		$xxx
Items for sale		x	**Government Equity**		
Work-in-process		x			
Raw materials, supplies		x	Unexpended budget authority		
Stockpile materials		x	Unapportioned appropriations		$ xx
Allowances (minus)		(x)	Unallotted apportionments		x
Real property, equipment			Unobligated allotments		x
Land		xx	Unliquidated obligations		x
Structure, facilities		xx	Less unfinanced budget authority		
Equipment		xx	Unfilled customer orders		(x)
Leasehold improvements		xx	Contract authority		(x)
Acquired security		x	Borrowing authority		(x)
Allowances (minus)		(xx)	Invested capital		xx
Other assets			Other-equity		
Work-in-process		x	Receipt account equity		x
Materials, supplies		x	Unappropriated receipts (minus)		(x)
Other		x	Foreign currency equity		x
Allowances (minus)		(x)			
			Total Government Equity		$ xx
			Total Liabilities and		
Total Assets		$xxx	**Government Equity**		$xxx

Note: Typically agencies financed from Congressional appropriations do not have the statement of financial condition independently audited in accordance with generally accepted auditing standards.

▲ *Consolidated Statement of Financial Position*—a summary of assets owned by the government, liabilities, and fiscal deficit.

▲ *Consolidated Statement of Operations*—a summary of federal revenues, expenses by functions, by object classification, and by agency.

Although this type of reporting was an undertaking aimed at extending accrual accounting concepts to governmental accounting, the Secretary of the Treasury warned that such statements were not the government's report on its financial condition and could not be so interpreted. The consolidated reports left unresolved many significant issues affecting the reported values and amounts. For example,

▲ The valuation of assets (such as public domain lands, the outer shelf) were reported at cost; but at the time a preference was expressed for alternate reporting on a current-value basis.

▲ Reported liabilities for pensions, social security, and veterans' benefits were not shown and various bases existed for valuing the government's future liability.

▲ Depreciation was calculated in a broad manner, without resolving asset lives, valuation, obsolescence, and other issues.

▲ Procedures were not uniformly defined at the time for determining accrued costs and taxes.

Note that no independent audit was made or required for the experiment. Further, the consolidated statements were not the result of agencies throughout the government applying generally accepted accounting principles to their activities.

GENERAL REPORTING REQUIREMENTS

While each federal agency is responsible for designing the reports for its programs, the General Accounting Office requires that such reports be prepared to show clearly significant financial facts about agency operations and activities. Additionally, the GAO requires that the reports be prepared and issued as often as necessary. Generally, reports should be prepared as of the end of an accounting period, typically a calendar month, although GAO permits the preparation of reports for four-week periods.

Agencies operating activities of the business type are also required to prepare statements of operations disclosing revenues and costs for appropriate fiscal periods. As part of its general systems design and the systems description that must be approved by the GAO, an agency must describe its reporting plan, list its reports, and provide a sample of formats to be produced by the system. The reporting should conform to detailed classifications used in the agency's budget submissions and program structure to allow for comparisons of plans to actual results.

PART VI

ACCOUNTING FOR REVOLVING FUNDS

chapter 24 **Revolving Funds**

INTRODUCTION   The preceding chapters outlined the method of accounting and reporting required of government agencies whose operations are financed by annual or other types of appropriated funds. Legal and other constraints, such as appropriation and obligation-type and cash-basis reporting, complicate the accounting by these agencies for their programs and activities. While appropriation-funded agency operations are in the preponderance, government activities spending billions of dollars annually are supported by another mechanism, referred to generally as revolving funds. Additionally, within the federal financial structure working funds exist that are used to support the cost of intra-government services.

FUNDS: REVOLVING,   **Revolving Funds**
CONSOLIDATED
WORKING, AND   The General Accounting Office has defined a *revolving*
OTHERS   *fund* as a combined receipt and expenditure account established by law to finance a continuing cycle of operations, with the receipts from the operations

409

usually being available in their entirety for use by the fund without further action by the Congress.

Consolidated Working Funds

Revolving funds would not include the consolidated working funds provided by one agency to another by the Economy Act of 1932. According to GAO, *consolidated working funds* consist of advances by agencies to a receiving agency responsible for accounting for the advances in a consolidated working fund account. The fund is established for the period of availability applicable to the purposes for which the advances were received. The supporting subsidiary accounts must be maintained by the receiving agency to differentiate the several appropriations from which the funds were received. Thus the symbols and titles assigned for these funds must be those published by the Treasury.

Management Funds

Management funds are described by GAO as combined receipt and expenditure accounts established by law to facilitate accounting for and administration of intragovernmental operations of an agency. The consolidated working funds are a type of management fund used to account for advances from other agencies.

Working-capital Funds

Working-capital funds have been defined by Congress as types of revolving funds. By PL 81-216, *working-capital funds* were described as revolving funds, consisting of two types: (1) *stock funds* for financing inventories of consumable materials, and (2) *industrial funds* for financing operations of industrial and commercial types of activities within the Department of Defense.

The distinctions between the "revolving" funds above appear to be related to (1) the nature of the activities financed and (2) the detailed accounting relationships to funding appropriations.

For example, working-capital and management funds are financed by the existing appropriations of agencies, and permits one agency to perform a service for other organizations. The servicing organization is required to maintain the distinction among the sources of funds used to finance its own operations. Seldom is a business or commercial type of activity supported by this type of arrangement.

In contrast, a revolving fund is established to carry out a cycle of business or a commercial type of operation and the receipts from the "sale" of the products or service of the fund are earmarked by Congress for continued use by fund managers.

Concept of Revolving Funds

The basic concept of a revolving fund is that once a corpus or fund is provided the corpus will remain intact through a series of authorized buying and selling activities. The corpus finances the purchase of the initial supplies, goods, or services. The cost of these procured items is accumulated by fund managers to establish a selling price to be charged to other government organizations. The buying organizations will pay for ordered items or services from their appropriated funds.

Exhibit 24.1 illustrates the revolving nature of the fund. Note that at any time, the total assets of the fund will remain the same (under normal operating conditions); however, the mix of assets consisting of cash, receivables, inventories, fixed assets or other assets, could vary.

Examples of Revolving Fund Activities

Historically financing by one method of funding rather than another has been deemed as more appropriate for certain activities. It should be noted that no absolute principle exists clearly to identify or establish qualifying criteria. However, some examples would include the following.

▲ *Stock Funds* are used to finance consumables such as medical and dental supplies, clothing and equipment, petroleum, repair parts and numerous other types of stock by the Department of Defense; centralized procurement of supplies, equipment, and nonpersonal services for other federal agencies by the General Services Administration; or payment of salaries and other expenses necessary for central administrative services for all agencies of the Department of Agriculture.

▲ *Industrial Funds* are used to finance arsenals and armories, depots, shipyards, printing plants, and other industrial enterprises of the Department of Defense; operations to produce currency, securities, stamps, and other engraved works by the Bureau of Engraving and Printing.

As mentioned earlier, billions of dollars of business are transacted by government agencies through revolving funds. Over 100 such funds exist

Exhibit 24.1 **OVERVIEW OF REVOLVING FUND PROCESS**

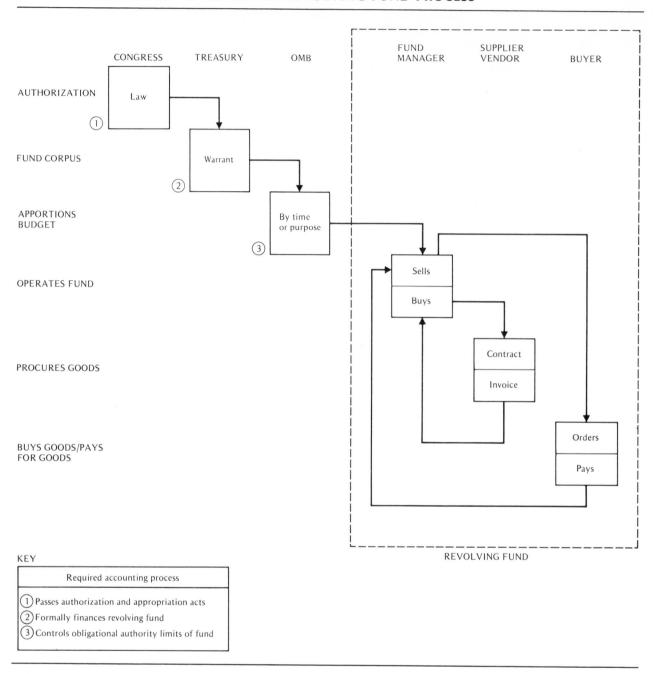

in the federal government. Additionally, each government-owned corporation operates with a revolving fund. These funds are often referred to as public enterprise funds because the continuing revenues are from a nongovernmental source; examples of such corporations would include the Federal Deposit Insurance Corporation, Student Loan Marketing Association, Rural Electrification Administration, and Farmers Home Administration.

OBJECTIVES AND ADVANTAGES OF REVOLVING FUNDS

For applicable activities, the financing of operations under a revolving-fund concept provides unique opportunities to assess the relative economy and efficiency of operating costs and permits the buyers' continual evaluation of the reasonableness of the selling price and of the quality of the fund products. Excessive or rising costs are immediately apparent to both fund managers and customers of the fund. Unit costs are tracked, and overhead and indirect costs are typically closely monitored. Revolving fund enterprises have several advantages.

▲ The fund permits a clearer presentation of profitable or loss operations. This same clarity would not exist in an operation funded by an annual appropriation.

▲ The financing structure of a revolving fund is simpler than appropriation-funded activities, in which the myriad sources of funds, receipts, or revenues tend to obscure the cost of programs and the financial impacts.

▲ Management of the fund has the flexibility, within Congressional restraints, to react more effectively and efficiently to changing conditions. Seeking authority to change a level of operations could require months of delay if supplemental requests for additional funding must be made to Congress.

▲ The self-sustaining nature of the fund provides a standard for effective management of income and other fund resources. The income-expense measure is as clear for revolving fund management as it is for commercial executives.

From a Congressional view, the authorization of revolving-fund operations generally tends to lessen control of and visibility into the activities of the fund. By law Congress may exercise the same level of controls that exists for appropriation operations. However, in practice many of the fund managers have responded well to the businesslike arrangement, have generated sustaining revenues, and have inherited the responsibility for levels of operations, staffing, and maybe even the total size of the revolving fund.

ESTABLISHING A REVOLVING FUND

Congressional Interest

Proposals for establishing revolving funds must be submitted to the Congress for review and approval. Additionally, established funds must provide full disclosure in each budget for review by Congressional appropriation committees. The funds needed to form the corpus or initial capital of a revolving fund are provided through the normal appropriation process. During the enactment process, Congress could impose certain types of restrictions. Some could be directed toward ensuring continual economical and efficient operations and continual assessment of fund costs. For example, in the case of an operation funded by an appropriation, Congress could limit the amount of money incurred for indirect or overhead costs, and could require fund managers to enlarge the business, hold cost relatively stable, and convince the buyers of the reasonableness of the fund's selling prices.

Further, Congress may desire to control the longer-term planning and outlays of the fund and may elect to prohibit the fund from reinvesting receipts into capital equipment and may also prohibit the recovery of depreciation cost as part of the reimbursable selling price. The last restriction would eliminate the accumulation of a sinking fund related to the depreciating capital assets. Such receipts, therefore, would go to the Treasury and being unavailable to the fund for reinvestment.

Congressional restrictions might be imposed on the manner in which other agency orders could be construed. For example, a fund that may obligate only after reimbursement from other customers will have considerably less flexibility than another fund that is able to enter into obligations on the basis of orders placed by customer agencies.

The fund may hold unearned receipts. However, restrictions might be imposed to ensure that such advances not be treated as obligational authority until services have been performed and the advances earned.

In practice the objective is to establish such a fund to increase the economies and effectiveness of operation. Thus a fund probably would not be subjected to restrictions like those outlined above unless problems existed or were anticipated.

OMB Review and Reporting

Typically, revolving funds are subject to the same reporting of obligations and apportionments that is required of activities funded by appropriations. For example, revolving funds subject to apportionment will have their obligational authority apportioned by submitting to OMB the same apportionment and reapportionment schedule required of appropriation-supported activities. All revolving funds, whether exempt from apportionment or not, must report to OMB the status of their budgets on the same report on budget execution required of all agencies.

Budgetary Authority

The existence of a revolving fund does not relieve the fund managers from fully complying with governmentwide legislation concerning fiscal and financial management of government resources. The fund does not provide exemptions from the generally accepted controls of federal financial management. In this regard, the Office of Management and Budget exercises the same responsibility with respect to budgetary or obligational authority that exists for agencies financing their operations through the regular appropriation process. Without careful fund management, over-obligation and overexpenditure conditions could result and would violate the Antideficiency Act, with the violators being subject to the same penalties.

Unless Congress has provided otherwise, the OMB, by its Circular A-34, *Instruction on Budget Execution*, provides guidance over the amounts that are apportioned to the fund and, thereby, governs or limits the obligations that a fund may incur. The objective of OMB's definition of budgetary or obligational authority is to limit the liabilities and debts of the fund to those that can be met from its operations. In summary, Circular A-34 limits a fund's budgetary authority to cash, balances on deposit with the Treasury, accounts receivable, and unfilled customers' orders, including advances received from others.

OMB states that other assets, whether of a working-capital nature such as inventories or a fixed asset, are not considered budgetary resources or obligational authority. Such assets cannot be used in determining the unobligated balance available for obligation. However, obligations for procurement of inventories and acquisition of assets must be included in obligations reported under Circular A-34. Claims against budgetary resources, such as payables and undelivered orders, must be used in determining unobligated balances.

Viewed from another perspective, OMB has defined obligational authority as being merely the "quick current assets" of the fund. That is, the budgetary authority consists only of the unspent, uncommitted, and unobligated resources in possession of the fund.

Treatment of Accounts Receivable

Revolving funds are directed to operate and report the results of their operations on an accrual basis. However as mentioned above, OMB will not permit the consideration of inventories as part of the funds available to an agency for commitment before the inventories are liquidated into cash.

Another deviation from full accrual accounting is the treatment of receivables.

OMB Circular A-34, *Instruction on Budget Execution,* states that some funds treat the write-off of receivables as an expense, which is proper in accrual accounting. For purposes of reporting under A-34, write-offs of receivables will not ordinarily be treated as an obligation, but rather as a reduction in revenues when such write-offs are not chargeable to an allowance for losses. Amounts provided for losses on receivables are treated as a reduction in revenues in the period when the provision is made.

FUNDING VIOLATIONS

Antideficiency Act Violations

As with other appropriated funds, the obligations or expenditures of revolving funds cannot be made in excess of amounts appropriated by Congress. Excess transactions are violations of the Antideficiency Act. In its Circular A-34, OMB takes the position that

> Incurring obligations in excess of apportioned budgetary resources is a violation of the Antideficiency Act and is reportable whether or not the fund has unapportioned resources or nonbudgetary resources or nonbudgetary assets greater than the amount of the deficiency.

OMB requires each fund manager to assume responsibility for calculating requirements for funds and to request appropriations in a manner that permits funding of outstanding obligations at all times during the year with available budgetary resources. If capital is insufficient, the manager must defer incurring obligations until the budgetary resources are sufficient to fund the obligations.

Anticipated reimbursements and anticipated customers' orders for the remainder of a year are not considered as a budgetary resource by OMB for the purpose of determining the status of funds on any given day even though such reimbursements may be anticipated at the time apportionments are made by OMB. Stated another way, a fund manager may not allow a level of fund/obligations that exceeds the lower of (1) the obligational authority apportioned by OMB or (2) the OMB apportionment less the amount by which actual reimbursements fell short of estimated reimbursements. At year end the practice of OMB is to adjust the estimated reimbursements to actual reimbursements, and the latter figure often forms a part of the obligational authority for the future. Excess reimbursements received late in a fiscal year and not apportioned by OMB do not lapse but may be carried forward if apportioned as obligational authority for the next fiscal year.

Surplus and Deficits

The objective of revolving-fund financing is to ensure to the extent possible that revenues and expenses are equal. Neither Congress nor OMB expects perfection. With the appropriate working capital, a fund may operate with a loss one year and a profit the next. Fund management is expected to propose the necessary action to raise or lower selling prices to ensure that the costs are recovered in the next fiscal year or that profits are returned to customers.

REPORTING BY REVOLVING FUNDS

The reporting requirements for revolving funds are similar to those required for appropriation-funded operations. Periodic accounting must be made to both the Treasury and OMB.

Budget Statements

Under OMB Circular A-11, *Preparation and Submission of Budget Estimates,* budget statements similar to those made by businesses must be submitted by all enterprises such as government corporations and all other revolving and trust revolving funds. The required statements on the accrual basis will include a condensed statement of revenue and expense, and a condensed statement of financial condition and changes in government equity.

If the enterprise is engaged in two or more major programs, OMB requires that the following data be segregated for each program: revenues, expenses, and net operating income or loss. Nonoperating income or loss will be shown separately with the figures that comprise the total net income or loss. The financial data submitted by the fund to OMB must agree with the information provided on the statement of financial condition to the Treasury. The condensed statement of financial condition has information arrayed by three principal sections, in the following general order.

REVOLVING FUND
Contents of Condensed Statement of Financial Condition

ASSETS

Fund balance with the Treasury
United States securities (at par value):
        Public debt securities
        Agencies securities
Accounts receivable (net)
Advances made

(continued)

Loans receivable (net)

Equipment (net)

Inventories (net)

Real property and equipment (net)

Other assets (net)

    TOTAL ASSETS

LIABILITIES

Accounts payable including funded accrued liabilities

Advances received

Unfunded liabilities

Debt issued under borrowing authority:

    Borrowing from the Treasury

    Borrowing from the Federal Financing Bank

    Agency securities issued

Other liabilities

    TOTAL LIABILITIES

GOVERNMENT EQUITY

Unexpended balances:

    Unobligated balances

    Undelivered orders

Unfinanced budget authority:

    Unfilled customers orders

    Contract authority

    Borrowing authority

Invested capital

    TOTAL GOVERNMENT EQUITY

Apportionment Reporting

OMB requires that revolving funds report on the budgetary authority to be apportioned for a given fiscal year and on budget execution. OMB circulars A-11 and A-34, respectively, provide detailed guidance on these two responsibilities.

Certain revolving funds are subject to the apportionment process of OMB and will be apportioned on an obligation basis on the SF 132, Apportionment and Reapportionment Schedule. Two types of apportionments are provided for on the SF 132:

▲ *Category A apportionments*—the apportionment of budgetary authority by time periods, typically quarterly.

▲ *Category B apportionments*—the apportionment of budgetary authority by activities, projects, objects, or for a combination of category B apportionments.

In the case of no-year and multiple-year funds (funds are available for obligation beyond the current fiscal year), apportionments will cover the anticipated financial requirements for the current year.

Budget Execution Reports

Revolving funds, whether apportioned or not, will report information on budget performance on SF 133, Report on Budget Execution. Reporting on the SF 133 is on an obligation basis. The report on budget execution has three principal sections.

▲ *Budget authority*—a statement of the total budgetary resources of the fund or other reporting entity, and the sources and amounts of the authority

▲ *Status of budgetary resources*—a reporting of obligations incurred, unobligated balances available for obligation, and unobligated balances not available for obligation, and the reasons

▲ *Relation of obligations to outlays and accrued expenditures*—a reconciliation of obligations incurred, net unpaid obligations, outlays, changes in accounts payable, and the accrued expenditures for the end of the reporting period

ACCOUNTING FOR REVOLVING FUNDS In practice, revolving funds have been used to finance service or supply activities desired by several government organizations. Earlier, mention was made of the stock funds of the Department of Defense. Services such as those provided by a computer center could also be operated as a revolving fund. Additionally, revolving funds have been used successfully to finance manufacturing and equipment overhaul activities. The specific accounting practices will vary with the nature of services provided.

Operation of Service or Supply Fund

A revolving fund providing services or supplies to its customers is principally concerned with closely monitoring its total costs in much the same manner as any private service or retail organization. The purchase price and handling and other overhead costs are passed along to the fund's customers, typically on a first-in, first-out basis. The selling price generally equates to total cost, or to cost plus a recovery factor to offset a loss of a prior period. Similarly if a profit was realized during an earlier period, the current year's services or supplies may be sold to customers for less than current costs.

The following steps outline the process for operating a service or supply fund.

▲   An agency must receive the approval of Congress through enacted authorization and appropriation acts.

▲   The Treasury must provide the initial corpus or capitalization for the fund.

▲   Supplies and inventory or services must be procured for resale to fund customers. Payments for these items will decrease the fund balance in the Treasury.

▲   The agency will then sell stock or services to customers, and reduce inventory if applicable, but increase the funds with the Treasury upon payment by the fund customer.

▲   Once completed, the cycle is repeated.

It is not uncommon for Congress in authorizing a revolving fund to provide the capital to fund only current operations, and to require the fund management to make a formal request to Congress for monies needed to procure long-term fixed assets. For example, PL 656, establishing the revolving fund of the Bureau of Engraving and Printing, reads in part as follows.

> . . . whenever any work or services are requisitioned from the Bureau of Engraving and Printing, Treasury Department, the requisitioning agency shall make payment therefor from funds available to it for such purposes at prices deemed by the Secretary of the Treasury to be adequate to recover the amount of direct and indirect costs of the Bureau, including administrative expenses incidental to performing the work or services requisitioned.

Under this legislation, Congress financed the normal operating costs of the bureau. Special appropriations were required by the bureau to cover the cost of extraordinary expenditures relating to buildings and land, expenditures which were specifically excluded by Congress in the initial capitalization of the fund.

Accounting Procedures

The obligation and expenditure of federal funds by a revolving fund must comply with the practices and procedures governing agencies whose activities are supported through appropriations. Thus, a revolving fund providing supplies or services would be required to formally recognize in its financial system the following events.

▲ Capitalization of the fund

▲ Estimated reimbursements to the fund

▲ Apportionments received from OMB

▲ Establishment of a process of fund control, possibly by issuing allotments to various personnel

▲ Orders from customers

▲ Obligations entered to obtain fixed assets (if permitted), personnel services, supplies, and inventories

▲ Goods and services received

▲ Billing of customers for services rendered

▲ Payments received from customers

▲ Payment for assets, services, and supplies received

▲ Inventory items consumed in operations

▲ Recognition of depreciation on a fixed asset used

▲ Adjustments for any changes in estimated reimbursements

Exhibit 24.2 illustrates the accounting that would record the events above. Exhibit 24.3 summarizes the effect of these transactions on the accounts of the fund. Remember that the example above is an extremely simplistic presentation of supply or service fund accounting. In practice, the annual transaction volume of some funds could easily exceed a quarter million in number and billions of dollars in value.

Assuming that the events above constituted the total financed activity for the accounting period, several accounts would be closed to determine the invested capital account balance at the end of the period. When the closing entries are posted to the invested capital account, the ending balance of invested capital comprises the asset investments that will be consumed during future operations.

The unexpended balance of the revolving fund will consist of several accounts.

▲ Unallotted apportionments

▲ Unobligated allotments

▲ Unliquidated obligations

Unless funds have been advanced from customers, the balance of the unfilled customers' orders account should not be considered as available budget authority when preparing reports at the end of the fiscal year. As mentioned earlier, costs incurred for customers who later fail to reimburse the revolving fund could cause the revolving fund to reflect a deficiency status in violation of the Antideficiency Act.

Exhibit 24.2 **ILLUSTRATION OF ACCOUNTING FOR SUPPLY OR SERVICE REVOLVING FUND**

FUND EVENT	NUMBER	ENTRIES	DEBIT	CREDIT
Capitalization of fund	(1)	Fund balance with the Treasury	$ 10,000	
		Unapportioned funds		$ 10,000
		To record fund corpus		
Estimated reimbursements to fund	(2)	Estimated reimbursements	20,000	
		Unapportioned funds		20,000
		To record anticipated reimbursements from customers that OMB must apportion		
Apportionment by OMB	(3)	Unapportioned funds	30,000	
		Unallotted apportionments		30,000
		To record apportionment by OMB and present unallotted funds		
Issuance of allotments	(4)	Unallotted apportionments	30,000	
		Unobligated allotments		30,000
		To record the issuance of obligational authority to fund managers		
Receipt of orders and advance payment by customers	(5)	Unfilled customers orders	25,000	
		Advances and reimbursements		25,000
		To record orders received that are valid obligations of ordering agency		
Placement of orders and other commitments	(6)	Unobligated allotments	27,000	
		Unliquidated obligations		27,000
		To record issuance of formal obligation documents and reduce the unobligated balance		
Receipt of assets, incurred expenditures, and expenses	(7)	Equipment	5,000	
		Inventory	8,000	
		Operating expenses	10,000	
		Accounts payable		13,000
		Accrued liabilities—payroll		10,000
		To record assets and expenses of accounting period		
		—plus—		
Reduction of previous outstanding obligations	(8)	Unliquidated obligations	23,000	
		Expended appropriation—capital		5,000
		Expended appropriation—operating		18,000
		To reduce outstanding obligations and reflect accrual of expenditures		

(continued)

Exhibit 24.2 *(continued)*

FUND EVENT	NUMBER	ENTRIES	DEBIT	CREDIT
Billing customers for services performed	(9)	Accounts receivable—other agency Earned revenues	22,000	22,000
		Billed other agency for performance and recognized revenue		
		—plus—		
Recording filled customer orders	(10)	Advances and reimbursements Unfilled customers orders	22,000	22,000
Recording deposits by customers and reduction of amount due to fund	(11)	Fund balance with the Treasury Accounts receivable—other agency	19,000	19,000
		To record deposits by customers and reduce receivable outstanding		
Recording disbursements	(12)	Accounts payable Accrued liabilities—payroll Fund balance with the Treasury	10,000 9,000	19,000
		To record payment of liabilities and reduction in fund balance		
Recording inventory issued for operations	(13)	Operating expenses Inventory	5,000	5,000
		To record inventory consumed during period		
Recording consumption of fixed assets	(14)	Operating expenses Accumulated depreciation	1,000	1,000
		To record depreciation for period relating to equipment		
Recognition of excess of actual reimbursements over estimated	(15)	Estimated reimbursements Unallotted apportionments	5,000	5,000
		To reflect increase in actual reimbursements over earlier estimates and change in amount apportioned by OMB		
Closing out earlier estimate for reimbursement	(16)	Reimbursement to appropriation Estimated reimbursement	19,000	19,000
		To adjust earlier estimate of customers orders for work completed		
		TOTALS	$300,000	$300,000

Exhibit 24.3 **ILLUSTRATION OF ACCOUNTING FOR SUPPLY OR SERVICE REVOLVING FUND**
(Effect of transactions)

ACCOUNT DESCRIPTION	TRANSACTION NUMBER	EFFECT ON ACCOUNT BALANCES	
		DEBIT	CREDIT
Assets			
Fund balance with the Treasury	1, 11, 12	$ 29,000	$ 19,000
Estimated reimbursement	2, 15, 16	25,000	19,000
Accounts receivable—other agency	9, 11	22,000	19,000
Unfilled customers orders	5, 10	25,000	22,000
Inventory	7, 13	8,000	5,000
Equipment	7	5,000	—0—
Accumulated depreciation	14	—0—	1,000
Liabilities			
Accounts payable	7, 12	10,000	13,000
Accrued liabilities—payroll	7, 12	9,000	10,000
Advances and reimbursements	5, 10	22,000	25,000
Investment of Government			
Unapportioned funds	1, 2, 3	30,000	30,000
Reimbursements to appropriation*	16	19,000	
Unallotted apportionments	3, 4, 15	30,000	35,000
Unobligated allotments	4, 6	27,000	30,000
Unliquidated obligations	6, 8	23,000	27,000
Expended appropriation—capital*	8	—0—	5,000
Expended appropriation—operating*	8	—0—	18,000
Revenues*	9	—0—	22,000
Operating Expenses*	7, 13, 14	16,000	
TOTALS		$300,000	$300,000

* Accounts ultimately closed to invested capital account

Note: The transactions closed to invested capital would produce the following balance in that account.

Invested capital			
Reimbursements to appropriation	$19,000	$22,000	Revenues
		5,000	Expended appropriation—capital
Operating expenses	16,000		
		18,000	Expended appropriation—operating
Total	$35,000	$45,000	Total
		$10,000	Balance[†]

[†] The balance consists of the following assets: uncollected accounts receivable of $3,000, fixed assets less accumulated depreciation of $4,000, and inventory of $3,000.

Thus the investment of the government in a service or supply fund at the end of a fiscal period will consist of any balance in the invested capital account plus the unexpended balance of the revolving fund.

As mentioned, service or supply funds function, conceptually, much like retail or wholesale organizations. The funds serve as an entity that permits larger, more economical purchases, development of specialization in the services or supplies provided by the fund to its customers, and minimizes the problems resulting from long lead-time procurements. Services and supplies are sold to fund customers essentially at cost, plus transportation, handling, and other incidental expenses.

There are two types of revolving funds: (1) service or supply funds, and (2) industrial funds. Industrial funds are involved in manufacturing, overhaul, or repair activities. Because enhancements, improvements, and alterations are made or a product is built, the accounting for industrial funds necessarily differs from that for service or supply funds. Industrial fund practices are described in the next chapter.

chapter 25 Industrial Funds

INTRODUCTION

As discussed in Chapter 24, two types of revolving funds operate within the federal government: (1) the service or supply funds and (2) the industrial funds. Chapter 24 outlined accounting considerations for service or supply funds. This chapter discusses industrial fund accounting.

There is an assumption, for the illustration in this chapter, that the fund was initially financed from a Congressional appropriation. It will be noted that, to a large degree, the accounting procedures parallel corporate accounting practices.

THE NATURE OF INDUSTRIAL FUNDS

The industrial fund, like the service or supply revolving fund, exists to permit one government organization to service other government organizations. Like the service or supply fund, the industrial fund must price its products at a value to return the fund's cost. Unlike service and supply funds though, the industrial fund activities will involve a manufacturing or conversion activity: raw materials are converted into finished or altered goods.

426

In the Department of Defense, as well as in other agencies, Congress in authorizing and capitalizing industrial funds was trying to exploit the buyer-seller relationship of the private sector. Under that relationship, contracts or agreements exist to purchase products at a given price, of a specific quality, in a specified number, and by a designated date. In government, analogous quasi-contracts are called project orders, work orders, or job orders. These form the "legal" agreement between the manufacturing entity and the fund customer.

Such a relationship exists between the arsenals, depots, shipyards, and printing plants of the Department of Defense and fund customers. Similarly, among the civil agencies, the Bureau of Engraving and Printing of the Treasury Department produces currency, Federal Reserve notes, postage stamps, and other financial instruments for several agencies, including the Treasury, the Federal Reserve Board, the Postal Service, and others.

The customers of a revolving fund need not be only federal organizations. The enabling legislation could permit sales to state and local governments as well as to foreign governments. Charges to customers other than the federal government most often provide for full cost recovery, including any unfunded federal labor costs, depreciation, overhead, and other administrative costs that may not be paid directly by the fund. When such is the case, the receipts relating to the unfunded costs must be accounted for in a manner designated by Congress, the Treasury, or the Office of Management and Budget.

While the capitalization of a specific fund will vary, the budgetary resources available for obligation on a revolving basis will often include, as a minimum, the fund balance with the Treasury, accounts receivable for completed orders, and the value of unfilled customer orders formally accepted by the industrial fund.

OPERATIONS OF INDUSTRIAL FUNDS

The operation of an industrial fund is, in concept, similar to the supply or stock fund. The industrial fund, because it is a kind of revolving fund, must recover its investment and costs through reimbursement from its customers. The process is the same as that for the supply or stock fund.

- ▲ Congress must, through authorization and appropriation legislation, give its approval to establish and operate an activity as an industrial fund.
- ▲ The agency must obtain an initial corpus or capitalization from the Treasury.
- ▲ Supplies must be procured, labor costs incurred, and other expenses paid to convert, service, or manufacture the products of an industrial fund.

Payments of these expenditures will decrease the fund balance with the Treasury.

▲ Completed services or products must be "sold" to customer agencies an an established selling or transfer price that is sufficient to recover the costs and expenses incurred by the industrial fund.

▲ Once reimbursement is accomplished, the cycle is repeated.

When establishing an industrial fund, Congress may provide funding for acquisition of capital equipment for only the current period, and may require fund managers to make a formal request to Congress for any additional monies needed to procure long-term fixed assets. Thus reimbursements to the fund for consumption of fixed assets (as through a depreciation charge) may not be available to the fund for the automatic replacement of capital assets. By this fiscal control, Congress limits the flexibility of managerial decisions to those affecting current operations; no sinking fund nor replacement fund is accumulating that might be used for the future acquisition of assets with the knowledge of Congress. The reimbursements in excess of current costs would revert to the Treasury unless the fund had specific authority to obligate and expend such funds.

COST ACCOUNTING CONSIDERATIONS

With an industrial fund, the accounting complexities increase severalfold. The conversion costs to mold raw materials into finished goods are one of several factors that did not exist with service or supply fund accounting. Additionally, a distinction must be made between direct and indirect materials and labor; possibly research and development costs and administrative expenses exist that must also be recovered in the established selling prices. There is no governmentwide system prescribed for the accounting of industrial funds, probably because of the great diversity of operations and processes in existence.

Elements of Costs

Systems for industrial funds carefully consider the several types of costs required by any conversion process, costs such as direct and indirect labor and materials; manufacturing overhead, development costs, and other administrative or selling expenses. The applied definitions are similar to industrial practices.

▲ *Direct labor costs* or productive labor costs refers to payroll costs that result from labor expended in the production or conversion process.

▲ *Direct material costs* includes supplies, components, and other material that form an integral part of the finished goods or are expended in its conversion or production.

▲ *Indirect labor costs* include payroll costs necessary to the completion of the conversion or manufacturing process, but that do not affect or alter the converted or finished goods.

▲ *Indirect material costs* are costs of material necessary to the conversion or manufacturing process, but whose application to the product is difficult to cost directly to the product.

▲ *Manufacturing overhead costs* could include personnel, material and supplies, equipment, buildings, real estate, and other costs necessary to the conversion or manufacturing effort, but the benefit or causal relationship of which is not directly related to units produced.

Fixed and Variable Expenses

As they do in commercial enterprises, the manufacturing expenses of an industrial fund might require that manufacturing overhead be monitored or accounted for on the basis of whether it is fixed, variable, or semivariable in nature. While it is not possible to give absolute definitions of these terms, there is acceptance of the following descriptions, which must be consistently defined by each industrial fund and related to its production activity.

▲ *Variable expenses* are those manufacturing expenses that can be related to an operating period and vary directly with the volume of the accounting period. Viewed another way, if there is no production, there are no variable costs.

▲ *Fixed costs* are manufacturing expenses that do not vary with the production of a single accounting period, but must be assigned to production on some rational basis and will not be absorbed by the production of a single period. Fixed costs will exist regardless of production.

Actual and Standard Cost
Accounting Methods

Depending on the nature of the product of a particular industrial fund, one might find either actual or standard costing principles being applied.

If an *actual cost accounting system* is employed, the supporting records will be designed to collect costs as incurred, that is, on a historical basis. Direct material and labor costs will be recorded as incurred. Indirect material, labor, and overhead costs will generally be assigned on an allocated, predetermined basis, with the predetermined rate adjusted to actual rate at the end of the accounting period.

With a *standard cost accounting system*, parts, components, operations, or processes have been precosted or predetermined and a "standard" established for the quantity as well as dollars required in the manufacturing process. Throughout the accounting period, the production units are costed at standard cost. Actual costs are accumulated in separate accounts, and a comparison is made to determine variances between the standard and actual costs. The variances (over or under) from standard become an additional cost adjustment that must be applied to adjust standard costs to actual production costs.

Overhead Variances

Monitoring of activities of the commercial type often entails the analysis of reasons for variance between actual and estimated production levels and costs. Because products must be costed currently and often cannot await the determination of actual expenses, overhead is applied or allocated to the period's activity on a predetermined basis, with some distinction made for varying levels of capacity or efficiency.

The overhead variance analyses would be (1) for volume variance and (2) for budget variance.

▲ *Volume variance* relates to the level of efficiency or capacity attained during the accounting period.

▲ *Budget variance* relates to the difference between the actual expenses incurred and the budgeted expenses planned for the capacity or level of efficiency attained in the accounting period.

Exhibit 25.1 illustrates a method of computing these overhead variances.

METHODS OF COST ACCOUNTING   The use of actual or standard cost principles and the application of overhead on predetermined bases, with end-of-period adjustments for variances, could be used with either of the two accepted cost accounting methods: (1) work order or job cost method and (2) process cost method.

The *work order* or *job cost* accounting method provides for determining the cost to produce a specific lot, job, project, contract, or other identifiable items. This method presumes that the cost incurred or charged can be identified to a specific work or job order number.

Exhibit 25.1 **COMPUTATION OF OVERHEAD EXPENSE VARIATIONS**

	ESTIMATED EFFICIENCY (100%)	ACTUAL EFFICIENCY (80%)	ACTUAL EXPENSES FOR PERIOD
Fixed expenses	$10,000	$10,000	$10,000
Variable expenses	25,000	20,000	24,000
Total overhead expenses	$35,000	$30,000	$34,000
Production units	100	80	80

Rate per Unit:

Applied ($35,000 ÷ 100 = $350)	$350

Estimate for 80% ($30,000 ÷ 80 = $375)	$375

Actual incurred ($34,000 ÷ 80 = $425)	$425

Computation of Variances:

Volume Variance

Rate applied—unit	$ 350
Rate for 80% efficiency—unit	375
Unfavorable variance per unit	$ (25)

Total unfavorable volume variance	
(1) 80 units @ $25/unit	(2,000)
(2) or $350 × 80 = $28,000 − 30,000	(2,000)
(standard − actual)	

Budget Variance

Actual expenses—unit	$ 425
Estimated for 80% efficiency—unit	375
Unfavorable budget variance	$ (50)

Total unfavorable budget variance	
(1) 80 units @ $50 per unit	$ (4,000)
(2) or $34,000 − $30,000	$ (4,000)

Total Variance

Actual for period	$34,000
Estimated for 100% efficiency	28,000
(80 units @ $350)	
Total variance—unfavorable	$ (6,000)

The *process cost* accounting method requires the determination of production cost by department for a specific time period and the calculation of an average unit cost based on units of production. Typically, the process costing method is required when the products of earlier processes become the raw material for later processes or the process results in producing joint products or by-products.

A cost accounting system should be viewed as a more precise recording, accumulating, and accounting for the activities of an organization than the appropriation accounting process described in the earlier chapters. The objective of a cost system is to determine the cost of performing a service or function. With respect to industrial funds, cost is required to permit the calculation of a selling or transfer price that will be charged by the manufacturing agency to other agencies. The underlying principle of an industrial fund, as mentioned earlier, is that it is a revolving fund—that is, the industrial fund must collect full cost for services or functions performed to maintain the "revolving" nature of the fund corpus.

WORK ORDER OR JOB COST ACCOUNTING

A prerequisite of a work order or job cost accounting system is that the servicing or manufacturing organization be organized in a manner to work on or manufacture in specific units, lots, jobs, or projects. The functions performed must be identifiable, relatable, and capable of being costed and charged to a specific customer (or work order). Exhibit 25.2 summarizes the major costing considerations of work order or job cost system.

A work order or job cost system for a manufacturing process producing units for a finished goods inventory for later "sale" or distribution to customer agencies entails a structure that provides for these activities.

▲ Allotment of funds, recording of obligations, and accruing of expenditures in the same manner as an agency whose operations are funded by appropriations

▲ Recovery of costs to preserve or "revolve" the initial capital investment or corpus of the revolving fund

▲ A system of procurement (through contracts and purchase orders) that is in compliance with federal procurement regulations

▲ A system of inventory and stores control and fixed asset accounting providing for the charging of consumed resources at the time of use

▲ A payroll system, which also includes detailed labor costing and distribution procedures for charging projects or jobs for labor performed, generally through a system of labor tickets, permitting the accumulation of labor costs by task, groupings of tasks, operations, jobs, projects, by work unit, departments and the plant as a whole for desired time periods (day, week, month, year)

Exhibit 25.2 **GENERAL FLOW OF WORK ORDER, JOB ORDER COST SYSTEM**

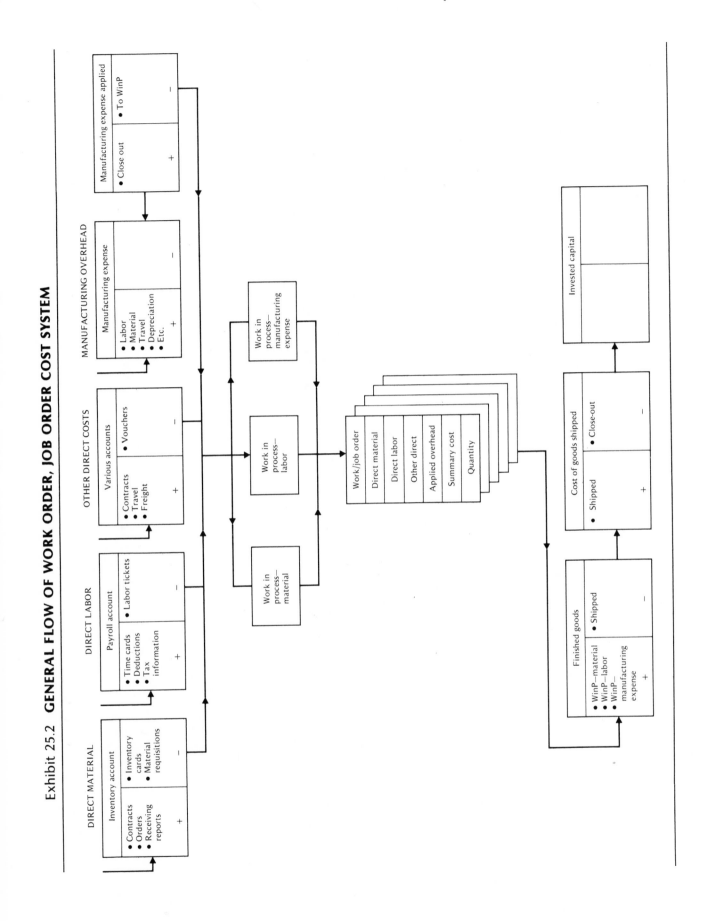

▲ The predetermination of overhead or burden expenses to be applied to a given level of activity or production, with the variance between the applied and actual expenses determined at least annually and adjustments made to the applied rates

▲ A system of general ledger control accounts for initially recording and managing the overall cost being incurred, supported by detailed cost accounting procedures to permit the further refinement or distribution of material, labor, and overhead costs to the manufacturing process

▲ A system for accumulating the cost of work in process, by major categories of cost (material, labor, overhead) by individual work order or job order

▲ Transfer of physical units and related costs upon completion from the work-in-process status to finished-goods status or direct to customers

▲ Controls over finished goods until "sold" or shipped to customer agencies, possibly with the cost of goods manufactured being transferred to the cost-of-goods-shipped status

▲ Financial reports that permit the periodic determination of the excess of revenues or expense to permit the adjustment of transfer prices to ensure a recovery of the cost incurred

Not a part of the work-order or job-order system, but still a necessary costing component of the selling price is an accurate assignment of general and administrative expenses to the appropriate accounting period. These nonmanufacturing costs are related to (1) finished goods delivered during the period, (2) finished goods in inventory, and (3) work still in process. When such cost must be allocated, a common allocation base is total cost because the general and administrative expenses are related to the overall management of the total facility, including the manufacturing activity, although such costs are not controllable by those responsible for production.

Accounting Procedures

Like all governmental activities, an industrial fund must comply with the general accounting requirements relating to obligations and expenditures and the reporting outlined in Chapter 23.

Certain transactions are typical of an industrial fund performing a maintenance, repair, or manufacturing function. An industrial fund performing one of these conversion functions would be required to recognize formally several events in its accounting records.

▲ Initial capitalization of an appropriation and apportionment of those monies to the industrial fund.

▲ Allotment responsibility, within the fund organization, to be distributed to officials designated as authorized to enter into obligations on behalf of the fund.

▲ Orders to manufacture or perform a conversion or other work for customer agencies. An initial control is to authorize a work order or job cost card, assigning a serial number or other unique designator to the order. The work orders may vary in size, shape, and content but often contain information such as

Name of a customer agency
Job number assigned
Beginning and ending date for ordered work
Accounts or appropriation numbers to be charged
Estimated costs
Actual costs
Quantity
Description of work to be performed
Departments to perform work
Variances between actual and estimated costs.

▲ Materials consumed and labor performed by the fund employees to be charged to a work order. (Nonproduction labor will be recorded in an idle or unassigned account for later accounting and analysis.)

▲ Issuance of contracts, purchase orders, and other agreements to procure materials and supplies must comply with governmentwide procurement regulations and must be formally recorded.

▲ Materials, supplies, equipment, and other acquisitions received to be recorded in fixed-asset accounts or inventory-asset accounts unless the items are to be used immediately; in that case the cost of the items charged directly to work-in-process or other control accounts.

▲ Materials to be released to work-in-process activities on the basis of formal materials requisitions describing the material desired, identifying numbers and descriptors, costs, accounting nomenclature, and other data.

▲ Labor to be accounted for by parts, components, assemblies, job, and project, permitting summarization by employee, department, and fund on the basis of time recorded on labor tickets. (The labor tickets, or a facsimile, are the basis for distributing labor costs to the various jobs in process. Additionally, labor costs, of course, are required by overhead and administrative activities as well.)

▲ Unfunded costs to be recorded and reported in much the same manner as funded costs are. (Two of the more common unfunded costs are (1) accumulated depreciation related to the use of fixed assets in the industrial activities and (2) the accrued liability for employees' earned leave. As leave is taken, the debit or charge is made against the accrued liability account.)

▲ Overhead or burden costs to be charged to production activities on the basis of an estimated or applied or standard rate because the actual level of overhead costs will not be known until after the close of the fiscal period. (At the end of the period the applied estimate of overhead costs is offset against the actual overhead costs. Variances between the applied and actual amounts are recovered by adjusting the applied rate in the future. Often the overhead is applied on the basis of an activity indicator (e.g., dollars of labor, hours of labor, machine hours, or other quantitative bases).)

▲ Cost of completed units transferred from work in process to finished goods must match the specific units completed. (The costs accumulated on the work or job orders are summarized and transferred from the work-in-process accounts to the finished-goods-inventory account.)

▲ Funds provided by customer agencies to be treated as advances (a liability) until earned. (Generally, revenues are earned when the completed goods are shipped pursuant to the direction provided by the customer agency. At this time the advance account may be reduced (or a receivable established if the agency is on a reimbursement basis). A companion entry is required to reduce the furnished goods inventory for the value of the goods shipped.)

▲ Formal orders, constituting obligational authority for the performing agency, to be recorded in the accounting records to ensure that these amounts along with other obligational authority are controlled and monitored.

Results of Operations

Certain conclusions may be made concerning the adequacy of the pricing or work performed during the fiscal period. For example, the total cost of goods manufactured must incorporate the material, labor, and overhead used, incurred, or applied. However, certain of the total costs of manufacturing benefited jobs still in process at the end of the period; therefore based on the work-in-process inventories, an adjustment of the total costs of manufacturing must be made to reflect the actual cost of manufacturing for the period. Also because all of the units produced are not necessarily shipped during the period of manufacture, adjustments must be made for the finished goods inventory.

While industrial funds may at times show losses, Congress expects that the fund managers will monitor activities and adhere to pricing policies that are both competitive with a commercial market and adequate to recover the cost and expenses of operations. When constructing a price, the fund managers must prepare reliable estimates of cost of manufacture, predict varying levels of manufacturing volumes, and carefully forecast the administrative expenses of the fiscal period.

Invested Capital

Industrial funds, like other government entities, must monitor the status of the government's investment. Earlier chapters indicate that certain accounts are closed at the end of the period to determine the excess revenues earned or the loss incurred. Additionally, the account closings are necessary to determine the invested capital of the government. After closing, the balance of invested capital is determined by these conditions.

INVESTED CAPITAL ACCOUNT

Manufacturing overhead— actual	$xxxx	Expended funds—capital	$xxxx
Administrative expenses	xxx	Expended funds—operating	xxx
Cost of goods shipped	xxxx	Earned revenue	xxxx
Total	$xxxx	Manufacturing overhead— applied	xxxx
		Total	$xxxx
		Balance	$ xx

The overhead applied account may also be closed to the manufacturing overhead—actual account to determine the amount of any overapplied or underapplied overhead costs. In this instance, the applied overhead was more than actual overhead incurred. Thus the units shipped were overcharged slightly for the excess applied overhead. If the application variance is signficant, studies will be made to reassess the application rate or allocation bases used. Often, adjustments are reflected in a revised application rate for a future accounting period.

Overhead Variances

Seldom will the amount of the overhead applied to production be the same amount as the actual overhead incurred during the fiscal period. In truth, part of the underapplied or overapplied overhead is applicable to both the current and the succeeding fiscal period. This situation is particularly likely if there is an ending work-in-process inventory. In practice though, the overhead variance is written off at the end of each period. Such an accounting is acceptable to the General Accounting Office.

GAO, in its *Accounting Principles and Standards*, Title 2, describes three procedures for disposing of the overhead variance.

▲ Redistribute the variance to materials issued for the various jobs of the year.

This procedure is impratical because no sales made during the year could be considered closed until after the end of the fiscal period. If such precision were ever required, the most effective costing might be to make no billings until after all accounts have been closed for the period.

▲ Carry the overhead variance forward to the next fiscal period, with the balance reflected as either a deferred charge or a deferred credit.

This practice is an acceptable alternative. However, as mentioned above, if the full variance is carried forward to the succeeding period, the costs of the later period are inflated or reduced by that portion of the overhead variance related to the production of the prior period.

▲ Charge the overhead variance to the overhead at the end of the period. An overapplication of overhead would be treated as a reduction in the overhead.

This last procedure is the most acceptable, providing the variance is minimal, probably no more than a few percentage points of the actual overhead.

Variances must be analyzed and not routinely accounted for as a deferred item or an adjustment to the period's overhead. The cause for variances can often highlight conditions requiring management's attention. Variances should be monitored and the application bases adjusted to ensure that the applied rates parallel as closely as possible the actual or anticipated overhead or expenses.

Formal Orders

As mentioned earlier, the receipt of a formal order may constitute an increase in a funding authority, and permit the industrial fund to enter into obligations and make expenditures. There is a risk, however. OMB permits formal orders to be considered as additional obligational authority, but states that obligations and expenditures may not be incurred in excess of revenues from the formal orders actually completed.

Thus, unless the industrial fund actually realizes revenues equal to the obligations and expenditures incurred for the formal contracts, the fund has exceeded its budgetary authority and the provisions of the Antideficiency Act have been violated. For this reason, industrial fund managers adhere to a conservative forecasting methodology, anticipating few revenues.

When formal orders constitute additional obligational authority for the performing industrial fund, the value of the order should be recorded in the accounting records to ensure that these amounts are monitored and controlled along with other funding authority.

PROCESS COST ACCOUNTING The costing principles and techniques applicable to the work or job order method are equally appropriate to the process cost method. The distinguishing feature is that under the process cost method costs must be accumulated by the various processes of production. In practice, these often relate to different departments of the manufacturing entity. Under the process method, it is not possible to retain the identity of a job order. Each job order is only a portion of the continuous manufacturing process.

Two federal government organizations whose operations are conducive to process cost accounting are the Bureau of the Mint and the Bureau of Engraving and Printing. The manufacturing effort in each organization is directed to the continuous manufacture of a unit of production requiring the completion of several processes. Under this method, careful definition must be made in determining

▲ The departments or cost centers
▲ The method of accumulating cost throughout the manufacturing process
▲ The volumes of units produced

Exhibit 25.3 summarizes the extent of cost accounting that must be performed to determine the total product cost and the unit cost at the Bureau of Engraving and Printing.

Description of Process Cost Accounting System

A prerequisite to the implementation of a process cost accounting system is the establishment of departments or cost centers responsible for performing specific manufacturing activities. Costs and expenses incurred are either charged directly or allocated to these departments. The input cost, plus additional manufacturing or conversion costs, must be accumulated for the accounting period and allocated to the units produced during the same period. The allocations become more complex if joint products or by-products result from the manufacturing process or if the total production includes both the finished units and units still in process at the end of the period.

A process cost accounting system must address several events in the production process.

▲ Several cost centers must be established to be responsible for incurring labor, material, and overhead costs. The centers could perform a single operation or a number of manufacturing operations.
▲ All elements of cost (labor, material, overhead) are recorded initially in the agency's general ledger control accounts, which in the case of Engraving

Exhibit 25.3   **GENERAL FLOW OF BUREAU OF ENGRAVING AND PRINTING COST ACCOUNTING SYSTEM**

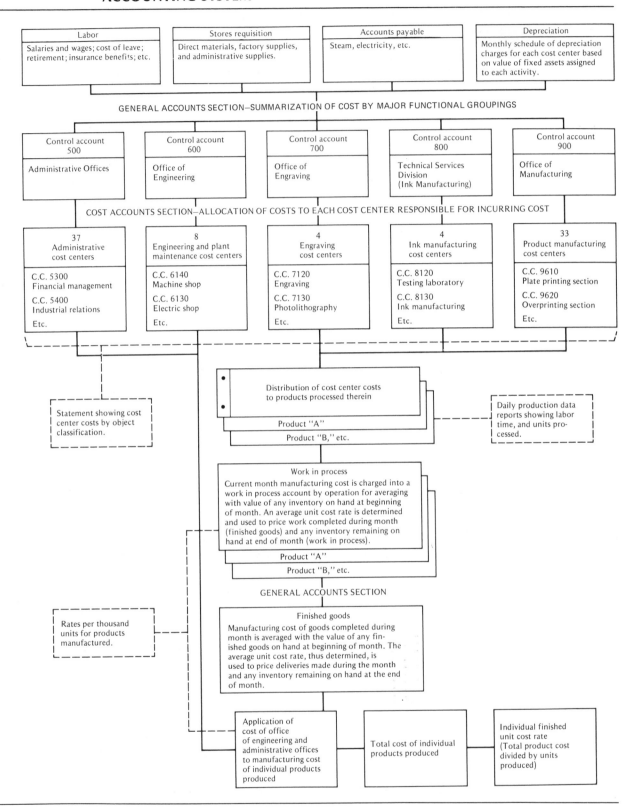

Labor	Stores requisition	Accounts payable	Depreciation
Salaries and wages; cost of leave; retirement; insurance benefits; etc.	Direct materials, factory supplies, and administrative supplies.	Steam, electricity, etc.	Monthly schedule of depreciation charges for each cost center based on value of fixed assets assigned to each activity.

GENERAL ACCOUNTS SECTION—SUMMARIZATION OF COST BY MAJOR FUNCTIONAL GROUPINGS

Control account 500	Control account 600	Control account 700	Control account 800	Control account 900
Administrative Offices	Office of Engineering	Office of Engraving	Technical Services Division (Ink Manufacturing)	Office of Manufacturing

COST ACCOUNTS SECTION—ALLOCATION OF COSTS TO EACH COST CENTER RESPONSIBLE FOR INCURRING COST

37 Administrative cost centers	8 Engineering and plant maintenance cost centers	4 Engraving cost centers	4 Ink manufacturing cost centers	33 Product manufacturing cost centers
C.C. 5300 Financial management C.C. 5400 Industrial relations Etc.	C.C. 6140 Machine shop C.C. 6130 Electric shop Etc.	C.C. 7120 Engraving C.C. 7130 Photolithography Etc.	C.C. 8120 Testing laboratory C.C. 8130 Ink manufacturing Etc.	C.C. 9610 Plate printing section C.C. 9620 Overprinting section Etc.

Statement showing cost center costs by object classification.

Distribution of cost center costs to products processed therein

Product "A"

Product "B," etc.

Daily production data reports showing labor time, and units processed.

Work in process

Current month manufacturing cost is charged into a work in process account by operation for averaging with value of any inventory on hand at beginning of month. An average unit cost rate is determined and used to price work completed during month (finished goods) and any inventory remaining on hand at end of month (work in process).

Product "A"

Product "B," etc.

GENERAL ACCOUNTS SECTION

Rates per thousand units for products manufactured.

Finished goods

Manufacturing cost of goods completed during month is averaged with the value of any finished goods on hand at beginning of month. The average unit cost rate, thus determined, is used to price deliveries made during the month and any inventory remaining on hand at the end of month.

Application of cost of office of engineering and administrative offices to manufacturing cost of individual products produced	Total cost of individual products produced	Individual finished unit cost rate (Total product cost divided by units produced)

Source: *Synopsis of Financial Management*, (May 1968 ed.). Department of the Treasury, Washington, D.C., adapted from p. 5.

and Printing include administration, engineering, engraving, technical services, and manufacturing. This recording is not sufficiently precise for costing purposes, however.

▲ After being recorded in the general ledger control accounts, the costs and expenses must be distributed to the responsible individual cost center or department. In this example, the monthly assessment of costs to centers is by OMB object classifications: personnel compensation, benefits, materials, utilities, etc.

▲ The initial distribution of cost will in some instances be to support offices or organizations whose cost in turn must be allocated on some beneficial or causal basis to cost centers. Such cost might be referred to as manufacturing overhead.

▲ Once the total cost of manufacture has been accumulated in the production cost centers, these costs must then be prorated over the units of production of the several cost centers. Manufacturing activities must accumulate production costs on a frequent basis. Typically, center cost reports are compiled daily to show labor, material, and overhead costs.

▲ For direct labor, a daily reporting from data accumulated by various cost centers is generally made of products produced and the hours of work invested by individuals. The direct labor cost is determined by multiplying the reported hours worked times labor rates for each operation or process. To the direct labor cost is added fringe benefit costs associated with the labor.

▲ With respect to direct materials, production centers are charged based on the requisitions for materials drawn from inventory. If more than one process benefits or uses the same material, allocations of material cost are based on the activity or output of the individual cost centers.

▲ Manufacturing overhead (indirect labor, indirect material, depreciation, etc.) must also be allocated to cost centers. In practice, the more common bases include direct labor hours, direct labor dollars, cost of materials, labor plus material cost, volume (square footage, cubic contents, space occupied, usage of equipment, etc.). Absolute precision is not critical, but timeliness of reasonably accurate data is important. For this reason many manufacturing entities adhere to predetermined rates or bases for charging or applying overhead during the period. Adjustments for variances between this predetermined rate and actual levels of overhead costs may have to be made after the end of the period when total costs are known with more precision.

▲ Total manufacturing costs and the units produced are posted to work-in-process inventory accounts. The costs and units of the current period are accumulated with the units and cost on hand at the beginning of the period to determine an average cost per unit for purposes of "pricing" the units transferred to a subsequent process or to finished goods, or goods that remain in process.

▲ One of the last costing efforts is distributing general, administrative, and other costs (engineering in the case of Engraving and Printing) over the total manufacturing costs of the period. These nonmanufacturing costs are related to (1) finished goods delivered, (2) finished goods in inventory, and (3) work still in the process of manufacture. A common allocation basis is total cost because these administrative costs are related to the overall general administration and management of the manufacturing operations and are not controllable by those responsible for production only.

Determining Production Costs

Exhibit 25.4 illustrates the cost of production using a process cost accounting method. Several differences exist between this accounting and the work order or job cost system described earlier.

▲ Costs are charged or applied to a department, not to the work order or job.

▲ Costs are accumulated by the manufacturing department, rather than being identified to a lot, job, or unit.

▲ Costs are transferred to succeeding departments in the process.

▲ Cost for units are determined periodically on an average basis for the equivalent units of production.

▲ The costs charged to earlier, manufacturing departments are transferred to succeeding manufacturing departments as units are moved from one department to another.

Note that the "finished unit" of any one department may or may not constitute the finished product ultimately shipped to the customer agency. In fact, in the typical operation, the end product of one department often becomes the raw material for the succeeding departments.

Exhibit 25.4 or a facsimile may be referred to as a cost of production statement or report. The exhibit shows total and unit costs for more than one department. In practice, such a report would be of interest to management, with individual departments often receiving the cost information for their own operations.

Accounting Considerations

Like other government entities, an industrial fund, regardless of the method of cost accounting used, must still comply with accounting standards and principles and the procedures relating to obligation and expenditure accounting and reporting. Although the nature of the transactions outlined below may be similar to that of a work order or job cost operation, significant differences exist, particularly with respect to (1) charging costs to departments (rather than to lots, job, etc.), (2) transfer of cost from one department to another (the products of an earlier department become the raw material of a succeeding department), and (3) effect of

COST OF PRODUCTION

Exhibit 25.4 (ILLUSTRATION OF PROCESS COST ACCOUNTING)

Units of Production

	DEPARTMENT A	DEPARTMENT B	DEPARTMENT C
Units started	2,000	-0-	
Units from other department	-0-	1,600	1,400
Units transferred to next department	1,600	1,400	-0-
Units transferred to finished goods	-0-	-0-	1,200
Units in process—end of period	400	200	200

Cost of Department

	DEPARTMENT A For Department	DEPARTMENT A For Unit	DEPARTMENT B For Department	DEPARTMENT B For Unit	DEPARTMENT C For Department	DEPARTMENT C For Unit
(1) Cost from other department	$ -0-	$ -0-	$ 9,600	$ 6.00	$15,400	$11.00
(2) Cost by department						
a) Material	4,000	2.00	-0-	-0-	1,400	1.00
b) Labor	3,600	2.00	4,500	3.00	2,500	2.00
c) Manufacturing overhead	3,600	2.00	3,000	2.00	2,500	2.00
Total—this department	11,200	6.00	7,500	5.00	6,400	5.00
(3) Total department cost	$11,200	$ 6.00	$17,100	$11.00	$21,800	$16.00

Disposition of Department Costs

	DEPARTMENT A	DEPARTMENT B	DEPARTMENT C
(1) Transferred to next department	$ 9,600	$15,400	-0-
(2) Transferred to finished goods	-0-	-0-	$19,200
(3) In process—end of period			
a) From other department	-0-	($6.00 × 200) 1,200	($11.00 × 200) 2,200
b) Materials	($2.00 × 400) 800	-0-	(1.00 × 200) 200
c) Labor	($2.00 × 400/2) 400	($3.00 × 200/2) 300	(2.00 × 200/4) 100
d) Manufacturing overhead	($2.00 × 400/2) 400	($2.00 × 200/2) 200	(2.00 × 200/4) 100
Total in process	1,600	1,700	2,600
(4) Total department cost	$11,200	$17,100	$21,800

Equivalent Units of Production

DEPARTMENT A
Material = 2,000 units complete
Labor = 1,600 + 1/2 of 400 = 1,800
Overhead = 1,600 + 1/2 of 400 = 1,800

DEPARTMENT B
Material = -0-
Labor = 1,400 + 1/2 of 200 = 1,500
Overhead = 1,400 + 1/2 of 200 = 1,500

DEPARTMENT C
Material = 1,400 units complete
Labor = 1,200 + 1/4 of 200 = 1,250
Overhead = 1,200 + 1/4 of 200 = 1,250

Computation of Unit Cost

DEPARTMENT A

$$\text{Material} = \frac{\$4000}{2000} = \$2.00$$

$$\text{Labor} = \frac{\$3600}{1800} = \$2.00$$

$$\text{Overhead} = \frac{\$3600}{1800} = \$2.00$$

DEPARTMENT B

Material = ——

$$\text{Labor} = \frac{\$4500}{1500} = \$3.00$$

$$\text{Overhead} = \frac{\$3000}{1500} = \$2.00$$

DEPARTMENT C

$$\text{Material} = \frac{\$1400}{1400} = \$1.00$$

$$\text{Labor} = \frac{\$2500}{1250} = \$2.00$$

$$\text{Overhead} = \frac{\$2500}{1250} = \$2.00$$

computing equivalent units of production. Additionally, the example assumes that the customer agency placed a formal order for the units produced.

Like other inventories, finished goods must be controlled until shipment to customer agencies. Periodically, generally each month, financial reports and statements are prepared to determine the relationship of revenues earned and billed to costs incurred. The "selling" or transfer pricing formula must be adequate to ensure that the revenues collected are sufficient to cover all costs and expenses.

Accounting Procedures

The operation of an industrial fund activity, using the process cost accounting method, requires that accounting records formally recognize several events.

▲ The initial capitalization and apportionment of monies authorized and appropriated by the Congress and apportioned by the Office of Management and Budget as being available for obligation and expenditure.

▲ The allotment responsibility distributed to officials designated as authorized to enter into obligation on behalf of the fund.

▲ The initiation of work on the basis of a formal order from customer agencies. (These orders should be acknowledged in the accounting records because the unfilled order is considered part of the composite obligational authority of the industrial fund.)

▲ The award of contracts, purchase orders, and other authorized agreements for the acquisition of materials, supplies, equipment, or services.

▲ The receipt and record of materials, supplies, equipment, and other acquisitions received.

▲ The accounting for material consumed or labor costs incurred. (However, unlike the work order system, in which costs are accumulated by specific jobs or lots, costs under a process cost system are charged directly to a department. It is the department, rather than the job, that is significant under a process cost system.)

▲ The recording and reporting of unfunded costs in the same manner as the funded costs. (The more common unfunded costs are accumulated depreciation related to fixed assets and the accrued liability for employees' earned leave.)

▲ The application or allocation overhead or burden costs to the departments on the basis of a predetermined rate because the actual overhead costs will not be known for some time after the close of the accounting period, probably long after the units have been completed and shipped to customers. (At the end of the period, the applied estimate of overhead costs is offset against actual overhead costs incurred. The variance between applied and actual costs is recovered from or returned to customers by adjusting the applied rate of future periods. Generally, overhead is applied to the manufacturing departments on some quantitative basis bearing a relationship to dollars of direct labor, hours of labor, machine hours, or some other indicator of activity.)

▲ The accounting for goods completed and the related costs, which must be removed from the work-in-process accounts and transferred to finished goods.

▲ In some instances, the customer agency may have provided an advance of funds, which must be treated as a liability owed until earned. Generally, the advance or revenues are earned when goods are completed and shipped pursuant to directions provided by the customer agency. Upon shipment, the completed units and the related cost must be removed from the finished goods inventory.

Periodically, usually monthly, a reporting is made of the manufacturing process. Industrial funds prepare a financial statement of revenues, costs, and expenses. This statement provides essentially the same information as the statement of cost of goods manufactured and sold, which one would expect to obtain from a commercial manufacturing plant. The industrial fund's statement must contain the following information, although the specific account titles may vary by the individual fund.

INDUSTRIAL FUND: STATEMENT OF REVENUES, COST, AND EXPENSES
(For the period ended September 30, 19xx)

REVENUES			$xx,xxx
COST OF GOODS SHIPPED			
Material:			
Beginning of period	$ —0—		
Purchases	+ x,xxx		
Available	$ x,xxx		
End of period	(x,xxx)		
Charged to departments		$ x,xxx	
Labor:			
Salaries charged to departments	$xx,xxx		
Accrued leave	+ xxx		
Total labor in period		xx,xxx	
Overhead:			
Applied		x,xxx	
Total cost incurred: (A)			xx,xxx (A)

(continued)

INDUSTRIAL FUND: STATEMENT OF REVENUES, COST, AND EXPENSES

(For the period ended September 30, 19xx) *(continued)*

Inventory adjustment:	Beginning	Ending	Net Change	
Work-in-process—Department A	+ $0	($x,xxx)	($x,xxx)	
Department B	+ 0	(x,xxx)	(x,xxx)	
Department C	+ 0	(x,xxx)	(x,xxx)	
Finished goods	+ 0	– (0) –	– (0) –	
Adjustment (B)		($x,xxx)	($x,xxx)	(x,xxx) (B)

COST OF GOODS SHIPPED (A – B) $xx,xxx (A – B)

EXCESS REVENUES OVER COST $ x,xxx

VARIANCE — ACTUAL OVERHEAD   (x,xxx)

ADMINISTRATIVE EXPENSES   (xxx)

EXCESS REVENUES OVER COST AND
**   EXPENSES** $ x,xxx

In practice, control accounts are used to provide a summary of period costs, such as those for personnel, fringe expenses, travel, contracts, etc. The costs are applied to manufacturing departments and other benefitting activities, such as overhead and administrative cost centers. The cost or expense variances can, pursuant to the guidance provided by the General Accounting Office, be shown as either a deferred charge or a credit in the succeeding period, depending upon whether there was an overapplication or underapplication of the cost or expense during the preceding period. The preferable treatment, however, is to adjust the cost or expenses for any variances at the end of the fiscal period unless the variance would have a material effect on the financial position of the agency. If the current period costs or expenses are adjusted for a variance, the adjustment should be made to the general overhead or administrative expenses account, as appropriate.

Invested Capital

The invested capital of the fund is determined by closing several of the cost, expenditure, and revenue accounts (into the invested capital account). After closing, the balance of the invested capital account is determined by the net balance of the following entries.

446

INVESTED CAPITAL

Cost of goods shipped	$xx,xxx	Expended funds—capital	$ x,xxx
Manufacturing overhead—		Expended funds—operating	xx,xxx
variance	x,xxx	Revenues	xx,xxx
Administrative expenses	xxx	Total	$xx,xxx
Total	$xx,xxx		
		Balance	$xx,xxx

Index

Index